Y0-BCL-350

VICTIMS OF THE SYSTEM

VICTIMS OF THE SYSTEM
Crime Victims and Compensation in
American Politics and Criminal Justice

ROBERT ELIAS

Transaction Books
New Brunswick (U.S.A.) and London (U.K.)

Second printing 1984

© 1983 by Transaction, Inc.
New Brunswick, New Jersey 08903

Library of Congress Catalog Number: 83-383
ISBN: 0-87855-470-X (cloth)
Printed in the United States of America

Library of Congress Cataloging in Publication Data

Elias, Robert, 1950-
   Victims of the system.

   Bibliography: p.
   1. Victims of crimes—United States.   2. Reparation—
United States.   3. Criminal justice, Administration of—
United States.   I. Title.
HV6250.3.U5E45   1983   362.8'8   83-383
ISBN 0-87855-470-X

For my parents

TABLE OF CONTENTS

LIST OF TABLES

ACKNOWLEDGEMENTS

The disadvantage of taking a long time to complete a study is that it allows a long list of people you must thank to accumulate. I thank the following people and organizations gladly: First, to the Vera Institute of Justice and its staff, which by hiring me as a research associate provided me with a foundation for conducting research on victims, as well as the source for one of my samples. I would like to thank Debbie Grayson, in particular, for her assistance. Next, I would like to thank the sources of my three remaining samples, and the persons most responsible for accommodating my research: the Manhattan and Albany offices of the New York Crime Victims Compensation Board, and especially to Executive Secretary Norma Keane, and to the investigators and members interviewed there. Thanks also to Charles Knox and the Newark Police Department, and to Carl Jahnke and the other members, investigators and staff of the New Jersey Violent Crimes Compensation Board.

In addition, I would like to thank many who assisted in the data analysis, including Robert Danziger and the computer staff of the University of Mannheim, West Germany; Victor Russell of the Vera Institute; Thomas Tugman and the computer staff of the University of Maryland; and Bruce Linn, George Stalker, and the computer staff of Tufts University.

Furthermore, I would like to thank the Law Enforcement Assistance Administration of the U.S. Department of Justice for awarding me a Research Fellowship to complete a portion of the study. I would most especially like to thank those people at the Pennsylvania State University who patiently helped me administer the grant, including Ann Bragg, Margo Groff, Pat Swanson, and Don Leitzell.

Special thanks also goes to two friends and advisers who gave me special assistance and encouragement: Richard Tobin of the State University of New York at Buffalo, and Kent Portney of Tufts University.

In addition, my greatest thanks to Robert Friedman, Robert O'Connor, and Philip Stebbins of the Pennsylvania State University, who read my study, offered encouragement, and made some very useful suggestions.

My greatest appeciation goes to James Eisenstein of the Pennsylvania State University. One could not hope for any more of the kind of encouragement, ideas, and support he provided. I owe him a great debt and a new pair of shoes for all the times he booted me in the pants to get me going.

I also appreciate the encouragement I received from my family. Most of all, my warmest thanks to Angelica Pinochet, who besides providing continuing and valuable assistance throughout the study, also gave me her love and emotional support, without which no one completes a major research project.

And finally, I would be amiss if I did not thank the Brooklyn and Newark victims who I interviewed. They graciously gave their time to describe their (in most cases) horrible ordeal of being victimized, by the offender and by the criminal-justice, political, and economic systems.

CHAPTER ONE
Introduction

Murderer and victim shout "Aaah" at the same time[1]

If the victim's role in modern literature reflects our true feelings, then it is little wonder that one kind of victim—the victim of crime, in particular—has received such little sympathy. Realistic literature, as Saul Bellow tells us, "pits any ordinary individual against the external world and the external world conquers him, of course."[2] Attention and even heroism are more likely to be focused on the victimizer than on the victim. One might argue that this happens for the crime victim as well.

At least one writer claims that "in our culture, attention is much more likely to be paid to the criminal as victim than to the victim as victim."[3] Some modern Western literature, at least, seems to bear this out. Many works about crime, both fictional and non-fictional, seem to direct our feelings and consciousness toward the criminal instead of the victim. For example, in Truman Capote's *In Cold Blood*[4] the story of a Kansas family's brutal murder compels the reader toward the offenders as victims since we are carefully distanced from the family, and learn little things about its members which alienate us even further.

In Anthony Burgess' *A Clockwork Orange*[5] young delinquents terrorize the persons and property of haphazardly chosen victims, and yet we are induced as readers to consider Alex—the ringleader—as a victim of the modern age. Similar treatment is afforded Gary Gilmore, the multiple murderer who helped restore the death penalty in the United States, by Norman Mailer in *The Executioner's Song*[6], where the offender is again treated as a product of a sick society.

And finally, another contemporary novel, which focuses almost entirely on the actual crime victim, nevertheless leaves an impression that is far from sympathetic. In Judith Rossner's *Looking for Mr. Goodbar*[7] our sentiments for this victim of rape and murder (after being "picked up" at a singles bar) are constantly undermined. We know from the beginning about her inevitable attack, and as we follow her from bar to bar toward this end, we begin to feel that she is asking for her fate, that she wants to be a victim. "Even her murderer must be, we are persuaded, a victim of her barely suppressed need for extinction."[8]

In other media, such as television, the criminal is less often portrayed as such a

1

hero, but neither is the victim. The dominant figure thus becomes the appropriate law-enforcement official, who somehow ends the offender's evil ways—usually with a bullet[9]. But, what about the victim?

Literary observers hardly have a case for modern literature's reflecting any real-life heroism for the average criminal[10]. Reality shows that offenders hardly generate more sympathy than victims. Those writers who elevate the criminal at the victim's expense do, nevertheless, often correctly highlight the offender's own victimization—by his society and his environment. But, the fact is that both the criminal and the victim are often victimized, and thus they are both justified in shouting "Aaah." While in fact the criminal hardly has been treated with sympathy, the victim has been the apparent beneficiary of almost two decades of belated, new attention.

Although crime victims once played prominent roles in the criminal process (see chapter two), that participation was stripped away centuries ago. When crime became viewed as an offense against the state[11], the victim was assigned a subordinate, and eventually a non-existent, role in the process of trying the offender. Such was predominantly the case until around 1965 when, largely induced by foreign practices, the victim began to gain greater prominence in law enforcement and public policy, and more concern about the effects of his victimization.

By the late 1960's, primarily as a response to the nation's law and order mood (which was substantially induced by the Nixon Administration's repressive approach to ghetto uprisings and to civil rights and anti-war activists, and by a backlash to the Warren Court's controversial criminal-justice decisions), paying attention to the crime victim became a very popular pursuit[12]. This focus was aided by the series of victimization surveys aimed at discovering more about the extent and consequences of crime, which were completed at this same time by the President's Commission on Law Enforcement and the Administration of Justice[13].

These surveys were a part of three studies of urban victimization completed by the Bureau of Social Science Research[14], the University of Michigan's Institute for Social Research[15], and the University of Chicago's National Opinion Research Center[16]. The results were alarming: as high as reported crime was, it represented only the tip of the iceberg. Actual victimization rates were at least twice the level reported by the Uniform Crime Reports. The latter were criticized both for the haphazard and the political means of their compilation[17]. But, a substantial portion of the blame for this discrepancy fell on the public's failure to report crime because it lacked confidence that doing so would bring about any positive result[18].

A second major group of victimization surveys was begun in 1970 by the Law Enforcement Assistance Administration and the Bureau of the Census. A joint program called the National Crime Panel[19] produced both national and city victimization surveys and corroborated the high unreported crime-rate discovered earlier by the President's Commission. This time, actual crime was found to be 3-5 times higher than the amount actually reported. These and other surveys[20] were alarming not only for revealing the true extent of crime as being higher than the already high level of known offenses[21], but especially because they indicated the public's serious doubts about the system's ability to work.

A new concern for the crime victim thus arose substantially to stem the tide of dissatisfaction with law enforcement. Even though evidence was available to show that the increase in the American crime rate was illusory compared to previous periods in our history[22], the fact nevertheless remained that the amount of crime—including considerable violent crime—was extraordinarily high. And, this level was bloated even further by exaggerated government pronouncements, and by media sensationalism[23]—including television's ability to bring crime, both fictional and real, into our living rooms.

A new emphasis arose that stressed the need (to paraphrase former President Nixon) to strengthen the forces of peace against the forces of crime—including the introduction of sophisticated (and usually militaristic) hardware and technology, surveillance, a crack-down on malcontents, and a beefing up of police authority (including Burger Court reversals of the meagre gains made by suspects and defendants during the Warren Court era) and power. New approaches to the problem also stressed police-community cooperation (although hardly for all segments of each community—ghetto areas often being excluded) in crime prevention[24]. The public—and the crime victim, in particular—was told that it was indispensable for effective law-enforcement. In an attempt to capture this cooperation, and also—not coincidentally—to try to build a more positive citizen perspective toward government and criminal justice, many victim programs were established in the 1970's.

These victim-assistance programs were sometimes independent, but most often were attached to the local police department or district attorney's office. These plans' objectives varied extensively, but included goals such as alleviating problems for victims during their court involvement (such as by providing an alert system to notify them of appearance dates), giving victims a clear understanding of their obligations as witnesses, and providing in-depth assessments, counselling[25], and referrals to social-service agencies[26].

The largest of these programs was the Victim/Witness Assistance Project, created by the Vera Institute of Justice in Brooklyn. This center offers a range of services to crime victims that are designed to mitigate difficulties encountered as a result of being victimized or of coming to court. These include a crime-victim hotline and an emergency repair service for burglary victims, as well as the more typical services such as a reception center, child-care services, transportation to court, and counselling. The Project offers about the most sophisticated victim services in the country. The Institute also has conducted on-going research projects to assess their programs and to analyze the crime victim's role in the criminal process[27].

Some of these assistance plans were designed for more than merely aiding crime victims. Although not extensively followed by actual results, many calls came for establishing permanent "victim advocates" to promote the victim's interests both in and out of court[28]. Attempts were also made to help involve victims more often and more productively in the criminal process—sometimes leaving the impression that perhaps the victim somehow owed the criminal-justice system something in return for its assistance. With the devotion to victim involvement—largely as a supposed aid to the prosecution in pursuing its cases—so high, one had cause to wonder whether the assistance was not regarded merely as secondary. Again, we were reminded about how crucial the public was to law enforcement, specifically in statistics such as those from New York, for example, where it was reported that 63% of all felony dismissals were caused by the victim's unavailability to pursue the case[29]. This concern has been reflected in extensive new research focusing not on a victim's needs or losses, but rather on how he can be made a better witness[30].

Although the actual, pervasive disuse of victims in the criminal process (especially in its earlier stages)—even when victims are willing—renders the aforementioned statistic and concern somewhat questionable (and more like blaming the victim for what were other causes of discontinued cases, and perhaps subsequent crime), the impression of the victim's great, potential role in criminal justice was maintained. Victim participation would not only help in crime prevention, it was said, but it would also help end the "revolving door" for criminals.

A great deal has been made in the last decade about how the offender has been given all the breaks, and how Warren Court decisions in the previous decade had given criminals rights that they did not deserve, which "handcuffed" the police, and which made convictions impossible. This "paradise" for suspects was contrasted with the victim's dilemma of being innocently attacked, often injured, frequently separated from his property, and beset with problems from the victimization that often were ignored[31].

Although the criminal's supposed advantages and the system's supposed benevolence toward him were grossly exaggerated, the depressing description of the average crime victim was largely accurate[32]. Much reason for concern did exist to justify a new public policy addressed to the crime victim's needs, and even perhaps to his rights[33]. Unfortunately, those very real necessities often came second to the political advantages of favoring victim assistance[34].

But, the concern for the victim was not merely political nor the sole concern of socially conscious citizens. It also became the focus of a tremendous outpouring of research and writing from the academic community. Much of this work was first initiated by criminologists. Although some writers previously had considered the victim in their work[35]—most notably Hans von Hentig's study of the victim-offender relationship[36]—it was not until relatively recently that the literature became so extensive.

Ironically, some of the initial writing was less than sympathetic with the victim as well since it considered the possible ways he could be implicated in his own victimization[37]. This led to a trend toward creating typologies to characterize the various degrees of victim involvement in the crime[38]. A concern for the victim-offender relationship persists, sometimes correctly noting the frequent blurring of roles and difficulty in assigning culpability to either side, as well as the frequent arbitrariness of who "plays" the criminal and the victim in each criminal episode—when the roles can be distinguished at all[39].

Much research also has been devoted to the varying susceptibility of different persons to different kinds of victimization, based not only on their behavior, but also on their characteristics, and even on chance[40]. Some of this attention, for example, has gone into analyzing the "recidivist" victim, and into comparing him to his criminal counterpart[41]. Others have observed a so-called "victimological cycle."[42] And, still others have emphasized an economic analysis of victimization[43]. Although some writers have approached these subjects rather deterministically, others insist that one's susceptibility to being victimized can be controlled[44].

Certain kinds of victimization have received scholarly attention far beyond their actual proportion of the crime rate, but the nature of these crimes or their victims make the preoccupation understandable. These "outstanding" kinds of crimes include elderly and child victimizations[45], as well as homicides committed against all victims[46]. But, by far, the greatest attention has gone to rape victims[47]. These studies have revealed valuable findings about these kinds of crimes, but they are less relevant to the average victimization.

The research on crime victims has certainly not been limited to American sources, nor even to American and European studies. The crime victim has been analyzed widely across the world, irrespective of political or economic systems, or levels of development[48]. Many of the victim's problems are universal.

The writing on crime victims has, in fact, become so extensive, and the attention so systematic, that this new body of literature has been dubbed "victimology."[49] Although criticized by some for either methodological shortcomings[50], or for its short-sighted, conservative emphasis (which ignores the victimization's real causes the way criminology has often ignored crime's root causes)[51], victimology's development thus far has followed closely in criminology's footsteps—only now the questions are asked about the other party in the ciminal event.

Some of this research has gone beyond merely discussing the disasters often experienced by crime victims, and the need to provide them assistance. More far-reaching studies have begun to study the victim's role in the criminal process, and not merely the victim as an isolated entity or as something merely to be manipulated[52].

Not all victimological research has been devoted to those who are commonly considered to be *crime* victims—or, in some cases, any kind of victim for that matter. Besides questioning whether the criminal is any less the victim than the recipient of the attack[53], other studies have identified still other victims in the criminal process, including professional killers[54]; bystanders[55]; ghetto residents[56]; government and private institutions[57]; prison inmates[58]; political criminals[59]; terrorists and their victims[60]; victims of female offenders[61], mass murderers[62], and white-collar criminals[63]; ex-convicts[64]; the society (i.e., do crimes without victims really exist?)[65]; and those wrongly apprehended and detained for a crime they did not commit[66].

Although not tied directly to the criminal process, other victims such as American Indians[67], abortionists[68], Vietnam veterans[69], homosexuals[70], consumers[71], prisoners of war[72], and genocide victims[73] have been investigated as well. Victimology thus has been broad enough to include various kinds of victims, crimes or offenses, and locations for crime, which is perhaps what induced one writer to propose a universalistic and international approach to handling victimization and its causes[74].

While such breadth is admirable, even narrow areas of victimology carry a great deal of importance. The research described herein will emphasize a smaller area of concern—providing compensation to crime victims as one means of giving assistance, redressing the wrong, and coaxing good will toward government and criminal justice from victims and the general public. Although they are described in considerable detail in the next chapter, victim-compensation programs in the United States are state-created plans that provide financial payments to crime victims from largely public monies. Compensation programs have several purposes, including not only restoring the victim monetarily after the victimization, but also improving the attitudes and cooperation of victims and the general public, aiding in crime prevention, and creating positive attitudes toward the government.

These are important and ambitious objectives, requiring the outlay of much money, and skillful implementation, to be successful. Victim compensation is a well-defined program constituting a clear public policy toward the victim. But, as is the case with most public policies here and abroad, this program is not politically neutral. To start, compensation programs have not been designed for all victims, and the commitment to those eligible varies considerably. Despite the programs' limitations and the political allocation of the resources required to run them, victim-compensation plans can and should be analyzed to assess the extent to which the policy is being realized. This study's purpose, therefore, is to offer a policy evaluation of compensation, emphasizing its effect on crime victims, and on criminal justice and government generally.

This research will assess the performance of two compensation programs—the New York Crime Victims Compensation Board and the New Jersey Violent Crimes Compensation Board—in achieving their objectives. The programs' success will be measured primarily through the eyes of the victims (large numbers of whom were systematically questioned about their experiences and attitudes) served by these plans, as well as by the views of program administrators and the author's observations.

The study will address, either directly or indirectly, a series of political questions deriving from the existing compensation programs and the possible creation of new ones. In addition to examining the "who gets what" question suggested above, the research also will be concerned with the decision-making politics which produced such programs, how the plans have been administered, how successfully the objectives have been met, and what influences have helped make it so. Public attitudes and relationships with government and the criminal-justice system also will be examined. And, the overall role of criminal justice and its new component—victim compensation—in the political system will be assessed as well. It is clear that victim compensation should not be treated narrowly, since it has broad implications as a public policy for public opinion and participation, law enforcement, and government.

The following chapters have been organized to facilitate a logical analysis of the research questions. Chapter two will describe in detail both the literature on victim compensation and the development of such programs to the present date. Chapter three will present the research design used to conduct this study. Briefly, it consisted of selecting four samples of victims, two each from both Brooklyn and Newark—thus allowing an experimental and control group in each city. One sample in each city consisted of victims who had applied to their state's compensation board, while the other group included only victims who had not made such a claim. Members of each of these samples, and officials at each state's compensation board, were questioned in extensive interviews.

The next three chapters will examine crime victims as we follow them through the victimization and post-victimization processes. Chapter four will describe the victims' characteristics and general attitudes. Chapter five will describe the victimizations, the characteristics of the Brooklyn and Newark criminal processes that the victims confronted, and the victims' actual role in those processes. Chapter six will assess the impact on victims of the criminal justice experience, including the outcomes of the process for the victim and his attitudes associated with it. The following three chapters will focus directly on victim compensation. Chapter seven will begin to describe the New York and New Jersey compensation boards and programs in particular, and their few differences will be compared. Chapter eight will describe the board officials in the two programs, and based on interviews with these members, a detailed description of the compensation process, and of official backgrounds, attitudes, preferences, and activities, will be provided. Chapter nine will resume the victim's journey through the criminal process, at least for those who applied for compensation. The victim's role in the compensation process, and his perspectives about the experience and its outcomes will be described.

Finally, chapter ten will assess compensation's impact on crime victims, partly by comparing applicants to other victims who made no compensation claims. Some attempt will be made to begin to explain some of the apparent outcomes and attitudes resulting from the victim's role in the criminal process, but especially resulting from his involvement in the compensation process. And then, chapter eleven will summarize and assess the research, and will evaluate victim compensation as a public policy.

As the next chapter will demonstrate, victim-compensation research has come to occupy a considerable portion of the overall victimology literature. Little of the writing on compensation, however, has gone beyond passionate calls (usually citing how fortunate the criminal is, in comparison,) to aid the crime victim financially, or beyond simply describing how each new victim-compensation program looks on paper. Few examinations of actual, functioning compensation programs have occurred. This study has been done to begin to fill that void, by evaluating two programs, not from a distance but through the eyes and mouths of those who actually confront and administer victim-compensation plans.

As has been typical since at least the end of the last century in American society (and no doubt in others), at least some classes of victims have been ignored, even implicated in their fates. Blaming the victim (such as by concluding that the poor are poor because they are unfit), is a convenient way of avoiding the root causes of many problems, much less alleviating the problems[75]. In the case of the crime victim, things now have been done on his behalf[76]. But, this study will show, among other things, that alleviating the crime victim's problems—like those of the offender—has a long way to go. Both murderer and victim still shout "Aaah" to get our attention.

NOTES

1. Taken from a description of Ionesco's play "The Lesson" in Martin Esslin, *The Theatre of the Absurd* (Garden City: Anchor Books, 1969), 118.

2. Gordon L. Harper, "Saul Bellow—The Art of Fiction: An Interview," *Paris Review*, 37(1965), 48; See also, Saul Bellow, *The Victim* (New York: Vanguard Press, 1947).

3. Susan Kress, "Doubly Abused: The Plight of Crime Victims in Literature," unpublished paper delivered at the Second International Symposium on Victimology, 1976; See also, Arthur Lapan, "The Victim in Contemporary Literature," in Israel Drapkin & Emilio Viano (eds.), *Victimology: Theoretical Issues in Victimology* (Lexington: D.C. Heath, 1974), 197; John Lewin, "The Victim in Shakespeare," in Emilio Viano (ed.), *Victims and Society* (Washington: Visage Press, 1978), 451.

4. Truman Capote, *In Cold Blood* (New York: Signet Books, 1965).

5. Anthony Burgess, *A Clockwork Orange* (New York: Ballantine Books, 1962).

6. Norman Mailer, *The Executioner's Song* (New York: Ballantine Books, 1978).

7. Judith Rossner, *Looking for Mr. Goodbar* (New York: Simon & Schuster, 1975).

8. Kress, note 3 *supra*, 13.

9. Jeffrey Reiman, *The Rich Get Richer and the Poor Get Prison* (New York: John Wiley, 1979).

10. Lois G. Forer, *Criminals and Victims: A Trial Judge Reflects on Crime and Punishment* (New York: Norton, 1980), 2.

11. William Chambliss, *Whose Law? Whose Order?* (New York: John Wiley, 1974).

12. See, for example, Mitchell C. Lynch, "Tough Luck If You're Ripped Off," *Wall St. J.*, 16 December 1979, 7; "Aid to Victims of Crimes: Something Being Done at Last," *U.S. News & World Report,* 8 December 1975, 42; "Now We're Doing More for the Victims of Crime," *Changing Times,* February 1978, 23.

13. President's Commission on Law Enforcement and the Administration of Justice, *Task Force Reports* (Washington: U.S. Gov't Printing Ofc., 1967).

14. Albert D. Biderman, et al., *Report on a Pilot Study in the District of Columbia on Victimization and Attitudes toward Law Enforcement* (Washington: U.S. Gov't. Printing Ofc., 1967).

15. Albert Reiss, *Studies in Crime and Law Enforcement in Major Metropolitan Areas* (Washington: U.S. Gov't. Printing Ofc., 1967).

16. Philip H. Ennis, *Criminal Victimization in the United States: A Report of a National Survey* (Washington: U.S. Gov't. Printing Ofc., 1967).

17. Wesley G. Skogan, "Comparing Measures of Crime: Police Statistics and Survey Estimates of Citizen Victimization in American Cities," (Washington: Amer. Statistical Assn., 1974); Richard Quinney, *A Critique of Legal Order: Law & Order in America* (Boston: Little, Brown, 1974), 63; A.L. Schneider, "Methodological Approaches for Measuring Short-Term Victimization Trends," (Eugene: Oregon Res. Inst., 1975); Michael E. Milakovich, "Politics and Measures of Success in the War on Crime," *Crime & Delinq.*, 21(1975), 1; James Inciardi, "Criminal Statistics and Victim Survey Research," in Viano, note 3 *supra,* 173; Paul D. Reynolds & Dale A. Blyth, "Sources of Variation Affecting the Relationship Between Police and Survey-Based Estimates of Crime Rates," in Israel Drapkin & Emilio Viano (eds.), *Victimology: Crimes, Victims and Justice* (Lexington: D.C. Heath, 1978), 201; Wesley Skogan, "Validity of Official Crime Statistics: An Empirical Investigation," *Soc. Sci. Q.* (1974), 12; Wesley Skogan, "Measurement Problems in Official and Survey Crime Rates," *J. Crim. Justice,* 3(1975), 17; Wesley Skogan, "Dimensions of the Dark Figure of Unreported Crime," in *Sample Surveys of the Victims of Crime* (Cambridge: Ballinger, 1975), 75; M.A. Howard, "Police Reports and Victimization Survey Results: An Empirical Study," *Criminology,* 12(1975), 433.

18. Anne L. Schneider, "Victimization Surveys and Criminal Justice System Evaluation," in Skogan, note 17 *supra,* 135.

19. See Michael J. Hindelang, *Criminal Victimization in Eight States* (Cambridge: Ballinger, 1976); Carol B. Kalish, *Crimes and Victims* (Washington: U.S. Dept. Justice, 1974); Wesley Skogan, *Survey Studies of the Victims of Crime* (Washington: U.S. Dept. Justice, 1975) and Reference Services, *Victimization: A Bibliography* (Washington: U.S. Dept. Justice, 1978) for reports and analyses of the victimization studies completed under this program in the following twenty-six cities: Atlanta, Baltimore, Boston, Buffalo, Cleveland, Chicago, Cincinnati, Dallas, Denver, Detroit, Houston, Los Angeles, Miami, Milwaukee, Minneapolis, Newark, New Orleans, New York, Oakland, Philadelphia, Pittsburgh, Portland, St. Louis, San Diego, San Francisco, and Washington, D.C.

20. Small Business Administration, *Crimes Against Small Business* (Washington: U.S. Gov't. Printing Ofc., 1968); *Criminal Victimization in Maricopa County* (Berkeley: Inst. Local Self-Gov't., 1969); Philip Reynolds, *Victimization in Metropolitan Regions* (Minneapolis: Center Soc. Res., 1973); *Crimes of Violence: A Staff Report Submitted to the National Commission on the Causes and Prevention of Violence* (Washington: U.S. Gov't. Printing Ofc., 1969); Paula Kleinman, *Protection in a Ghetto Community* (New York: Columbia Univ. Press, 1972); *Study 2043* (New York: Louis Harris & Assoc.,

1970); *Study 861* (Princeton: Amer. Inst. Pub. Opin., 1972); Gilbert Geis, "Victims of Crimes of Violence and the Criminal Justice System," in Duncan Chappell & David Monahan (eds.), *Violence and Criminal Justice* (Lexington: D.C. Heath, 1975); Lynn Curtis, *Criminal Violence: National Patterns and Behavior* (Lexington: D.C. Heath, 1974).

21. But see James Levine, The Potential for Crime Over-Reporting in Criminal Victimization Surveys," *Criminology,* 14(1976), 307; Frederic DuBow & David Reed, "the Limits of Victim Surveys," in Skogan, note 17 supra, 151.

22. See, for example, Ted Gurr, *Rogues, Rebels and Reformers* (Beverly Hills: Sage, 1976) for a description of the high American crime rates in past eras, as well as now.

23. Guy Cumberbatch & Alan Beardsworth, "Criminals, Victims and Mass Communications," in Viano, note 3 *supra,* 72.

24. Center for the Study of Criminal Justice, *The Iron Fist and the Velvet Glove: An Analysis of U.S. Police* (San Francisco: Garrett, 1977); Robert C. Trojanowicz & Samuel Dixon, *Criminal Justice and the Community* (Englewood Cliffs: Prentice-Hall, 1974); Guy D. Boston, *Community Crime Prevention: A Selected Bibliography* (Washington: Nat. Crim. Justice Ref. Serv., 1977).

25. See *Evaluation and Change: Services for Victims* (Minneapolis: Minn. Medical Res. Found., 1980); Yona Cohn, "Crisis Intervention and the Victim of Robbery," in Drapkin & Viano, note 17 *supra,* 17, for efforts toward coping with victims' mental health.

26. National District Attorneys Association, *Final Evaluation: Commission on Victim-Witness Assistance* (Washington: Arthur D. Little, 1977); Anne Newton, "Aid to the Victim: Victim Aid Programs," *Crime & Delinq. Lit.,* 8(1976), 508; Mary E. Baluss, "Integrated Services for Victims of Crime: A County- Based Approach," (Washington: Nat. Assn. Counties Res. Found., 1975); Commission on Victim-Witness Assistance, *The Victim Advocate* (Washington: Nat. Dist. Attnys. Assn, 1978); Leonard Bickman "Research and Evaluation: Cook County State's Attorney Victim- Witness Assistance Project," *Victimology,* 1(1976), 457; Commission on Victim-Witness Assistance, *Help for Victims and Witnesses* (Washington: Nat. Dist. Attnys. Assn., 1976); Section on Criminal Justice, Commission on Victims, "Reducing Victim/Witness Intimidation: A Package, (Washington: Amer. Bar Assn., 1979); Lois P. Kraft, et al., "An Evaluation of the Victim-Witness Advocate Program of Puma County," (Tucson: Ofc. Puma Co. Attny., 1979); John Dussich, "Victim Service Models and Their Efficacy," in Viano, note 3 *supra,* 471; David Friedman, "A Program to Service Crime Victims," in Viano, note 3 *supra,* 27; John Dussich, "The Victim Ombudsman: A Proposal," in Israel Drapkin & Emilio Viano (eds.), *Victimology: Society's Reaction to Victimization* (Lexington: D.C. Heath, 1976); 105; Anthony A. Cain, *Victim/Witness Assistance: A Selected Bibliography* (Washington: U.S. Dept. Justice, 1978); "Victim Assistance Programs in Minnesota," *Victimology,* 2(1976), 88.

27. "Impact Evaluation of the Victim/Witness Assistance Project's Appearance Management Activities," unpublished report, Vera Institute of Justice, 1976; "An Evaluation of the Victim/Witness Assistance Project's Court-Based Services," unpublished report, Vera Institute of Justice, 1976; "Victim/Witness Assistance Project Operations Report," unpublished report, Vera Institute of Justice, 1975.

28. Frederic L. DuBow & Theodore Becker, "Patterns of Victim Advocacy," in William McDonald (ed.), *Criminal Justice and the Victim* (Beverly Hills: Sage, 1976), 115; Leo F. Callahan, "The Victim Advocate: Programmed Police Response for the Crime Victim," *Police Chief,* 42(1975), 50; "Crime Victims Advocate Urged," *Trial,* 12(1976), 52; "A Spokesman for Victims: Past and Future," *Law Enforce. J.,* 5(1975), 4; H. Jones, *Victim Advocate* (Washington: Nat. Dist. Attnys. Assn., 1977).

29. Cited in "Pilot Complainant Survey," unpublished report, Vera Institute of Justice, 1976.

30. James L. Lacy, *National Standards Concerning the Prosecution Witness* (Washington: Nat. Center Prosec. Mgt., 1972); *Dismissed for Want of Prosecution* (Chicago: Chi. Crime Comm., 1974); *Report on Why Victims Fail to Prosecute* (Cincinnati: Cincinnati Police Div., 1975); Frank Cannavale & William Falcon, *Witness Cooperation* (Lexington: D.C. Heath, 1976); "Why Witnesses Can't Be Located," (Washington: Nat. Crim. Justice Ref. Serv., 1977); A.S. Cutter, "Why the Good Citizen Avoids Testifying," *Annals,* 287(1953), 103; Commission on Victim Witness Assistance, "No Show Survey," (Washington: Nat. Dist. Attnys. Assn., 1975).

31. Robert Reiff, *The Invisible Victim: The Criminal Justice System's Forgotten Responsibility* (New York: Basic Books, 1979); J.L. Barkas, *Victims* (New York: Chas. Scribners, 1978); Jack Grotus, *The Victims* (London: Hutchinson, 1969); Bernard Leftkowitz, *The Victims* (New York: Putnam, 1969); Gladys Schultz, *How Many More Victims?* (Philadelphia: Lippincott, 1965).

32. "Victims of Crime or Victims of Justice?" (Washington: Amer. Bar Assn., 1977).

33. Zvonimir P. Separovic, "Some Reflections on the Victim, Law Enforcement, and the Rights of the Victim in the U.S.A.," in Drapkin & Viano, note 26 *supra,* 29; "Victim's Rights," *U. Rich. L.R.,* 11(1977), 679; F.E. Inbau, "Victim's Rights Litigation: A Wave of the Future?" *U. Rich. L.R.,* 11(1977), 447; J.P. Busch, "Victim Rights in Stolen Property in California," *Calif. L.R.,* 64(1976), 1018; Sidney Hook, "The Emerging Rights of the Victims of Crime," *Fla. B.J.,* 46(1972), 192; Sidney Hook, "The Rights of the Victim," *Encounter,* 38(1972), 11.

34. Duncan Chappell, "Providing for the Victim of Crime: Political Placebo or Progressive Programs?" *Adelaide L.R.,* 4(1972), 296.

35. Calvin Schmid, "A Study of Homicides in Seattle, 1919 to 1924," *Social Forces,* 4(1926), 745; Rollin Perkins, "The Law of Homicide," *J. Crim. L., Criminol., & Police Sci.,* 36(1946), 412.

36. Hans von Hentig, *The Criminal and His Victim* (New Haven: Yale Univ. Press, 1948).

37. Lynn Carter, "Victim Precipitation," in Lynn Curtis (ed.), *Crimes of Violence* (Lexington: D.C. Heath, 1975), 73; Annon Rubinstein, "The Victim's Consent in Criminal Law: An Essay on the Extent of the Decriminalizing Element of the Crime Concept," in Edward Wise & Gerhard O.W. Mueller (eds.), *Studies in Comparative Criminal Law* (Springfield, Ill.: Chas. Thomas, 1975); Lynn Curtis, "Victim Precipitation and Violent Crime," *Soc. Problems,* 21(1973), 594; J. Baldwin, "Role of the Victim in Certain Property Offenses," *Crim. L.R.,* (1974), 353; Robert Silverman, "Victim Precipitation," in Drapkin & Viano, note 3 *supra,* 99.

38. Robert Silverman, 'Victim Typologies: Overview, Critique, and Reformulation," in Israel Drapkin (ed.), *Victimology* (Lexington: D.C. Heath, 1976), 55; Jack A. Mack, "A Victim Role Typology of Rational Economic Property Crimes," in Drapkin & Viano, note 3 *supra,* 127.

39. Guglielmo Gulotta, "The "Offender-Victim System," in Viano, note 3 *supra,* 50; Wolf Middendorf, "The Offender-Victim Relationship in Traffic Offenses," in Israel Drapkin & Emilio Viano (eds.), *Victimology: Violence and Its Victims* (Lexington: D.C. Heath, 1976), 187; Hans von Hentig, "Remarks on the Interaction of Perpetrator and Victim," in Drapkin, note 38 *supra,* 45; Simha F. Landau, "The Offender's Perception of the Victim," in Drapkin & Viano, note 3 *supra,* 137; Joachim Weber, "On the Psychodiagnosis of the Offender-Victim Relationship," in Drapkin & Viano, note 3 *supra,* 155; LeRoy Schultz, "The Victim-Offender Relationship," *St. Louis L.R.,* 18(1967), 135. Arthur Solarz, "Driving Under the Influence of Drugs and the Offender-Victim Relation-

ship," in Israel Drapkin & Emilio Viano (eds.), *Victimology: The Exploiters and the Exploited* (Lexington: D.C. Heath, 1978), 181; Sung Tai Cho, "Criminality, Victim and Victimizer," in Drapkin & Viano, note 3 *supra,* 93.

40. David R. Watson, "Some Conceptual Issues in the Social Identification of Victims and Offenders," in Viano, note 3 *supra,* 60.

41. Joan H. Johnson, et al., "The Recidivist Victim: A Descriptive Study," (Huntsville, Tx.: Inst. Contemp. Correct. & Behav. Sci., Sam Houston St. U., 1973); Eduard Ziegenhagen, "The Recidivist Victim of Violent Crime," *Victimology,* 1(1976), 538.

42. Richard A. Ball, "The Victimological Cycle," *Victimology,* 1(1976), 379.

43. M.K. Block & G.L. Long, "Subjective Probability of Victimization and Crime Levels: An Econometric Approach," *Criminology,* (1973), 87; Neil S. Komesar, "A Theoretical and Empirical Study of Victims of Crime," *J. Legal Stud.,* 4(1976), 301; Edna Erez & Simon Hakim, "A Geo-Economic Approach to the Distribution of Crimes in Metropolitan Areas," in William Parsonage (ed.), *Perspectives in Victimology* (Beverly Hills: Sage, 1979), 29; Carl Pope, "Victimization Rates and Neighborhood Characteristics: Some Preliminary Findings," in Parsonage, note 43 *supra,* 48.

44. Joel M. Teutsch & Champion K. Teutsch, "Victimology: An Effect of Consciousness, Interpersonal Dynamics, and Human Physics," in Drapkin & Viano, note 3 *supra,* 169.

45. William Berg & Robert Johnson, "Assessing the Impact of Victimization: Acquisition of the Victim Role among Elderly and Female Victims," in Parsonage, note 43 *supra,* 58; David Decker, et al., "Patterns of Juvenile Victimization and Urban Structure," in Parsonage, note 43 *supra,* 88; Fay Lomax Cook, "Criminal Victimization of the Elderly: A National Problem?" in Viano, note 3 *supra,* 130; David Reifen, "Court Procedures in Israel to Protect Child-Victims of Sexual Assaults," in Drapkin & Viano, note 17 *supra,* 67; Emilio Viano, "The Battered Child," in Drapkin & Viano, note 39 *supra,* 145; Susan Harlap & Israel Drapkin, "Child Injury in West Jerusalem," in Drapkin & Viano, note 39 *supra,* 177; LeRoy G. Schultz, "Child as a Sex Victim: Socio-Legal Perspectives," in Drapkin & Viano, note 39 *supra,* 187; W.H. Feyerherm, "On the Victimization of Juveniles: Some Preliminary Results," *J. Res. Crime & Delinq.,* 11(1974), 40; J.F. Gubrium, "Victimization in Old Age: Available Evidence and Three Hypotheses," *Crime & Delinq.,* 20(1974), 245; Jack Goldsmith, "A Symposium on Crime and the Elderly," *Police Chief,* 43(1976), 18; V. DeFrancis, "Protecting the Child Victim of Sex Crimes Committed by Adults," *Fed. Probation,* 35(1971), 15; Mattii Virkkinen, "Victim Precipitated Pedophilia Offenses," *Brit. J. Crim.,* 15(1979), 175; "Crimes Against Aging Americans: The Kansas City Study," (Kansas City: Midwest Res. Inst., 1977); M.A.Y. Rifai, *Justice and Older Americans* (Lexington: D.C. Heath, 1977); C.E. Pope, "The Effects of Crime on the Elderly," *Police Chief,* 43(1976), 48; L.P. Brown, "Crime Prevention for Older Americans: Multnomah County's Victimization Study," *Police Chief,* 43(1976), 38; R. Forston, "Criminal Victimization of the Aged: The Houston Model Neighborhood Area," (Austin: Texas Crim. Justice Council, 1974).

46. Stephen Schafer, "Changing Victims of Changing Homicide," in Drapkin & Viano, note 39 *supra,* 25; Marvin Wolfgang, *Studies in Homicide* (New York: Harper & Row, 1967); B.M. Cormier & C.C. Angliker, "Psychodynamics of Homicide Committed in a Semi-Specific Relationship," *Canad. J. Crim & Correct.,* 14(1972), 335; J.M. McDonald, *Murderer and His Victim* (Springfield, Ill.: Chas. Thomas, 1961); Marvin Wolfgang, "Victim Precipitated Homicide," in Drapkin, note 39 *supra,* 79; Gloria Count Van Manen, "Macrostructural Sources of Variation in Homicide Victim Rates in the Capital City," in Viano, note 3 *supra,* 255; Neville H. Avison, "Victims of Homicide," in

Drapkin & Viano, note 39 *supra*, 55; A.M. Rosenthal, *Thirty-Eight Witnesses* (New York: McGraw Hill, 1964).

47. Michael Agopian, et al., "Interracial Rape in a Northern City: An Analysis of 63 Cases," in Terence Thornberry & Edward Sagarin (eds.), *Images of Crime: Offenders and Victims* (New York: Praeger, 1974), 91; Dianne Herman, "The Politics of Rape and Wife-Beating: The Criminal Justice System's Response to Violence Against Women," unpublished paper delivered at the American Political Science Association annual meeting, Washington, 1977; Nancy Wolfe, "Victim Provocation: The Battered Wife and the Legal Definition of Self-Defense," *Soc. Symposium,* 25(1979), 98; Samuel Smittyman, "Characteristics of Undetected Rapists," in Parsonage, note 43 *supra*, 99; Shirley Feldman-Summers, "Conceptual and Empirical Issues Associated with Rape," in Viano, note 3 *supra*, 91; Lynn Curtis, "Toward a Theory of Response to Rape," in Viano, note 3 *supra*, 220; Kurt Weis & Sandra Borges, "Rape as a Crime Without Victims and Offenders?" in Viano, note 3 *supra*, 230; Mary L. Keefe & Henry T. 0'Reilly, "The Plight of the Rape Victim in New York City," in Viano, note 3 *supra*, 391; Kurt Weis & Sandra Weis, "Victimology and Justification of Rape," in Drapkin & Viano, note 39 *supra*, 3; Leslie Sebba & Sorel Cahan, "Sex Offenses: The Genuine and the Doubted Victim," in Drapkin & Viano, note 39 *supra*, 29; Steve Nelson & Manachem Amir, "The Hitchhike Victim of Rape," in Drapkin & Viano, note 39 *supra*, 47; Joseph Peters, "The Philadelphia Rape Victim Study," in Drapkin & Viano, note 17 *supra*, 181; Stephanie Riger, et al., "Women's Fear of Crime: From Blaming to Restricting the Victim," *Victimology,* 3(1978), 274; Murray Straus, "Sexual Inequality, Cultural Norms and Wife Beating," in Viano, note 3 *supra*, 519; Lisa Brodyaga, *Rape and Its Victims: A Report for Citizens, Health Facilities, and Criminal Justice Agencies* (Washington: Nat. Inst. Law Enforce. & Crim. Justice, 1975); Wenzell Brown, *True Story of the Interplay of Aggressor and Victim in Sexual Attacks* (Derby, Conn.: Monarch, 1961); Ann Wolbert Burgess & Lynda Lyttle Holstrom, "Rape: The Victim and the Criminal Justice System," in Drapkin & Viano, note 17 *supra*, 21; Ann Wolbert Burgess & Lynda Lyttle Holstrom, "Rape: The Victim Goes on Trial," in Drapkin & Viano, note 17 *supra*, 31; Lois Veronen, "Treating Fear and Anxiety in Rape Victims: Implications for Criminal Justice," in Parsonage, note 43 *supra*, 148; J.M. McDonald, *Rape, Offenders, and Their Victims* (Springfield, Ill.: Chas. Thomas, 1971); Bruce J. Rounsaville, "Theories in Marital Violence," *Victimology,* 3(1978), 11; Barbara Star, "Comparing Battered and Non-Battered Women," *Victimology,* 32.

48. V.V. Stancia, "Victim Producing Civilizations and Situations, in Viano, note 3 *supra*, 28; Nwokocha K.U. Nkpa, "Armed Robbery in Post Civil War Nigeria: The Role of the Victim," in Viano, note 3 *supra*, 158; Jan P.S. Fiselier, "Victims of Crime in the Netherlands," in Viano, note 3 *supra*, 268; Gerd Kirchhoff & Claudia Thelen, "Hidden Victimization by Sex Offenders in Germany," in Viano, note 3 *supra*, 277; Kiochi Miyazawa, "Victimological Studies of Sexual Crimes in Japan," in Viano, note 3 *supra*, 295; Charles Okaeri, "Community Responsibility and the Victim in Nigerian Society," in Viano, note 3 *supra*, 440; Nwokocha K.U. Nkpa, "Victims of Crime in the Igbo Section of Nigeria," in Drapkin & Viano, note 39 *supra*, 115; Israel Drapkin, "The Victim Under the Incas," in Drapkin & Viano, note 17 *supra*, 135; Louis Freed, "A Victimological Assessment of the Problem of Crime in South Africa," in Drapkin & Viano, note 26 *supra*, 55; Stanley Z. Fisher, "The Victim's Role in Criminal Prosecutions in Ethiopia," in Drapkin & Viano, note 17 *supra*, 73; Richard F. Sparks, "Crimes and Victims in London," in Skogan, note 17 *supra*, 43; H.D. Schwind, "Interim Report on Research on Unreported Crime in Goettingen," *Kriminalistik,* 28(1974), 241; A.A. Congalton, "New South Wales: Unreported Crime," (New South Wales: Bur. of Crime, 1975); E. Stephan,

"Results of the Stuttgart Survey of Victims Taking Comparable American Data into Account: An Interim Report," *Kriminalistic,* 29(1975), 201; A.A. Congalton, "Who Are The Victims?" (New South Wales: Bur. of Crime, 1975); S.S. Ostroumov & L.V. Frank, "On Victimology and Victimization," *Soviet Law & Gov't.* 15(1976-77), 70; Hazel G. Genn, "Findings of A Pilot Survey of Victimization in England," *Victimology,* 1(1976), 253.

49. Inkeri Anttila, "Victimology: A New Territory in Criminology," in Drapkin & Viano, note 3 *supra,* 5; Hans Goppinger, "Criminology and Victimology," in Drapkin & Viano, note 3 *supra,* 9; Zvonimir P. Separovic, "Victimology: A New Approach in the Social Sciences," in Drapkin & Viano, note 3 *supra,* 15; Beniamin Mendelsohn, "Victimology and the Technical and Social Sciences," in Drapkin & Viano, note 3 *supra,* 25; Richard Sparks, et al., *Surveying Victims: A Study of the Measurement of Criminal Victimization, Perceptions of Crime, and Attitudes Toward Criminal Justice* (New York: John Wiley, 1977); Michael Hindelang, et al., *Victims of Personal Crime* (Cambridge: Ballinger, 1978); Koichi Miyazawa, "Society and the Victim: Attitudes and Policies," in Drapkin & Viano, note 26 *supra,* 5; Michael Hindelang, *Criminal Victimization in Eight American Cities* (Cambridge: Ballinger, 1976); William F. McDonald, "The Role of the Victim in America," *in Assessing the Criminal: Restitution, Retribution, and the Legal Process* (Cambridge: Ballinger, 1977), 295; Robert LeJeune & Nicholas Alex, "On Being Mugged: The Event and Its Aftermath," *Urban Life & Culture,* 2(1973), 259; Terence Thornberry & Robert Figlio, "Victimization and Criminal Behavior in a Birth Cohort," in Thornberry & Sagarin, note 47 *supra,* 28; Irwin Waller, "Victim Research, Public Policy, and Criminal Justice," *Victimology,* 1(1976), 240; Task Force on Criminal Justice Research and Development, Standards, and Goals, "Research on Criminal Justice Problems: Victim Research," (Washington: Rand Corp., 1976); James Garofalo, *Local Victim Surveys* (Washington: U.S. Dept. Justice, 1977); Gerhard O.W. Mueller & H.H.A. Cooper, *The Criminal, Society and the Victim* (Washington: U.S. Dept. Justice, 1979); Stephen Schafer, *The Victim and His Criminal* (New York: Random House, 1968); Simon Dimitz & Walter Reckless, "Focus on the Victim," *in Critical Issues in the Study of Crime* (Boston: Little, Brown, 1968), 201; LeRoy Lamborn, "Toward a Victim Orientation in Criminal Theory," *Rutgers L.R.,* 22(1968), 733; William F. McDonald, "Towards a Bicentennial Revolution in Criminal Justice: The Return of the Victim," *Amer. Crim. L.R.,* 13(1976), 649; Stephen Schafer, "Victimology," in *Introduction to Criminology* (Boston: Reston, 1976), 105; Beniamin Mendolsohn, "The Origin of the Doctrine of Victimology," in Drapkin, note 39 *supra,* 3; Willem Nagel, "The Notion of Victimology in Criminology," in Drapkin, note 39 *supra,* 13; Daniel Glaser, "Victim Survey Research: Theoretical Implications," in Drapkin, note 39 *supra,* 31; William H. Parsonage, *Perspectives in Victimology* (Beverly Hills: Sage, 1979); Emilio Viano, *Victims and Society* (Washington: Visage, 1976); Beniamin Mendolsohn, "Victimology and Contemporary Society's Trends," in Viano, note 3 *supra,* 28; David Lewis Smith & Kurt Weis, "Toward an Open Systems Approach to Studies in the Field of Victimology," in Viano, note 3 *supra,* 43; Herbert Maisch & Horst Schuler-Springorum, "Procedural Victimology and Its Contributions to Victimological Knowledge," in Drapkin & Viano, note 17 *supra,* 13; Albert Biderman, "Victimology and Victimization Surveys," in Drapkin & Viano, note 17 *supra,* 135; Marie G. Argana, 'Development of a National Victimization Survey," in Drapkin & Viano, note 17 *supra,* 171; Ellie S. Cohn, et al., "Crime Prevention vs. Victimization: The Psychology of Two Different Reactions," *Victimology,* 3(1978), 285; Heather McKay & John Hagan, "Studying the Victim of Crime: Some Methodological Notes," *Victimology,* 3(1978), 135; Eduard Ziegenhagen, *Victims, Crime and Social Control* (New York: Praeger, 1977); William G. Doerner, "Correspondence Between

Crime Victim Needs and Available Public Services," *Soc. Serv. R.,* 50(1976), 482; K. Aromaa & S. Leppa, "A Survey of Individual Victims of Property Crimes," Institute of Criminology (1973), series M: 26; H. Brownell, "The Forgotten Victims of Crime," *Record,* 31(1976), 136; M. Mansfield, "Justice for the Victims of Crime," *Houston L.R.,* 9(1975), 75; Clyde W. Franklin, "Victimology Revisited: A Critique and Suggestions for Future Directions," *Criminology,* 14(1976), 125; John B. Cordrey, "Crime Rates, Victims and Offenders," *J. Police Sci. & Admin.,* 3(1975), 100; Wesley G. Skogan, "Victimization Surveys and Criminal Justice Planning," *U. Cinn. L.R.,* 45(1976), 167; Wesley G. Skogan, "Victims of Crime: Some National Panel Data," (Washington: U.S. Dept. Justice, 1975); "Michigan Public Speaks Out on Crime," (Washington: U.S. Dept. Justice, 1973); D.D. Schram, "Study of Public Opinion and Criminal Victimization in Seattle," (Washington: U.S. Dept. Justice, 1973); D. Blumin, "Victims: A Study of Crime in a Boston Housing Project," (Boston: Mayor's Safe Streets Act Advisory Comm., 1973); N.J. Beran, "Criminal Victimization in Small Town, USA," *Intl. J. Crim. & Penol.,* 2(1974), 7; Deborah Galvin, "Concepts in Victimization and the Slave," in Viano, note 3 *supra,* 571; Vahahn N. Dadrian, "An Attempt at Defining Victimology," in Viano, note 3 *supra,* 40; A.D. Biderman, "Time Distortions of Victimization Data and Mnemonic Effects," (Washington: Bur. Soc. Sci. Res., 1970); Frank Carrington, *Victims* (New Rochelle: Arlington House, 1975); M. Wright, "Nobody Came: Criminal Justice and the Needs of Victims," *Howard J. Penol. & Crime Prev.,* 16(1977), 22.

50. Ken Levine, "Empiricism in Victimological Research: A Critique," *Victimology,* 3(1978), 77.

51. Lynn A. Curtis, "Victims, Policy, and the Dangers of a Conservative Mentality," unpublished paper presented to Second International Symposium on Victimology, Boston, 1976; Lynn Curtis, "The Conservative New Criminology," *Society,* 14 (1977), 3.

52. James Stookey, "The Victim's Perspective on American Criminal Justice," (Minneapolis: Minn. Dept. Correct., 1976); Eduard Ziegenhagen, "Toward a Theory of Victim-Criminal Justice System Interactions," in McDonald, note 28 *supra,* 261; David Landy & Elliott Aronson, "Influence of the Character of the Criminal and His Victim on the Decisions of Simulated Jurors," in Drapkin & Viano, note 3 *supra,* 95; John Conklin, *The Impact of Crime* (New York: MacMillan, 1975); Anthony Schembri, "The Victim and the Criminal Justice System," in Viano, note 3 *supra,* 348; Eduard Ziegenhagen, *Victims, Crime, and Social Control* (New York: Praeger, 1977); Richard Knudten, "The Victim in the Administration of Justice: Problems and Perspectives," in McDonald, note 28 *supra,* 115; "Crime Victims: Recovery for Police Inaction and Underprotection," *Law & Soc. Order,* (1970), 179.

53. Richard Quinney, "Who Is The Victim?" *Criminology,* (1972),314; Joseph Newman, "The Offender as the Victim," in Drapkin & Viano, note 17 *supra,* 113; Jeffrey Reiman, "Victims, Harm, and Justice," in Drapkin & Viano, note 3 *supra,* 77; Essat A. Fattah, "The Use of the Victim as an Agent of Self-Legitimization: Toward a Dynamic Explanation of Criminal Behavior," *Victimology,* 1(1976), 29; W.J. Blum, "Victims of Crime and Other Victims," *Chi. Bar Rec.,* 51(1971), 463.

54. John Kidner, "Victims? Hell! We're the Victims!: A Conversation with Charles "Chuckie" Crimaldi," *Victimology,* 3(1978), 161.

55. James Ratcliffe, *The Good Samaritan and the Law* (Garden City: Doubleday, 1966); Leonard Bickman, "Bystander Involvement in a "Crime," in Viano, note 3 *supra,* 144; Biff Latane & Joan Dorky, *The Unresponsive Bystander* (New York: Appleton-Century-Crofts, 1970).

56. Robert Crosby & David Snyder, "Crime Victimization in the Black Community,"

in Drapkin, note 39 *supra,* 175; P.H. Kleinman, "Victimization and Perception of Crime in a Ghetto Community," *Criminology,* 11(1973), 307.

57. E.L. Quarantelli & Russell Dynes, "Organizations as Victims in American Mass Disturbances," in Drapkin & Viano, note 39 *supra,* 121; Stuart J. Miller, et al., "Games People Play: Notes on Staff Victimization," in Drapkin & Viano, note 39 *supra,* 157.

58. Simon Dimitz, et al., "Inmate Exploitation: A Study of the Juvenile Victim," in Drapkin & Viano, note 39 *supra,* 135; Israel Drapkin, "The Prison Inmate as Victim," in Viano, note 3 *supra,* 560.

59. Ward Sinclair & John Jacobs, "Are These America's Political Prisoners?" *Washington Post,* 8 January 1978, 71.

60. Rona Fields, "Victims of Terrorism: Effects of Prolonged Stress," *Evaluation & Change: Services for Victims* (Minneapolis: Minn. Medical Res. Found., 1980), 76.

61. Vernetta D. Young, "Victims of Female Offenders," in Parsonage, note 43 *supra,* 72.

62. Bruno M. Cormier, "Mass Murder, Multicide, and Collective Crime: The Doers and the Victims," in Drapkin & Viano, note 39 *supra,* 71; Chanoch Jacobsen, "Condoned Mass Deviance and Its Victims," in Drapkin & Viano, note 39 *supra,* 91.

63. Gilbert Geis, "Victimization Patterns in White Collar Crime," in Drapkin & Viano, note 39 *supra,* 89; Maurice Goldsmith, "The Thalidomide Affair," in Drapkin, note 39 *supra,* 205.

64. Yoel Yinon and Ilana Tennenbaum, "Employers Attitudes Towards the Employment of Ex-Convicts in Israel," in Drapkin & Viano, note 26 *supra,* 41.

65. Hugo Bedau, "Are There Really Crimes Without Victims?" in Drapkin & Viano, note 3 *supra,* 63; Milo Tyndel, "Offenders Without Victims," in Drapkin & Viano, note 3 *supra,* 55; S. Wachter, "High Cost of Victimless Crimes," *Record,* 28(1973), 357.

66. David Schichor, "The Wrongfully Accused and the Criminal Justice System," in Drapkin & Viano, note 17 *supra,* 121; T. Chiossone, "Defendant's Right to Reparation for Damage Caused by Detention Following a Verdict of Not Guilty," *Annuario del Instituto de Ciencias Penales y Criminologicas,* 5(1973), 23; Richard Moran & Stephen Zeidman, "Victims Without Crimes: Compensation to the Not Guilty," in Drapkin & Viano, note 26 *supra,* 21.

67. Vahahn N. Dadrian, "The Victimization of the American Indian," *Victimology,* 1(1976), 517.

68. Terry Norris & Jack Bynum, "The Medical Abortionist: Villian or Victim?" in Viano, note 3 *supra,* 413.

69. Susan Salasin, "Treating Vietnam Veterans as Survivors," *Evaluation & Change* (Minneapolis: Minn. Medical Res. Found., 1980), 135.

70. Edward Sagarin & Donal E.J. MacNamara, "The Homosexual as a Crime Victim," in Drapkin & Viano, note 39 *supra,* 73.

71. Knowlton W. Johnson, et al., "Consumer Protection: Responsiveness of Control Agents to Victims of Fraud," *Victimology,* 3(1978), 63; Diane Vaughan & Giovanna Carto, "Victims of Fraud: Victim Responsiveness, Incidence, and Reporting," in Viano, note 3 *supra,* 403; "Fraudulent Advertising: The Right of a Public Attorney to Seek Restitution for Consumers," *Pac. L.J.,* 4(1973), 168.

72. Julius Segal, et al., "Universal Consequences of Captivity," in *Evaluation & Change* (Minneapolis: Minn. Medical Res. Found., 1980), 84.

73. Vahahn N. Dadrian, "The Common Features of the Armenian and Jewish Cases of Genocide: A Comparative Victimological Perspective," in Drapkin & Viano, note 39 *supra,* 99; Thomas Adler & Jahudit Stern, "The Psychopathology and Psychodynamics of Youth and Children in Holocaust Survivors," in Drapkin & Viano, note 26 *supra,* 69.

74. Stanley W. Johnson, "Toward a Supra-National Criminology: The Right and Duty of Victims of National Governments to Seek Defense Through World Law," in Drapkin & Viano, note 3 *supra*, 37.

75. William Ryan, *Blaming the Victim* (New York: Vintage, 1971); Sidney Lens, "Blaming the Victims," *The Progressive*, August 1980, 27.

76. Nevertheless, as will be suggested, these "advances" are still notable for largely ignoring the underlying causes—the social sources of crime—of the problem.

CHAPTER TWO
Historical Development of Victim Compensation

Much writing in the area of victimology has occurred in the last two decades. Victim compensation research, in particular, has occupied a significant portion of that output. Several different approaches to victim-compensation studies have been taken: Some research emphasizes the legal issues involved, including various kinds of legislation that have created compensation programs. Other studies focus on various new proposals to create compensation plans. Still other research analyzes the pros and cons of compensation, and the possible alternatives for the crime victim. And, just as many other reports summarize victim compensation's requirements, methods, and operations.

Besides addressing the question of compensation generally, some research focuses on specific programs, such as one or more of the existing American state plans. Other studies dwell on proposals to enact a federal compensation scheme, and still others make comparisons with the numerous foreign plans that exist. Finally, some limited research attempts to assess the outcomes of actual compensation programs, and to evaluate their operations. The study presented herein attempts to expand significantly this latter portion of the literature by evaluating victim compensation's impact—largely through the eyes of crime victims themselves.

Many of the existing studies take a historical approach to compensation, and considered altogether, the research can be viewed as a chronicle of victim compensation's historical development. Consequently, the following literature review will clarify the evolution of such plans, as well as highlight their underlying theories, controversies, and modern day manifestations. This survey will enable an analysis of the defenses and critiques of victim compensation, the possible alternatives, the purposes and administration of such plans, and the existing evaluations of compensation programs. This review will provide a context for the specific research that is being presented in this study.

Historical Development

Early Law

Despite what appears to be only a recent concern for repaying the crime victim for his losses, the practice is historically quite ancient[1]. Before government began regulating the criminal process, reparation occurred in a "blood revenge" taken by the victim against the offender[2]. But, after the state took control of criminal justice, such revenge became, in itself, a criminal act. Thereafter, victim restitution occurred through negotiations in either a "composition" or "adhesive" procedure, which produced a combined monetary and punitive judgment. Restitution was included as an element of the offender's atonement[3].

But, as the state increased its dominance over human activities, it also enhanced its control over criminal justice. Thus, the restitution previously given by the offender to the victim was taken increasingly by the King or other leader as fines to help bolster government treasuries. And, the victim was left to recover for his losses on his own. Even the oft-cited Hammurabian Code of 2250 B.C., which compensated crime victims and thus provides a precedent for the practice, really was motivated more by a desire for better law enforcement and commerce than by the victim's needs[4].

The "composition" process divided eventually into the two separate systems we know today. Thus, the victim must now resort to a separate civil action to recover damages previously received through restitution. Crime has become an offense not against the victim but against the state, while the civil wrong has become a separate offense against the individual. From its origins in western civilization's primitive law, criminal justice has moved from an individualistic orientation to a social one, and the victim has literally been the victim.

Alternatives to Victim Compensation

Victim compensation's opponents have suggested many other possible methods of recovery for the crime victim. But, in fact, close analysis shows that crime victims have for centuries been without any really effective means of recouping their losses, or for seeking some action against the offender. The fact that this dilemma persists to the present day is only one indication of the meagre public policy and resource commitment toward the crime victim.

Among the alternatives to compensation that have been suggested is the civil suit, but having the victim take the criminal to court to seek reparations has obvious weaknesses[5]. Since such a small portion of all offenders are captured, a criminal will probably be unavailable for the victim to sue in the first place. Even when apprehended, some offenders are not convicted. And, many of those who are convicted go to prison, which usually means that the offender cannot collect (if the suit is successful) until at least after the incarceration ends.

A civil suit may be brought against the criminal when he is not imprisoned, or after being released, but the system and the offender's typical characteristics then seem to frustrate the victim's success[6]. If the criminal is available, and if the victim can somehow afford legal representation (and the victim's loss often prevents this), then a civil suit may be filed. But, the procedure is cumbersome. The principle of "mutuality" renders all evidence of the offender's conviction inadmissable in many states[7]. The criminal is entitled to separate proceedings for each case brought against him.

The criminal trial results from the state's indicting the offender. The civil proceeding results from an individual's accusation against the criminal. Therefore, the victim and his counsel must build an entirely new case, which tends to be a long and costly process. Most suits are failures, and in those few successful ones, the damages awarded rarely include sufficient restitution or an allowance for expenses such as legal fees[8]. What's worse, however, is that even if the civil process was a more viable proceeding, most offenders are too poor to pay a judgment against them in the first place. Although the United States could copy the use by some foreign legal systems of a "joinder" proceeding that allows a simultaneous criminal and civil trial[9], this approach would still fall considerably short of a realistic solution for the victim.

Other so-called "remedies" for the victim include suggestions that the victim merely absorb the loss, justified either based on a desire to avoid having people rely on the government dole, or on the claim that any money diverted from crime prevention to provide for the victim is unwarranted[10]. The latter argument stresses the scarce resources available for criminal justice, and that preventing crimes will avoid the need to compensate victims in the first place. Unfortunately, we already have poured millions of dollars into crime prevention and it has had no noticeable effect.

Seeking personal revenge is another apparent solution for the victim, but it breeds lawlessness and disorder. Informal restitution by private arrangement sometimes occurs such as in embezzlement and other property cases, but technically, the victim legally obstructs justice by accepting such a payment. Although such "payoffs" might occur more than we think, it hardly can be suggested as the recourse that victims should rely upon. Some professional criminals use "blood money" to pay victims for not pressing charges[11]. But, again this causes the victim to violate the law, and generally provides no realistic and reliable solution.

Incorporating restitution into suspended or probationary sentences has increased in the last few years, and many have advocated its more intensive use[12]. It is an encouraging sign (not only for the victim, but also as an alternative to imprisoning the offender) but the idea has a long way to go, and suffers from some obvious weaknesses as well. It fails to account for sentencing inequities, the offender's frequent lack of assets, and the fact that many offenders are not apprehended and some are not convicted.

Some states are experimenting with allowing offenders to earn restitution while on work release from prison, but again the limitations remain[13]. And, for imprisoned offenders, the victim's hope for restitution is often nonexistent. Most prisoners do not earn wages while incarcerated, and those few prison industries that do exist are constrained severely by policies that embody private industry's fear of competition[14]. And, a related suggestion seeks to pay victims from the statutory fines ordinarily paid by the offender to the government, but this proposal suffers from most of the same weaknesses as does restitution[15].

Still another remedy advocated is using private insurance to indemnify the victim for his losses[16]. This is pressed as a way to avoid increasing the government's welfare costs, perhaps even requiring compulsory crime insurance similar to automobile coverage. This solution has many problems, however. First, it is far from clear that the victim should have to bear the burden of indemnifying himself. Also, it erroneously assumes that most people can afford insurance, and know how to cover themselves adequately against crime. And, even if they did, most insurance companies will not issue policies in high-crime areas, or place severe limitations on coverage[17], or charge exorbitant rates for coverage[18]. The people most likely to be victims either cannot get sufficient insurance or, for personal or economic reasons, avoid purchasing what is available.

Frequently, victims must accept state welfare as a result of their losses. This tends to be a demeaning and inequitable method of recovery[19]. Private organizations sometime provide charity, but this also is demeaning, unreliable, and inequitable. The government sometimes furnishes "charity" itself through relief such as tax deductions for stolen property, but this is hardly a suitable remedy. State legislators have been known to sometimes vote aid to specific victims, but this obviously is limited and perhaps even unconstitutional[20].

Finally, the notion of a crime-tort has been recognized in statutes that establish liability for damages caused by government against private individuals[21]. Under those laws, the state's responsibility derives from its failure to protect individuals during activities such as fighting fires and suppressing riots. Further extending government liability can occur only by diminishing the state's "sovereign immunity"—the doctrine that assumes that government can do no wrong, and that liability would hamper governmental functioning[22]. If this doctrine were eliminated or compromised, then government liability could begin to include its inability to provide sufficient law enforcement. This is perhaps a worthy idea, but requires a considerable change in state policy, and many of the aforementioned problems of bringing a civil suit—this time against the government—would still remain.

In sum, the proposed alternatives for the victim in seeking to recover his losses are clearly inadequate. It is from recognizing these drawbacks that a more viable and comprehensive approach has been suggested—the grant of victim compensation.

Victim Compensation and Its Critics

The idea of victim compensation is to have the government reimburse the crime victim from state or national funds that are raised through taxes. Needless to say, many people oppose such an approach[23].

Some critics insist that the victim's present remedies are not so inadequate, and ought to be relied upon. This is especially the case for advocates of private insurance. Brock, for example, claims that state compensation would encroach on private insurers[24]. Mueller and Sheleff object to "crime" victims being singled out for attention among the many other kinds of unaided victims in society[25]. Mueller also argues that failure caused the old compensation approach to disappear, so why repeat the same mistake[26]? Smodish claims that such a policy would only enhance an already too far advanced "creeping socialism."[27] Others object simply to creating another massive bureaucracy, and to the difficulties of administering such a program[28]. And, perhaps the strongest objections come from those who envision enormous costs for victim compensation[29].

Additional opposition comes from those who either doubt the victim's general innocence, or the government's ability to distinguish the innocent from those who may have contributed to their own victimization. Thus, for example, Menninger reiterates a frequently voiced fear about the likelihood of fraudulant claims[30]. More specifically, some—like Michael Fooner—suggest that individuals might engage in activities (such as prostitution perhaps) that could invite victimization, or might fake victimization[31] in order to get an award[32].

And, at least one writer—Harry Weihofen—has cited the frequent personal relationship that exists between victims and offenders in violent crimes, thus questioning whether, for example, the husband who attacks his wife might not benefit from his wife's compensation[33]. Overall, considerable doubt exists in some observers' minds, based on statistics showing victims' high level of prior court involvement—sometimes as defendants themselves—whether victims are really any different from criminals, and thus deserve special consideration in the first place[34].

Gerhard Mueller continues his critique of state compensation by stressing its potentially adverse effects on law enforcement. It is suggested, for example, that the money spent on compensation could be better invested in more effective law-enforcement techniques[35]. Furthermore, others claim that state compensation would not only avoid improving law enforcement, but actually cause its deterioration. That is, some argue that since revenue is limited, it will have to come from existing programs to finance compensation plans.

Some—like Fooner—go even further to conclude that state compensation would actually induce crime[36]. Some of that crime might be caused by public or offender complacency, either concluding perhaps that victimization is not so bad for the recipient if he is guaranteed compensation. Or, as Maggadino describes it, victim compensation might produce a "moral hazard," whereby people will be willing to submit themselves to the more hazardous state of having less crime protection with the prospect of benefitting from compensation if they are ever victimized[37]. This, of course, assumes that expenditures are positively related to crime prevention, and that withdrawing some of them (for use as compensation) will necessarily increase the crime rate.

Roger Meiners, arguing along similar lines, indicates that people will be forced to forego purchasing crime insurance and prevention because they will have to use the money they would ordinarily have for such purchases to pay the higher taxes necessitated by adopting a compensation program. Thus, in his mind, victim compensation might constitute nothing more than a "subsidy for criminal activity."[38]

And finally, some objections to compensation derive from claims that the policy is only a thin disguise for redistributing income. Having everyone pay for state compensation through their taxes (ignoring for the moment the inequities therein) would dispense the cost of crime, and thus put a greater burden on those who are less affected (especially in the case of violent crime) by it. And, in addition, others claim that if this does not constitute redistribution among economic classes, then at the very least it amounts to a regional redistribution. That is, as Maggadino argues, the lower-crime rural and suburban areas would have to subsidize the compensation for the nation's higher-crime urban areas[39]. But, even if income redistribution is an acceptable basis or goal of these programs, Meiners claims that a better approach would be to transfer the money directly, without any compensation plans at all, because this would avoid the aforementioned side-effect of possibly increasing criminal activity[40].

The Case for Victim Compensation

Despite the numerous objections and cautions voiced by some against state compensation, the overall support has been extensive. The general[41] and official[42] public seem to be very much in favor of the idea. Individual victims also have expressed their support[43]. And, scholarly and governmental promotion are likewise abundant[44].

More than simply citing the aforementioned inadequacies of the crime victim's existing remedies, many have derived theories to justify victim compensation generally:

Strict Liability Theory. This rationale, which is said to have originated from Jeremy Bentham, claims that compensation should be awarded because the social contract between the victim and his government has been broken. That is, the victim has a legal claim against the state for its failure to prevent the crime that produced the victimization[45]. Since the government limits the individual's ability to protect himself, and instead gives that power to law-enforcement personnel, and taxes the individual to support that personnel, then the government can be held liable by the victim when its law-enforcement activities are unsuccessful[46]. And, the case against the government is enhanced when one considers the barriers it creates against the victim's being restituted by the offender, including the aforementioned doctrine of mutuality—which limits the chances of civil recovery, and the state's imprisonment of the offender—which impedes his ability to reimburse the victim[47].

Furthermore, some take this so far as to not only accuse the state of not preventing crime, but also of actually producing or inducing crime in the first place. That is, it is claimed that government helps produce a social environment that is conducive to crime, and it therefore produces crime victims. Thus, based on these arguments, and recognizing the drawbacks of a civil suit against the government, some have concluded that victim compensation is the only way to hold the state liable for victimizations, while giving the victim a reasonable chance of recovery.

Government Negligence Theory. Some critics argue that perhaps we cannot hold the government responsible for all crime, but that at least it should be held liable for victimizations caused by negligence of law-enforcement personnel. This, of course, would provide a more selective basis for a victim's eligibility for compensation[48].

Equal Protection Theory. Another approach maintains that victim compensation would be a way of equalizing the burdens of victimization[49]. Since some people live in high crime areas while others do not, it is claimed that government should do something to redress the imbalance in peace and general welfare enjoyed by its citizens[50]. Another argument along these lines recognizes that efficiency in law enforcement requires that not all victimizations be investigated and that not all crime be prevented in the first place. To promote equity, however, it would seem appropriate to reimburse victims to compensate for the resulting crime. Thus, victim compensation is a way to promote equal benefits[51].

Humanitarian Theory. This rationale does not place any blame or legal responsibility on the government for victimizations, but rather suggests the granting of compensation on humanitarian grounds. Thus, this would constitute a kind of "government charity" in a more organized fashion, and presumably be given to needy individuals after victimization[52].

Social Obligation Theory. Some claim that historically (at least until recent developments in the modern era) the victim and society had a special relationship in law enforcement. Evidence exists that one of the main reasons why the victim lost that role was because governments increasingly sought to use the restitution previously paid to the victim as fines to bolster their own depleted treasuries[53]. It is suggested that the time has come to cease taking advantage of the victim, and moreover, to go further to meet his needs. Although the victim might have no clear legal claim against the government for assistance under this theory, it is argued that the state should use its "police powers" to provide for the victim's welfare[54], and create such a "right." Thus, the state would be providing for the victim, but he need not be destitute to qualify.

Social Welfare Theory. This is the most widely advocated basis for victim compensation. It is grounded on a rationale similar to that offered for the social obligation theory, except that compensation would be limited to only those who are in need, or who would otherwise qualify for government "welfare." This difference is rationalized by the desire to limit the welfare state's reach, and to provide assistance (especially with scarce resources) only for those who need it most[55].

Crime Prevention Theory. Still another rationale suggests that state compensation is warranted because it will actually aid in law enforcement[56]. The public will be more likely to report crime, to aid in apprehending and identifying criminals, to press charges, and to aid criminal-justice personnel generally if they have some hope of recovering compensation for their efforts[57]. Furthermore, it is claimed that compensation might prevent further crime, since it will mitigate the victim's desire to break the law to seek revenge against the offender or to seek money to survive after his victimization losses.

Political Motives Theory. A final basis relies on the various political advantages of granting compensation. Public opinion is strongly in favor of such plans[58], and thus it is good political strategy to respond to such sentiments[59]. Furthermore, even if a person is never victimized and thus never has a need for compensation, politicians can benefit from the good will the policy builds in people toward the criminal-justice system, the government, and politicians themselves. Thus, compensation can provide a symbolic, psychological benefit to the public, even if it never needs or receives any actual aid[60]. And, of course, that kind of response helps bolster the regime's political stability by helping curb the alienation that a failing criminal process—and society, might engender.

With one or more of these rationales in mind, numerous proposals outlining the ingredients of a workable compensation program have been advanced. Model plans have been offered by organizations such as the Council of State Governments, the Harvard Journal of Legislation, the Canadian Corrections Association, the Conference of Commissioners on Uniformity of Legislation in Canada, the National Conference of Commissioners on Uniform State Laws[61], and the National Association of Attorneys General[62], as well as by individual researchers[63].

Victim-Compensation Programs

Foreign Plans. The credit for instigating the first, actual victim-compensation programs is often given to Margery Fry[64], a British criminal reformer who worked diligently to establish such plans. Actually, the first plan was begun in New Zealand[65] in 1963. Great Britain[66] launched its scheme a year later, followed by the United States in 1965, by Canada[67] and Australia[68] in 1967, by Northern Ireland[69] in 1968, and by Sweden[70] in 1971.

Other nations outside the United States have been considering such plans for a number of years as well[71]. But, a somewhat less pressing need exists in many other nations because, among other things, they[72]—unlike the United States— have long ago formalized the victim's claim for restitution from the offender as a part of the criminal proceeding. Thus, although not all offenders are apprehended or convicted, the victim's chances of recovery are still much greater than when he must rely on a separate civil suit, as in the United States[73].

American Plans. The first compensation program in the United States began in 1965 in California[74]. It was joined by New York[75] and Hawaii[76] in 1967, and by Massachusetts[77] and Maryland[78] in 1968. In the past decade, at least twenty other states have legislated such programs[79]. Also, one territory, the Virgin Islands, has had a plan since 1968. Nevada (1969) and Georgia (1972) have adopted only limited compensation plans that make awards solely to "good samaritans"— those who incur losses while trying to aid an individual or the police in preventing a crime[80]. Rhode Island has had a program since 1972, but has specifically withheld its operation until a federal statute—providing the state with matching funds—is enacted. And finally, Louisiana, which had legislated a plan in 1974, never appropriated any funds to enable actual compensation, and in 1976 repealed the program altogether[81].

The idea of a federal program has existed since at least 1965 when Senator Yarborough began introducing a bill that would create a national compensation plan which would provide the states financial incentives to adopt similar programs[82]. In 1972, Senator McClellan assumed the battle for such legislation, but he was no more successful[83]. And, most recently, Congressman Rodino and Senator Kennedy have proposed bills, but as of this writing no federal program has been created. The major obstacle has been fears about such a program's costs. Those doubts still exist despite recent studies that conclude that the actual costs— providing the federal program was patterned after the typical state program now existing—would not be nearly as astronomical as it is often assumed[84].

Political Context of Victim Compensation

Apart from the weight of opinion, the short-run political advantages, and the aforementioned justifications for victim compensation, what caused this and other forms of victim assistance to emerge in the United States in the 1960's? The answer seems to lie primarily in its relationship to the disruption and crisis of the period.

Beginning with the civil-rights movement in the early 1960's, instability grew throughout the decade from events such as urban riots, the welfare-rights movement, and Vietnam War protests[85]. Simultaneously, the Warren Court had been extending significant constitutional rights to criminal suspects and defendants at precisely the time when law and order toughness against protest and crime became the rallying cry of the day[86]. The backlash against civil rights for blacks seemed to coincide with the backlash against "handcuffing the police" in their battle against crime—whose perpetrators were largely characterized as blacks.

By the 1968 presidential election, crime was considered the nation's number one issue[87], and Richard Nixon campaigned and won as a "law-and-order" candidate. Nixon was not the only one rallying behind this issue: Nelson

Rockefeller—at that time governor of New York—had been pushing for tougher law enforcement in his state, and especially in New York City, for some time. The Nixon election, however, signalled a new mood for law enforcement which was bolstered by a new federal involvement—ironically to counteract many of the criminal-justice decisions of the federal judiciary. Nixon changed that judiciary, however, with the appointment of Warren Burger as Chief Justice, and the President pushed for other changes, such as the Omnibus Crime Control and Safe Streets Act of 1968 and the new Law Enforcement Assistance Administration in 1969, as well. Thus begun a law-and-order perspective that, despite the economic distractions of the 1970's, has lasted strongly through the present day—and may, in fact, be reintensifying[88].

Government actions in criminal justice were not merely a response to rising crime, which was particularly highlighted by the victimization studies of the late 1960's that indicated vastly higher crime levels than we had imagined. New policies were perhaps even more a result of the protest that much of the crime seemed to reflect. Just as government had instituted programs during the New Deal and then again, beginning with Lyndon Johnson's Great Society programs in 1964, moves were made to stem the tide of disenchantment.

Ostensibly labelled as welfare designed by the government to meet the needs of the poor, the programs of the 1960's had much more to do with seeking calm in a crisis situation[89]. Part of that crisis derived from massive urban problems, whose increase could be traced, in part, back to the irresponsibility and negligence of state governments. The massive new involvement of the federal government was a response to state inaction to a considerable degree. But, while the states might have been content to transfer most of the problems of their cities to the national government, the issue of law enforcement was not so easily passed on. Although extensive national government funding would later be directed toward local law-enforcement in the 1970's, the responsibility for concrete, local action in the 1960's could not be skirted. With crime prevention requiring decentralized action directly in the cities, states and localities were forced to act—especially with law enforcement being the major public demand of the period. It was in this area, therefore, that the states offered some of their strongest arguments for federalism and a halt to national government (read: Warren Court) interference in their activities[90].

Besides fighting off federal interference prior to the Nixon and Burger era, the states took some steps of their own in law enforcement. One of them was to begin to talk loudly about the plight of the crime victim and to experiment with possible victim assistance. The greatest threat perceived was from violent crime, and thus it is not surprising to find the American states eventually creating victim-compensation programs for precisely that problem.

But, victim compensation also was widely perceived not as general assistance, but rather as a welfare program, since violent-crime victims were mostly poor.

These programs also produced a potential psychological satisfaction for other economic classes, but the focus was on those lower class people who, not coincidentally, were the subject of a wide variety of other social-appeasement programs at the same time[91].

In other words, victim compensation was one of many welfare programs designed to help reduce urban unrest. As Daniel Moynihan has suggested:

> In 1965 there had been four major riots and civil disturbances in the country. In 1966 there were twenty-one major riots and civil disorders. In 1967 there were eighty-three major riots and civil disturbances. In the first seven months of 1968 there were fifty-seven major riots and disturbances...In retrospect the domestic turbulence of the United States in the late 1960's may come to appear something less than cataclysmic. But this was not the view of the men then in office. Mayors, governors—presidents—took it as given that things were in a hell of a shape and that something had to be done.[92]

In New York, for example, Nelson Rockefeller created the State Urban Action Center in 1967, which was established to reduce urban crime and violence[93]. This also happened to be the same year he pushed victim compensation through the New York State legislature.

In sum, although the American states actually took their cues from the compensation plans of other nations, the impetus was less social justice and more a matter of seeking social stability. The meagre, tangible commitment and results of the programs—even in the beginning—serve to emphasize their largely symbolic purpose, during a time of crisis. And, after the crisis (which was much more widely perceived as one of social protest and not simply one of high crime) passed, even the psychological commitment waned.

The Administration of Victim Compensation

How victim compensation is granted may have an important effect on a program's success, but no comparative research has investigated this possibility. Nevertheless, four different kinds of administration do occur among the existing programs: 1) criminal courts; 2) civil courts; 3) dependent boards; and 4) independent boards. In the United States, however, only the latter three are represented.

For a long time, establishing an independent board was clearly the dominant approach to administering awards. This method provides for an agency that is completely occupied with awarding compensation. Recently, however, other administrative approaches have been increasing. Jurisdictions such as California, Washington, North Dakota, Wisconsin, and Virginia have merely added a compensation office to another pre-existing agency, and thus are dependent boards[94].

The final two administrative approaches use the existing courts. One method, which exists in Massachusetts, Ohio, Illinois, and Northern Ireland, allows compensation claims to be made in the civil courts, where compensation is determined through an investigation by a state's attorney[95], and a decision by a trial judge[96]. And, the final method, used only in New South Wales and Queensland, awards compensation initially through the criminal courts. That is, the victim makes a claim for compensation at the offender's trial, and that request is acted upon by the attorney general's office and the treasury department, in separate decisions[97].

Argument persists over the best administrative method. Some indicate, for example, that the courts are already overburdened[98], and thus are inappropriate for awarding compensation, whereas others argue that local courts provide victims with the greatest access to possible awards[99]. Some claim that the best results will be achieved by creating an independent board, while others counter that incorporating the board into a pre-existing agency prevents the growth of yet another bureaucracy. In any case, despite some recent experiments away from independent boards, they still remain by far the most common method of administering compensation.

Almost all compensation plans are funded from tax revenues. But, a couple of jurisdictions[100], such as Virginia and Florida, do finance their programs solely from money raised by fining criminals in addition to other sanctions they might receive for committing the crime[101].

While the organizational characteristics of court-administered compensation plans obviously correspond to normal trial courts, the features of independent and dependent boards are distinct. The boards require victims to file applications indicating their victimization and other circumstances. Each board consists of at least three members who are usually appointed by the governor (or other chief executive) for from four to seven years. Some plans require a political party balance among the board members, and many require that members be attorneys. Some schemes operate on a full-time basis while others work only sporadically.

Claims are usually divided among the board members, and then redistributed again among the board's investigators. Additional information may be requested from the claimant, an investigation is conducted, and then the board member usually issues a unilateral decision on each of the claims in his caseload[102]. It is usually the final decision of the board for most applicants.

Most programs allow claimants to request a review of their decision, in which case the entire board will usually reconsider the lone board member's previous decision. The board might grant the applicant a hearing, either when review is requested, or when the board seeks the claimant's personal testimony. But, hearings are very infrequent, and thus it is usually only the sole investigator who has any personal contact with each victim's case. If the claimant is still dissatisfied with the decision after review, he usually can seek an appeal in the courts[103].

The administrative approach to compensation is clearly less formal and less technical than the judicial approach (or at least compared to what is supposed to happen in the courts). While the burden of providing evidence does fall on the applicant, strict rules as to the admissability of that evidence do not prevail. Most programs allow victims to be represented by counsel, both at hearings and otherwise, but again, legal technicalities are kept to a minimum[104].

Board members are given varying amounts of discretion in considering and making awards. Some boards, such as England's, are very limited in their ability to go beyond the particular legal criteria for a claimant's eligibility for an award. Other programs, such as California's, are given some leeway in applying the rules. And some, such as New York's, appear at times to have considerable discretion in some cases[105].

Most compensation boards seek some kind of relationship with the judicial system, even though most programs are created administratively apart from the courts. This connection is sought for several reasons: First, some concern exists about prejudicing a defendant's case by a premature award to a claimant[106]. That is, granting an award might imply that a crime actually took place, and that information might be used against the person at trial. Thus, the board will often seek to cooperate with the prosecutor's office in the timing of awards. Next, the board wants to interact with the criminal-justice process because it seeks (at least sometimes) to better inform victims about compensation. Thus, for example, the board might rely on the police to inform victims[107], including possible efforts to get policemen to read "victims rights cards" similar to those required for criminal suspects since the Miranda decision.

Finally, the board seeks to be integrated into the criminal-justice process because of the broader goals of victim compensation. That is, granting compensation is not only supposed to allow victims to recover their losses, but also to induce victims (and the public generally) to participate in the process and cooperate with other law-enforcement personnel. In fact, such a connection is necessary perhaps if such programs seek (as they claim to do) to redeem people's attitudes toward criminal justice after being victimized, and after suffering the inevitable burdens of pursuing a criminal case against the offender.

Eligibility for Victim Compensation

Despite some opposing voices, victim compensation has been an overwhelmingly popular policy since its disinterment by New Zealand in 1964[108]. What obstacles the policy has had to overcome stem largely from the issue of cost. From their outward appearance, the programs that have, in fact, been legislated would seem to have overcome this barrier. But, unfortunately, the problem of finances lingers on, even in those programs.

One of this problem's major repercussions is that while legislators have often enthusiastically promoted compensation programs, their eagerness has noticably declined when appropriations for such plans have been considered[109]. Consequently, extensive limitations have been imposed on a claimant's eligibility so as to reduce the number of successful claims, and thereby insure that meagre appropriations will nevertheless be sufficient to fund the program.

Although eligibility restrictions have been the main device to avoid high program costs, another factor is perhaps equally important. That is, legislatures—and boards themselves for that matter—have been extraordinarily stingy in publicizing victim compensation in most cases. The idea of asking the police to inform victims about compensation seems to be the exception to the rule, and when done, is often a request that is ignored anyway. Thus, boards and legislatures have sheltered themselves from the costs of extensive claims by providing poor information about the board's particular application procedures in the first place[110].

But, the actual eligibility requirements are formidable in themselves. First, many boards will only award compensation to citizens of that jurisdiction, and even then, often only when the crime was actually committed there. Overwhelmingly, compensation is limited to violent crimes, and thus property crimes are rarely considered[111]. Although most programs operating outside the United States will consider awards for pain and suffering[112], only Hawaii and Delaware will do the same in this country. Some plans also compensate "good samaritans."[113] Automobile claims are usually excluded, however, unless a vehicle was used as a weapon[114]. Most programs also do not require that offenders actually be convicted in order for the victim to get an award[115], but most plans will, nevertheless, delay a victim's claim to await the criminal case's outcome so as to protect the defendant (or is it more likely the prosecutor?).

Most plans require the claimant's continued cooperation in order to be considered for an award. Thus, the victim is required to have reported the crime to the police within a specified time after his victimization[116]. And, the claim to the compensation board itself must be made in a timely manner[117], although recent changes have extended that time to as much as one year after victimization in at least one jurisdiction. The victim must also cooperate with other criminal-justice personnel to aid in apprehending, identifying, and convicting the offender. In fact, delaying a claim's consideration until after the offender's case is complete has been suggested as a legitimate incentive to the victim to continue cooperating with law-enforcement officials[118].

A fine line appears to exist between eligibility requirements designed to avoid high program costs, and those that are supposedly enforced to prevent fraudulent claims. The fear of fraud is pervasive among those who have created compensation programs. A major (but not sole[119]) reason, for example, for excluding property claims from coverage, is the concern for illegitimate claims. Having a present or past relationship with the offender (including blood ties or sexual relations) disqualifies the victim in order to prevent fraud[120]. And finally, fraud is supposedly curbed by imposing strict standards of responsibility on the victim[121].

That is, no evidence must exist that the victim in any way contributed to his own victimization. Thus, a victim who has been found to have invited, facilitated, provoked, perpetrated, cooperated, or instigated the crime against himself usually will be eliminated from consideration[122].

Since most boards do not rely on the offender's criminal conviction for determining whether in fact a person has been victimized, they must use other criteria instead[123]. Thus, they seek whatever information might be available from law-enforcement personnel, and then rely on investigations by their own staff, and on evidence provided by the victim himself[124]. Despite the usual lack of rigid rules of evidence, the substantial burden of proving a victimization actually took place falls upon the claimant. Obviously, a claimant is only eligible, therefore, if he can convince the board that an appropriate crime occurred in the first place.

If such proof is successfully provided, the claimant is still not guaranteed an award, by any means. First, many programs require that the victim satisfy a "means test" or demonstrate "serious financial hardship" as a result of the crime[125]. Thus, in most of these programs, practically nobody who would not otherwise qualify for basic government welfare qualifies for compensation. Some boards applying the means test will, however, exclude certain basic possessions when considering the victim's assest, which will give some more claimants a chance to qualify for assistance. Other programs exist, however, that do not apply a hardship test at all, and thus claimants from all economic classes will pass this potential hurdle.

If a victim qualifies financially, he still must satisfy other requirements. Most compensation payments are limited to covering out-of-pocket costs, medical expenses due to injuries, and lost income due to time missed at work. And, many times limits exist even on these. For example, reimbursement for work loss usually requires missing at least two weeks work, and even then, is compensated on a fixed rate unrelated to the victim's actual losses. Also, medical costs are often reimbursed on schedules[126] which may not correspond to actual costs. Most programs also require a minimum loss[127], sometimes as high as $500 in order for one's claim to be considered. And, most programs have maximum limits on their awards which may fall short of the legitimate losses[128].

Compensation also is permitted in cases of death caused by victimization. In such cases, funeral expenses are usually paid, and an amount also is granted to dependents[129] for lost support due to the victim's death. Without lost support or funeral expenses, no awards are usually given in death cases.

Claimants must report any other payments they receive from other agencies after their victimization. Those payments are then subtracted from the total award[130]. Unfortunately, most boards will delay final awards to await the outcome of the victim's other claims. Many boards also will subrogate any of the victim's claims against the offender. That is, if the victim were to ever recover a civil judgment or restitution from the criminal, these payments would go to the board to help defray the cost of the victim's compensation[131]. When awards are made, they are usually in a lump-sum form[132], although most boards also make periodic payments in some kinds of cases. Only a few boards grant emergency awards pending the outcome of the claim[133].

In sum, the requirements that must be met to qualify for compensation are extensive. When they are put in perspective, therefore, the limited nature of most compensation programs can be recognized, in spite of their ambitious and glossy facades.

Evaluating Victim-Compensation Programs

The modern era of victim compensation has evolved considerably since its rebirth about two decades ago. Mere discussion of compensation's value and of criteria and proposals for its implementation has evolved into actual, functioning programs. And those few, initial experiments have unfolded into many plans operating today in the United States and various other parts of the world.

Much has been written[134] about this development. But, little research or writing has extended further than merely validating that victim-compensation programs, with certain characteristics, have in fact been created, and are operating. That is, practically no attention has been given to how the programs really work, what effects or results they produce, and whether or not the plans have succeeded or failed[135].

Among the few attempts to assess such programs' effectiveness, several writers have "evaluated" plans by summarizing their impressions of the compensation board's activities. Thus, for example, MacNamara and Sullivan complain that few victims are able to apply for aid because of eligibility requirements or a lack of publicity, that fewer than half those applying are given awards, and that some awards for medical costs have been inflated[136]. Hasan and Sebba argue more specifically that coverage should include property, that mimimum loss and maximum award standards and the relationship exclusion should be eliminated, and that compensation should be considered not as welfare but rather as a right[137]. And, Lamborn complains about no compensation for children conceived in rape[138].

A few researchers have observed that concerns for the crime victim—including exposing drawbacks in current compensation plans—have failed to exceed mere promises or lofty statements. In their minds, compensation has become politically popular, and thus officials have incentives to push for such programs[139]. But, as Chappell argues, the programs have been designed to drastically limit the possibility of achieving their objectives, and thus the result has been a continuing predominance of social values in criminal justice over the concerns of individual crime victims[140]. The simple presence of compensation programs seems to provide "political capital" and satisfies "legislative consciences[141]," when actually they fall (especially in their present, unworkable form) far short of serving the victim's true range of needs.

Further corrections are suggested by Reiff, who seeks emergency awards, simplified application procedures, and eliminating the means test, payment for attorneys by the board, the board's contracting of other victim services, and increasing the time for reporting the crime to the police, among other things[142]. And, Lamborn includes among his impressions that compensation's cost has not proven exorbitant, nor have the programs' sizes ballooned, nor have fraud and victim provocation been major problems. On the other hand, Lamborn also concludes that compensation programs have been no more adequate for victims than the ineffective alternatives they were designed to replace. Not only are few people being compensated, but *"no available analysis* of the evidence supports the thesis that a crime victim compensation plan will affect either the crime rate or the effectiveness of police or prosecutors" (emphasis mine)[143].

This observation is not surprising since so few evaluations exist upon which to measure compensation's impact in the first place. Although many of the aforementioned ''evaluations'' are valuable for the questions they raise and for some of the impressions they provide about how compensation boards are working, they nevertheless do not provide a comprehensive, first-hand, and in-depth assessment of these plans. Only a few researchers have gone any further.

One study by Brooks, for example, seems to promise—by its title—to reveal ''who gets what'' from compensation programs, but instead delivers only ''who may get what.'' That is, the study merely provides a comparison of eligibility requirements and award criteria for several proposed models of compensation legislation and plans[144], and does not look at the actual results for applicants to any particular program, as one might expect. Another offering by the same author appears to be a survey of board members about improving compensation plans, but instead is limited largely to a summary of program rules and regulations[145]. And, in yet another article, Brooks does examine board reports and present some impressions about their activities, but hardly fulfills its title of ''how well are criminal injury compensation programs working?''[146] The author suggests the goals of such programs but fails to assess their achievement in any more than an impressionistic way.

Finally, Brooks does ultimately deliver in another study what he had promised in his earlier work: ''an opinion survey of program administrators.'' This investigation identifies a preference for independent boards to administer compensation, a desire to eliminate the ''need'' requirement, and a wish to award compensation for pain and suffering. Although these preferences do not characterize the typical American program, the other opinions surveyed indicated that administrators largely accept the remaining elements of their own programs[147]. This kind of information taken directly from board members themselves is, of course, considerably more valuable for evaluating programs than merely appearances.

Other research has shown the small beginnings of more comprehensive and detailed assessments of victim compensation. Edward's review of the British plan analyzes victims applying to the board. In limited questioning, it was discovered that claimants are dominated by males, who are largely employed as policemen, and who were victimized on the street[148]. Little was done, however, to take the analysis any further, such as in determining which characteristics may have been most associated with receiving an award. Doerner has analyzed the volume of claims, board decisions, and public awareness from annual reports of California, Maryland, Hawaii, Massachusetts, and New York programs. This research observes the enormous processing delays, and the lack of publicity. The author recommends new administrative procedures to reduce delay, providing attorneys for claimants at no cost, and having the police advise all victims about compensation at the crime scene[149].

In another study of English practice, Vennard sought not to evaluate victim compensation so much as to survey a victim's reaction to a compensation order. The results of this very small inquiry indicate that again publicity about compensation was very poor. And, it appears that among those victims who were aware of compensation, and who desired such assistance, considerable disillusionment results from a failure to get an award. Not receiving compensation thus appears to contribute to a sense of injustice[150].

One planned study by Geis seemed to offer much potential for useful evaluations of victim compensation. This research proposed to evaluate California's plan by interviewing 60 victims who were among the first to be compensated in 1965 and 1966, and comparing them to interviews of another 60 victims who would have been compensated in 1963 and 1964 if the program had existed at that time. This study was intended to assess not only board procedures, but also the program's effect on financial status and victim attitudes[151]. Unfortunately, only a small amount of that research was actually completed. From those minor glimpses, victims seemed to display a considerable desire for revenge, a tendency toward racism, positive feelings toward the police, but negative attitudes toward other criminal-justice personnel[152]. Overall, this research reveals considerable discontent among victims toward both the criminal and the criminal-justice process[153], but the study was unable to assess victim compensation's effect on these attitudes.

Another California project, conducted by Fogelman, went somewhat further. Forty-nine recipients of compensation in that state were interviewed to determine whether their financial needs surpassed their awards by the government. The results showed wide-ranging emotional and social needs, in addition to financial woes[154].

One small study by Redja and Meuer attempted to evaluate victim compensation's effectiveness in reducing economic insecurity. The research provides a comparative analysis of the Hawaiian and New York programs, but unfortunately is limited to drawing conclusions from annual reports. The study finds that Hawaii receives a higher per capita number of claims and gives a higher percentage of awards than the New York program. The authors assume that this must be due to Hawaii's granting awards as a matter of right as compared to New York's welfare or needs approach. On the other hand, New York awards more total compensation, and pays a higher average amount in its awards, than Hawaii. The research devises "income maintenance standards" that include the need for adequate benefits, universal population coverage, equitable financing, encouraging loss prevention, and redistributing income. The study concludes with some recommendations designed to achieve these standards[155].

A major source of controversy has been the possible costs of financing victim-compensation programs. Several attempts have been made to assess these expenses, by both individual researchers[156] and by organizations[157]. But, these evaluations do not appear to be particularly reliable, either because of their faulty assumptions or due to the political motivations that might have directed their conclusions.

Two apparently more reliable assessments, however, focused specifically on the projected costs of a national compensation program[158]. Based on criteria such as the National Crime Survey, board statistics, alternate eligibility requirements, and loss data, the researchers derived twelve possible models of cost. The research has been the most sophisticated cost assessment to date. And, besides cost estimates, its other conclusions are significant as well. The authors find that excluding minimum-loss requirements and intrafamilial victimizations (whose presence is typical of almost all programs) would have a negligible effect on overall costs. This finding alone clearly belies the extensive fears maintained by most legislators and observers contemplating such plans[159].

Finally, the most systematic and comprehensive research into victim compensation's impact has been provided in a few studies by Doerner and various associates[160]. Using an interrupted time-series design, the researchers attempted to assess victim compensation's effect on crime reporting and on conviction rates. In the case of reporting, four states— New York, Hawaii, Maryland, and Massachusetts—with compensation plans were compared to a control group of ten states without compensation. Compensation's advocates often claim that such programs will lower the crime rate. Based on the view that if such an effect was possible it would occur by raising the "known" crime rate (i.e., cause an increased reporting of crime), Doerner hypothesized that the compensation states would show a higher known rate of all crimes and a higher known violent-crime rate as well. Although some changes did occur, Doerner attributed them to the appearance of several confounding rival hypotheses, and not to his own[161].

Doerner's other research examines Ontario's and Saskatchewan's compensation plans as compared to a control group of plans in Nova Scotia, the Northwest Territories and the Yukon, Prince Edward Island, British Columbia, and Newfoundland. Since virtually all compensation plans cover only violent crimes and require some proof of an actual victimization before recovery, the author hypothesized that violent-crime conviction rates in the experimental group would increase, while the property-crime conviction rates would not. Again, rival hypotheses seemed to better explain the minor changes in outcomes than Doerner's theories[162].

Conclusion

These final studies seem to provide some evidence of compensation's effect on criminal justice, and as systematic evaluations of this public policy, they are a valuable contribution. It is clear, however, that such research has been very limited. Even the more sophisticated attempts at empirical studies have been extremely small or restricted.

Some writers, although they have not filled the gap themselves, have at least recognized the need for in-depth, evaluative research. Among those observers are those who have proposed models for evaluating program performance. For example, Lamborn has concluded that successful compensation plans must not only award payments but also operate in an atmosphere that provides an informal process, ensures expeditious decisions, and preserves the claimant's dignity[163].

Another model is presented by Edelhertz and Geis, who also provide the most extensive histories and descriptions of the earliest American programs. Their criteria for board effectiveness include fairness, speed, simplicity, coordination, economy, education, accountability, and communication with other appropriate agencies[164].

Some of the right questions, such as "who gets what?" "how are programs performing?" and "political placebos or progressive programs?" already have been asked in writings that unfortunately fail to provide the answers. Other writers recognizing the need for evaluative research pose other questions as well: What administrative approach to awarding compensation is actually the best in practice? What are the program's specific goals, and to what extent are they actually (not just potentially or apparently) being achieved? To what extent are awards actually meeting victims's real needs? What are the characteristics of those who actually apply for compensation? What is the plan's impact on criminal justice[165]?

Other questions whose answers necessitate new research include: Does the financial-hardship requirement affect the grant of compensation? What is the impact for victims whose claims are denied? What are the various factors, in addition to program regulations, that influence board members in making compensation decisions[166]?

Research undertaken to answer these kinds of questions has not yet occurred. What is needed are systematic, experimental, and comprehensive evaluations of existing compensation programs. The research herein seeks to help satisfy that need.

This study presents goal-oriented research, which focuses not so much on the policymaking process producing compensation programs as on board decision-making and on the plan's effectiveness in achieving its objectives. Nachmais has identified two primary types of evaluative research: Process evaluation assesses whether a particular program is implemented according to its intended guidelines. Impact evaluation, on the other hand, assesses whether the program's implementation produces a change in the desired direction. That is, such evaluation requires operationalizing the program's particular objectives, defining criteria for measuring success, and measuring the policy's progress in achieving those goals[167]. It is by conducting program assessments according to these two major evaluative approaches that this study will hopefully provide a significant addition to the existing victim-compensation literature.

Notes

1. Frank W. Miller, "Comment on the Proposal," *J. Pub. L.,* 8(1959), 203; Helen Silving, "Comment on the Proposal," *J. Pub. L.,* 8(1959), 236; Geoffrey MacCormack, "Revenge and Compensation in Early Law," *Amer. J. Comp. L.,* 21(1973), 69.

2. Stephen Schafer, "Victim Compensation and Responsibility," *S. Cal. L.R.,* 43(1970), 55.

3. Stephen Schafer, "Compensation of Victims of Criminal Offenses," *Crim. L. Bull.,* 10(1974), 605.

4. Robert Childres, "Compensation for Criminally Inflicted Personal Injury," *N.Y.U. L.R.,* 39(1964), 445.

5. Joan Covey, "Alternatives to a Compensation Plan for Victims of Physical Violence," *Dickinson L.R.,* 69(1965), 391; Ruben Castillo, et al., "The Use of Civil Liability to Aid Crime Victims," *J. Crim. L. & Criminol.,* 70(1979), 57; Gerhard O.W. Mueller & H.H.A. Cooper, "Civil Alternatives for Victims of Crimes," unpublished paper, New York University, 1973.

6. Ralph Glatfelter, "For the Victims of Crime: A New Approach," in Israel Drapkin & Emilio Viano (eds.), *Victimology: Society's Reaction to Victimization* (Lexington: D.C. Heath, 1974), 139.

7. Notes, "Use of Record of Criminal Conviction in Subsequent Civil Action Arising from Same Facts as the Prosecution," *Mich. L.R.,* 64(1966), 708.

8. Covey, note 5 *supra,* 393.

9. C. Howard, "Compensation in French Criminal Procedure," *Modern L.R.,* 21(1958); Silving, note 1 *supra,* 237.

10. Gerhard O. Mueller, "Compensation for Victims of Crime: Thought Before Action," *Minn. L.R.,* 50(1965), 213.

11. Bruce R. Jacob, "Reparation or Restitution by the Criminal Offender to His Victim: Applicability of an Ancient Concept in the Modern Correctional Process," *J. Crim. L., Criminol., & Police Sci.,* 61(1970), 152.

12. John Stewart & Stanley Rosen, "Adequacy of Compensation, Worthiness of Recipient, and Their Effects on Transgressor Compliance to Render Aid," *J. Soc. Psych,* 97(1975), 77; Stephen Schafer, "Restitution to Victims of Crime: An Old Correctional

Aim Modernized," *Minn. L.R.*, 50(1965), 243; Stephen Schafer, "Corrective Compensation," *Trial*, 8(1972), 25; Stephen Schafer, "Creative Compensation," *Crime-Trial Mag.*, (1972), 5; Burt Galaway & Joe Hudson, "Restitution and Rehabilitation: Some Central Issues," *Crime & Delinq*, 18(1972), 406; Albert Eglash, "Creative Restitution," *J. Crim. L., Criminol., & Police Sci.*, 48(1958), 619; Naomi Goldstein, "Reparation by the Offender to the Victim as a Method of Rehabilitation for Both," in Drapkin & Viano, note 6 *supra*, 193; Richard Laster, "Criminal Restitution: A Survey of Its Past History and an Analysis of Its Present Usefulness," *U. Rich. L.R.*, 5(1970), 88; Herbert Edelhertz, *Restitutive Justice* (Seattle: Battelle, 1974); Joe Hudson, *Restitution in Criminal Justice* (St. Paul: Minn. Dept. Correct., 1976); R. Deming, "Correctional Restitution: A Strategy for Correctional Conflict Management," *Fed. Prob.*, 40(1976), 27; Joe Hudson, "When Criminals Repay Their Victims: A Survey of Restitution Programs," *Judicature*, 60(1977), 312; Burt Galaway, "Is Restitution Practical?" *Fed. Prob.*, 41(1977), 3; Alan Harland, "Restitution by the Criminal: A Better Way of Paying for Crime?" *Vital Issues*, 27(1975), 2; William Jacobson, "Use of Restitution in the Criminal Process: *People v. Miller*," *U.C.L.A. L.R.*, 16(1969), 456; Kathleen Smith, *A Cure for Crime* (London: Duckworth, 1965); Joe Hudson & Burt Galaway (eds.) *Restitution in Criminal Justice* (Lexington: D.C. Heath, 1977); Stephen Schafer, "The Victim and Correctional Theory: Integrating Victim Reparation with Offender Rehabilitation," in William McDonald (ed.), *Criminal Justice and the Victim* (Beverly Hills: Sage, 1976), 227; Virgil Williams & Mary Fish, "A Proposed Model for Individualized Offender Restitution through State Victim Compensation," in Drapkin & Viano, note 6 *supra*, 155; Burt Galaway, "The Uses of Restitution," *Crime & Delinq.*, 23(1977), 57; Joe Hudson & Burt Galaway (eds.) *Considering the Victim: Readings in Restitution and Victim Compensation* (Springfield, Ill.: Chas. Thomas, 1976); R. Campbell, *Justice Through Restitution—Making the Criminal Pay* (Milford, Mich.: Mott Media, 1977); A. Newton, "Alternatives to Imprisonment: Day Fines, Community Service Orders, and Restitution," *Crime & Delinq. Lit.*, 8(1976), 109; J. Heinz, "Restitution or Parole: A Follow-Up Study of Adult Offenders," *Soc. Serv. R.*, 50(1976), 148; Stephen Schafer, "Correctional Rejuvenation of Restitution to the Victim of Crime," in Walter C. Reckless & Charles L. Newman (eds.), *Interdisciplinary Problems in Criminology* (Columbus: Amer. Soc. Criminol., 1964), 10; Mark Arnold, "Making the Criminal Pay Back His Victim," *Christian Science Monitor*, 14 February 1978, 3; J.M. Perillo, "Restitution in a Contractual Context," *Columb. L.R.* (1973), 1208; Minocher J. Sethna, "Treatment and Atonement for Crime," in Emilio Viano (ed.), *Victims and Society* (Washington: Visage, 1978), 529.

13. David Fogel, et al., "Restitution in Criminal Justice: A Minnesota Experiment," *Crim. L. Bull.*, 8(1973), 681; Bill Read, "How Restitution Works in Georgia," *Judicature*, 60(1977), 322; Joe Hudson, "Undoing the Wrong," *Soc. Work.*, 19(1974), 313; S. Chesney, *Assessment of Restitution in the Minnesota Probation Services* (St. Paul: Minn. Gov. Comm., 1976); R.O. Steggerda, *Victim Restitution: An Assessment of the Restitution in Probation Experiment Operated by the Fifth Judicial District Department of Court Services* (Des Moines: Polk Co. Dept. Prog. Eval., 1975); T. Balivet, *Connecticut: Recommendations for Improving the Use of Restitution as a Dispositional Alternative* (Washington: Amer. U. Inst. Stud. in Justice, 1975); M.S. Serrill, "Minnesota Restitution Center," *Corr. Mag.*, 1(1975), 13.

14. Michael Smodish, "But What About the Victim? The Forsaken Man in American Criminal Law," *U. Fla. L.R.*, 22(1969), 6.

15. Gerhard O. Mueller & H.H.A. Cooper, "Society and the Victim: Alternative Responses," in Drapkin & Viano, note 6 *supra*, 89.

16. James E. Starrs, "A Modest Proposal to Insure Justice for Victims of Crime," *Minn. L.R.*, 50(1965), 285; Minocher Sethna, "Compensation of Victims of Offences," in Drapkin & Viano, note 6 Supra, 168; Fred E. Inbau, "Comment on the Proposal," *J. Pub. L.*, 8(1959), 201.

17. Herbert Denenberg, "Compensation for Victims of Crime: Justice for the Victim as Well as the Criminal," *Insurance L.J.*, (1970), 628.

18. LeRoy Lamborn, "Remedies for the Victims of Crime," *S. Cal. L.R.*, (1970), 43.

19. This is, nevertheless, the means used in New York, and in most other American programs.

20. Smodish, note 14 *supra*, 8.

21. Luis Kutner, "Due Process for Crime Victims," *Trial*, 8(1972), 28; A.M. Linden, "Victims of Crime and Tort Law," *J. Canad. Bar Assn.*, (1969), 17.

22. Luis Kutner, "Crime Torts: Due Process of Compensation for Crime Victims," *Notre Dame Law.*, 41(1966), 494.

23. David J. Bental, "Selected Problems in Public Compensation to Victims of Crime," *Issues in Criminol.*, 3(1968), 217.

24. H. Donnie Brock, "Victims of Violent Crime: Should They Be An Object of Social Effection?" *Miss. L.J.*, 40(1968), 92.

25. Gerhard Mueller, "Comment on the Proposal," *J. Pub. L.*, 8(1959), 218; L. Shaskolsky Sheleff, "Victim Compensation—Its History, Rationale, Implementation, and Potentialities," *Crime, Punish. & Correct.*, 5(1976), 8.

26. Mueller, note 25 *supra*, 229.

27. Smodish, note 14 *supra*, 11.

28. Mueller, note 10 *supra*, 219.

29. *Ibid.*, 214.

30. Karl Menninger, *The Crime of Punishment* (New York: Viking, 1968), 181.

31. But see Glenn B. Martin, "Victim Compensation in Several States: A Comparative Analysis," (M.A. Thesis, U. Texas, 1978) for an analysis of the chances of fraud.

32. Michael Fooner, "Victim-Induced, Victim-Invited, and Victim-Precipitated Criminality: Some Problems in Evaluation of Proposals for Victim Compensation," *Science*, 2(1966), 1080; Brock, note 24 *supra*, 118.

33. Henry Weihofen, "Comment on the Proposal," *J. Pub. L.*, 8(1959), 211.

34. *Ibid.*, 215.

35. Mueller, note 25 *supra*, 236.

36. Fooner, note 32 *supra*, 1082.

37. Joseph Magaddino, "Crime, Victim Compensation, and the Supply of Offenses," *Public Policy*, 57(1976), 437.

38. Roger Meiners, *Victim Compensation: Economic, Legal, and Political Aspects* (Lexington: D.C. Heath, 1978), 82.

39. Magaddino, note 37 *supra*, 440.

40. Meiners, note 39 *supra*, 86.

41. Anthony Meade, et al., "Discovery of a Forgotten Party: Trends in American Victim Compensation Legislation," *Victimology*, 1(1976), 429; Gallup Poll Index, *Compensation for Crime Victims: Report No. 5* (Princeton: Amer. Inst. Pub. Opin., 1965).

42. Gilbert Geis, "Compensation to Victims of Violent Crime," in Rudolph Gerber (ed.), *Contemporary Issues in Criminal Justice* (Pt. Washington: Kennikat, 1976), 104.

43. J.L. Barkas, "Considering the Victims," in *Victims* (New York: Scribners, 1978), 185.

44. Robert Childres, "Compensation for Criminally Inflicted Personal Injury," *Minn. L.R.*, 50(1965), 271; L. Stanley Chauvin, "Compensation for Victims of Crime: An

Overview," *State Gov't* (1974), 9; Gilbert Geis, "State Compensation to Victims of Violent Crime," in President's Commission on Law Enforcement and the Administration of Justice, *Task Force Report: Crime and Its Impact—An Assessment* (Washington: U.S. Gov't. Printing Ofc., 1967), 157; Gilbert Geis, "Compensation for Victims of Violent Crimes," *in Crimes of Violence* (Washington: U.S. Gov't. Printing Ofc., 1969), 13:1559; James Brooks, "The Case for Creating Compensation Programs to Aid Victims of Violent Crimes," *Tulsa L.J. 11(1976),* 477; Walter J. Blum, "Victims of Crime and Other Victims," *Chi. Bar Rec.,* 52(1971), 463; Glenn Floyd, "Compensation to Victims of Violent Crime," *Tulsa L.J.,* 6(1970), 100; Gilbert Geis & Richard A. Weiner, "International Conference on Compensation to Innocent Victims of Violent Crime," *Intl. R. Criminol. Pol.,* 26(1970), 123; Gilbert Geis, "State Compensation for Crime," *Hospitals,* 46(1976), 50; Gilbert Geis, "Victims of Violent Crime: Should They Be Compensated?" *Vital Issues,* 20(1970), 1; Gilbert Geis & Herbert Sigurdson, "State Aid to Victims of Violent Crime," *State Gov't.,* 43(1970), 16; Ronald Goldfarb & Linda Singer, "Victim Compensation," in *After Conviction* (New York: Simon & Schuster, 1973), 131; Michael Mansfield, "Justice for the Victims of Crime," *Houston L.R., 9(1971), 75; Norval Morris & Gordon Hawkins, Honest Politicians Guide to Crime Control* (Chicago: U. Chi. Press, 1970), 42; Herbert A. Rosenthal, "Compensation for Victims of Crime," *A.B.A. J.,* 58(1972), 968; U.S. Senate, Committee on District of Columbia, "Compensation of Victims of Crime," Hearings, 91st Cong., 1st sess. (Washington: U.S. Gov't. Printing Ofc., 1970); A.M. Linden, "International Conference on Compensation to Innocent Victims of Violent Crime," *Crim. L.Q.,* 11(1969).,145; Paul F. Rothstein, "State Compensation for Criminally Inflicted Injuries," *Texas L.R., 44(1965), 38; J. Griew, "Compensation for Victims of Violence," Crim. L.R.* (1962), 801; Robert Sandler, "Compensation for Victims of Crime: Some Practical Considerations," *Buffalo L.R.,* 15(1971), 645; Pablo Drobny, "Compensation to Victims of Crime," *St.L.U. L.R.,* 16(1971), 201; Robert Cancilla, "Compensating Victims of Crime," *Crime Prevent. R.,* (1975), 286; A. Newton, "Aid to the Victim: Compensation and Restitution," *Crime & Delinq. Lit.,* 8(1976), 368; A.J. Duplissie, "Compensating Victims of Crimes of Violence," *Intl. Crim. Police R.,* 24(1969), 8; "Compensating Crime Victims," *Justice Assist. News* (1980), 2; *Crime Victim Compensation* (Washington: Nat. Inst. of Justice, 1980).

45. Notes, "Compensation for Victims of Crime," *U. Chi. L.R.,* 33(1966), 537.

46. LeRoy Lamborn, "The Propriety of Governmental Compensation of Victims of Crime," *G. Wash. L.R.,* 41(1973), 714.

47. Jacob, note 11 *supra,* 152.

48. Kutner, note 23 *supra,* 495.

49. Arthur Goldberg, "Equality and Governmental Action," *N.Y.U. L.R.,* 39(1964), 205.

50. James Polish, "Rehabilitation of the Victims of Crime," *U.C.L.A. L.R.,* 21(1973), 335; Lester Thurow, "Equity Versus Efficiency in Law Enforcement," *Public Policy,* 18(1970), 454.

51. *Ibid.*

52. Polish, note 50 *supra,* 337.

53. John Schmutz, "Compensation for the Criminally Injured Revisited: An Emphasis on the Victim?" *Notre Dame Law.,* 47(1971), 90.

54. Comment, "Compensation to Victims of Violent Crimes," *NW U. L.R.,* 61(1966), 76; An analogy also is often drawn to the present awards under workman's compensation. See Marvin Wolfgang, "Victim Compensation in Crimes of Personal Violence," *Minn. L.R.,* 50(1965), 230; Robert Reiff, "Restitution and Compensation," in *The Invisible Victim* (New York: Basic, 1979), 142.

55. Notes, note 45 *supra,* 593.

56. Duncan Chappell & L. Paul Sutton, "Evaluating the Effectiveness of Programs to Compensate the Victims of Crime," in Israel Drapkin & Emilio Viano (eds.), *Victimology: Theoretical Issues in Victimology* (Lexington: D.C. Heath, 1973), 213; T.F. Coon, "Public Defender and Victims Compensation Legislation: Their Part in the Criminal Justice System," *Bull. Soc. Profess. Investig.* (1971), 25.

57. Schafer, note 2 *supra,* 59.

58. Geis, note 42 *supra.*

59. Stephen Schafer, "The Proper Role of a Victim-Compensation System," *Crime & Delinq.,* 21(1975), 48.

60. Chappell & Sutton, note 56 *supra,* 212.

61. James Brooks, "Who Gets What? An Analysis of Five Model Proposals for Criminal Injury Compensation Legislation," *State Gov't.* (1974), 18.

62. Winsor C. Schmidt, *Legal Issues in Compensating Victims of Crime* (Raleigh: Nat. Assn. Attnys. Gen., 1976), 40.

63. Childres, note 4 *supra,* 459; LeRoy Schultz, "The Violated: A Proposal to Compensate Victims of Violent Crime," *St.L.U. L.R.,* 10(1965), 238; LeRoy Schultz, "A Compensation Program for Sex Victims," in Harvey Gochros & LeRoy Schultz (eds.), *Human Sexuality and Social Work* (New York: Assn. Press, 1972), 334.

64. Margery Fry, "Justice for Victims," *J. Pub. L.,* 8(1959), 191.

65. B. Cameron, "Compensation for Victims of Crime: The New Zealand Experiment," *J. Pub. L.,* 12(1963), 375; Kent Weeks, "The New Zealand Criminal Injuries Compensation Scheme," *S. Cal. L.R.,* 43(1970), 107; Louis Waller, "Compensation of Victims of Crime in Australia and New Zealand," in Drapkin & Viano, note 6 *supra,* 175; Geoffrey W.R. Palmer, "Compensation for Personal Injury: A Requiem for the Criminal Law in New Zealand," *Amer. J. Comp. L.,* 21(1973), 1.

66. Donald Williams, *Criminal Injuries Compensation* (London: Oyez, 1972); Bernard Downey, "Compensating Victims of Violent Crime," *Brit. J. Criminol.* (1965), 92; Donald Williams, "Compensating Victims of Crimes of Violence: Another Look at the Scheme," in Drapkin & Viano, note 6 *supra,* 147; Glanville Williams, "Comment on the Proposal," *J. Pub. L.,* 8(1959), 194; J.L. Montrose, "Comment on the Proposal," *J. Pub. L.,* 8(1959), 197; Herbert Edelhertz & Gilbert Geis, *Public Compensation to Victims of Crime* (New York: Praeger, 1974), 213; Alec Samuels, "Compensation for Criminal Injuries in Britain," *U. Toronto L.J.,* 17(1967), 20; D. Glazebrook, "Compensation for Victims of Crimes of Violence," *Brit. J. Criminol.,* 2(1962), 295; Terence Morris, "Compensation for Victims of Crimes of Violence," *Modern L.R.,* 24(1961), 744; David Harrison, "Criminal Injuries Compensation in Britain," *A.B.A. J.,* 57(1971), 476.

67. Saskatchewan (1967), Ontario (1968), Newfoundland (1968), Alberta (1969), Manitoba (1970), New Brunswick (1971), Quebec (1971), British Columbia (1972), Northwest Territories (1973), Prince Edward Island (1973), Yukon (1975); see G. Clark, "Compensation for Personal Injuries, Damages, and Social Insurance," *Law Soc. Gaz.,* 64(1967), 339, 408, 476; G. Clark, *Compensation to Victims of Crime and Restitution by Offenders* (Ottowa: Canad. Correct. Assn., 1968); D.T.G. Feeney, "Compensation for Victims of Crime," *Canad. J. Correct.,* 10(1968), 261; P. Burns, "Comprehensive Study of Victims of Crime Indemnification in Canada: British Columbia as a Microcosm," *U. Brit. C. L.R.,* 8(1973), 105; D.R. Miers, "Ontario Criminal Injuries Compensation Scheme," *U. Toronto L.R.,* 24(1974), 347; Linden, note 21 supra; Douglas Marshall, "Compensation: New Atonement for Old Guilt?" *J. Canad. Bar. Assn.,* 2(1971), 24; W.J. McGrath, "Compensation to Victims of Crime in Canada," *Canad. J. Correct.,* 12(1970), 11; James Eremko, "Compensation of Criminal Injuries in Saskatchewan," *U. Toronto L.R.,* 19(1969), 263; D.B. Kirkham, Compensation for Victims of

Crime (Edmonton: Bishop, McKenzie, 1968); Notes, "Awards of the Crimes Compensation Board," *Saskatch. L.R.*, 35(1970), 75; George J. Bryan, "Compensation to Victims of Crime," *Alberta L.J.*, 6(1968), 202.

68. New South Wales (1967), Queensland (1968), Southern Australia (1969), Western Australia (1970), Victoria (1972), Tasmania (1976); see Duncan Chappell, "Emergence of Australian Schemes to Compensate Victims of Crime," *S. Cal. L.R.*, 43(1970), 69; Waller, note 65 *supra;* Duncan Chappell, "Compensating Australian Victims of Violent Crime," *Aust. L.J.*, 39(1967), 3; John Barry, "Compensation Without Litigation," *Aust. L.J.*, 37(1964), 347; P.G. McGowan, "Criminal Injuries Compensation Act of 1970 (W.A)," *U. West. Aust. L.R.*, 10(1972), 305.

69. David Miers, "Compensation for Victims of Crimes of Violence: The Northern Ireland Model," *Crim. L.R.* (1969), 576; David Miers, "Compensation for Consequential Loss Under the Malicious Injuries Code," *Irish Jur.*, 6(1971), 50.

70. Edelhertz & Geis, note 66 *supra*, 250.

71. Stephen Schafer, "Compensation and Restitution to Victims of Crime," in *The Victim and His Criminal: A Study in Functional Responsibility* (New York: Random House, 1968), 105.

72. West Germany, France, Hungary, Israel, Holland, Dominican Republic, Norway, Belgium, Austria, Denmark, Finland, Italy, Switzerland, Turkey, Greece, Argentina, Yugoslavia, Mexico, Cuba, Iran, and South Africa; see also H. Johnson, "Compensation for Victims of Criminal Offenses in English and Soviet Law," *Current Leg. Prob.*, 17(1964), 144; Uzy Hason & Leslie Sebba, "Compensation to Victims of Crime: A Comparative Survey," in Drapkin & Viano, note 6 *supra*, 103.

73. Stephen Schafer, *Compensation and Restitution to Victims of Crime* (Montclair: Patterson Smith, 1970).

74. Brock, note 24 *supra*, 106; William Doerner, "State Victim Compensation Programs in Action," *Victimology*, 3(1977), 106; Geis, note 42 supra; Willard Shank, "Aid to Victims of Crime in California," *S. Cal. L.R.*, 43(1970), 85; Gilbert Geis & Dorothy Zietz, "California's Program of Compensation to Crime Victims," *Legal Aid Briefcase*, 25(1966), 66; Sylvia Fogelman, "Compensation to Victims of Crimes of Violence," (M.S.W. Thesis, U. S. Cal., 1971); Gilbert Geis, "California's New Crime Victims Compensation Statute," *S. Diego L.R.*, 12(1974), 880; Evelyn J. Younger, "Commendable Words: A Critical Evaluation of California's Victim Compensation Law," *J. Bev. Hills Bar Assn.*, 7(1973), 12; Edelhertz & Geis, note 66 *supra*, 76.

75. See chapter seven for citations and a detailed description.

76. George E. Rejda & Emil Meuer, "An Analysis of State Crime Compensation Plans," *J. Risk & Insurance* (1975), 599; Edelhertz & Geis, note 66 *supra*, 130.

77. Samuel Vitali, "A Years Experience with the Massachusetts Compensation of Victims of Violent Crime Law, 1968-1969," *Suff. U. L.R.*, 4(1970), 237; Glenn Floyd, "Massachusetts Plan to Aid Victims of Crime," *Boston U. L.R.*, 48(1968), 380; Note, "A State Statute to Provide Compensation for Innocent Victims of Violent Crimes," *Harv. J. Legis.*, 4(1966), 127.

78. Notes, "Criminal Victim Compensation in Maryland," *Md. L.R.*, 30(1970), 266.

79. New Jersey (1971), Alaska (1972), Illinois (1973), Texas (1973), Washington (1973), Minnesota (1974), Ohio (1975), North Dakota (1975), Delaware (1975), Michigan (1976), Tennessee (1976), Pennsylvania (1976), Wisconsin (1976), Kentucky (1976), Virginia (1977), Oregon (1977), Kansas (1978), Florida (1978), Indiana (1978), Connecticut (1979); see also Edelhertz & Geis, note 66 *supra*, 154, 174; John Durso, "Illinois Crime Victims Compensation Act," *Loyola L.J.*, 7(1976), 351; Boyd L. Wright, "What About the Victims? Compensation for the Victims of Crime," *N. Dak. L.R.*, 48(1972),

473; R. Cosway, "Symposium on Recent Washington Legislation: Crime Compensation," *U. Wash. L.R.*, 49(1974), 551; Note, "Compensating Victims of Crime: Individualized Responsibility and Government Compensation Plans," *Maine L.R.*, 26(1974), 175; Harl Haas, "An Argument for the Enactment of Criminal Victim Compensation Legislation in Oregon," *Willamette L.J.*, 10(1974), 185; R.J. Gross, "Crime Victims Compensation in North Dakota: A Year of Trial and Error," *N. Dak. L.R.*, 53(1976), 7; Note, "Criminal Law: Victims Rights—Virginia Adopts Statute to Compensate Victims of Crime," *U. Rich. L.R.*, 11(1977), 679; Note, "Tennessee's Criminal Injuries Compensation Act," *Memphis St. L.R.*, 7(1977), 241; Dale O. Cloniger, "Victim Compensation in Florida: Economic Efficiency or Social Obligation?" *Econ. Leaflets*, 32(1973), 1; Gary Watchke, "Compensation for Victims of Crime: A Current Status Report," (Madison: Wisc. Legis. Ref. Bur., 1976); Nancy A. Gattusso-Holman, "Criminal Sentencing and Victim Compensation Legislation: Where is the Victim?" in Viano, note 12 *supra*, 363; Glenn Floyd, "Victim Compensation Plans," *A.B.A. J.*, 55(1969), 159; Martin, note 31 supra; Stewart W. Pinkerton, "Aiding the Innocent: More States Award Cash Compensation to Victims of Crime," *Wall St. J.*, 26 August 1970, 1; Note, "An Analysis of Victim Compensation in America," *Urban Laywer*, 8(1972), 17; Richard Knutden, "Crime Victim Compensation Laws and Programs," unpublished report, Marquette University, 1976; and see also chapter seven for citations and detailed description of New Jersey's plan.

80. Herbert Edelhertz, "Compensating Victims of Violent Crime," in Duncan Chappell & John Monahan (eds.), *Violence and Criminal Justice* (Lexington: D.C. Heath, 1975), 75.

81. This perhaps was prompted by a Louisiana court decision that required the processing of claims even if no compensation was granted. See Meiners, note 38 *supra*, 37.

82. Ralph Yarborough, "S. 2155 of the 89th Congress—The Criminal Injuries Compensation Act," *Minn. L.R.*, 50(1965), 255; Ralph Yarborough, "The Battle for a Federal Violent Crimes Compensation Act: The Genesis of S.9," *S. Cal. L.R.*, 43(1970), 93.

83. John McClellan, "Society's Moral Obligation: Victims of Crime Act of 1972," *Trial*, 8(1972), 22.

84. James Garofalo & L. Paul Sutton, *Compensating Victims of Violent Crime: Potential Costs and Coverage of a National Program* (Albany: Crim. Justice Res. Ctr., 1977); James Garofalo & Joan McDermott, "National Victim Compensation: Its Costs and Coverage," *Law & Policy Q.*, 1(1979), 439; Edward D. Jones, "A Cost Analysis of Federal Victim Compensation," in Wesley Skogan (ed.), *Sample Surveys of Victims of Crime* (Cambridge: Ballinger, 1976), 189; "HR.4267: Compensation for Victims of Crime," *Concern*, 2(1980), 7; Barbara McClure, "Crime: Compensation for Victims" (Washington: Lib. of Cong., 1979).

85. Frances Fox Piven & Richard A. Cloward, *Poor People's Movements* (New York: Vintage, 1979), 272; Joseph Boskin, *Urban Racial Violence in the 20th Century* (Beverly Hills: Glencoe, 1969); Richard Kirkendall, *A Global Power: America Since the Age of Roosevelt* (New York: Knopf, 1980); Kenneth Dolbeare & Murray Edelman, *American Politics: Policies, Power, and Change* (Lexington: D.C. Heath, 1977), 108; Herbert Gans, *More Equality* (New York: Vintage, 1973), 36.

86. Paul Murphy, *The Constitution in Crisis Times: 1918-1969* (New York: Harper, 1972), 404.

87. Richard Scammon & Ben Wattenberg, *The Real Majority* (New York: Coward, McCain, 1970).

88. "The Curse of Violent Crime," *Time*, 23 March 1981, 57.

89. Frances Fox Piven & Richard A. Cloward, *Regulating the Poor: The Functions of*

Public Welfare (New York: Vintage, 1971), 183; Edward Greenberg, *Serving the Few: Corporate Capitalism and the Bias of Government Policy* (New York: Wiley, 1974), 181.

90. David A. Walker, "Intergovernmental Response to Urban Riots," in Robert Connery (ed.), *Urban Riots: Violence and Social Change* (New York: Acad. Political Sci., 1968), 169.

91. Piven & Cloward, note 85 *supra;* Richard Quinney, *Class, State and Crime* (New York: Longman, 1980), 127.

92. Daniel Moynihan, *The Politics of a Guaranteed Income* (New York: Harper & Row, 1973), 101-2.

93. Ira Katznelson & Mark Kesselman, *Politics of Power* (New York: Harcourt-Brace-Jovanovich, 1979), 182.

94. Meiners, note 38 *supra,* 33.

95. Schmidt, note 62 *supra,* 13.

96. LeRoy Lamborn, "The Methods of Governmental Compensation of Crime," *U. Ill. L. Forum* (1971), 655.

97. Burt Galaway & L. Rutman, "Victim Compenstion: An Analysis of Substantive Issues," *Soc. Serv. R.,* 48(1974), 60.

98. *Ibid.,* 64.

99. Gilbert Geis, "Experimental Design and the Law: A Prospectus for Research on Victim-Compensation in California," *Calif. West. L.R.,* 2(1966), 85; W.T. Westling, "Some Aspects of Judicial Determination of Compensation Payable to Victims of Crime," *Aust. L.J.,* 48(1974), 428.

100. In 1979, New Jersey became the third state to raise revenue ($25 per conviction) for compensation at least partially from criminal fines; "From State Capitols," *Concern,* 1(1979), 5.

101. Edelhertz & Geis, note 66 *supra,* 36.

102. Arnold Enker, "A Comparative Review of Compensation for Victims of Crime," in Drapkin & Viano, note 6 *supra,* 121.

103. J.L. Lambert, "Compensation Orders: A Review of the Appellate Cases," New L.J., 126(1976), 69; Schmidt, note 62 *supra,* 29.

104. Edelhertz & Geis, note 66 *supra,* 278.

105. Donal MacNamara & John Sullivan, "Making the Crime Victim Whole: Composition, Restitution, Compensation," in Terence Thornberry & Edward Sagarin (eds.), *Images of Crime: Offenders and Victims* (New York: Praeger, 1974), 84.

106. Robert Scott, "Compensation for Victims of Violent Crimes: An Analysis," *Will. & Mary L.R.,* 8(1967), 277.

107. Gilbert Geis, "Compensation for Crime Victims and the Police," *Police,* 13(1969), 55.

108. Notes, note 45 *supra,* 557. But, this success might be because the programs are small scale, limited, and do not threaten existing interests like programs such as medicare and no-fault insurance.

109. Duncan Chappell, "Providing for the Victim of Crime: Political Placebos or Progressive Programs?" *Adelaide L.R.,* 4(1972), 294.

110. Lamborn, note 96 *supra,* 668; Schmidt, note 62 *supra,* 29.

111. Smodish, note 14 *supra,* 19; Galaway & Rutman, note 97 *supra,* 65; LeRoy Lamborn, "The Scope of Programs for Governmental Compensation of Victims of Crime," *U. Ill. L. Forum* (1973), 25.

112. Lamborn, note 111 *supra,* 33.

113. Redja & Meuer, note 76 *supra,* 607.

114. Lamborn, note 111 *supra,* 29.

115. But see Meade, note 41 *supra,* 426.

116. *Ibid.*

117. Schmidt, note 62 *supra,* 22.

118. Inbau, note 16 *supra,* 203.

119. Polish, note 50 *supra,* 340; Enker, note 102 *supra,* 126.

120. Lamborn, note 111 *supra,* 84.

121. *Ibid.,* 76.

122. LeRoy Lamborn, "Toward a Criminal Orientation in Criminological Theory," *Rutgers L.R.,* 22(1968), 760; Schmidt, note 62 *supra,* 24.

123. Lamborn, note 111 *supra,* 44.

124. Schmidt, note 62 *supra,* 20.

125. Polish, note 50 *supra,* 337.

126. J.C. Walker, "Valuations of the Criminal Injuries Compensation Board," *Solic. J.,* 110(1966), 970.

127. Lamborn, note 111 *supra,* 53.

128. Wolfgang, note 54 *supra,* 234; Lamborn, note 111 *supra,* 46; Schmidt, note 62 *supra,* 26.

129. Lamborn, note 111 *supra,* 73

130. *Ibid.,* 65.

131. Edelhertz & Geis, note 66 *supra,* 279.

132. Lamborn, note 111 *supra,* 61.

133. Glenn Floyd, "Victim Compensation: A Comparative Study," *Trial,* 8(1972), 14.

134. See previous notes in this chapter.

135. Chappell & Sutton, note 56 *supra,* 207.

136. MacNamara & Sullivan, note 105 *supra,* 88.

137. Hason & Sebba, note 72 *supra,* 118.

138. LeRoy Lamborn, "Compensation for the Child Conceived in Rape," in Viano, note 12 *supra,* 368.

139. See, for example, Meiners, note 39 *supra,* 51.

140. Chappell, note 109 *supra,* 299.

141. LeRoy Lamborn, "Crime Victim Compensation: Theory and Practice in the Second Decade," *Victimology,* 1(1976), 509.

142. Reiff, note 54 *supra,* 61, 164.

143. Lamborn, note 138 *supra,* 508.

144. Brooks, note 61 *supra,* 17.

145. James Brooks, "Compensating Victims of Crime: The Recommendations of Program Administrators," *Law & Soc. R.,* 7(1973), 445.

146. James Brooks, "How Well are Criminal Injury Compensation Boards Performing?" *Crime & Delinq.,* 21(1975), 50.

147. James Brooks, "Crime Compensation Programs: An Opinion Survey of Program Administrators," *Criminology,* 11(1973), 271.

148. J. Edwards, "Compensation to Victims of Crimes of Personal Violence," *Fed. Prob.,* 30(1966), 8.

149. Doerner, note 74 *supra,* 108.

150. Julie Vennard, "Victims Views on Compensation and the Criminal Justice System," (London: Home Ofc. Report, 1976).

151. Geis, note 99 *supra,* 85.

152. Gilbert Geis, "Crime Victims and Victim Compensation Programs," in William McDonald, note 12 *supra,* 253.

153. Gilbert Geis, "Victims of Crimes of Violence and the Criminal Justice System," in Chappell & Monahan, note 80 *supra,* 61.

154. Fogelman, note 74 *supra,* 47.

155. Redja & Meuer, note 76 *supra*, 608.

156. Edelhertz & Geis, note 66 *supra*, 288; Duane G. Harris, "Compensating Victims of Crime: Blunting the Blow," (Philadelphia: Phila. Fed. Res. Bd., 1972), 19; Meiners, note 38 *supra*, 46.

157. Law Enforcement Assistance Administration, "Victims of Crime Act of 1972," (Washington: U.S. Dept. Justice, 1972), 719; U.S. House of Representatives, Committee on the Judiciary, "Victims of Crime Act of 1977," report 95-337, HR.7010, 95th Cong., 1st sess., 12; U.S. House of Representatives, Committee on the Judiciary, "Crime Victim Compensation," Hearings, 94th Cong., 1975-76, serial no. 39, 1273; Schmidt, note 62 *supra*, 9.

158. Garofalo & Sutton, note 84 supra; Garofalo & McDermott, note 84 *supra*.

159. Garofalo & McDermott, note 84 *supra*, 461.

160. William Doerner, "A Quasi-Experimental Analysis of Selected Victim Compensation Programs," *Canad. J. Criminol.*, 20(1978), 239.

161. William Doerner, et al., "An Analysis of Victim Compensation Programs as a Time-Series Experiment," *Victimology*, 1(1976), 310; William Doerner, "An Examination of the Alleged Latent Effects of Victim Compensation Programs Upon Crime Reporting," *LAE J.*, 41(1978), 71.

162. Susan Stelzenmuller Silverman & William Doerner, "The Effect of Victim Compensation Programs Upon Conviction Rates," *Sociol. Sympos.*, 25(1979), 40.

163. Lamborn, note 96 *supra*, 671.

164. Edelhertz & Geis, note 66 *supra*, 264.

165. Chappell & Sutton, note 56 *supra*, 214.

166. Geis, note 152 *supra*, 247, 255.

167. David Nachmais, *Public Policy Evaluation: Approaches and Methods* (New York: St. Martins, 1979), 5.

CHAPTER THREE
Research Design

Research Questions and Hypotheses

Evaluating victim-compensation programs depends initially on identifying the intentions and goals of the policymakers responsible for such plans. From these objectives, one might assess the extent to which the programs have been successfully implemented and have had the desired impact.

As indicated in the previous chapter, several rationales have prompted the creation of victim-compensation programs. These justifications suggest the extent to which a government should take responsibility for crime victimization. They also signify the particular objectives being sought by adopting compensation plans. Among those various objectives, most existing compensation programs emphasize the following:

Restoration

This goal seeks to restore crime victims to a status similar to that existing before the victimization. A program's major resource for achieving this objective consists of adequately compensating victims for their losses due to crime[1]. But, because compensation programs do not reimburse for property losses, the payments are limited to those made for out-of-pocket losses—including medical expenses, and for lost earnings.

Crime Prevention

This objective seeks to control crime. Policymakers indicate that victim-compensation will renew the public's faith in law enforcement by indicating a concern for crime victims. Having compensation programs, and especially reimbursing actual victims, will allegedly improve the public's attitude toward the criminal process and its officials. This, in turn, will supposedly increase the public's cooperation with law-enforcement personnel, and enable a more effective crime control[2].

Social Stability

A final goal also depends on compensation's impact on public attitudes. Although this objective rarely is stated explicitly by policymakers[3], most compensation programs nevertheless have as an implicit goal the desire to prevent public disillusionment with government in general. Politicians not only expect to gain votes by supporting victim compensation, but also hope that such a program will improve the public's image of its government[4]. Crime continues to spiral in the United States, and law-enforcement officials and politicians seem either unable or unwilling to cope with the problem[5]. The public often believes that through court decisions, judicial leniency, and other factors, criminals are receiving protection while potential or actual crime victims are left to their own defenses. Thus, under these conditions of disillusionment and lawlessness, it is important—symbolically if not tangibly—to provide some social appeasement. Victim compensation will apparently serve as a "safety valve" to reduce public instability, and to improve public attitudes toward criminal justice and government.

Not only are the aforementioned objectives the most prominent ones displayed in those states having compensation programs, but they are also, in particular, the three dominant goals of the two states (New York and New Jersey) being examined in this study. An attempt has been made here to evaluate the extent to which these objectives have been achieved.

Several working research questions guided this evaluation of the two compensation programs:

- *Do compensation programs adequately compensate victims?* That is, who gets victim compensation, and why? And, to what extent are victims compensated adequately—based on their losses and their own evaluation of their awards—after being victimized?
- *Does the underlying theory for a program's grant of awards affect its impact?* That is, an important distinction among compensation plans is whether reimbursements are granted as a matter of right or as a kind of welfare. Does it make any difference which approach is used for its effect on achieving compensation's various goals, such as adequately reimbursing victims, controlling crime, and changing public attitudes?
- *Do adequately compensated victims develop better attitudes toward the criminal-justice process, and become more willing to cooperate with law-enforcement personnel?* That is, does receiving compensation produce the desired changes in public attitudes toward law enforcement and government? Does compensation actually improve public attitudes (at least among actual victims who receive payments), and thus reduce public instability as well as induce more public cooperation in controlling crime?
- *Does a victim's denial of any or adequate compensation produce adverse effects for criminal justice and government?* That is, what are victims' reactions when they apply for compensation, but are denied an award, or receive what they consider an inadequate award? Does this produce negative attitudes toward criminal justice and government, and thus create disillusionment and a reluctance to cooperate with law-enforcement officials in the future?
- *Does financial reward determine a victim's willingness to participate in the criminal-justice process?* That is, to what extent does prospective financial benefit (even if only to cover one's expenses) induce favorable attitudes toward criminal justice, and a vic-

tim's willingness to assist law-enforcement officials? Would financial payments (including reimbursements other than victim compensation) produce greater victim participation?

Information was gathered to attempt to answer these and other related questions about victim compensation's impact. In addition, this study proceeded based on five hypotheses deriving from those research questions:

- *Victim compensation programs are not adequately compensating victims.* This theory was based on several factors surrounding the grant of compensation. First, it was unlikely that victims would be totally satisfied with their inability to recover property losses, which are categorically excluded from coverage. Second, for those losses covered by compensation plans, extensive eligibility requirements appeared to be a barrier to successful recovery. Third, inadequate publicity seemed to limit the number of crime victims who would know how to apply for compensation, or even of its existence in the first place. And finally, budgetary constraints appeared to limit significantly the amount of money allocated for compensation, and thus the extent to which victims could be adequately reimbursed, or even paid at all.
- *A "rights" approach would be more successful than a "welfare" approach to awarding compensation.* It was theorized that if compensation was granted based on right and not on financial need, a program would be more likely to be associated with positive attitudes toward government and the criminal process. A 'rights' approach would allow a plan to avoid the stigma of being another welfare program, and would recognize that even less than impoverished victims are affected by their losses, and expect some assistance.
- *Adequately compensated victims do have better attitudes toward criminal justice and government.* This hypothesis derived from evidence that indicated that monetary considerations are paramount with many crime victims, many of whom are poor. Financial inducements and rewards (if only to pay expenses or basic losses) would seem to be a strong incentive for present and future participation, for favorable attitudes toward criminal-justice officials and government.
- *A victim's denial of any or adequate compensation will produce negative attitudes toward criminal justice and government.* Once a compensation program is created, and once a crime victim discovers it, a natural expectation would be that payments would be made, and that they would be satisfactory. Thus, it was theorized that if a victim knows about compensation, but fails to receive it because he fails to qualify, then this will cause resentment. In fact, it was hypothesized that not only would this produce negative attitudes, but that those attitudes might be more adverse toward criminal justice and government than had the compensation program never existed in the first place. This would be an unanticipated impact of the program that policymakers probably did not consider.
- *Financial reward will make a victim more likely to participate in the criminal-justice process.* As mentioned previously, it would seem that crime victims are motivated by financial considerations. But, other potential financial rewards exist besides victim compensation. Getting involved in the criminal process might produce payments such

as witness fees, payoffs from the defendant, court-ordered restitution, or insurance reimbursements. It was theorized that these kinds of financial incentives would be important influences on a victim's decision to participate, in addition to his possible hope for victim compensation.

A research design and strategy was devised to investigate these inquiries, and to evaluate compensation programs in a systematic fashion. The following describes how and where the research data were collected, what criteria were used for sampling and study location, and the characteristics of the interviews and questionnaires used to collect information for the project.

Data Collection

Since this study evaluates victim-compensation programs, the decisions as to which programs to study, and how, were important ones. First, three different administrative approaches to dispensing compensation existed among those states having such programs when this research began. One approach granted payments from an office created within an existing state agency (dependent board). Another approach provided disbursements through the existing court system (judicial board). And, the final method occurred by creating an entirely new, administrative board solely concerned with this program (independent board). Although comparing these three administrative approaches might be useful for assessing their relative effectiveness in achieving compensation's goals, it was decided in this study to investigate plans employing only the "independent board" approach. When this study began, practically all states were using this method, and most still do prefer this approach.

Another difference among the existing compensation boards was their varying coverage of crimes. In the United States, however, only Hawaii and Delaware were awarding payments for some property crimes, and for pain and suffering due to victimization. Since the remaining boards only reimbursed for losses due to violent crimes, only compensation plans awarding on that basis were considered.

Finally, a major difference among the plans rested with the underlying philosophy upon which payments were made. Some boards awarded compensation on a welfare basis, whereby the applicant had to demonstrate financial need in order to qualify. Other boards, however, provided compensation as a matter of right, regardless of financial well-being. Since it was hypothesized that this latter distinction might be crucial in determining, among other things, who was compensated and an applicant's satisfaction level, a comparative design was adopted. In sum, two "independent" boards were chosen which awarded payments only for violent crimes, but which differed in their award philosophies: one taking the welfare approach and the other using a rights basis.

Having established these criteria, the final question was to decide which boards to choose in particular among those left qualifying. New York's and New Jersey's compensation boards were chosen for many reasons. First, since the author's mobility was restricted by financial limitations, studying two boards located near each other was desirable. Second, since in granting compensation, New York employs a welfare approach while New Jersey uses a rights basis, the two states provided the desired difference in award philosophy. Third, the boards were both well-established, and had been dispensing compensation for a number of years—as compared to most other programs, which were relatively new. Fourth, in almost all other respects (including their status as "independent" agencies) other than the welfare/rights distinction, the two boards appeared to operate almost identically.

Moreover, since most violent crimes occur in urban areas, it was desirable to chose two major urban areas as data collection sites. Brooklyn, New York and Newark, New Jersey were chosen for this reason and also because just prior to beginning this research, the author did crime-victim research in Brooklyn for the Vera Institute of Justice. Vera runs the Victim/Witness Assistance Project to provide services for Brooklyn crime victims, and the author worked at the Project's research arm—the Intensive Evaluation Unit. Since the Unit was engaged in research evaluating its own services and the crime victim's role in the Brooklyn criminal process, the author was well-informed about that jurisdiction, and used this background as a stepping-stone for the present study.

Newark was chosen as the other site for the research since it has many similarities in crime, location, and population to Brooklyn. That the cities comprise part of the same larger New York City metropolitan area also contributed to their selection, since differences among a victim's experiences and attitudes might, thereby, be more easily traced back to the respective criminal-justice systems or compensation boards that served them instead of to variations in their environments.

Finally, Newark and Brooklyn were chosen because the structure of New Jersey's and New York's compensation programs made it possible to isolate victims who lived and were victimized in those cities from other victims living elsewhere in either state. Each compensation board has particular offices devoted in part to each of the two cities. Securing victims from the same city in each state was important for being able to follow each victim's experience beginning with victimization, through their criminal-justice involvement, and finally, to their contact with the compensation board. Thus, it was necessary to isolate a common criminal-justice system in each state through which each of the victims studied would pass.

Sources of Data

Evaluating victim-compensation depends on collecting data from a variety of sources. Thus, information was accumulated from official reports, compensation-board observations, program records, official interviews, and victim interviews. The two compensation boards being analyzed issue annual reports describing their operations, and providing some limited statistics about their applicants, and administrative and financial data. In New York, a detailed legislative review of the program also was available[6].

Since this study's purpose was not primarily an administrative analysis, only those observations of everyday operations necessary to broadly understand how claims were processed at each board were made. Furthermore, only one hearing for each board was observed since the vast majority of board decision-making occurs unilaterally by the individual board members, and not from the relatively few hearings conducted.

A third data source included interviews with board members and investigators (see questionnaire in Appendix E). Two members and one investigator from each compensation board were questioned in personal interviews taking about one hour. These respondents were chosen for two reasons: First, since board-member turnover is fairly high (at least in New York), it was necessary to identify officials who were serving and making decisions on the cases during the time-period when the victims in this study had applied. And second, since officials serve in different parts of each state, it was necessary to isolate those who had made decisions for Brooklyn and Newark crime victims in particular.

Board officials were questioned not only to better understand the decision-making process, but also to identify backgrounds and attitudes which might affect official behavior. Thus, these administrators were asked to describe their board's purposes, goals, procedures, and eligibility requirements. And, they were questioned about decision-making influences—beyond merely statutory requirements—as well as about their view of their board's overall impact. Inquiries about their backgrounds, how they were selected, and possible career aspirations beyond the board also were made. And finally, officials were asked about their attitudes toward crime, law enforcement, and government.

The final source of data was the most extensive. Since this study was most concerned with victim compensation's effects (both economic and psychological) on crime victims, extensive interviews were conducted with actual crime victims from both Brooklyn and Newark.

Sampling Crime Victims

Four samples of crime victims were chosen. All the victims in these groups were victimized in 1976 or 1977. Two samples represented comparison groups by which to contrast compensation's effects in New York and New Jersey. Thus, one of the samples consisted of Brooklyn claimants, or victims who had contact with the New York Crime Victims Compensation Board after having experienced the Brooklyn criminal process. The other sample consisted of Newark claimants, or victims who had contact with the New Jersey Violent Crimes Compensation Board after having experienced the Newark criminal process.

Since this study sought not only to compare compensation-board experiences in the two states, but also to contrast the effects of having versus not having applied to a compensation board, in general, the remaining two samples were drawn accordingly. One of them consisted of Brooklyn non-claimants, or victims who experienced the Brooklyn criminal process, but who had not applied to the New York compensation board. And, the other sample consisted of Newark non-claimants, or victims who experienced the Newark criminal process, but who had not applied to the New Jersey compensation board.

Brooklyn Claimants

Each of the four samples came from a different source. The claimant victims were drawn from the respective compensation boards. In New York, although Brooklyn is serviced by an office in New York City, the author had to visit the New York Crime Victims Compensation Board's main office in Albany, where case records are stored. Initially, the author met some resistance in Albany because of the officials' reluctance to divulge information without victims' permission. After providing many assurances as to the study's confidentiality, Board officials finally consented to releasing some information from their files, including the victims' names and telephone numbers, which were needed to conduct the interviews. The author was limited by being unable to examine the entire files. This barrier was posed, however, merely to protect the confidentiality of medical and financial records, and thus no request for desired information was denied.

Before collecting information, some narrowing of the cases was necessary. Since information was collected in March 1978, only cases that were complete as of that time were included. The cases also were narrowed to those filed with the board after 1 January 1977. In addition, of course, only cases involving Brooklyn victims were chosen, which was not difficult since cases were catalogued by county.

Furthermore, two kinds of crimes were eliminated from consideration: homicides and rapes. Homicides were eliminated because they produce nobody to interview other than the victim's survivors. These cases were labeled in the files and were easily eliminated. Rapes also were excluded because they have unique characteristics that might have skewed this study's evaluation of victim attitudes and cooperation. Eliminating rape cases was more difficult, but was nevertheless achieved.

Moreover, including victims who had received awards as well as victims who had not was desirable. Thus, the cases remaining after the aforementioned screening were separated into those resulting in awards and those resulting in denials. Physically, it was unnecessary to rearrange the cases since awards and denials are filed separately. But, it was important to insure that the sample included representative amounts of denials and awards.

Since about 80 completed interviews were sought in this and the other samples, 150 cases were selected, thus allowing for almost a 50% margin of safety in securing the desired number of interviews. The New York board had been granting awards for an average of 40% of all claims made (including the period covered by this study), and thus 40% of the 150 cases (or 60 cases) were to be taken from the "award" files, while the remainder (90 cases) were to be taken from the "denial" files. In this sense, the sample was stratified.

The total number of Brooklyn cases contained in the files for the filing period covered by the study could be estimated from board records. Thus, from the period 1 January 1977 to 31 March 1978, approximately 6000 decisions were rendered. About three-quarters of all cases come from New York City, thus resulting in about 4500 cases decided from that jurisdiction. Within New York City, Brooklyn accounts for about 30% of the decisions, thus leaving about 1350 cases from that county decided during this time-period.

Nothing suggested that the overall pattern of awards and denials characterizing all the board's decisions would be any different than for Brooklyn in particular. Thus, it was assumed that 60% of Brooklyn's 1350 cases would be denials (or 810 cases), and that 40% would be awards (or 540 cases). A visual glance at the space occupied in the respective award and denial files seemed to support this assumption.

A systematic sample of both the "awards" and "denials" files was taken. To guard against having made a high estimate of the number of cases in each file, more conservative figures of 480 cases in the awards file and 720 in the denials file were used. Then, the number 8 was chosen at random to begin the sampling in each file. The files each were ordered only by the date on which the case was decided. Thus, beginning with the eighth case, every eighth case thereafter was selected in each file, producing an evenly dispersed array of cases throughout the decision period. In the awards file, cases were chosen on this basis until 60 total cases were selected, while 90 cases were selected from the denials file. This produced the desired 150 cases, and a systematic, stratified sample that was guarded from all known selection biases.

Newark Claimants

A similar procedure was employed to produce a second claimant sample from the New Jersey compensation board. The author visited the Newark office of the New Jersey program, which is also the main office. Unlike the New York experience, reviewing New Jersey's case files was not resisted. Thus, all of the data taken from these files was retrieved by the author and one assistant who had been working previously with him on the project. Despite this access to information not available in New York, none of the extra materials were relevant to the study, and thus they were ignored.

Cases were selected in New Jersey from the same time-period used in New York. Newark victims were not filed separately from other New Jersey victims whose cases were decided by this office, so the separation had to be done by hand. At the same time, both homicide and rape cases were eliminated as had been done in New York. And, awards and denials also were filed separately, so selecting a representative group around that distinction was simplified.

Eighty completed interviews were sought for this sample as well, and thus 150 cases were chosen overall. Similar to New York, the New Jersey board had been granting awards in about 40% of their cases, with the rest resulting in denials, and thus a stratified sample based on these percentages was planned.

An estimate was taken of completed Newark cases contained in the files for the aforementioned filing period, similar to that made in New York for Brooklyn cases. Since New Jersey's operation is vastly smaller than New York's, only about 700 decisions were made by the board from 1 January 1977 to 31 March 1978. About 65% of all cases come from the Newark office, where two of the board's three members make decisions. Thus, at least 455 (65% of 700) of the decisions came from the Newark office, but with two members making decisions, the amount was probably more like 550 cases. Although no firm statistic indicated the percentage of Newark victims among the Newark office's entire caseload (which included other victims from northern New Jersey), the consensus among board members was that the figure was about 85%. Thus, approximately 470 (85% of 550) of the total cases decided during the filing period were Newark victims.

Again, as in New York, nothing suggested that the overall pattern of awards and denials that characterized the board's entire caseload would be any different for Newark in particular. Thus, it was assumed that 60% of Newark's 470 cases would be denials (or 282 cases), and that 40% would be awards (or 188 cases). A visual glance at the space occupied in each of the files seemed to confirm this estimate.

A systematic sample of both the "awards" and "denials" files was taken in Newark, as had been done for Brooklyn. To guard against having made a high estimate of the number of cases in each file, more conservative figures of 180 cases in the awards file and 270 cases in the denials file were used. Then, the number 3 was chosen at random to begin the sampling in each file. The files each were ordered only by the date on which the case was decided. Thus, beginning with the third case, every third case thereafter was selected in each file, producing an evenly dispersed array of cases throughout the decision period. In the awards file, cases were chosen on this basis until 60 total cases were selected, while 90 cases were selected from the denials file. And, once again—as in Brooklyn—this produced the desired 150 cases, and a systematic, stratified sample that was guarded from all known sampling biases.

The information provided by board files in both states included the following: the claimant's name, address, and phone number, demographic characteristics, the crime's circumstances, the physical and financial losses suffered, the extent of the claimant's cooperation with law-enforcement officials, the claim's opening and closing dates, the claimant's other potential sources of financial aid, the aforementioned medical and financial records, and the outcome and reasons in each compensation case. Some of this information was provided by the claimant himself on the original application form, but additional information was added through board investigations.

Although the file information was somewhat useful, it was most beneficial in two areas: First, the data on how each claim was decided and why, were valuable for understanding the disposition of cases. Second, access to the files (even if only indirectly, as in New York) provided the most crucial information about victims, which enabled them to be contacted for interviews. Otherwise, the file data was used mainly for verifying answers to questions later asked of each victim interviewed.

Brooklyn Non-Claimants

This sample arose from the author's work with the Vera Institute of Justice. A sample of victims had been selected by the Victim/Witness Assistance Project's research unit for its own study. The unit had received permission from the Brooklyn District Attorney's office to interview crime victims arriving at the Brooklyn Criminal Court's complaint room after being victimized.

Respondents for the Vera study were selected during a six-week period in 1976, and included only victims whose alleged offenders had been arrested. On each day of the sampling period, a maximum of ten victims appearing in the complaint room and ten not appearing, were chosen. Personal interviews were conducted with those arriving in the complaint room in a separate office to ensure privacy. For those not interviewed in the complaint room, interviews either were arranged by phone or in person by Vera staff. The hours and days of sampling were staggered to insure representative selection from both peak and off-peak complaint-room volume. Every third victim was chosen for an interview during each sampling day, until the desired number was questioned.

The projected sample size was 480 victims, but useful information was compiled from only 325 respondents, the difference consisting of victims not interviewed in the complaint room, and who could not otherwise be contacted, as well as from incomplete interviews and refusals. The interviews themselves occurred during a period from the end of 1976 through the middle of 1977.

The sample of Brooklyn non-claimants sought for the research herein derived from Vera's group of 325 victims. Permission to use the sample was granted from both the Director of Vera's Intensive Evaluation Unit, and from the Brooklyn District Attorney's office. To be comparable with the aforementioned claimant samples, it was necessary that only violent-crime victims be selected, but only about 170 of Vera's 325 victims qualified. Lacking a better (or any other, for that matter) source of Brooklyn crime victims, this sample of 170 cases was adopted. This was done despite some sampling limitations, and despite the threat this sample posed to the study's internal validity, since the victims it contained had previously been "tested." That is, they had been questioned with related inquiries before[7].

Nevertheless, these difficulties were accepted, and the sample of 170 cases was reduced subsequently to around 150 after eliminating rapes (obviously, no homicide victims had been interviewed, and thus they already were eliminated) as had been done in the previous, claimant samples. Also, the responses to Vera's questionnaire were available as background information about these victims.

According to statistics compiled by the New York compensation board, over 134,000 violent crimes were reported in Brooklyn in 1976. And yet, only 1072 victims filed compensation claims, which indicates that less than 1% of all violent-crime victims in that county are even applying for an award[8]. Based on this statistic, it was reasonable to assume that practically none of the aforementioned 150 crime victims culled from the Vera study would have applied for compensation. This assumption was borne out, and it produced precisely the kind of comparative sample of Brooklyn non-claimants that had been sought.

Newark Non-Claimants

Just as for Brooklyn, a sample of violent-crime victims who had experienced Newark's criminal process but not the state's compensation was sought. The sample of Newark victims was requested from the Victim Service Center, which is an organization run through the Newark Police Department, and designed to provide victim aid similar to that given by Vera's Victim/Witness Assistance Project in Brooklyn. Due to questions of confidentiality, however, identifying information about the victims served by this office was refused.

By appealing directly to the Newark Police Chief, access was finally given to records at the Department's main headquarters. With considerable difficulty, a process of elimination similar to the one used for the previous samples was achieved. Only closed cases where the offender had been apprehended were selected. And, among those, all rapes and homicides were excluded, as well as other, non-violent crimes. These selections were made for a time period corresponding to the other samples; that is, cases were restricted to people who had been victimized during the last half of 1976, but whose cases had lingered as long as December 1977.

Fortunately, felonies had been separated from misdemeanors in the Department's files, and homicides and rapes also were segregated. Since once again, 80 completed interviews were sought, a sampling scheme designed to select almost twice (150) that many victims was devised. Based on files containing approximately 5000 cases, the 30th case was selected first at random. Then, every thirtieth case thereafter was selected until 150 cases were accumulated, and which were evenly spaced throughout the filing period.

As with the sample culled from the Vera study, this sample had potential problems of reliability. In this case, the limitation arose from uncertainties about police files. Nevertheless, no known sampling biases otherwise entered the case selection. Also, although police files contained some information about crime victims, it was—not unexpectedly—meagre, especially compared to information about the suspect.

And finally, just as it had been reasonable to conclude in Brooklyn that practically no victims taken from the Vera study had applied for victim compensation, so too had such an assumption been made for the Newark sample. Once again, this guess was correct, and it produced another useful sample of non-claimants to compare with Newark claimants.

In sum, four samples of victims were accumulated between March and May 1978. These groups were identified to enable at least two initial comparisons: a contrast between two different compensation programs, and a contrast between crime victims who had applied for victim compensation (claimants) and those who had not (non-claimants). It was intended that generalizations could be made from these victims samples. But, some notable restrictions on these victims' representativeness must be mentioned. Besides the dangers of generalizing about victims outside Newark and Brooklyn, these respondents also do not include any rape or homicide victims. In addition, these are victims whose experiences are now over six years old, and which may not always typify current realities either in the cities' criminal process or the state's compensation programs. And finally, these are all victims who reported the crimes to the police[9] or in some other way became involved in their cases, and whose alleged offenders were all arrested. These circumstances are certainly atypical since it is estimated that only about one-half of all crimes are reported, and only a small fraction result in apprehending a suspect—although rates are higher for violent-crime victims such as the ones involved in this study. In any case, these characteristics of this study's victims must be considered before generalizing from its results.

Interview Procedure

Once the four samples were selected, and some background and identifying information on each victim was accumulated, an attempt to interview the victims was made. Initially, contacting victims and interviewing them in person was considered. But, this approach—despite being the most common survey method—was quickly abandoned. A substantial number (320) of interviews was desired, but little time, money and other resources were available at the time to make this possible on a face-to-face basis. Consequently, interviews were conducted by telephone—a method whose validity has been confirmed by recent studies on interview methods that have found no significant differences in results between face-to-face and telephone interviews for research projects[10].

Since the Vera Institute employed a large team of experienced interviewers, who were administering a questionnaire with some similarities to the ones used in this study, the author availed himself of their skills. When sufficiently "trained," the author completed the survey instrument, and conducted a small pre-test of the questionnaire and his phone-interviewing technique on five crime victims in March 1978. Thereafter, the questionnaire was reformulated to correct surveying problems encountered in the pre-test. Then, the author worked with a research assistant who translated the questionnaire into Spanish, and who later administered it (under the author's supervision) by telephone to victims speaking that language. The final version of the longest questionnaire took about 50 minutes to complete for each victim.

The telephone interviews with the victims in the four samples took place between March and April 1978. Of the potential 150 interviews possible in each sample, actual interviews were completed for 98 non-claimants and 85 claimants in Brooklyn, and for 80 non-claimants and 79 claimants in Newark[11].

Questionnaires

Aside from the "official" questionnaires used for board administrators, three other questionnaires were administered, all to crime victims. One of the forms— the longest—was labelled the "comprehensive" questionnaire, because it included the questions asked of all the crime victims involved in the study. The second form, labelled the "victim-compensation insert," included additional questions asked only of the two claimant groups—for obvious reasons.

The final questionnaire was called the "Brooklyn piggyback,"[12] and was administered only to the sample of Brooklyn non-claimants. This form contained some, but not all, of the questions on the "comprehensive" questionnaire. The nature of this sample, and the previous information available about these victims accounts for this shortened form of questioning.

That is, as explained above, this sample of victims was taken from an on-going Vera Institute study. Vera had been examining victim experiences in the criminal process, and had asked some questions that clearly overlapped with those intended for the present study. Instead of repeating those questions, they were deleted, and thus the "piggyback" included only those questions that had not been previously asked of these victims but that had been asked of everyone else in this study on the "comprehensive" questionnaire.

The "comprehensive" questionnaire had been composed with this "overlapping" of questions in mind. Since maximum comparability among the samples was desired, all those questions previously asked in the Vera study of Brooklyn non-claimants that were desired for the study herein were reprinted exactly on the "comprehensive" questionnaire. The answers to these questions given by the other samples surveyed in this research were merely compared to those answers already available from Vera for the Brooklyn non-claimant sample. The "piggyback" form merely allowed the remaining questions in the comprehensive questionnaire to be asked of Brooklyn non-claimants—thus saving time and avoiding duplication.

This "piggyback" approach was used with some reluctance. Obviously, exposing this sample to two separate questionings, with a time-gap between the two interviews, was a less than optimal method of gaining the desired information—especially for purposes of comparison with the other samples. What made matters worse was that actually Vera's questioning of these Brooklyn non-claimants had come in two interviews as well. That is, each victim was given an "entrance" and an "exit" interview. Thus, some of the data gathered from these Brooklyn victims actually was accumulated in a total of three (two by Vera and one by the author) separate interviews, as compared to this data's having been collected from victims in the other three samples in only a single interview.

Clearly, this is a further complication. But, some countervailing considerations can be mentioned. First, most of the questions on the "entrance" interview that were used in this study were merely factual inquiries about the respondent's victimization and background, and not about attitudes or post-victimization experiences that were likely to change over time. Most of the questions about attitudes and post-victimization experiences relevant to this study appeared on Vera's "exit" interview, which occurred a lot closer in time to the "piggyback" interviews conducted for the study herein. Thus, some questions in this study were asked of Brooklyn non-claimants in three separate interviews, but the vast majority of those inquiries occurred in only two interviews, and little time had passed between those two sessions to significantly bias the results.

A final redeeming consideration must be mentioned. Although previously it was indicated that the shortened, "piggyback" version of the questionnaire had been used to avoid duplicating questions that had already been asked of Brooklyn victims, some duplications were retained purposely. Although this risked presenting a possible bias due to previous "testing," it was done to purposely assess differences, if any, that might result from questioning victims partially at one point in time, and then completing the questioning some time later. The duplicates were minor but did include both factual and attitudinal questions. And, comparing the initial and follow-up responses to these duplicate inquiries indicated practically no differences, despite the gap in time between the two interviews. So, while this is certainly not a final guarantee against the effects of time and the separate interview sessions for these victims, it is nevertheless, some evidence to support the validity of this complicated questioning procedure.

These drawbacks were accepted based on the realities of conducting the kind of research attempted in this study. In addition to the author's scarce resources, this complicated method of surveying Brooklyn non-claimants was accepted because rejecting this available sample would have meant not being able to secure a control group for Brooklyn at all. It is extremely difficult for a researcher to gain access to the kinds of samples used in this research in the first place, much less the kind of identifying information about the victims which is needed to be able to contact the victims and have any hope of interviewing them. And, the complications arose only in the control sample, and affected none of the questions directly aimed at victim compensation. Thus, the questioning—as had the sampling—proceeded nevertheless under the circumstances.

Nature of Victim Survey

The questionnaires were carefully designed to elicit certain kinds of information from crime victims. Although some borrowing from the Vera questionnaire occurred (primarily for comparability), the vast majority of the questions were original to this study—including all the inquiries about victim compensation. The survey instruments allowed a wide array of data to be accumulated so as to best understand a victim's experiences and attitudes, and to allow the research hypotheses that guided this study to be fully assessed.

As the "comprehensive" questionnaire indicates, information was sought about the following: First, although some information about each respondent's victimization was already known, the victim's own version of the crime was desirable. Second, the questions were concerned also with the respondent's post-victimization experience in the criminal process, from reporting the crime, through pressing charges, to his court appearance. This required inquiries about the victim's participation in the process, his inconveniences and treatment, and his attitudes about the process and its other participants—both official and unofficial.

Third, respondents also were asked their general attitudes about crime and criminal justice. Closely related were inquiries about each respondent's view of government generally, and about his perceived political viability in the society. And, victims also were asked question about their social status.

These kinds of questions obviously were not asked to discover anything directly about a victim's compensation experience, even though that is this study's main focus. Instead, these pre-compensation questions were intended to gain a broader view of a victim's circumstances, and even more importantly, to isolate victim experiences that might compete with his compensation-board experience in explaining his attitudes toward criminal justice and government, and his likely future cooperation with those institutions. That is, questions other than those relating directly to victim compensation were asked to help test other, competing explanations for a victim's attitudes and desire to participate. And obviously, questions particularly directed at measuring (and not merely seeking the causes of) those attitudes and levels of cooperation were asked eventually as well.

But, of course, inquiries specifically oriented toward victim compensation also were necessary. They were asked in combination with a group of questions designed to assess generally each respondent's attitudes and experiences about recovering his losses due to the crime and its repercussions. Although everyone was asked general questions about economic loss and recovery, and some attitudinal questions about victim compensation in general, most victim-compensation questions were administered only to claimants.

The most direct questions about victim compensation asked respondents to discuss in detail their compensation-board experience, including the process, their problems, and the outcomes. And, they also were asked their attitudes about board members and requirements, as well as about their overall view of their experience. Obviously, since only claimants could answer any of these questions, the inquiries appeared on the separate "victim-compensation insert," and were administered only to the two, appropriate samples—one in Newark and one in Brooklyn. The only exceptions to this were a couple of victims in the "control" samples in each of the two cities who "beat the odds" by also having happened to have applied for compensation as well. Of course, the rest of the respondents in these control groups—the non-claimants—had no contact with the compensation board whatsoever.

In sum, this research design was created to allow an in-depth and systematic study of violent-crime victims. Using a comparative design for the first time in this kind of research made it possible to contrast claimant and non-claimant experiences, as well as the compensation plans in two different states. The study and questions were structured to evaluate victim-compensation's success in achieving its objectives, as well as to assess its overall impact on crime victims, the criminal-justice process, and government generally.

Notes

1. Gilbert Geis, et al., *Public Compensation to Victims of Crime* (New York: Praeger, 1974), 25, 155.

2. *Ibid.* Note, however, that only compensation's effect on the attitudes and potential cooperation of actual victims—not of the public generally—will be tested in this study.

3. See Chapter seven, pp. 5, 6.

4. Geis, note 1 *supra,* 34.

5. See one author's claim that law-enforcement personnel are not unable, but rather are unwilling to reduce crime, in Jeffrey Reiman, *The Rich Get Richer and the Poor Get Prison* (New York: Wiley, 1979), 11.

6. Legislative Committee on Expenditure Review, *Crime Victims Compensation Program* (Albany: State of New York, 1979).

7. The danger to the study's internal validity is caused by "testing," or the possible effects of prior questioning on a second test's results. See Donald Campbell & Julian Stanley, *Experimental and Quasi-Experimental Designs for Research* (Chicago: Rand McNally, 1963), 5.

8. Crime Victims Compensation Board, *1977-78 Annual Report* (Albany: State of New York, 1978), 17.

9. But, the evidence shows that violent crimes are the most highly reported, and thus these victims are representative at least of violent-crime victims; see Herbert Jacob, *Crime and Justice in American Cities* (Englewood Cliffs: Prentice-Hall, 1980), 18.

10. See the results and sources in Theresa F. Rogers, "Interviews by Telephone and In Person: An Experiment to Test Quality of Responses and Field Performance," unpublished paper delivered at American Association of Public Opinion Research, 1975; "Random-Digit Dialing for Survey Research," (Washington: Police Found., 1978); S. Sudman, "New Uses of Telephone Methods in Survey Research," *J. Marketing Res.*, 3(1966), 1966; Alfred Tuchfarber, et al., "Reducing the Costs of Victim Surveys," in Wesley Skogan (ed.), *Sample Surveys of Victims of Crime* (Cambridge: Ballinger, 1976), 207-21.

11. Contrary to popular belief, most victims were not generally reluctant to talk about their victimization and post-victimization experiences, and thus few interviews were lost due to refusals.

12. See all the questionnaires in Appendix E.

CHAPTER FOUR
Characteristics of Violent Crime Victims

Crime is considered these days to be a major threat to our lives, limbs, and possessions. Although most Americans have fears about crime, these apprehensions might more legitimately be held by some than by others[1]. For instance, young, urban, lower class, non-white males are much more likely to be victimized (at least by violent crimes) than others[2].

Of major relevance to this study is the tendency of Brooklyn and Newark residents to be victimized. Statistics indicate that the two cities are largely consistent with national averages (for urban areas) and with each other in their residents' likelihood of being violent-crime victims given their particular background characteristics. For example, among thirteen major American cities, the average robbery rate is 6 per thousand population, while the mean number of assaults is 32 per thousand people. For Brooklyn and Newark, the robbery rates are 9 and 8 per thousand, respectively, while the number of assaults is 23 and 29 per thousand population. The two cities also reflect national averages in the sex, race, age and income of their violent-crime victims, as well[3].

As indicated in the previous chapter, the samples examined herein are somewhat restricted in the victims they represent from each city. Respondents were limited to violent-crime victims since this study's major focus is on victim compensation, for which only these kinds of victims are eligible in both New York and New Jersey. But, because surveying deceased victims is difficult, and because including sexual-assault victims might bias the study, the violent crimes of murder and rape were excluded. Also, since inconsistencies in exposure could affect a victim's exposure apart from his compensation-board experiences, only victims who had some contact with the criminal-justice process prior to contacting the compensation program were questioned. This meant that only victims whose crimes were reported, and who pressed charges—at least initially—were included in the study[4].

In sum, the victims surveyed were drawn to be representative of assault and robbery victims who pursued their cases against their offenders. And, for those applying for compensation, the victims questioned were sampled so as to be characteristic of all claimants coming before New York's and New Jersey's compensation boards, respectively. The four samples analyzed in this study consist of two groups from both Brooklyn and Newark. One of the two samples in each city consists of victims who were applicants at their state's compensation board (Brooklyn and Newark claimants), while the other sample consists of victims who had made no such claims (Brooklyn and Newark non-claimants).

The study's ultimate goal is to compare these samples so as to assess the impact of victim-compensation programs, and to differentiate claimants and non-claimants, and the victims and programs in each state. But, before encountering a compensation board, many victims (including all those selected for this study) become involved in the criminal process to pursue a case against their assailant, and even earlier, all victims, obviously, are actually victimized. These experiences produce a set of contacts and outcomes which potentially can have a strong effect on a victim's attitudes toward criminal justice and law-enforcement officials. Since one of victim compensation's major goals is to (favorably) affect these attitudes, it will be necessary in the next two chapters to begin to separate these competing influences so as to isolate most clearly the impact of compensation, and to assess its effectiveness.

Before describing criminal victimization experiences and post-victimization involvements in the criminal process, it is necessary to better understand the kinds of victims included in the study. That is, aside from their common traits of having been violent-crime victims who pursued their cases against their assailants in either Brooklyn or Newark, what are their other characteristics? This chapter will discuss those attributes, including general backgrounds and socio-economic characteristics, as well as general attitudes toward government and criminal justice.

Besides merely providing a useful summary of the victims in this study, comparing their characteristics serves an additional and very important function. A victim's background and general attitudes may exert a strong influence on his specific attitudes about government and law-enforcement processes and officials. As with the potential effects of the victimization and post-victimization experiences, background characteristics will compete with the influence of victim-compensation programs in determining a victim's ultimate views of criminal justice. Consequently, one must carefully examine these characteristics and attempt to identify any significant differences that might exist among the separate samples. Any such differences may ultimately explain any resulting variance in attitudes, and thus provide a competing hypothesis to victim compensation's supposed effect. If no differences in background traits emerge, however, then this potential, rival influence can be dispelled.

This chapter's examination of victim characteristics will provide not only a broad summary of the kinds of victims the study includes, but also a comparative analysis of the four samples. This presentation thus will facilitate an initial description of the two major, non-attitudinal objects of this research: who applies for compensation and who gets awards? That is, by simply distinguishing between claimants and non-claimants, one will begin to understand who applies and who does not, and who potentially may receive an award. Who actually receives awards will not be fully discussed until chapter nine when the compensation process and its outcomes are examined. Consequently, this chapter will only begin to describe who gets what from victim compensation, while it will be left to subsequent chapters—especially chapter ten—to explain why.

General Victim Attributes

To begin to characterize the victims questioned in this study, respondents were asked about their various social traits. Thus, among the demographic information elicited from victims was their age, sex, marital status, racial background, and religious affiliation. The results of these inquiries show that the victims were largely young or early-middle aged, married, non-white males who were only somewhat influenced by religion. The only significant differences existing between the samples was in the victims' age and sex.

A more detailed description of these traits can begin with the respondents' ages, which averaged 37.5, and ranged from 15 to 80. Most victims were young (ages 15-30) (42%), followed by early-middle aged (31-45) (32%), late-middle aged (46-60) (15%), and elderly (over 60) (11%) (Table 4.1). A statistically significant[5] (.02) difference among the samples appeared with Brooklyn claimants emerging as older while Brooklyn non-claimants were younger, but the variations were weak (V=.25)[6]. This indicates that at least in New York, compensation-board applicants tended to be older than non-applicants[7].

On the average, more than twice as many victims were male (68%) as were female (32%) (Table 4.2), but the differences among the samples were statisti-

TABLE 4.1 AGE

	ALL	Claimants		Non-Claimants	
		BKLN	NEWK	BKLN	NEWK
	%	%	%	%	%
YOUNG	143 (42)	31 (36)	30 (28)	52 (53)	30 (28)
EARLY MID	106 (32)	28 (33)	24 (20)	32 (33)	22 (27)
LATE MID	57 (15)	14 (16)	15 (19)	10 (10)	18 (22)
ELDERLY	36 (11)	12 (14)	10 (13)	4 (4)	10 (13)
	342	85	79	98	80

(S=.02) (V=.25)

TABLE 4.2 SEX

	ALL	Claimants BKLN	Claimants NEWK	Non-Claimants BKLN	Non-Claimants NEWK
	%	%	%	%	%
MALE	231(68)	67(79)	57(72)	57(58)	50(62)
FEMALE	111(32)	18(21)	22(28)	41(42)	30(38)
	342	85	79	98	80
(S=.01) (V=.22)					

cally significant (.01). Males (79%) dominated over females (21%) most clearly among Brooklyn claimants, while the greatest sexual balance (58% to 42%, respectively) characterized Brooklyn non-claimants. Although the difference was again weak (V=.22), it does indicate a tendency, at least in New York, for claimants to be significantly more male than female.

More victims were married (46%) than any other status, with a little less than one-third being single. The rest were either separated/divorced (16%), or widowed (6%) (Table A.1)[8]. None of the individual samples differed significantly from these averages.

Overall, caucasians (43%) outnumbered other racial groups, including blacks (40%), hispanics (15%)[9], orientals (1%), and others (1%) (Table A.2). Although whites were the single largest group, the minorities combined (57%) were more often victims. No significant differences among the samples occurred, despite the fact that among Brooklyn non-claimants, the typical excess of whites over blacks actually was reversed.

Respondents also were asked how important religion was in their lives. The vast majority indicated that religion was somewhat important (62%), while 23% said it was very important, and only 15% claimed that it did not influence them at all (Table A.3). None of the separate samples deviated significantly from these averages.

Socioeconomic Status

Several questions, including inquiries about each victim's education, employment status, occupation, income, and dependents, were asked to assess each respondent's socioeconomic status. The results clearly indicate that the social and economic class of respondents is not very high. The typical victim had not finished high school (only a couple due to their youth), was unemployed, receiving welfare, and supporting a couple of dependents. Claimants victims appeared to be somewhat better off than the average but not significantly. Ironically, in New York, a claimant must satisfy a "means test" in order to qualify for compensation, and yet Brooklyn claimants were better off economically than all the other samples, including Brooklyn non-claimants.

More specifically, it was discovered that most victims (41%) had some high school, but had not graduated. Three in ten victims did graduate from high school, while about one in ten either had some college or less than an eighth-grade education. College graduates and postgraduates (3% each) accounted for the remaining responses (Table A.4). The differences in education among the separate samples were not statistically significant.

The other indicators of potential economic well-being were no brighter. For example, more victims were unemployed (42%) than in any other employment category, including fully employed (35%), partially employed (10%), self-employed (8%), or students (5%) (Table A.5). None of the individual samples differed significantly from these averages.

These employment levels were elaborated by having victims indicate their occupations. Although over one-third of those questioned specified no occupation, many other vocations were mentioned. The largest group, those in service jobs, comprised almost one of every five victims specifying an occupation. Among others employed, skilled (12%) workers were next, followed by clericals and salespersons (11% each), laborers and managers (9% each), students (8%), professionals and retired persons (7% each), and crafts persons (3%) (Table A.6). No statistically significant differences from this pattern of responses emerged among the individual samples.

Another factor that helps define a victim's economic well-being is his income. The income levels indicated were consistent with the previous measures. Slightly over one in five respondents' incomes was not recorded either because of refusals (15%) or missing data (6%). But, among those responding, more than twice as many people were receiving welfare payments, at least sporadically (41%), as were found in any other income category. The next largest group were those earning between $10,000 and $15,000 (20%), followed by those earning between $7500 and $10,000 (13%), those earning either less than $5000 or between $5000 and $7500 (8% each), those earning between $15,000 and $25,000 (7%), and those earning over $25,000 (3%) (Table A.7). None of the individual samples deviated significantly from this pattern.

A final influence on economic status is the effect of a victim's family size on his finances. The repondents were asked about the number of dependents supported by their incomes. The average number of dependents was 2.4, but the amount ranged from none to eight. Most victims (32%) had only one dependent, but even this would appear to be a considerable burden given the average victim's age and income. Moreover, 17% had two dependents, 13% had three, 12% had four, 11% had either none or five, 3% had six, and 1% had either seven or eight (Table A.8). None of the separate samples deviated significantly from these averages.

Community Ties

Victims were questioned about their ties to their communities, including how long they had resided in either Brooklyn or Newark, and at their present address; whether they were members of social groups; and whether they had ever used local social services, and if so, which ones. These inquiries were made since a victim's inclination to cooperate with law-enforcement officials, to have favorable attitudes toward criminal justice, and to use a social-service agency such as a victim-compensation program might be related to his community ties.

The amount of community ties registered by victims was mixed. Although few respondents belonged to community groups, they usually had resided in their communities for a sufficient time to develop local roots. And, social-service agencies were widely used, although more by non-claimants than by claimants. Claimants—who were generally a little more economically secure than non-claimants—did dominate one social service: medical care. But, most significant perhaps was the fact that those most likely to use social-service agencies were those (non-claimants) who failed to apply for victim compensation, perhaps indicating that such programs are either unknown or (as the claimant samples seem to confirm by their failure to identify victim compensation as a social service either) not perceived as a community service[10].

In particular, respondents were asked how long they had lived at their present address (Table A.9), and for how much total time they had been living in either Brooklyn or Newark (Table A.10). The largest category of respondents (30%) had been living at both their present address and in one of the two cities from two to five years. The length of residence for the remaining respondents was divided almost equally between those who lived in their present address, or in Brooklyn or Newark generally, either less than two years or more than five years (35% each). Almost one in ten listed residence for over twenty years. No significant differences from the averages emerged among the individual samples.

Likewise, victims were questioned about their memberships in community social groups. Only about two of every five respondents were involved in such groups (Table A.11). In contrast, victims were more likely to use social services in their community. Almost two-thirds had used some kind of social-service agency (Table A.12). The individual samples again were consistent with the averages for these responses. When asked to name the specific agencies they used, the largest number cited some kind of medical assistance (26%). Other prominent services mentioned were daycare and welfare (22% each), and social workers (18%), followed by community centers (7%), legal aid (3%), victim-service agencies (either Brooklyn's Victim/Witness Assistance Project or Newark's Victim Service Center or counseling (1% each) (Table A.13). None of the individual samples deviated significantly from these averages. But, it is interesting to note that only a few mentioned some kind of victim-referral agency—despite the fact that actually an average of 84% did use this service (see chapter five, Table 5.10). And, none of the claimants mentioned either compensation board—despite the fact that about 50% did use this service.

Victim Attitudes about Politics and Government

Victims were asked another series of questions to assess their general views of government and their perceived viability in the political system. This was done to better understand political attitudes that might affect a victim's willingness to cooperate with government and law-enforcement efforts, and to seek government assistance in times of need. Respondents were asked about their party affiliation; their views about government responsiveness; their ability and inclination to vote, campaign, and otherwise influence or interact with the government; and their personal efficacy in general.

Overall, the typical victim lacks party affiliation; views his government as unresponsive; feels he could not affect government policy; and thus would not and has not attempted to do so; lacks political-campaign experience; denies that he would receive equal treatment; and assesses his future prospects as discouraging. In sum, these attitudes do not reflect a victim's tendency to trust his government, nor to seek to influence or benefit from it, nor especially to participate in its functions. This is discouraging news for those (such as victim compensation's supporters) who hope to have victims actively assist in government activities such as law enforcement.

While the political efficacy of victims is generally low, some evidence exists to show that some victims are even more alienated than others. That is, Brooklyn claimants were significantly more inclined to label government as unresponsive, and less inclined to try to influence their city councils in the future. Newark claimants, on the other hand, were significantly less discouraged in their future prospects than other victims, including Brooklyn claimants. These differences might be due to the effects of each state's compensation program, or could merely reflect the victims' experience in the criminal-justice process, or even previously held aversions to government (see chapter 10).

More specifically, a plurality of victims indicated their membership in the Democratic Party (39%), but the next largest category mentioned was no party at all (28%). Almost one in five were Republicans, 12% were independents, and 2% mentioned other political parties (Table A.14). The differences among the four samples were not statistically significant, but some of the findings, in the aggregate, are important nevertheless.

For example, the combination of no party, other party, and independents constituted the largest group (42%) of respondents, who were apparently united in rejecting the two major parties. In fact, this group is almost as large as all major party identifiers combined (57%). Such results reflect the fact that considerable numbers of victims have either sought alternatives to the main parties, or have avoided political involvement (e.g., "I don't get involved in that game") altogether.

A considerable majority (57%) of all victims felt that government was generally unresponsive (e.g., "this government is only good for the rich") to their needs. Only 27% indicated that government was sometimes responsive, and even fewer (16%) said that government usually was responsive (Table 4.3). Brooklyn claimants had significantly (.05) less confidence (65% indicated rarely responsive) in government than Newark claimants (only 22% indicated rarely responsive), but the relationship was not very strong (V=.20).

Respondents were asked about their ability to affect their city council on a matter of importance to them. Again, a considerable majority (60%) indicated that they would have no effect (e.g., "it's no use," and "we couldn't get in the door"). A little more than one in three said that they would have some influence, while 5% did not know what impact they would have. Only 2% thought they would have considerable impact (Table A.15). The differences among the samples were insignificant.

Victims' responses as to whether they would try to affect their city council on an important matter, or whether they had ever actually tried to do so, were largely predictable given the aforementioned low sense of efficacy. Seventy-three percent of the respondents said they would not try to affect their local government (Table A.16). And, nine out of ten indicated that they had also never in the past tried to influence their city council (Table 4.4). Brooklyn non-claimants were significantly (.05) less inclined to have ever tried to affect their

TABLE 4.3 GOVERNMENT RESPONSIVENESS

	ALL %	Claimants		Non-Claimants	
		BKLN %	NEWK %	BKLN %	NEWK %
USUALLY	56 (16)	10 (12)	17 (22)	14 (14)	15 (19)
SOMETIMES	91 (27)	20 (24)	22 (28)	26 (27)	23 (29)
RARELY	195 (57)	55 (65)	40 (51)	58 (59)	42 (53)
	342	85	79	98	80

(S=.05) (V=.20)

TABLE 4.4 EVER TRY TO AFFECT CITY COUNCIL

	ALL	Claimants BKLN	NEWK	Non-Claimants BKLN	NEWK
	%	%	%	%	%
YES	35 (10)	10 (12)	10 (13)	5 (5)	10 (13)
NO	307 (90)	75 (88)	69 (87)	93 (95)	70 (87)
	342	85	79	98	80
(S=.05) (V=.20)					

city council in the past than the other three samples, although the relationship was somewhat weak (V=.20).

This apparent frustration with government was reflected in answers to related questions as well. More than half the respondents were not registered to vote (Table A.17). Moreover, an average of 96% of all respondents also had never taken part in a political campaign (Table A.18). And, more than one-half (52%) of the victims surveyed indicated that they probably would not receive equal treatment by government officials such as by police officers (Table A.19). No significant differences emerged among the separate samples on these responses.

The comments made on these questions were consistent. One respondent summarized the sentiment of many when he answered "why bother?" to the question of whether he was registered to vote. Another victim echoed the views of many others when he indicated, ironically, that he "had too many of his own problems" to get involved in political campaigns. And, still another respondent reflected a popular skepticism about receiving fair treatment when she said that she was "treated like a criminal even when I am a victim."

Respondents' political attitudes and efficacy might be summarized by the personal question asked about their future prospects in society, in general. Only slightly more respondents viewed their future with mixed feelings (43%) than viewed their prospects with discouragement (40%). Only 17% assessed their futures as hopeful (Table 4.5). Newark claimants differed significantly (.02) from the other samples. Although the difference was somewhat weak (V=.22), these victims were both less hopeful and less discouraged than other victims, and instead were much more likely to simply be uncertain or have mixed feelings. Overall, however, the comments among all victims were generally dreary (e.g., "this is typical of the messes I get myself into"), although some were more disheartening than others (e.g., "after all this, I just want to die...why bother?").

Finally, when one combines victims' responses as to whether they think they

TABLE 4.5 FUTURE PROSPECTS

	ALL	Claimants		Non-Claimants	
		BKLN	NEWK	BKLN	NEWK
	%	%	%	%	%
HOPEFUL	57 (17)	14 (17)	10 (13)	23 (24)	10 (13)
MIXED	148 (43)	36 (42)	44 (56)	34 (35)	34 (43)
POOR	137 (40)	35 (41)	25 (32)	41 (42)	36 (45)
	342	85	79	98	80
(S=.02) (V=.22)					

would have an effect on city council, and whether they would ever try to exert such influence, and whether they believe they would receive fair treatment from government officials, an index of respondents' sense of political efficacy emerges[11]. That combination shows that a clear majority (52%) has a poor sense of efficacy (Table A.20). No significant differences among the samples emerged.

Victim Attitudes Toward Criminal Justice

To more directly test the likelihood of victims participating positively in criminal justice, respondents were asked their particular views on crime and on the government's response to the crime problem[12]. Victims were questioned about what they thought causes crime, how they felt about the crime rate, whether friends had been victimized recently, their view of government's responsibility for crime, and whether law-enforcement officials were performing adequately.

Overall, victims were disheartened about the crime problem. They were strongly convinced of crime's extensiveness, which seems at least partially reinforced by the number of respondents whose friends had been victimized (not to mention their own victimization). Respondents attributed the cause of crime to many sources, but most did not blame the government directly. A sizable minority, however, did accuse government directly. Brooklyn victims and all claimants were significantly more likely to cast such blame. A considerable majority of victims also was dissatisfied with law-enforcement efforts to cope with the crime problem. Brooklyn victims were significantly less satisfied than Newark victims. The victims surveyed held what appear to be clearly negative views about criminal justice, which might reflect adversely on their willingness to support law-enforcement officials.

In particular, more victims felt that crime was caused by permissiveness (23%) than from any other source, followed by social decay (17%), poor law enforcement (15%), poverty (13%), government lenience (12%), and born criminals (10%). While 2% indicated they did not know the cause of crime, another 2% blamed it on boredom. And, perhaps most interesting were those comments blaming crime on racism (5%) and on government repression (1%) (Table A.21). One respondent, for example, said "what do you expect in a racist society?" No significant differences occurred among the individual samples.

The overwhelming majority of respondents felt that the crime rate was high (86%), while 9% thought it was moderate, 4% had no opinion, and 1% indicated that the rate was low (Table A.22). Perhaps some respondents' views on the crime rate reflect the high percentage (41%) of their friends who had been victimized recently (Table A.23). No significant differences emerged among the samples on these responses.

When asked directly to comment about government's responsibility for crime, a clear majority (60%) answered in the negative, but a notable amount (40%) did cast some blame in that direction (Table 4.6). Although the relationship is fairly weak ($V=.21$), some significant (.05) differences did emerge from the individual samples. Brooklyn victims cast significantly more blame on government for causing crime than Newark victims, and claimants registered more accusations than non-claimants.

Among those (40%) ($N=138$) who held the government responsible, most felt that it failed to protect the public (35%), or was too lenient (31%), or was too unconcerned (21%). Only a few blamed the government for creating a poor social atmosphere (10%), or for either repression or racism (4%) (Table A.24). Again, the differences among the individual samples were insignificant.

Among those (60%) ($N=206$) who did hold government responsible for crime, 197 explained why: Slightly more than one-half claimed that crime was not the government's fault, while the rest repeated the things besides government

TABLE 4.6 GOVERNMENT RESPONSIBILITY FOR CRIME

	ALL	Claimants		Non-Claimants	
		BKLN	NEWK	BKLN	NEWK
	%	%	%	%	%
YES	136 (40)	41 (48)	29 (37)	40 (41)	26 (33)
NO	206 (60)	44 (52)	50 (63)	58 (59)	54 (67)
	342	85	79	98	80
	(S=.05) (V=.21)				

that they felt were the real causes (Table A.25). The differences emerging among the samples were not statistically significant.

Finally, respondents were asked whether they thought that criminal-justice officials were doing all they could to cope with the crime problem. Despite some reluctance to blame government directly for crime, many victims (66%) thought that officials could be doing more, while only one-third believed that officials had been doing everything possible (Table 4.7). And, Brooklyn victims were significantly (.05) less supportive of law enforcement efforts than Newark victims, although the difference ($V=.21$) was weak.

Conclusion

The victims in this study show a variety of general backgrounds and attitudes. But, most victims were young, married, non-white males with a low socioeconomic status and poor attitudes toward both government and criminal justice. Although the status characteristics of the respondents are interesting in themselves, victims' negative attitudes are of greatest importance to this study. Although these are only general sentiments about government and law enforcement, they may translate into specific attitudes and behavior in practice.

The foregoing description of victim characteristics also shows some significant differences among the four, separate samples involved in the research. Without reviewing the specific differences again (see Tables 4.1-4.7), it can be observed that Brooklyn claimants differed notably in age and sex, and in confidence in government, willingness to blame government for crime, and in their beliefs about whether law-enforcement officials are doing all they could to cope with crime. Brooklyn non-claimants differed significantly in their history of having

TABLE 4.7 JUSTICE OFFICIALS DOING ALL THEY CAN

	ALL	Claimants		Non-Claimants	
		BKLN	NEWK	BKLN	NEWK
	%	%	%	%	%
YES	115(34)	26(31)	29(37)	30(31)	30(38)
NO	227(34)	59(69)	50(63)	68(69)	50(62)
	342	85	79	98	80
(S=.05) (V=.21)					

tried to influence government, and Newark claimants deviated notably in their view of their future prospects.

These differences are important in two ways: First, the variations in age and sex may be related to one's victimization and post-victimization experiences, and the attitudes they produce. But, of particular significance is the fact that age and sex may be related to whether a victim applies for compensation and whether he receives an award, as well as to how he experiences the compensation process and to what attitudes he develops as a result.

Second, the statistically significant differences in attitudes toward government and criminal justice are perhaps even more crucial. If claimants appear[13] to be considerably less positive toward our political institutions than non-claimants, on at least some measures, then unless some intervening influence is causing these results, one must seriously question the acclaimed, affirmative effects of victim compensation on improving those attitudes, or on at least assuring that they do not get worse. And, if on important attitudinal measures it is found that Brooklyn claimants are considerably less satisfied than Newark claimants, then one must wonder whether—if, in fact, it can be traced to victim compensation—any differences in the two state's compensation programs account for the attitudinal variations. Such a program difference—and practically no others actually exist—is each plan's underlying philosophy (welfare vs. right) for granting awards.

Furthermore, even many of the statistically insignificant findings have much potential importance. That is, if victim compensation is really performing adequately, then the attitudes among claimants towards government and criminal justice should not only not be worse than non-claimants, and not only not be the same as non-claimants, but in fact, they should clearly be significantly better than non-applicants. This is obviously not the case since the best that claimants have done is to register attitudes that are no worse than their fellow victims. Of course, one must again guard against attributing these results too directly to victim compensation (although it seems that some advocates believe such programs can overcome other, possible intervening (and depressing) influences on attitudes), since other factors may have contributed to this result.

Overall, among the characteristics and attitudes discussed in this chapter, the differences are not extensive. The significant variations that do exist raise questions and warrant taking them into consideration before drawing final conclusions about victim compensation, and they will be resolved in subsequent chapters. Since the number of differences is not considerable, however, one cannot presume that backgrounds are a major determinant of differences in who applies for compensation and who gets awards, nor a predictor, on their own, of attitudinal differences toward government and criminal justice. Consequently, the potential influence of victim compensation thusfar has no strong competitor.

If background characteristics and general attitudes do not appear to vary extensively enough to potentially affect a victim's attitudes toward government and law enforcement, then one must look to other possible influences. The next two chapters will discuss the possible effects of the victimization and post-victimization processes, and simultaneously allow us to begin to observe victims as they move into and through the criminal process, toward the position of perhaps applying for victim compensation.

Notes

1. James Garofalo & John Laub, "The Fear of Crime: Broadening Our Perspectives," *Victimology*, 3(1978), 242; Terry Baumer, "Research on the Fear of Crime in the United States," *Victimology*, 3(1978), 274; Stephanie Rigor, et al., "Women's Fear of Crime," *Victimology*, 3(1978), 274; Ellen Cohn, et al., "Crime Prevention vs. Victimization: The Psychology of Two Different Reactions," *Victimology*, 3(1978), 285; Jeffrey Henig & Michael Maxfield, "Reducing Fear of Crime: Strategies for Intervention," *Victimology*, 3(1978), 297; Diedre Gaquin, "Measuring Fear of Crime: The National Crime Survey's Attitude Data," *Victimology*, 3(1978), 314; Marlys McPherson, "Realities and Perceptions of Crime at the Neighborhood Level," *Victimology*, 3(1978), 319; Victoria Jaycox, "The Elderly's Fear of Crime: Rational or Irrational?" *Victimology*, 3(1978), 329; Robert Rubel, "Victimization and Fear in Public Schools," *Victimology*, 3(1978), 339; Robert Zion, "Reducing Crime and Fear of Crime in Downtown Cleveland," *Victimology*, 3(1978), 341; Margaret Gordon & Stephanie Rigor, "The Fear of Rape Project," *Victimology*, 3(1978), 346; Wesley Skogan, "Public Policy and the Fear of Crime in Large American Cities," paper delivered to Midwest Political Science Association, Chicago, 1976; James Garofalo, "Victimization and the Fear of Crime," *J. Res. in Crime & Delinq.* (1979), 80.

2. M.K. Block & G.J. Lenz, "Subjective Probability of Victimization and Crime Levels: An Econometric Approach," *Criminology*, 11(1973), 87; Frank Furstenberg, "Public Reaction to Crime in the Streets," in George F. Cole (ed.), *Criminal Justice: Law and Politics* (Belmont: Wadsworth, 1972), 43; Michael Hindelang, et al., *Victims of Personal Crime* (Cambridge: Ballinger, 1978).

3. National Criminal Justice Information and Statistical Service, *Crime in Eight American Cities* (Washington: U.S. Gov't Printing Ofc., 1974); National Criminal Justice Information and Statistical Service, *Criminal Victimization in the Nation's Five Largest Cities* (Washington: U.S. Gov't. Printing Ofc., 1975); Office of Planning and Program Assistance, *1977 Comprehensive Crime Control Plan* (New York: Div. Crim. Justice Serv., 1978).

4. See chapter 3 for more details on sampling.

5. The measure of statistical significance used is the chi-square test.

6. The measure used to assess size of relationship is Cramer's V.

7. Significance tests for all tables in this chapter were calculated not only for all four samples considered together, but also for all possible pairs of samples in each table. Only statistically significant results are reported, however.

8. See numbered tables, all of which show no statistically significant relationships, in Appendix A.

9. See Bureau of Justice Statistics, *The Hispanic Victim: A Comparative Study of Criminal Victimization against Hispanics and Non-Hispanics* (Washington: U.S. Gov't. Printing Ofc., 1980).

10. A similar finding can be found in a smaller study of applicants to the New York Crime Victims Compensation Board: Barbara Dulberg, "Social and Psychological Fac-

tors Inhibiting Use of Crime Victims Compensation Board,'' (M.A. Thesis, John Jay College of Criminal Justice, 1978).

11. This composite index of a victim's political efficacy was comprised of the variable just noted. Some of the answers on these variable were recoded so that the values of each variable would range in order from good to poor. When combined into a single index, a range of four numeric values resulted—the lowest two being labelled as good efficacy, and the highest two being labelled as poor efficacy.

12. Doris A. Graber, ''Evaluating Crime-Fighting Policies: The Public's Perspective,'' paper presented at the American Political Science Convention, Washington, 1977; C.W. Thomas & C.C. Nelson, *Public Attitudes toward Criminal Justice Agencies, Policies and Levels of Criminal Victimization* (Washington: Nat. Inst. Law Enforce. & Crim. Justice, 1975); T. Bartell, *Citizen Perceptions of the Justice System* (Albuquerque: U. N. Mexico's Inst. Soc. Res. & Develop., 1975).

13. One must note a methodological problem that limits one's ability to draw firm conclusions about victim attitudes in this study. As explained in some detail in chapter 3, considerable difficulty confronts the researcher in trying to complete a study such as this. Two of the major obstacles are getting samples of victims in the first place, and then having the time and resources to properly question the respondents. These problems have rendered the research design less than optimal. A preferable method of conducting the study would have been to question victims at various stages of the process, such as before victimization, after victimization (but before confronting the criminal process), after the criminal case is resolved and the victim's participation in the criminal process has ended, and after contact and a final decision by the compensation board. This kind of testing in stages would have provided some useful controls.

Since a comparative study using such an approach would have been highly impractical, controls were sought instead through the process of contrasting separate groups, two of which (claimants) were exposed to an experimental influence (the compensation process) and two of which (non-claimants) were not. If both claimants and non-claimants have similar experiences and contact, and yet express significantly different attitudes, then this provides some basis for attributing the differences to the experimental influence. This is especially so if, as has been done in this study, the samples are drawn randomly to protect against systematic biases. But, the controls inherent in this design are far from perfect, and they do not account for the possibility, for example, that the general attitudes toward government and criminal justice which are reflected in this chapter have been registered as preconceptions by victims, and not responses to the victimization or post-victimization (including compensation) experiences at all. This kind of limitation must be noted and taken into consideration in drawing conclusions. Unfortunately, the nature of this kind of research makes eliminating such problems difficult, if not impossible.

CHAPTER FIVE
Victims in the Criminal Process

For many victims, their victimization by the offender often lasts only a few minutes. But, crime's impact, and the future actions it may require or provoke often can cause a victim's involvement for many months, even years. When a person is victimized, he may begin a post-victimization experience that requires extensive participation in the criminal-justice process and various transactions with other private and public agencies. One of those other agencies may be a victim-compensation program, at least for Brooklyn and Newark victims. Whether a victim ever applies for compensation, and the success of his application, may depend significantly on his previous experience in the criminal process.

Since one of this research's major objectives is to assess who applies for compensation and who gets awards, examining victimization and post-victimization experiences will add appreciably to our present information (see chapter four) about the characteristics of applicants and beneficiaries. It will be important to scrutinize the four samples of victims in this study to isolate differences among respondents that might have contributed to "who gets what" from victim compensation. As with the previous chapter, however, the observations made here will be reserved to describing differences in characteristics, while it will be left to subsequent chapters to explain just what contribution these traits may have made to various compensation outcomes. The proponents of victim compensation, including those who created and who are administering such programs in New York and New Jersey, claim that compensating will improve attitudes toward government and criminal justice, and induce a willingness to cooperate in law enforcement, which will aid in crime prevention. In order to examine victim compensation's supposed effects, however, one must analyze other, competing factors that might influence attitudes and cooperation. These factors must include a victim's experience from the time he is victimized, through his criminal-process involvement, to the point when he may become eligible for compensation. A special understanding of that experience will be provided herein through the respondents' own description of their victimization, and through a detailed account of the physical characteristics and atmosphere of the Brooklyn and Newark courts.

In sum, it is necessary to examine the nature of the crime committed against the victim, the offender's characteristics, any previous victim experience in the criminal process, and his current experiences in the process. The latter includes whether the crime was reported, an arrest was made, and charges were pressed[1], and what kind of experiences the victim encountered in pursuing the case—including his activities in the complaint room and the courtroom—as well as the problems he may have faced in so appearing.

One also must consider the various outcomes of each case—including the grant of bail, property return, and other possible reimbursements, and the offender's penalty. And finally, one must assess the victim's attitudes toward his criminal-justice experience—including his views of the process, of the defendant, and of law-enforcement officials, as well as his likelihood of future involvement.

In addition to presenting victim experiences that help describe who applies for compensation and who potentially may receive an award, those experiences also are discussed in this chapter to begin assessing what contribution they may make toward producing certain attitudes about government and law enforcement. Since victim compensation's advocates claim that such programs will have a beneficial effect on these attitudes, that presumption can only be tested by eliminating (or at least controlling for) other, potential determinants of a victim's feelings. By examining the victimization and post-victimization experiences, and how they might vary among the separate samples in this study, one can, in fact, consider such rival determinants. If the experiences are not significantly different, and thus are fairly uniform among the samples, then any differences in attitudes might be attributable to victim compensation afterall.

Criminal Victimization

To best understand the victimization of the respondents in this study, an attempt was made to compile information about their experience, such as the particular kind of violent crime, the amount of injury and property loss, the nature of the victim-offender relationship, the number of offenders, and their traits. And, to accumulate an even broader picture of the victimization, respondents were asked actually to describe the crime committed against them. In other words, an attempt was made to prevent the raw data on these victimizations, offered alone, from disguising the more profound, human dimensions of these crimes. As explained by victims in their own words, the crimes clearly range from the ridiculous to the sublime. These descriptions will combine with the statistics to provide a more complete understanding of criminal victimization.

The following figures and descriptions will indicate the tremendous variety of criminalization which exists within the broad labels of assaults and robberies. Most of the respondents in this study were assault victims, which helps explain why most of those questioned suffered some kind of injury, while many fewer sustained a property loss. When personal belongings were taken, cash was the item usually stolen. Although some respondents were cross-complainants, most were not. But, the victim's past familiarity with the offender, including frequent close relationships, was widespread. And finally, most victimizations were produced by only one assailant, he was usually male, and so was his victim.

The only significant differences among the individual samples in the victimization experience included the tendency of Brooklyn non-claimants to be cross-complainants more frequently, and for claimants (in both cities) to differ importantly from non-claimants (in both cities) in their tendency to have known or had a close relationship with the offender. The former finding defies any clear explanation, while the latter observation obviously seems explained by the compensation rules that govern eligibility in relationship crimes, and thus apparently cause some victims to eliminate themselves. In sum, other than these two differences, no major divergences seem to exist among the victimization experiences in the various samples.

Kinds of Crimes

More specifically, the victimizations include the following characteristics: Since certain kinds of violent crimes were not considered (see chapter four), the remaining crimes were either assaults or robberies[2]. Despite the obvious seriousness of these offenses, it did not mitigate the absurdity of some incidents:

> The defendant hit me with a milk crate after he had asked for more onions on his frankfurter. I gave him so much they were falling off on the floor. Then I hit him back with a Coke bottle.

Almost two-thirds of those surveyed were assault victims of one kind or another, while a little over one-third were robbery victims (Table B.1)[3]. Obviously, taking property was not the dominant reason for the crimes committed against these victims. The separate samples did not differ significantly in the distribution of crimes.

Many of these offenses were street crimes:

> I was choked, beaten, sat on and threatened by him with a knife. He took all my keys and said he would come around for more, and then tied me up before leaving, and stole $125, $35 worth of food stamps, a wrist watch, and jewelry.

Other crimes occurred in business establishments:

> Three men came into my office and attempted to steal some eyeglass frames. They cut the telephone line and made personal calls on another telephone.

> Two men came into the bar. One came behind the bar with a gun and told me to lay on the floor. They emptied the register, took my ring and money, and then robbed other customers in the bar at the time.

The vast majority of the victims experienced some injury from the crime committed against them[4]. Only 4% reported no injury whatsoever, while 22% indicated minor harms requiring no medical attention, 58% required medical assistance, and 16% were hospitalized (Table B.2). None of the individual samples differed significantly from the average.

The victims' own descriptions of their injuries illustrate the tremendous range of the harms. One respondent indicated: "Three men mugged me and my nose got bent." But, other injuries were more profound:

> I was beaten repeatedly on the head, and robbed, and I received brain damage as a result.

> I was severely beaten in a mugging. I got a brain concussion, a deeply lacerated scalp, a broken left elbow, a broken bone in my back, a damaged right eye, blood clots behind the right eardrum, bel palsy on the right side of my face, and a damaged right eyelid. I can't see well, can't hear, and can't walk properly.

> I was sitting on a bar stool in the social club when I felt a burning in my leg and fell off the stool. When I woke up, I was in Lutheran Hospital. My leg was shattered in many places by gunshot, and I was forced to have an above the knee amputation of my left leg.

Three out of five victims reported no property loss from their victimization, while just short of 40% did suffer such losses (Table B.3). Among those reporting property losses, the following stolen items were indicated: cash (43%), wallet or purse (20%), jewelry (14%), electrical equipment (6%), clothing or bicycles (4% each), and credit cards or household items or office supplies or other losses (2% each) (Table B.4). No important differences were found among the samples on these responses.

As with the range of injuries, however, the magnitude of the properties lost was quite varied. Whereas many reported only minor losses, some were huge:

> I have a store for sale. Four men came in as buyers and said they wanted to buy the next day. But, the next day they called and said they wouldn't buy, but asked me to bring $10,000 to their apartment, saying that if I did, I could earn $40,000. I went to the apartment with the money and there was a table for card playing with $40,000 on it. I refused to play. One of the men pulled a gun, took my money, and left. The next day a stranger called and said he knew who took my money, and asked to meet him at Kennedy. I went to Kennedy, saw the informer, and called a cop.

The vast majority (95%) of the victims were sole complainants in their case, as compared to a few (5%) who were cross-complainants (Table 5.1). The latter indicates that the person who the respondent claimed victimized him also pressed counter-charges against the respondent. Brooklyn non-claimants were significantly[5] (.01) more likely to be cross-complainants (11%) than the other samples, although the relationship was fairly weak (V=.20)[6].

TABLE 5.1 TYPE OF WITNESS

	ALL %	Claimants		Non-Claimants	
		BKLN %	NEWK %	BKLN %	NEWK %
COMPLAINANT	325 (95)	84 (99)	77 (98)	87 (89)	77 (96)
X-COMPLAINT	17 (5)	1 (1)	2 (2)	11 (11)	3 (4)
	342	85	79	98	80

(S=.01) (V=.20)

In some cases, it is either unclear who is the real offender and who is the real victim, or almost a matter of chance as to which side strikes first:

> Him and my cousin and I were drinking and fooling around, and we began fighting. I tried to stop the fight and he stabbed me with a knife.

Victim-Offender Relationships

Respondents also were asked to specify any relationship they might have had with the offender. A little over one-half the offenders were strangers to the respondents, but the rest were recognized in one way or another. These various "relationships" included: saw (offender) before (11%), acquaintance (9%), neighbor (8%), spouse or friend (4% each), ex-spouse or girl/boy friend or ex-girl/boy friend or business associate/co-worker (2% each), and sister/brother or mother/father or other relative or indirect relationship (e.g., in-law, wife's cousin, etc.) or friend of the family (1% each) (Table B.5).

After eliminating those respondents who failed to reply, these "relationships" were categorized to distinguish among strangers (51%), acquaintances (32%)[7], and close relationships (17%)[8]. These groupings show that almost one-half of these violent crimes involved offenders and victims who knew each other, with almost one in five cases involving intimate associations (Table 5.2)[9]

The victims' description of the crimes illustrate the different relationships that occur. Some crimes are committed by strangers:

> I got out of my car and he started shooting at me and my boyfriend for no reason at all. I never saw him before.

> I was stabbed in the back by a person who was drunk, and it required the amputation of my left arm above the elbow.

Other crimes are produced by acquaintances such as business co-workers:

TABLE 5.2 VICTIM-OFFENDER RELATIONSHIP

	ALL	Claimants		Non-Claimants	
	%	BKLN %	NEWK %	BKLN %	NEWK %
STRAN	169 (49) 51	54 (64) 65	49 (62) 62	36 (37) 38	30 (38) 40
INTIM	55 (16) 17	4 (05) 05	3 (04) 04	24 (24) 24	24 (30) 32
ACQUA	109 (32) 32	25 (29) 30	27 (34) 34	36 (37) 38	21 (26) 28
BLANK	9 (03)	2 (02)	0	2 (02)	5 (06)
	342	85	79	98	80

(S=.001) (V=.33)

I had to fire the super because the tenants didn't like him. He came and asked for $700 he claimed I owed him, and I was told to settle it the next day. Then, he assaulted me after chasing me with a switch-blade, and took my money.

And finally, myriad kinds of intimate relationship cases also occurred:

He (husband) beat me with a hair curler, and left marks on my hands and arms. He beats me all the time. He (ex-boyfriend) wouldn't leave my house. He punched me back from the door on to the floor, said he wanted money and took my pocketbook. Then he hit me on the side of my face with his fist. He tried to get me on to the bed, and after a struggle on the steps, he hit me in the head with a wrench. Then, he took a butcher's knife from the kitchen and cut my arm, before I finally convinced him to leave.

I was living with him and he said he was going to die and wanted to marry me so I could get the benefits. Eventually, he forced me to marry him but did not allow me to report it to the welfare department. He began mistreating me and my daughters and my sisters by beating us. Last week, he cut up all my clothes and hit my sister again. I reported the case and an appearance notice for him was sent. I told my daughters that if he behaved, I wouldn't mention the notice; if he didn't, I'd show him. Since he did not stop mistreating me, I showed him the court appearance notice and he got angry and told me that I wanted to land him in jail. He went to work and when he returned at night, he attacked me with a razor, and cut my back and my left cheek.

In fact, however, the average relationship figures are a very misleading description of the victims in this study. The pattern of relationships differs considerably between claimant and non-claimant groups for an apparently very good reason. Claimants cannot recover from their respective state's compensation plans if they have a present or past relationship with the offender[10]. Since it can be assumed (it is specified as a basis of disqualification in program brochures) that at least some potential claimants with such relationships disqualified themselves by not applying, this seems to account for the very great reduction (from an average of 29% for non-claimants to an average of 5% for claimants) in "intimate" relationships specified.

A truer picture of actual victim-offender relationships seems reflected in the non-claimant samples. An average of 62% (as compared to the four-sample average of 49%) of the non-claimants knew their offender. The difference in "intimate" relationship between claimants and non-claimants might roughly indicate the actual victims who are disqualified by compensation rules. In any case, the differences between these two groups clearly are significant (.001) and the relationship is moderately strong (V=.33), but the variation is artificially imposed by compensation-board regulations.

Assailant Characteristics

Finally, in regard to relationships, charges were brought against a perhaps unexpected group: police officers. In the victim's words:

> I was putting my car away when the police came up and started attacking me. I have internal pains and headaches.

> I was thrown down on the corner of Hoyt and Livingston by plainsclothes detectives who claimed I had committed a crime. My shoulder was bruised; I pulled a muscle on my right side; and my toe was broken on my right foot.

One must assess how compensation (if granted) in these kinds of cases might affect the victim's attitudes toward the criminal process and law-enforcement officials.

Most respondents (77%) were victimized by only one offender, although as many as eight assailants were specified by one respondent. Almost one in five respondents were victimized by two offenders, while 5% reported three attackers, 2% four, and 1% five (Table B.6). The number of offenders was very consistent among the individual samples except that none of the Brooklyn victims reported any more than three criminals.

Each respondent was asked the sex of his offender beginning with the primary attacker. Almost nine out of ten primary offenders were male (Table B.7). No significant differences were discovered among the separate samples. But, if one compares the victim's sex (see chapter four, Table 4.2) with the offender's sex, one finds that females are almost three times more likely to be victims than offenders. Overall, however, most crimes were committed by males against other males.

As for the victim's secondary attacker, only 24% had one, and females (7%) were even less present here than males (92%) (Table B.8). And finally, only 9% had more than two attackers, and females did not appear at all among these assailants (Table B.9). Obviously, multiple offenders were dominated by males.

These figures, which describe the kinds of crimes, their harms, and several victim and offender characteristics, communicate much of the victimization experience, but do not quite capture the complete variety of these crimes. A few more descriptions will begin to complete the picture. A very frequent circumstance of victimization, for example, is some kind of accident or quarrel:

> My nephew was moving the car and sideswiped a dog by accident. The owner of the dog started to fight my nephew, then ran to the house, and got a gun and started shooting at us.

> I was invited to his girlfriend's home. He accused me of interfering with his personal problems and set his dog on me. When the dog didn't respond, he hit me with a gun in the right eye. He hit me a few more times outside the apartment, then escorted me home at gunpoint. My eyeball was ruptured and I lost vision.

Others get involved in crimes because of their "good samaritan"[11] activities:

> He shot another man and I saw it happen. I got out of my car to help but was shot in the hand. I observed an armed holdup. I need surgery to my left hand.

Some are even victimized for refusing to commit a crime:

> He pulled a knife on me at Stalb and Nostrand, and told me to do a robbery with him. I said no; he took my radio and left.

And finally, crime for some is a sort of celebration:

> I was hit with a bat on my head and right arm. He knocked on my door and said "here's your birthday present," and then hit me with a baseball bat wrapped in Christmas paper.

Victim Motivations

After a person is victimized, he may not have a choice as to how to respond. That is, sometimes a victim may be rendered so debilitated by the crime that others essentially decide whether to initiate the case in the criminal-justice system. Among those other decision-makers are people who witness or discover the crime, including police officers. But, on the other hand, many other victims are able to make a conscious decision themselves about whether or not to formally initiate and pursue their cases in the criminal process. Many studies indicate the various reasons why victims may not report their victimizations[12], and victimization surveys have exposed the real crime rate to be at least twice, and perhaps as much as three times, as high as the amount reported to law-enforcement officials and recorded in the Uniform Crime Reports.

With this high rate of reluctance to report crime, it is important to investigate the reporting patterns found among the victims surveyed in this study[13]. Then, it is useful to know the extent to which cases were pursued to the next logical step of pressing charges[14]. Examining figures on reporting and pressing charges is important not merely for clarifying a victim's involvement in the criminal process, but more importantly, for understanding his motivations in pursuing the case. In other words, to what extent is each victim getting involved after his victimization, and why?

To help discover the answers to these questions, respondents were asked if they called the police, and if not, who did; whether they would have called the police if they had had the chance; why they reported the crime; whether they pressed charges; and why they pressed charges, including some specific closed-ended inquiries suggesting possible outcomes they might have been seeking.

Overall, much can be observed about the victims' motives in getting involved in the criminal process after their victimization. Only about one-half the respondents actually reported their crimes themselves. But, some were unable—due to their injuries, for example—to report the incident, and the vast majority indicated they would have reported the crime if they had had a chance to do so. When a victim reported a crime, he most often did so to pursue his own interests[15], then for motives directed against the offender, and then for the society's sake.

Since the research design purposely included only respondents who had pursued their cases against their assailant, it is no surprise that practically everyone brought charges[16]. These charges were pressed for a variety of reasons, but on the average they were for motives similar to those for reporting the crime in the first place. But, in the long run, the decision to press charges reflected a decreasing concern for the victim's own interests and a great increase in social concerns.

Few statistically significant differences emerged among the victims' motives for initiating and pursuing their cases. The differences that did appear concerned who reported the crime, and the importance to victims of seeking social justice, of protecting themselves and their families, of protecting the society, and of revenge as motives for participating in the criminal process.

Reporting the Crime

More specifically, the study shows that just over one-half of all respondents called the police on their own behalf. The rest were reported by a combination of others, including friends (18%), unknown (13%), family (11%), and others (7%) (Table 5.3). Brooklyn non-claimants were significantly (.05) more likely to specify "don't know" and less likely to specify "friend" as answers, although the relationship was weak (V=.15).

Victims not reporting their victimizations on their own were asked whether they would have called the police if they had had the chance. The overwhelming majority (87%) indicated that they would have, while 3% were not sure, and

TABLE 5.3 WHO CALLED THE POLICE

	ALL	Claimants		Non-Claimants	
		BKLN	NEWK	BKLN	NEWK
	%	%	%	%	%
VICT	168 (49) 51	43 (51) 52	42 (53) 55	44 (45) 47	39 (49) 51
DK	42 (12) 13	6 (07) 07	7 (09) 09	21 (21) 23	8 (10) 11
FAMIL	36 (11) 11	10 (11) 12	5 (06) 07	13 (13) 14	8 (10) 11
FRIEN	59 (17) 18	18 (21) 22	17 (22) 22	7 (07) 08	17 (21) 22
OTHER	24 (07) 07	6 (07) 07	6 (07) 08	8 (08) 09	4 (05) 05
NA	13 (04)	2 (02)	2 (03)	5 (05)	4 (05)
(S=.05) (V=.15)					

13% said they would not have called (Table B.10). The individual samples were consistent with these figures in all regards.

Respondents who did report their victimizations (N=168, 51%) were asked further why they reported the crime (Table B.11). Although 3% failed to answer, a wide variety of substantive responses were given, with no single answer really dominating. A common answer was that the offender had done wrong (19%), such as this revealing statement: "He had no right to beat me up; I'm not his daughter."

The next most important concerns among victims were their desire to protect themselves or their family, and to recover lost property (17% each). Among those voicing the former sentiment were victims who indicated that: "He threatened to kill me," and "He came against me and my family aggressively," and "It's better for me for my own protection. If I drop charges, he may do it to me again," and finally, "He scared the shit out of me." Those seeking to recover lost property said things such as: "That watch was my graduation present," and "I felt it was the thing to do; I was very upset about getting robbed." Other respondents justified reporting the crime as protecting society as a citizen's duty, and because they had been injured (14% each). Those interested in community protection offered comments such as: "I want to be able to walk the streets free," and "I reported a crime before; it's a bad neighborhood, and we need more people in the neighborhood to do this," and "They seem to be getting worse and worse." On the other hand, those concerned about their injuries included: "She hit me with a pipe and I was hurt bad," and "I was bleeding, with my head split open."

Some victims were most concerned in reporting the victimization with punishing the offender (12%), such as: "He should be put away," and "I can't take it anymore. He should be put in jail or given a doctor; he's an alcoholic." And, still others wanted to end a recurring situation (3%), such as: "He was impossible to live with. We were constantly fighting," and "I've been victimized before, and I want it stopped." And finally, some rare but revealing motives were sometimes mentioned that are not reflected in the statistics:

> Knowing that I had a case before in court as a defendant, I felt it was time that justice worked in my favor. I also felt it would be detrimental to me if I took the law into my own hands.

The reasons given for reporting the crime indicated no significant differences among the separate samples.

The motives for reporting the crime can be categorized to reflect the relative importance to the victim of his own interests, the society's needs, or just desserts for the offender as the basis for his pursuing the case. In other words, when reporting the crime, was the victim primarily concerned with himself and his family (victim orientation)[17], with the society (social orientation)[18], or with the criminal (offender orientation)[19]? Just as when each victim's motive was considered individually, these classifications reflect no significant differences among the individual samples. The victim's interests (55%) clearly are the dominating reasons for reporting the crime, followed by just desserts for the offender (33%), and then society's interests (15%) (Table B.12). The victim's own immediate needs obviously are his most important motivations after being victimized.

Pressing Charges

Respondents also were asked about pressing charges against the offender. Since virtually everyone brought charges at least initially (Table B.13), each victim's reasons for doing so were emphasized in the interviews. When asked why they pressed charges, respondents gave many of the same reasons they had given for reporting the crime, but added a couple of others (Table B.14). Also, unlike with the reasons for crime reporting—where only about one- half the respondents had done so and therefore were able to provide a rationale— practically all the respondents could and did give their reasons for pressing charges.

The leading motive for bringing charges was to punish the offender (23%), such as: "I want him sent to jail for a whole year for someone your own color doing something like that," and "I want them locked up; I really want them killed," and "I want to see him get life." Others were more interested in social justice (17%), including those indicating that: "I just want a fair result, and to be sure that the offender gets what he deserves." Another sizable group was concerned with their own or their family's protection (16%), such as: "I want to divorce him, have him locked up, so that I can get protection from him, his friends, and his family," and "I want to get him out of the apartment to protect myself and my daughters."

Somewhat fewer victims pressed charges to help protect the society generally (13%), including those who said: "Something's got to be done; he's mugged several people now," and "Somebody's got to make him realize that the public is out in the street; he's hazardous to everybody," and "I don't want to see him get off because there has been a lot of bike stealing going on." Only slightly fewer respondents expressed a desire to end a recurring situation (11%), such as: "I want this situation to end now," and "So he won't try it again." Still others pursued their cases to seek restitution or the return of their property (10%), as is reflected in comments such as: "I want to get my money back; it's borrowed," and "I want to get back the money and not bother him anymore," and "I want my radio or $100."

The final two groups of victims bringing charges indicated they had done so either to provide the offender treatment, or for miscellaneous other reasons (5% each). Those in the former group indicated that: "I would like to see this man get some help; he's not normal," and "I want him to see a psychiatrist, but don't want him to be put in jail." And, among the miscellaneous reasons were: "I have to do with everyone in the neighborhood. I want to be left alone. I need better police protection for myself and my customers," and "I just want him to learn his lesson, not to be put away, only probation," and "I want to file a civil suit to recover my losses."[20] Once again, the reasons given for pressing charges among the four individual samples indicate no significant differences.

Just as the respondents' motives for crime reporting could be categorized, so too, can their reasons for pressing charges. Thus, one can once again examine the extent to which a victim's own interests[21], or the society's interests[22], or the offender's just desserts[23] induced the victim to bring a formal case against the alleged assailant. Just as when each victim's motive for bringing charges was considered individually, these categories show no significant differences among the separate samples. But, the victim's own interests (40%) are once again the leading motives for pressing charges, followed by society's interests (31%), and then just desserts for the offender(29%) (Table B.15).

As when asked why they reported the crime, the victims' own immediate needs emerged as the most important reasons when deciding to pursue the case even further. But, unlike the figures for crime reporting, which showed an offender orientation twice as often as social concern, the results for pressing charges run in the opposite direction. That is, social motives are more important than the offender's just desserts in a victim's decision to bring charges. But, most of the victims' increase in social concern comes, in fact, not at the expense of an offender orientation, but rather from a reduced concern for his own interests as the process progresses. In fact, the victim's offender orientation also increases when it comes to pressing charges, largely due to an important increase in respondents' desire to have the offender punished.

Can these apparent motivational changes be explained by a change of heart between reporting the crime and pressing charges against the offender, or do they merely reflect the fact that almost twice as many respondents indicated why they brought charges as indicated why they reported the crime? When those victims who answered both questions are isolated, the figures reveal that changing motives between reporting and pressing charges remains. That is, the victims own interests dominated in 38% of the cases, society's interests 32% of the time., and concern for the offender 30% of the time. No significant differences emerged among the separate samples.

Besides asking victims to answer open-ended questions about pressing charges, several closed-ended inquiries (suggesting possible motives) also were made. Respondents were asked, for example, the importance of receiving restitution or having their property returned. Twice as many victims indicated that either one of those goals was very important (51%) as did those who felt that these goals were only somewhat important (24%), or not important at all (25%) (Table B.16). No significant differences existed among the individual samples.

Victims also were asked how important it was to have the offender put in jail. More than one-half said it was very important (55%), while a little more than a quarter felt it was only somewhat important (26%), and still less indicated that it was not important at all (19%) (Table B.17). Again, the separate samples were consistent with these figures.

In addition, respondents were asked the importance of achieving social justice. A large majority indicated that this goal was very important (70%), followed by many less who felt it was only somewhat important (21%), and even some who said it was not important at all (9%) (Table 5.4). Brooklyn non-claimants (81%) were most inclined to value social justice, significantly (.01) moreso than the other samples, although the relationship was not very strong (V=.25).

Next, victims were asked specifically the importance of protecting oneself or

TABLE 5.4 IMPORTANCE OF SOCIAL JUSTICE

	ALL	Claimants		Non-Claimants	
		BKLN	NEWK	BKLN	NEWK
	%	%	%	%	%
VERY	214 (63) 70	55 (65) 69	45 (57) 59	64 (65) 81	50 (63) 70
SOME	63 (18) 21	17 (20) 21	24 (30) 32	8 (08) 10	14 (18) 20
NONE	29 (09) 09	8 (09) 10	7 (09) 09	7 (07) 09	7 (09) 10
NA	36 (11)	5 (06)	3 (04)	19 (19)	09 (11)
	342	85	79	98	80
(S=.01) (V=.25)					

one's family. More respondents felt this was very important (72%) than any other motive for pressing charges suggested to them. A little over one in five felt that such protection was at least somewhat important (22%), whereas only 6% thought it was not important at all (Table 5.5). But, this only reflects an average for all respondents, and in this case, the mean disguises some important differences among the individual samples. Although the relationship is fairly weak (V=.22), Brooklyn claimants were significantly (.001) less likely to cite self-protection as very important (58%) and particularly less so compared to Brooklyn non-claimants (94%).

Victims also were asked the importance to them of protecting others. Slightly more than one-half indicated that this goal was very important (51%), while about one-third said it was only somewhat important (33%), and 16% felt it was not important at all (Table 5.6). Brooklyn non-claimants were significantly (.001) more inclined to regard protecting others as very important than the other samples, although once again the relationship was fairly weak (V=.21).

Finally, among the possible motives for pressing charges suggested to respondents was revenge against the offender. This incentive received the least support of all, with only about one in five believing it was very important (19%), while almost one-third felt it was only somewhat important (31%), and one-half said it was not important at all (Table 5.7). Once again, Brooklyn non-claimants were significantly (.001) more inclined to indicate that revenge was not at all important (71%), even moreso than the already low level among victims, but clearly the relationship (V=.16) was weak.

In sum, when these motives for pressing charges and pursuing one's case are compared and ordered by importance, it is clear that protecting oneself or one's family is the most prominent goal, followed by a desire for social justice, the offender's punishment, restitution or property recovery, protecting the society,

TABLE 5.5 IMPORTANCE OF PROTECTING SELF/FAMILY

	ALL	Claimants BKLN	NEWK	Non-Claimants BKLN	NEWK
	%	%	%	%	%
VERY	220 (64) 72	46 (54) 58	54 (68) 72	74 (76) 94	46 (58) 65
SOME	66 (19) 22	26 (31) 33	18 (23) 24	3 (03) 04	19 (24) 27
NONE	19 (06) 06	8 (09) 10	3 (04) 04	2 (02) 03	6 (08) 09
NA	37 (11)	5 (06)	4 (05)	19 (19)	9 (11)
	342	85	79	98	80

(S=.001) (V=.22)

TABLE 5.6 IMPORTANCE CF PROTECTING CTHERS

		Claimants		Non-Claimants	
	ALL	BKLN	NEWK	BKLN	NEWK
	%	%	%	%	%
VERY	155(45) 51	33(39) 41	34(43) 45	60(61) 76	28(35) 39
SOME	102(30) 33	30(35) 38	29(37) 39	14(14) 18	29(36) 41
NONE	48(14) 16	17(20) 21	12(15) 16	5(05) 06	14(18) 20
NA	37(11)	5(06)	4(05)	19(19)	9(11)
	342	85	79	98	80

(S=.001) (V=.21)

and revenge. The most victim-oriented goals among these motives are restitution or property recovery and protecting oneself and one's family, while the most socially oriented are social justice and protecting others, and the most offender-oriented are jailing the assailant and seeking revenge. When combined as such, respondents show their primary concern, once again, with their own interests, followed by social concerns, and then offender concerns. This reiterates, therefore, the foregoing findings about the priorities in pressing charges that were revealed in the open-ended questions.

Victim Experiences in the Criminal Process

Once the victim has decided to pursue his case, many possibilities for becoming further involved in the criminal process arise. How does the crime victim

TABLE 5.7 IMPORTANCE OF REVENGE

		Claimants		Non-Claimants	
	ALL	BKLN	NEWK	BLKN	NEWK
	%	%	%	%	%
VERY	57(17) 19	12(14) 15	18(23) 24	10(10) 13	17(21) 23
SOME	94(28) 31	32(38) 40	25(32) 33	12(12) 15	25(31) 34
NONE	154(45) 50	36(42) 45	32(41) 43	55(56) 71	31(39) 43
NA	36(11)	5(06)	4(05)	20(20)	7(09)
	342	85	79	98	80

(S=.001) (V=.16)

participate in the system? Where does he go, who does he talk to, and what does he do? What problems and obstacles arise in his path of involvement? How far will he pursue his case?

To help discover the answers to these kinds of questions, victims were asked about their involvement in the criminal process, including any previous appearances. They were asked specifically about their post-victimization encounters with the offender, whether they appeared in the complaint room and in the court. Questions also were asked about the inconveniences of making it to court, about what they did when they came to court, and about the extent to which they pursued their case to its conclusion.

Examining these experiences is important because they might significantly influence a victim's subsequent attitudes—about crime, law-enforcement personnel, the criminal process, and government generally. Understanding these experiences by themselves is important enough since they tell us about the victim's present and potential role in the criminal process, but they are important also because they provide possible rival (to victim compensation's effects) determinants of victim attitudes. Thus, it also is necessary to stress any differences among the samples in their criminal-justice experiences.

What is the general experience of victims in the Brooklyn and Newark criminal processes? Most of the respondents were not involved previously in the court system, but a notable amount were—including many who were previously victims, and even defendants. Some of the victims were threatened, usually with some personal threat. Most victims did arrive in the complaint room, and most of those who did not claimed that it was because they had not been asked. Most respondents stayed with the investigating officer while in the complaint room, and had no real input into the decision of drawing up charges against the offender.

Less than one-half the victims were at arraignment, however, although about one-third of the cases were decided there. Over one-half the defendants were released on bail. This result was overwhelmingly opposed by victims, who primarily expressed fear at that outcome, and even decided sometimes not to arrive in court to pursue their cases as a result. The vast majority of the respondents did arrive in court, however, in fact usually at least twice, and typically for periods between three and six hours long. Over one-half made it to court each time they were asked. This appearance record was achieved despite various inconveniences, largely regarding financial losses that would be incurred if the victim came to court. When in court, only a small number were asked to testify, and even fewer were consulted by either the prosecutor or the judge about their cases.

The atmosphere and procedures of the Brooklyn and Newark courts are mysterious and overwhelming for most victims. If a victim can overcome this foreboding environment, he usually will find that his ability to help dispose the case is very limited. It would seem to present a clearly frustrating experience, and one that sometimes even ends at the victim's initiation, such as by his decision to drop charges.

Aside from whatever satisfactions come from pursuing one's case in the criminal process, the victim must largely fend for himself to receive the kinds of services that will enable him to recover his losses, both physically and economically. Oftentimes, the victim does not even know that some, limited services are available, but even when he does, he may not use them. Such is the case with victim compensation, for example, almost one-half of those knowing about it having failed to apply.

Few statistically significant differences from this pattern of victim involvement emerged among the separate samples. The only notable variations occurred in the tendency to drop charges, the use of social services (including victim-service centers) after victimization, the level of satisfaction with these services, and the tendency of having heard about victim compensation.

Prior Court Involvement

Considering the victim's participation in the criminal process more specifically can begin with the respondent's prior court involvement[24]. Well over one-third of those surveyed indicated their past involvement (39%), while 61% had not (Table B.18)[25]. Respondents who were involved previously (N=130) were asked how and a little over one-third indicated they had been victims (35%), and even more (36%) said they had been defendants. The remaining involvements included being both a victim and defendant before (16%), being a witness (10%), and miscellaneous other kinds of participation (3%) (Table B.19).

Although no significant differences emerged among the individual samples in prior involvement, the findings are very important nevertheless. They show that among those involved previously, a large number (51%) were people who had been victimized before. And, even more respondents (52%) actually had been defendants before!

Criminal Threats

Since it was suspected that victims might be afraid to pursue their cases in the criminal process, respondents were asked whether they had ever been threatened by their assailants. Almost one-third indicated that they had been threatened, including 11% at the crime scene, and another 19% sometime afterwards. Seventy percent said they never had been threatened (Table B.20). No significant differences were found among the separate samples.

The victims who had been threatened (N=102, 30%) were then asked how they were threatened. Fifteen percent gave no answer. But, among those who did, almost two-thirds had been threatened verbally (62%), while 21% had been intimidated indirectly through others, and 15% actually had been physically threatened (Table B.21). The total number of victims was too small to assess the statistical significance of the differences among the samples.

Complaint Room

Respondents were asked about their specific appearances in the criminal process[26]. Their initial involvement would likely be their arrival in the "complaint room," where they would press charges against their assailant. It is valuable to begin here in describing the atmosphere, procedures and physical layout of the criminal courts into which the victims in this study entered[27].

The crime victim, if he enters the criminal process in Brooklyn and Newark at all, will find himself in a particularly striking environment. Behind the huge, old gray walls of the criminal-court buildings, one finds two of the busiest judicial systems in the nation. Almost all prosecutions occur in criminal court, including all misdemeanors and almost all felonies. All misdemeanor cases end in one way or another in this court. And, although felony prosecutions may proceed to the grand jury and then on to the next rung in the judicial ladder, in practice this occurs less than 25% of the time, with the remaining cases being disposed in criminal court.

The court is under very great pressure to dispose cases quickly, and many felony cases are, therefore, terminated as early as the arraignment stage. In effect, the criminal court acts as a proving ground for the prosecutor to sort out the few "serious" felony cases (which eventually will be sent to the upper court unless plea bargained) from cases where it is appropriate to send the defendant to state prison.

One way of viewing the prosecutor's function is simply that of "keeping the lid on the system." With relatively few resources and with the least-experienced assistant prosecutors, the district attorney's office makes sure that few cases survive lower-court screening so that upper-court prosecutors are not overburdened, and can devote more intensive effort to the serious cases that are passed on to them.

The administrative requirements of an efficient criminal court[28], however, may not produce an atmosphere that promotes the victim's involvement. The criminal process has a universalistic, not particularistic, focus. Thus, criminal-justice officials are concerned with broad trends and groupings, and not with individual victims, nor their well-being in the criminal process. What role a complainant might want to assume in his case may be quite distinct from his actual participation[29].

Observers of many urban, criminal-court systems in the United States have noted that despite the adversarial myths, the reality often is much cooperation among judges, prosecutors, and defense attorneys[30]. In fact, these officials must rely upon each other to achieve their respective goals. Disagreements, surprises, and combat are all inimical to achieving the efficiency deemed necessary for the system's and the actors' survival. The criminal courts in Brooklyn and Newark seem no different in this regard. Without any long-term, systematic observation[31], it cannot be clearly determined to what extent the court actors in these two cities form what Eisenstein and Jacob have called "workgroups."[32] But, the elements of cooperation basic to the workgroup arrangement were apparent in both cities.

How does or can the victim fit into these workgroups? It has been observed that the defendant often is excluded from basic participation or consideration in the workgroup. Is the victim's involvement any different? This is an important question since it may affect significantly his overall satisfaction with the system, and his willingness to invoke it in the future. To examine the victim's role, we must view his experience as he moves through each stage of the criminal process.

When an arrest is made, a formal affadavit of charges against the suspect is drawn up by an assistant prosecutor in the complaint room. This room is most victims point of entry into the criminal-adjudication process. As victims and witnesses enter this room, they encounter a long, narrow hall which is stuffy and dingy, and in peak hours, very noisy and crowded. Hard plastic seats line one wall, and are filled usually with complainants and police officers, who are talking or dosing while waiting to see the assistant prosecutors. The wait often is considerable, and can range up to a few hours. At the end of this rather dirty, grimy room are a pair of police desks where officers sign in and complete various forms for the Police Department.

Both cities have victim-service centers. But, whereas Newark's program (the Victim-Service Center) is located in a separate police-department building, Brooklyn's service (the Victim/Witness Assistance Project) is located right in the complaint room. These centers attempt to orient the victim to the court process, tell him about various services he may be entitled to, and ask him how he may be contacted in the future about his court dates. The programs try to comfort the victim during what is potentially a very disorienting and threatening situation[33]. Since the complaint room often is a victim's first court initiation, the victim-service center—at least the one on the scene in Brooklyn—may be playing a pivotal role (yet one frequently unfulfilled in other cities) in influencing the victim's decision whether or not to continue with the case.

One end of the complaint room is devoted to the prosecutor's office. It includes a bureau responsible for ensuring that inexperienced assistant prosecutors will act in ways consistent with management policy. In the bureau office, a more experienced assistant prosecutor screens all felony cases before preparing the affadavit of charges. The complainant is only rarely asked into this office, but if so, he is then questioned about the case. Otherwise, the bureau chief reviews the complaint, asks the police officer investigating the case questions, and assigns a "track" to the case. These "tracks" identify what the case is "worth" for assistant prosecutors who handle the case thereafter—ranging from a serious felony case with good evidence to a recommendation for dismissal.

Although victims rarely enter the bureau office, they are somewhat more likely to be questioned outside by prosecutors after their case has been tracked. For this, they are sent (along with the police officer) to one of the several booths that line one wall. There, the victim is questioned by the less experienced prosecutors, who record the information, dictate it to a typist, and combine it with the "tracking" recommendation which they have been handed, thus producing a folder ready for the prosecution to use in court.

Overall, the complaint room undoubtedly impresses the victim as a rather dismal place—hardly the majestic halls of justice many are led to expect of a courthouse. Perhaps this poor atmosphere causes arresting officers to rarely insist that the victim accompany them to the complaint room. If the victim does go to the complaint room, it normally takes place a few hours after the crime, or early the following day, while the trauma of the event is still fresh in his mind. From the police officer's perspective, however, he may feel he is sparing the victim the complaint room's turmoil by sending him home after the crime while the officer describes the incident to the prosecutor himself. Thus, police officers may have an important influence on this aspect of a victim's criminal-justice involvement.

Among the respondents questioned in this study, a large number (70%) did at least arrive at the complaint room (Table B.22). Those not arriving mostly indicated that they had not been asked (39%), while others said that the crime prevented them or that they were a cross-complainant (12%), followed by other reasons (10%), told not to come (9%), threatened (8%), reluctance to prosecute (6%), arrived in court or at arraignment instead (2%), or because they were unable to find the location (1%) (Table B.23). The individual samples showed no significant differences from this pattern.

Those victims who did arrive in the complaint room, on the other hand, were asked what they did there. Almost one-half indicated that they merely stayed with the investigating police officer (48%), while 22% said they talked to the prosecutor, 10% indicated they signed an affadavit, 8% claimed they did nothing, and still others said that they went to arraignment (which sometimes occurs after the case leaves the complaint room) or did miscellaneous other things (6%) (Table B.24). None of the individual samples differed significantly from these figures.

Victims appearing in the complaint room voiced comments that indicated their own sense of uselessness: "It was just one big waste of time," and "I was intimidated by all the people there, and did not know what was going on," and "Nobody asked me what I wanted, they just filled out papers." It seems clear that for those appearing in the complaint room, frustration results for anyone expecting to assume a role beyond merely making a complaint[34]. What is worse is that even achieving that limited objective involves long, uncomfortable, and distasteful waits, for little apparent purpose.

Arraignment

After the case leaves the complaint room, it may proceed to the arraignment court, in anywhere from a couple of hours to a couple of days. Arraignment is the next major stage in the adjudicative process where a victim might appear. It is conducted in large, high-ceilinged rooms similar to small auditoriums. The building's age can be seen in the time-stained wood panelling, and in the years of grafitti carved into the backs of the courtroom benches.

The atmosphere is very informal. Victims, defendants, and their families and friends, as well as policemen and other spectators, stand or sit leisurely, some mill about, and except for occasional commands for silence from the bailiff, conversations are frequent. This commotion, coupled with the room's terrible accoustics, makes it nearly impossible for the uninitiated to follow the proceedings, even if they could understand all the legal jargon.

Although some victims in this study were in court before, sometimes as past victims, this setting and the activities that follow may come as a great surprise to most victims. Visions of the stately judicial process, with formality and decorum clearly are shattered. The criminal trial is exposed as considerably less than the expected, adversarial contest between competing lawyers, presided over by an imposing judge, and decided by a jury of the defendant's peers.

Instead, victims discover that in many cases, the vast majority of the court's business is disposed of in proceedings that rarely resemble any kind of combat. Essentially, the defense attorney and prosecutor are bargaining over the outcome of the case—oftentimes having made an agreement outside court—and with the judge intervening only sporadically, and rarely to complicate the negotiations. The emphasis is clearly on efficiency, and that goal is promoted by a process that must scarcely resemble justice in the victim's (or the defendant's) eyes. It is not that the victim is so concerned about justice for his assailant, but he will be surprised nevertheless to see the system as it really operates. It may become "injustice" to the victim as well, if it produces an outcome he considers unfair, or if he is given little or no role in the process itself.

What the victim sees of the criminal process in operation unfolds at the front of the courtroom. There stand a police officer, assorted lesser personnel, the judge, defense attorney, and prosecutor, with the latter two frequently breaking away to lean over the bench for private conversations with the judge, out of earshot of the rest of the court. Prior to each case, the defendant, unless in the rare instance where he is represented by private counsel, meets briefly with his court-appointed lawyer. Cases are announced loudly like items called at an auction, and just as fast, and each defendant is paraded out in front of the judge.

The charges that initially will be pursued against the defendant will have been decided already. The "tracking" system will have identified those relatively few cases in which the defendant is considered a clear threat to society. Such cases rarely will be bargained with the defendant and his lawyer, at least not at this stage, like most of the less serious cases. The defendant may plead guilty at this stage and then a date is set for sentencing. Alternatively, a plea of innocence may be entered, and the case will be adjourned to a subsequent hearing, usually in another courtroom with an appearance and atmosphere similar to the arraignment court.

Arraignment is the victim's second potential opportunity to become involved in his court case. But, in fact, less than one-half of the respondents questioned were present at arraigment (49%), while 48% did not show, and 3% did not even know if they had been (Table B.25)! The individual samples were consistent with these figures.

One of the possible reasons for not arriving at arraignment is caused by allowing a victim to sign an affadavit in lieu of appearance. This reason was not mentioned, however, among the (unsolicited) comments made by respondents as to why they did not appear. The statements did emphasize practical excuses as well as signs of continuing frustration: "I have to work and couldn't make it that day," and "I was still in the hospital from the stabbing," and "Work is so scarce, I couldn't risk it," and "What good would it have done me?"

When a victim does arrive at arraignment, he may believe that he is needed in his case, and that perhaps he can contribute something meaningful to it. Unfortunately, this expectation is rarely realized. Victims often are only "used" in the pejorative sense, to aid one official or another in some administrative or personal concern.

Disposing of as many cases as possible in a short time is an all-encompassing requirement in and out of the courtroom. Thus, it is not surprising that, in this study, over one-quarter of the cases were disposed at the arraignment stage (28%). Almost two-thirds of the cases were not settled here (64%), while 8% of the respondents did not even know if their case was settled at this point (Table B.26)! The individual samples were consistent with these averages, as well.

Ironically, one of the few tangible means of victim participation during the arraignment stage seems not to be giving testimony or being consulted, but rather to drop charges against the offender. The respondents in this study were not asked when they had dropped charges (if, in fact, they had at all), but general observations in the Brooklyn and Newark courts indicate that doing so was one of the victim's few roles at this stage.

Except for his role in dropping charges, the victim has a meagre part to play at arraignment, if he shows up. Other influences (such as the defendant's prior record, the "tracking" decision, and any trace of a victim-offender relationship) seem to have a much greater impact on what happens during arraignment and on what dispositions result from this stage.

The victim whose case is disposed at arraignment seems to benefit from that outcome to an extent by being spared lengthy involvement in the process, and by being able to help dismiss a case when he so desires. It is ironic, however, that doing so helps mostly the defendant or the courtroom officials, and not himself. And, such a role is also little consolation for the victim who wants to actively pursue his case. In sum, the victim's desires are rarely followed and rarely solicited.

Bail. The arraignment stage is important, however, not only for the formal beginning (and sometimes quick ending) it gives a case in the court process. This stage is also where a decision is made whether or not to release the defendant on bail. From both the defendant's and the victim's perspectives, the bail decision may very well be the most important aspect of arraignment. Certainly, the defendant is concerned about bail if for no other reason than it means his freedom. He may use his release to help prepare his defense, or perhaps to persuade or bribe the victim to drop charges. The defendant also might use this released time to threaten the victim with retaliation. Since previously we have noted that, in fact, almost one in five respondents was intimidated by the defendant, the bail decision is very important to victims as well.

At least 54% of the assailants in this study received their release on bail, including 36% who received it outright, while another 18% received bail after spending at least some time in jail. Only one in five assailants was known by his victim as not having received his release (20%), while another 26% of the respondents did not know if their offenders had made bail (Table B.27). The latter is only one of the many signs of how most victims are kept guessing about their cases. The separate samples again were consistent with these figures.

Respondents whose assailants were released on bail (N=186, 54%) also were asked how they felt about that outcome. An overwhelming number (88%) were opposed to granting bail, while only 7% approved, and 5% did not care (Table B.28). None of the individual samples deviated significantly from these figures. But, some of the comments opposing bail indicated some confusion about what such an outcome meant. Many seemed to think that pre-trial detention was part of the defendant's punishment for committing the crime, and that by being released, he was "getting off" from his crime. The fact that using pre-trial detention for punishment is often what occurs, does not deny the fact that it is not supposed to be its purpose.

Nevertheless, typical negative reactions to bail release included: "She could have killed me; she should go to jail," and "He should be taught a lesson." Among those who appeared to better understand the role of pre-trial detention often advocated it for practical reasons such as: "He would try to get revenge." On the other hand, some were in favor of bail, sometimes out of sympathy: "She has a baby she has to take care of."

To gauge better the importance of bail release to the victim, respondents were asked whether granting bail affected their arrival in court to pursue their cases further. The overwhelming majority (81%) indicated that it had no effect on their appearance, while 1% said that they were not sure of its effect, and 18% claimed it did have an effect (Table B.29). No significant differences occurred among the individual samples.

Those indicating that they were (or may have been) affected by the grant of bail (N=39, 11%) were asked how it influenced them. Almost one-half (45%) indicated that it caused them to be fearful, while 28% expressed anger, and apparently a full 25% failed to show up in court because of it (Table B.30). The numbers were too small to test the significance of the differences among the samples on the effects of bail.

Whether the issue is a dismissal, or an adjournment, or setting bail, one thing seems to characterize every event at arraignment: the speed of the process. For victims who arrive in court expecting those ingrained ideals about justice and due process, their first initiation—even if they are the victim—may come as somewhat of a shock. No formal trials, nor an adversary process, nor the expected judicial decorum and formality, are encountered. Business is completed in court at a pace that even the initiated (and some did exist among the respondents in this study) may have to strain to follow.

What role can the victim have in such quick resolutions? In actuality, and even potentially, only an insignificant one. A more prominent role would impede arraignment's use as a quick screening device. In other words, in the context of the "workgroup," the victim seems to have no access to its activities, and certainly is not made a working member, despite the victim's obvious stake in how the case is handled. Thus, even at this stage the victim discovers that he can contribute very little, and that the defendant is not the only one who often fails to get his "day in court."

Post-Arraignment

If the case survives arraignment, it will be adjourned for a preliminary hearing in criminal court to establish probable cause, and then perhaps proceed through subsequent motions hearings, and maybe on to a subsequent trial in either the criminal court (for misdemeanors, including charges reduced to that status from original felony charges) or in a higher court (for felonies). But, cases can be resolved at any point along the way by dismissals or plea negotiation. And, frequently these "points" may be quite numerous since most cases are characterized by many adjournments or postponements[35]—many for which victims may appear only to discover that they have wasted their time by coming.

Court Appearance. To what extent do victims arrive in court after arraignment to pursue their cases? Among the respondents in this study, the vast majority (88%) did arrive at least once, while only 12% did not appear again (Table B.31). Those who did appear in court (N=296) also were asked how many times they showed up. Well over one-third (38%) indicated that they had appeared twice—which also was the average for all respondents—followed by 26% once, 23% three times, 8% four times, 2% five or six times each, and 1% eight times (Table B.32). The separate samples showed no significant differences on these responses.

Respondents also were asked how long they had spent in court when they did appear. They were asked to specify the minimum and maximum amounts of time in court. The minimum time ranged from one to nine hours. After controlling for those who had not appeared in court at all, one discovers that the largest group (18%) appeared at least two hours, followed by a minimum of three hours (17%), one or five hours (16% each), four hours (13%), seven hours (8%), six hours (7%), eight hours (4%) and nine hours (1%)(Table B.33). The average minimum amount of time spent in court was a little over three hours. The individual samples did not differ significantly from these figures.

When asked the maximum amount of time they spent in court, the answers ranged from one to fourteen hours. Again, when eliminating those victims who had not appeared in court at all, one finds that the largest group (16%) remained in court as much as six hours. This was followed by a maximum of seven or eight hours (15%), five hours (14%), nine hours (9%), three hours (5%), two hours (4%), ten or eleven or twelve hours (3% each), one hour (2%), and thirteen or fourteen hours (1% each)(Table B.34). Victims spent an average maximum of five to six hours in court. The individual samples also were consistent with these averages.

Respondents were asked whether they were able to make it to court each time they were asked. Many times, the victim will not show for a hearing, and thus how many times he actually appears should not be taken as necessarily the number of scheduled dates for the case. In fact, in both cities, the victim's failure to appear is sometimes a reason for granting a continuance, despite the fact that in most cases the victim is not even consulted.

In any case, over one-half (54%) indicated that they were able to make it to court each time they were asked. A little over one-quarter indicated that they were not always able to make it, while another 20% claimed that they were never asked to come (Table B.35). The separate samples showed no meaningful deviation from these results.

Court Problems. Why were many victims unable to make it to court each time they were asked? One reason might have been the various inconveniences they had to overcome in order to appear. Such interferences include the difficulties of taking time off from work, transportation to the court, childcare or elderly care, trouble finding the court, no place to wait, and miscellaneous other inconveniences. In fact, however, no more than 30% of the respondents indicated that any one of these factors provided an inconvenience, although victims might have been restrained by more than one problem at a time. The single, leading interference was taking time off from work[36] (see Tables B.36-B.40). The four separate samples showed no significant differences in any of these categories.

Having the services of the victim-service centers in the two cities might have contributed to less inconveniences[37]. But, when such interferences are mentioned, economic considerations and not merely the bother of showing up, seemed to dominate, as indicate in comments such as: "I didn't get paid for the days I had to miss work," and "I lost wages which I needed for food and rent," and "I was afraid that if I missed work, I would be fired," and "I didn't have enough to have the kids taken care of," and "It costs too much to ride to court."

Court Involvement. Once a victim takes the trouble (and pays the expense) of coming to court, it might be reasonable for him to expect that he is needed in his case, or that he can in some way participate. One possible means of involvement would be if the victim were asked to testify[38]. Less than one-third of those questioned, however, were asked to testify (30%) (Table B.41). The individual samples were not significantly different from these results.

Respondents also were asked if the prosecutor had consulted them about their cases while in court. Only 12% indicated they had been questioned (Table B.42). Among those (N=40) who had been consulted, only one-half indicated that their suggestions to the prosecutor had been followed (Table B.43) Victims also were asked to what extent the judge questioned them about the case[39]. Even less (10%) were involved in this way (Table B.44). No significant differences among the separate samples were disovered on these responses.

When one examines collectively whether respondents were consulted either by being asked to testify or by being questioned by either the prosecutor or the judge, one discovers that only one victim in five has been able to participate through as little as one of these methods (Table B.45). And, along with this small quantity of involvement, the quality of participation is questionable, as well. This is illustrated, for example, by the victim who was questioned by the judge and claimed that: "He tried to show me why it was not worth continuing with the case." No significant differences occurred among the separate samples.

One wonders whether this meagre and low-quality participation might contribute to a kind of "negative" involvement available to the victim. That is, victims also can pursue their cases by dropping the charges against the defendant during the case. Almost 15% of the respondents indicated that they had dropped charges (Table 5.8). And, claimants were significantly (.05) less likely to drop charges (perhaps because their cooperation with law-enforcement officials was a prerequisite to qualify for compensation) than non-claimants, but the relationship was weak (V=.13).

Among those who dropped charges (N=49, 15%), just over one-half (51%) indicated that under other circumstances they might have stayed with their cases, while 49% said that nothing could have kept them with their cases (Table B.46). The number of responses was too low to assess the statistical significance of the differences among the separate samples.

TABLE 5.8 DECIDE TO DROP CHARGES

	ALL	Claimants		Non-Claimants	
		BKLN	NEWK	BKLN	NEWK
	%	%	%	%	%
YES	48 (14) 15	12 (14) 14	8 (10) 10	78 (15) 17	12 (15) 15
NO	287 (84) 85	73 (86) 86	71 (90) 90	78 (80) 83	67 (84) 85
OTHER	5 (01)	0	0	5 (05)	0
NA	2 (00)	0	1 (01)	0	1 (01)
	342	85	79	98	80
(S=.05) (V=.13)					

Why do victims drop charges? Some simply believe the case has been pursued far enough: "I wanted to teach him a lesson, but I didn't want him to go to jail." Others were disgusted with the delays: "I went to the court several times, and nothing ever happened except that I lost money." Still others expressed some fear in pursuing the case any further: "He might come after me." Some victims thought it was futile: "He was only going to get off anyway, why knock myself out?" And finally, some simply could not see why they were needed: "They didn't care what happened or how I felt about the crime."

With such pervasive lack of victim involvement in the criminal process, it is not surprising that respondents would be discouraged. It is perhaps more surprising, however, to think that some claim that uncooperative victims are a major reason preventing successful prosecutions. Some cases are dismissed because the victim is absent, and it occurs primarily at the preliminary hearing, but also at the many different adjournments that victims are unable to make. This has less to do with victim cooperation, however, and much more to do with case scheduling, notifications, delays, and costs (for the victim). In fact, one study has indicated that 90% of the victims who were regarded as uncooperative by the prosecutor considered themselves as cooperative[40]. It is ironic that the role that victims are practically invited to assume (non-participation) during most of the criminal-court process is ultimately the one that contributes most to the offender's release. The process essentially does not facilitate the victim's involvement except largely for administrative appearances to keep some cases alive.

In sum, although some differences exist between arraignment and post-arraignment, the stages are largely similar in the victim's lack of involvement in them. Many cases are whisked through arraignment and quickly disposed in order to concentrate on more serious crimes. The pace diminishes in post-arraignment proceedings as the court and prosecution devote more of their resources to each case. And ultimately, the pace is the slowest of all for the most serious cases and for those with the most evidence, which may proceed through post-arraignment stages out of the criminal court to the upper court, where they may languish for additional, long periods awaiting formal trials.

Although at least one researcher[41] compares the victim's role when testifying as akin to the medieval practice of "trial by ordeal," due to the stressful interrogation it often involves, one wonders whether this is the real test for victims. That is, if the victims in this study are typical, then the "ordeal" might best be viewed not as too arduous participation in the criminal process, but too little. How satisfied the victim is with his case's pace, his contacts, the case's disposition, and his treatment and involvement, may determine his satisfaction overall with criminal justice, and perhaps more significantly, his present and future cooperation in the law-enforcement process. Those attitudes, and especially their relationship to the victim's experience before the compensation board, must be examined in subsequent pages.

Other Post-Victimization Contacts

After being victimized, victims also may become involved with other agencies that are less directly a part of the criminal process than the complaint room or courtroom. That is, victims may have used various social-service agencies following the crime to help them recover from its effects.

The overall findings show that most respondents had not used any social services after victimization, but most had at least used the facilities of a victim-service center. And, while this study's samples purposely ensured that about one-half the respondents would have contact with yet another service—victim compensation—actually many more had heard about the programs (primarily through the broadcast media), and yet had not applied. Some of the differences among the samples were statistically significant, including the tendency to use social services and to have heard of victim compensation.

More specifically, respondents were asked whether they used any social-service agencies after their victimization. Only 19% indicated they had (Table 5.9). Brooklyn victims were significantly (.01) more likely to have used such agencies than Newark victims, although the relationship was weak ($V = .15$).

Victims also were asked whether they had ever been aided by either the Victim/Witness Assistance Project (VWAP) in Brooklyn or the Victim Service Center (VSC) in Newark. Over 84% of the respondents indicated that they had been assisted by one of these two agencies, while almost 16% said they had not (Table 5.10). Perhaps due to VWAP's being in the Brooklyn complaint room, as compared to VSC's location outside the Newark court, victim contact with the former was higher than with the latter. And, differences among the samples were

TABLE 5.9 USE SOCIAL SERVICES AFTER VICTIMIZATION

	ALL	Claimants		Non-Claimants	
		BKLN	NEWK	BKLN	NEWK
	%	%	%	%	%
YES	65 (19)	19 (22)	12 (15)	24 (25)	10 (13)
NO	277 (81)	66 (78)	67 (85)	74 (75)	70 (87)
	342	85	79	98	80
(S=.01) (V=.15)					

statistically significant (.002), with Brooklyn non-claimants having considerably more contact, although the relationship was somewhat weak (V=.21).

Finally, victim compensation itself might be considered a kind of social service available to the victim after the crime. Obviously, only the victims in the claimant samples used this service. But, almost three quarters of all respondents had heard of victim compensation (72%), while only 28% had not (Table B.47). This average is misleading since it includes claimants, all of whom obviously heard of compensation. But, even when that is taken into consideration, almost one-half (46%) of the non-claimants also had heard of the compensation programs.

How did those who knew about victim compensation hear about it? Almost one in five (19%) heard about it from either radio or television, while 16% were informed by newspaper stories, 10% claimed to have been told by either VWAP or VSC, 4% heard from friends, and 2% were told by the prosecutor (Table B.48). The individual samples did not differ significantly from these averages.

TABLE 5.10 HELPED BY VICTIM SERVICES

	ALL	Claimants		Non-Claimants	
		BKLN	NEWK	BKLN	NEWK
	%	%	%	%	%
YES	286 (84)	63 (74)	64 (81)	93 (95)	66 (83)
NO	56 (16)	22 (26)	15 (19)	5 (5)	14 (18)
	342	85	79	98	80
(S=.002) (V=.21)					

Among those who did not avail themselves of victim compensation (N=174, 51%), most respondents (52%) claimed that they never had heard of the service, followed by either feeling that they were ineligible or thinking a claim would be futile (11% each), being unsure how to make a claim (9%), finding the forms too difficult (4%), either losing the forms or feeling the claim was a bother or wanting to avoid an investigation or objecting to the delay or having received other assistance (2% each), and either believing the claim would be costly or desiring to forget the crime or not feeling a claim was necessary or believing that compensating was an inappropriate government role (1% each) (Table B.49). Obviously, these answers only were provided by non-claimants. No significant differences emerged between the two samples, but it is notable that the vast majority of non-applicants failed to make a claim because the program was unknown to them.

Conclusion

It would be unreasonable to expect that any person's victimization by crime would be a positive experience. Although this chapter has demonstrated the wide range of incidents that occur in violent crime, most of the victimizations are similarly frightening and frustrating. The victim is justifiably angered, usually with the offender and often with law-enforcement officials, but sometimes also with himself.

It is important that the post-victimization experience be one whereby the victim can recover from the crime and help pursue his assailant. Thus, the victims in this study expressed as their primary motivations for invoking the criminal process the desire to protect themselves and their families, to recover their losses, and to pursue the offender. These victims, in other words, did not come to the conclusion that many thousands of other crime victims do: that reporting the crime will be futile for their interests. Unfortunately, based on their criminal-justice experiences, the Brooklyn and Newark victims examined in this research may come to the opposite conclusion if they are victimized ever again.

The foregoing pages clearly indicate that the goals sought by crime victims rarely are realized. The next chapter assesses head-on the outcomes of the criminal process for the victim, but data already analyzed question whether the protection and recovery that victims seek are ever received. The prevalence of continued threats from the assailant, especially when the latter has received bail, and the general disuse of social services that might help the victim recoup his losses, both indicate less than satisfying outcomes for the victim.

But, perhaps more importantly, this chapter has raised serious questions about the victim's ability to effectively participate in his case against the assailant. In addition to the many other frustrations of getting to court and appearing in court, the average victim is on solid ground when he complains about no information and no involvement in his case. Although again we must wait until the next chapter to assess victim attitudes about criminal justice directly, it seems highly unlikely that a victim's frustration with his victimization will be alleviated through his criminal-justice experience, and in fact, it might be intensified.

If differences in victim attitudes toward criminal justice emerge in the next chapter, they apparently will not be due to variations among victims in their criminal-justice experience. Few statistically significant differences separated the four samples of victims in this study. Thus, the victimization and post-victimization experiences can be added to the background characteristics examined in the previous chapter as unlikely explanations for any variance among victims in their feelings about criminal justice, its personnel, and their (the victims') future involvement in the process. Thus, the purposely contrived (by the research design) differences among victim in their contact with victim compensation, and perhaps the differences among those who did experience the compensation process, continue to have little competition from the victim's other criminal-justice experiences in producing significant variations in victim attitudes and future cooperation.

It is to these actual and specific attitudes, and to a final, possible determinant (criminal-justice outcomes) of these sentiments that we now must move. For now, much evidence seems to support the claim that after a person is victimized by crime, he is subject to a second victimization, by the criminal-justice process itself. Although some notable efforts have been made on behalf of victims in the criminal process, and Brooklyn and Newark are leaders in this endeavor, much remains to be done to facilitate a more meaningful involvement in the system.

Notes

1. As indicated in chapter three, a research design was adopted that purposely biased the samples to ensure that the crimes were reported (although not necessarily by the victim), the assailants were arrested, and charges were pressed.

2. See John Conklin, *Robbery and the Criminal Justice System* (Philadelphia: J.B. Lippincott, 1972) for prior research on victims and criminals in robberies.

3. See numbered tables, all of which show no statistically significant differences, in Appendix B.

4. See Michael Gottfriedson & Michael Hindelang, "Bodily Injury in Personal Crimes," in Wesley Skogan (ed.), *Sample Surveys of Victims of Crime* (Cambridge: Ballinger, 1976), 73; Mark Blumberg, "Injury to Victims of Personal Crimes: Nature and Extent," in William Parsonage (ed.), *Perspectives on Victimology* (Beverly Hills: Sage, 1979), 133.

5. The measure of statistical significance (S) used is chi square.

6. The measure of strength of relationship used is Cramer's V.

7. Including acquaintance, friend of the family, indirect relationship, saw before, business associate/co-worker, and neighbor.

8. Including spouse, ex-spouse, girl/boy friend, ex-girl/boy friend, sister/brother, mother/father, other relative, and friend.

9. This phenomenon of extensive relationships between offenders and victims in violent

crimes is consistent with national statistics. See, for example, the Uniform Crime Reports.

10. As will be explained in more detail in chapter 6, relationship cases are disqualified from coverage in both states.

11. This is an important kind of victimization since several compensation programs, including New York's, were begun with just such victims in mind. See chapter 7 and James Ratcliffe, *The Good Samaritan and the Law* (Garden City: Doubleday, 1966).

12. For related attempts to understand the victim's decision whether or not to report the crime, see Michael Hindelang & Michael Gottfriedson, "The Victim's Decision Not to Invoke the Criminal Justice Process," in William McDonald (ed.), *Criminal Justice and the Victim* (Beverly Hills: Sage, 1976), 57; A. Emerson Smith & Dal Maness, "The Decision to Call the Police," in McDonald, *Ibid.,* 79; Frank Furstenberg & Charles Welford, "Calling the Police: The Evaluation of Police Service," *Law & Soc. R.,* 8(1972), 24; Wesley Skogan, "Citizen Reporting of Crime: Some National Panel Data," *Criminology,* 13(1976), 535; Richard Block, "Why Notify the Police: The Victim's Decision to Notify the Police of an Assault," Criminology, 11(1974), 555; Richard O. Hawkins, "Who Called the Cops? Decisions to Report Criminal Victimization," *Law & Soc. R.,* 7(1973), 22.

13. Since the research design for this study purposely selected only cases that were reported to the police, the primary distinction on reporting to be made here is who reported the crime and *why.*

14. Likewise, the research design was biased heavily toward including cases that were pursued (including the pressing of charges) by the victim against an offender, and thus the primary emphasis here will be to check the extent to which the design produced the desired effect, and on *why* charges were pressed.

15. But, consider the following: "A basic conflict in priorities emerges. The victim's immediate interest in preventing increased injury or the recovery of losses is not entirely congruent with police priorities of excluding intervention in incidents not considered to be crimes, and of apprehending the accused. There is no doubt which set of priorities prevails, as it is the police, not the victim, who determine whether intervention will take place and what tasks are to receive immediate attention." Eduard Ziegenhagen, *Victim, Crime and Social Control* (New York: Praeger, 1977), 75.

16. See note 14.

17. Including protecting self/family, ending a recurring situation, property loss, and the victim's injury.

18. Including protecting society/citizen's duty.

19. Including punishing the offender, and the offender was wrong.

20. This is an interesting rationale since several victim compensation programs (including New York's and New Jersey's) were created based in part on the inadequacy of pre-existing methods (including civil suits) of recovering losses due to victimization.

21. Including protecting oneself/family, and restitution/property return.

22. Including protecting society/citizen's duty, and social justice.

23. Including punish offender, and treat offender

24. Consider that: "Although little is known about the operating norms that define the victim's role, there is some reason to believe that once the crime is identified, the personal characteristics of the victim and the accused and *prior relationships* with the police, particularly as a suspect, are likely to be significant." (emphasis mine.) Ziegenhagen, note 15 *supra,* 75; and see A.J. Reiss, "Discretionary Justice in the United States," *Intl. J. Crim. & Penology,* 2(1974), 181.

25. Compare this finding to: Leonard Buder, "Half of 1976 Murder Victims Had Police Records," *N.Y. Times,* 28 August 1977, 33.

26. See Leon Sheleff, "The Criminal Trial: Bystander, Victim and Criminal," in Israel Drapkin & Emilio Viano (eds.), *Victimology: Theoretical Issues in Victimology* (Lexington: D.C. Heath, 1976), 111; Girolaino Tartaglione, "The Victim in Judicial Proceedings," in Israel Drapkin & Emilio Viano (eds.), *Victimology: Crimes, Victims and Justice* (Lexington: D.C. Heath, 1976), 5.

27. What follows will be a "composite" of the Brooklyn and Newark criminal processes, which are quite similar to each other, and thus each system does not warrant separate description.

28. Abraham Blumberg, *Criminal Justice* (Chicago: Quadrangle, 1967); Malcom Feeley, "Two Models of the Criminal Justice System: An Organizational Perspective," *Law & Soc. R.*, 7(1973), 407.

29. Consider: "In the event that the accused is apprehended and the victim has an interest in proceedings against the accused, the victim is confronted with new sets of priorities (as compared to those of the police) shared by various other criminal justice practicioners, and the victim is even further removed from the decision-making process," Ziegenhagen, note 15 *supra*, 75.

30. See James Eisenstein & Herbert Jacob, *Felony Justice* (Boston: Little, Brown, 1977); Blumberg, note 28 *supra*.

31. But see Robert C. Davis & Forrest Dill, "Comparative Study of Victim Participation in Criminal Court Decision-Making," unpublished paper, Vera Institute of Justice, 1978, for impressions on victims in workgroups in Brooklyn

32. Eisenstein & Jacob, note 30 *supra*.

33. See a further discussion of victim-service centers later in this chapter.

34. But see Richard P. Lynch, "Improving the Treatment of Victims: Some Guides for Action," in McDonald, note 12 *supra*, 165.

35. As many as 16 adjournments for cases in Brooklyn is not unknown.

36. This result, however, must be qualified when one considers that many respondents had no job to miss in the first place.

37. See note 33.

38. See William McDonald, "Notes on the Victim's Role in the Prosecution and Disposition Stages of the American Criminal Justice Process," unpublished paper presented at the 2nd International Symposium on Victimology, Boston, 1976; Laura Banfield & C. David Anderson, "Continuances in the Cook County Criminal Courts," *U. Chi. L.R.*, 35(1968), 259; D.J. Hall, "The Role of the Victim in the Prosecution and Disposition Stages of a Criminal Case," *Vanderbilt L.R.*, 28(1975), 931.

39. Deborah Denno & James Cramer, "The Effect of Victim Characteristics on Judicial Decisionmaking," in McDonald, note 12 *supra*, 215.

40. Frank Cannavale, *Witness Cooperation* (Lexington: D.C. Heath, 1975), 39.

41. Doreen J. McBarnet, "Victim in the Witness Box—Confronting the Stereotype," unpublished paper presented to 2nd International Symposium on Victimology, Boston, 1976.

CHAPTER SIX
Impact of the Criminal Process

If a crime victim decides to pursue his case in the criminal process, he likely will have expectations about the results of his efforts. In other words, a victim rarely will undertake formal court participation without particular reasons for doing so. The last chapter has made it clear that the victims in this study are no exception to this tendency since they specified particular motivations for getting involved. Most of these reasons focused on their own needs, but many others also showed concerns about the offender and about the society in general. For the most part, victims sought specific outcomes from their participation, and thus, it is important to analyze the results of their involvement to see if those outcomes actually matched their expectations.

These outcomes will begin to tell us more about the impact of victims' participation in the criminal process, but perhaps the repercussions of the experience are even better gauged by measuring victim attitudes about various aspects of the system and its results in their cases. In other words, how does the victim feel about his court involvement, how well does he believe he and the offender were treated, and to what extent is he satisfied with his case's procedures and results—in relation to his own needs, as well as to those he believes are appropriate for the offender and the society, in general?

To understand the impact of the criminal process, beyond the particular victimization and post-victimization experiences thusfar described, it is necessary to examine the specific outcomes of the process for victims, and their attitudes associated with pursuing their cases.

Outcomes of the Criminal Process

Many crime victims do not pursue their cases in the criminal process (or otherwise) after they are victimized. But, others—including all the respondents questioned in this study—do attempt to take their cases to court. The particular reasons for doing so are varied, but many have to do with a desire to bring the offender to justice, as well as with pursuing one's economic and physical well-being.

To assess the extent to which these important, motivating goals were realized, respondents were asked (see questionnaire in Appendix E) about the offender's punishment (which also was verified by records), about their (the victims') lingering problems from the crime, and specifically about their ability to recover financial losses through payments and through returned property. The latter, financial inquiries concentrated on all the possible, alternative (to victim compensation, which will be examined in chapter nine) means of reimbursement or recovery available in the criminal process or from related agencies.

The following pages will show that the benefits of participating for crime victims hardly seem overwhelming. About one-third of all defendants were freed without punishment, and another one-half plead guilty—perhaps to charges less than the crime the victim believed was committed against him[1]. Also, while victims experienced many different kinds of problems from the crime, this should not dilute their frequency and intensity—including economic and physical losses.

Furthermore, only a very small proportion of victims whose property was stolen had it recovered, and even then, they were not necessarily able to get it back from authorities. Although witness fees are authorized in both cities to help defray the complainant's expenses, they are practically never paid, and thus the victim must bear these costs of involvement from his own resources. And, this occurs despite the fact that most respondents indicated their likely greater willingness to cooperate if such fees actually were paid.

And finally, other kinds of payments or recovery were just as elusive. Most respondents were not reimbursed at all for their losses, largely—in their minds— because of meagre assistance, and especially due to inadequate or non-existent concern for the crime victim. Among those who were paid, various kinds of welfare payments dominated, with some evidence of pay-offs by defendants or their counsel, but practically no effective aid forthcoming from private sources (such as insurance) or from the criminal process (such as through court-ordered offender restitution to the victim).

In sum, the actual outcomes for crime victims who get involved in the criminal process may be no better than for those who decide to ignore their victimization, and certainly the results cannot be described as favorable for most victims. These effects also seem to have been felt uniformly across the separate samples included in this study since virtually no significant differences in outcomes were discovered. These findings further indicate the apparent lack of meaningful differences among the separate groups of victims, at least insofar as their background, victimization, and post-victimization experiences are concerned.

Case Outcomes

More specifically, almost one-half (47%) of the cases brought by the respondents in this study ended through a guilty plea, while 31% were dismissed, 15% resulted in conviction, 4% were resolved in miscellaneous other ways (including mediation), 2% were acquitted, and 1% were concluded by having the respondent drop charges (Table C.1)[2]. Since at least one-third of the cases did not result in punishing[3] the alleged offender, many victims may have been dissatisfied with their case's resolution on this ground alone[4]. No significant differences in case outcome occurred among the separate samples.

The number of lingering problems resulting from victimization is another important outcome for the victim. Emotional difficulties(16%) constituted the largest number of problems specified, followed by physical injury or financial (other than lost income) losses (14% each), medical problems or other disruptions or lost income or no problems (11% each), lost property (6%), and damaged property (3%) (Table C.2). The problems were well-balanced, with personal or physical difficulties competing equally with financial problems. The individual samples were consistent with these averages.

Financial Recovery

It was possible to more specifically examine some of these problems. First, respondents were asked whether they had recovered their lost property. After accounting for the 60% who did not suffer property loss in the first place, only 20% had recovered their property (Table 6.1). The differences overall among the individual samples were statistically significant[5] (.002), and the relationship was moderately strong (V=.33)[6]. In particular, the difference between non-claimants in Brooklyn and Newark was pronounced, with 38% of the former recovering their property as compared to none of the latter.

When asked where their property was now, almost one-half (45%) claimed that after recovery, it was returned (at least eventually) to them, but 35% indicated that the property still was being held by the police, 17% cited the court, and 3% mentioned others (Table C.3). Again, the minor differences among the individual samples were not statistically significant.

Besides the question of recovering property, many victims also were concerned with other kinds of payments for their losses, or at least for participating in the case against the offender. Consequently, respondents were asked about the various kinds of payments (initially all but victim compensation) they may have received during the course of pursuing their case.

For example, victims were asked whether they had been paid by the prosecutor. Only 2% indicated they had been, despite the fact that such payments, commonly designated as witness fees, are authorized to be paid by district attorneys in both cities (Table C.4)[7]. This failure to receive such fees was consistent among the individual samples.

In addition to whether respondents were able to recover their lost property and receive witness fees for their court involvement, one must consider the extent to which victims were able to recover specific monetary losses (including possible reimbursements from victim compensation) from the crime in order to fully un-

TABLE 6.1 RECOVER STOLEN PROERTY

	ALL	Claimants		Non-Claimants	
		BKLN	NEWK	BKLN	NEWK
	%	%	%	%	%
YES	23 (08) 20	8 (09) 23	7 (09) 21	11 (11) 38	0
NO	106 (31) 80	27 (32) 77	27 (34) 79	18 (18) 62	34 (43) 100
NA	205 (60)	49 (58)	44 (56)	67 (68)	45 (56)
DK	5 (02)	1 (01)	1 (01)	2 (02)	1 (01)
	342	85	79	98	80

(S=.002) (V=.33)

derstand the economic impact of these cases. Thus, respondents were asked simply whether they were able to recover their financial losses. Almost two-thirds (66%) said they had not been able to, while 21% indicated that they were partially reimbursed, and 13% claimed that they were fully paid (Table C.5). Thus, a total of a little over one-third (34%) of the victims were at least partially repaid. No significant differences emerged among the separate samples.

Since almost two-thirds of the respondents claimed to have not been paid, only the remaining victims (N=117) were asked who paid them. Victim compensation was mentioned as a source by 7% of those reimbursed, but all of these victims were obviously from the two claimant samples. Among those recovering by other means (N=93), the largest category of responses indicated payment by medicaid (34%), followed by unemployment welfare (12%), medicare (12%), health insurance (9%), workman's compensation (8%), social-security insurance (6%), other social security or restitution (5% each), property insurance (4%), the defendant or his counsel (2%), and automobile insurance (1%) (Table C.6). The differences among the separate samples were not statistically significant.

Among those victims who could have indicated victim compensation as the means of payment (Brooklyn and Newark claimants), no significant differences emerged in their tendency to mention such an award. It is important to note, however, that the average (12) number of respondents in these two samples specifying victim compensation as their source of payment (see Table C.6) is only about one-third the number (32) of victims in each group that actually were reimbursed from this source! Since only one answer to this question was requested from respondents, this apparently infrequent mentioning of compensation cannot automatically be taken as a sign that they forgot about the award they received. It could merely mean that they specified another source of repayment first. Even so, not having compensation (if one, in fact, received it) as foremost in a victim's mind must be a disappointment to those who believe that an award will have a dramatic effect. Obviously, it has no such effect among what appears to be around two-thirds of the recipients.

Whereas the previous inquiry was designed to elicit the first or primary source of reimbursement coming to the victim's mind, subsequent questions probed particular kinds of possible payments to discover whether those sources of recovery were used at all. For example, respondents were asked whether they had been paid by private insurance. Only a little more than one-quarter (26%) of those responding said yes, while 71% indicated that insurance payments had not been received (Table C.7). This result clearly seems to support those advocating victim compensation based on private insurance's being an inadequate alternative. No significant differences emerged among the separate samples.

Respondents also were specifically asked whether the judge had ordered restitution from the offender to the victim. Only 7% indicated that restitution had been ordered, however (Table C.8). Among those few (N=8) whose offender was ordered to pay restitution, only one-half of the victims had received any payments (Table C.9). And, among the four, actual recipients of restitution, one indicated that the payment was somewhat satisfactory, two said it was unsatisfactory, and one did not answer at all (Table C.10). Obviously, restitution, like private insurance, was not a viable alternative to victim compensation for the victims in this study, and thus would seem to further verify the claims of those who believe that state compensation is the only solution. No significant differences among the separate samples occurred in their restitution experience.

Victims also were specifically asked whether they were paid directly by the defendant or his counsel. In other words, were respondents recipients of what is sometimes called "blood money," which often not only reimburses the victim for his losses, but also buys his silence or refusal to pursue the case against the offender in the courts? The answer for Brooklyn and Newark victims seems to be largely no, but 14% of the respondents did admit to this kind of payment, although not necessarily in cash. Among those recipients, over one-half (57%) were paid by the defendant alone, while 30% were paid by the defense attorney alone, and 13% were paid by both (Table C.11). The individual samples did not differ significantly from these averages, but this should not reduce the findings' importance. Even though the level was comparatively low, this informal approach to resolving a criminal case constitutes a notable alternative to the normal channels, and a route that is perhaps much more beneficial in the long run for the victim.

Finally, those respondents who were unable to recover any of their losses (N=224) were asked why not. Almost one-third indicated in one way or another that the reason was because the crime victim was ignored by the criminal-justice system and the society. Some indicated, for example, that: "There's just no place to go and nobody cares," and "Nobody cares until it happens to them," and "These people only care about the offender, and I get nothing." Another one-quarter of the respondents indicated that they were unable to recover their losses because they felt that assistance was unavailable. Others (18%) knew about assistance, but claimed they did not qualify. One in ten victims said that they had no insurance, 7% indicated that their property had not been returned, 5% said they had not been restituted by the offender, and 4% said that this was not covered by welfare (Table C.12). Again, the separate samples did not differ significantly from these results.

It would be difficult to imagine the foregoing outcomes being associated with very positive attitudes among victims toward the offender, law-enforcement personnel, and the criminal process, in general. It is to these actual sentiments which we now must move.

Victim Attitudes Toward the Justice Experience

Victims' general attitudes toward crime and criminal justice have been examined already in chapter four. Those viewpoints told broadly about their perspectives, but their more specific attitudes toward their actual, post-victimization experiences in the court system are perhaps even more important[8]. Beyond their general views of crime and criminals, for example, how do they feel about their actual assailant? Or, beyond their general attitudes about how criminal-justice personnel are doing their jobs, how do they feel about the specific officials they encountered in their case?

To assess these more specific attitudes, respondents were asked to voice their sentiments about the crime and the offender, about their relative satisfaction with their treatment and involvement in the criminal process, about their feelings about the case's outcome for themselves and the defendant, about their sentiments about the victimization's overall effects, about their relative satisfaction with certain agencies that might have been used after the crime, about the propriety of government payments to crime victims, and about their projected interest in ever becoming involved in the criminal process again in the future.

Overall, most victims were angry with their assailants, but some also were annoyed with themselves, including a few who even felt guilty in having pursued the case. Likewise, many victims feared the offender's revenge, but some also sought vengeance of their own. Overall, the victims' sentiments toward the offender were naturally negative, but certainly not overwhelmingly so.

Although most victims were strongly interested in knowing their case's outcome, few were satisfied with the results. Victims also were considerably dissatisfied with the criminal-justice officials who they encountered in pursuing their cases. Both prosecutors and judges were criticized for treating defendants too easily. Many respondents also felt that the judge had not treated them (the victims) fairly. Crime victims' overall view of law-enforcement officials was not much better, with only police officers getting any decent amount of support, followed by prosecutors, and then judges.

More than one-half the respondents indicated that their involvement was greater than expected, and yet also consistently complained about its poor quality. Consequently, less than one-half felt it was worthwhile coming to court. It is not surprising, given these sentiments and experiences, that almost one-half the respondents shunned any possible criminal-justice involvement again in the future. Some did, however, claim that they would embrace an alternative such as mediation. Possibly those who received "blood money" might find that a viable route in the future, as well.

Most of the victims were at least somewhat satisfied with the victim-service agencies in each city, but the aid offered them was (in their eyes), nevertheless, minimal. A few victims were able to avail themselves of alternative social services after their victimization, but those that did were largely dissatisfied with the results.

The strongest effects of the victimization experience seemed to be some kind of lingering emotional or physical harm, and also (significantly) negative feelings toward the court system and its personnel. The suggestion about how to improve things for future crime victims were dominated by a desire for better law enforcement and for more concern for the victim in court. For a number of attitudes expressed by victims toward the criminal-justice process and its personnel, statistically significant differences emerged. Considerable variation existed in feelings about the criminal case's outcome, the prosecutors' and judge's treatment of the defendant, the judge's fairness, and the prosecutor, judge, and police generally. What were generally negative feelings were even more negative among some samples—most frequently among Brooklyn claimants.

Attitudes Towards Offenders. More specifically, one can begin to review these attitudes in some detail beginning with the victim's view of the offender. This inquiry was the first of a series of questions designed to elicit a victim's feelings, since his case had been concluded, about pursuing charges against the assailant, about the criminal himself, and about the crime situation generally. Respondents were asked, for example, whether they were angry with the defendant. The largest category (37%) of responses indicated that no anger was felt for the offender, perhaps reflecting the passage of time since the victimization[9]. One-third of the respondents, however, indicated that they were very angry with the defendant, while 30% said they were somewhat angry (Table C.13). Thus, the latter two categories combined show that almost two-thirds of the victims were still angry at their assailants. No significant differences emerged among the separate samples.

On the other hand, respondents also were asked whether they were angry with themselves as a result of their case. A clear majority (60%) indicated that they were not, while 27% expressed some self-belittling, and only 13% were very angry with themselves (Table C.14). Again, the individual samples displayed no significant differences among themselves.

Another inquiry sought to gauge whether victims feared the offender's revenge for having pursued the case. Almost two-thirds (63%) of the respondents expressed no such fears, but one-quarter very much feared revenge, while 12% were somewhat fearful about such an outcome (Table C.15). On the other hand, victims also were asked whether they wanted revenge against the offender. Three-quarters of the respondents said no, but 14% wanted revenge very much, and 10% wanted it to some extent (Table C.16). Obviously, about one-quarter of the victims were not at all happy with the offender's (easy) treatment in the criminal process. No significant differences emerged among the separate samples in their responses to these questions.

Respondents also were asked whether they felt guilty having brought the case against the offender. The vast majority (83%) expressed no guilt whatsoever, but 10% felt somewhat guilty, and 7% even felt very guilty (Table C.17). And finally, respondents were asked whether they felt less safe on the streets since their victimization. Almost two-thirds (65%) indicated no such fears, but almost one-quarter (23%) were very fearful, and another 12% expressed some worry (Table C.18). The individual samples again showed no significant differences on these questions.

When viewed collectively, the foregoing attitudes can begin to provide an overall picture of the victim's feelings about the offender. That is, the victim's degree of anger at either the offender or himself, his fear or desire for revenge, and his relative fear of the streets collectively may reflect a certain attitude toward the assailant. When so combined[10], virtually no positive sentiment toward the assailant emerges among the respondents questioned. But, only 10% of the victims felt strongly negative, while the vast majority (90%) had become ambivalent about the offender (Table C.19). No significant differences among the separate samples were discovered.

Attitudes Toward Case Outcomes. A victim's interest in his case is another important attitude for assessing his view of his criminal-justice experience. As indicated in the previous chapter, most victims knew their case's outcome. But, about one in ten respondents did not know their case's outcome until told in the interview (Table C.20). To what extent were these victims interested in what had happened in their cases? Apparently, much interest existed since over three-quarters (76%) expressed a desire to know, while only 24% either did not care, or were uncertain (Table C.21). The responses were too few to draw any conclusions from the differences among the separate samples. But, overall, these findings are at least some indication that victims are interested in their case's outcomes.

How satisfied were victims with the actual outcome of their cases against the alleged offenders? A majority (51%) of the victims were firmly dissatisfied, while 26% were only somewhat satisfied, 14% were very satisfied, and 9% did not care (Table 6.2). The differences among the individual samples were statistically significant (.02), but only produced a moderate (V=.27) relationship.

TABLE 6.2 SATISFIED WITH CASE CUTCOME

		Claimants		Non-Claimants	
	ALL	BKLN	NEWK	BKLN	NEWK
	%	%	%	%	%
VERY	47 (14) 14	6 (07) 07	9 (11) 12	19 (19) 20	13 (16) 17
SOME	88 (26) 26	14 (17) 17	22 (28) 29	26 (27) 27	26 (33) 34
UNSAT	169 (49) 51	58 (68) 68	40 (51) 52	41 (42) 43	30 (38) 39
NC	29 (09) 09	6 (07) 07	6 (08) 08	10 (10) 10	7 (09) 09
BLANK	5 (02)	1 (01)	1 (01)	1 (01)	2 (03)
DK	3 (01)	0	1 (01)	1 (01)	1 (01)
	342	85	79	98	80

(S=.02) (V=.27)

Brooklyn claimants were particularly dissatisfied (68%) with their case outcomes, while Newark non-claimants were the least dissatisfied (39%).

When those respondents who indicated at least some satisfaction (N=135) with their case outcomes were asked why they felt that way, only some (N=128) answered, but 38% indicated their approval of something having at least been done about the situation (Table C.22), such as those who said: "I'm glad he's out of the house but it doesn't help me support the kids," and "The sentence is unimportant, only that he doesn't bother me and interfere in my life and my family's." Almost one respondent in five (19%) said they were satisfied because they received protection, including those who indicated: "I got an order for protection and he was fine after that." And, 15% of the victims were satisfied with their case's outcome because the defendant was punished, such as those who said: "At least he had to pay for it by being punished," and "Going to jail may give him some kind of responsibility."

Almost one in ten respondents (9%) expressed satisfaction with their case because justice was done, including those who said: "I didn't want to hurt the defendant because she is a young girl who didn't know what to do and I think it was a fair decision," and "I'm glad I didn't have to go to jail myself, but if I hadn't been arrested[11], I would have wished he had gone to jail." Another was strikingly detached in his conception of justice: "If he got locked up fine, if he got off, well good for him."

Some victims (7%) were pleased with their case because the defendant was not punished, including those who indicated: "I didn't want him in jail, only in a rehabilitation center," and "She wasn't the one who took the money, so I am satisfied with the outcome for her." Others who claimed the same source of satisfaction, however, were less convincing: "I am happy for my friend (the defendant) who had a bum rap. I would have wanted the case to go on with the guys who really did it, but my friend wasn't the one who stabbed me."

Still others satisfied with their case's outcome included those (5%) who were thankful for having the dispute resolved, such as one who said: "I'm just glad it's all over and he doesn't bother me anymore." Few (3%) also were satisfied because they would be receiving restitution, such as: "Just as long as I get my money back, it will be okay." And finally, a couple (2%) were satisfied for miscellaneous, yet sometimes wistful, reasons such as: "Even in more serious cases than this, no big thing is made of them. This is no worse. In other words, the poor are not very highly thought of."

Despite this satisfaction, most other victims (63%) were not happy with their case's outcome. Among those dissatisfied or unsure about their case who answered (N=202), nearly one-half (43%) thought the defendant's punishment was insufficient, including those who indicated: "They only gave him eight months when he deserved more because I'm still ailing," and "He almost killed me and got only twenty days." Quite a few (15%) respondents also complained that they were not restituted, such as: "I wanted him to pay all of the hospital bill," and "I lost a lot, especially with the dismissal. They should have given me some money for the days I lost; nobody paid me for that." Others (11%) cited their experience and its outcome as a waste of time, including: "I just wasted a lot of time and money going back and forth," and "It's ridiculous! They call that justice! It's stupid for me to come to court; nobody asked me what I wanted; I lost time and money: the man almost killed me."

Much smaller groups of respondents were discontent with their cases for other reasons. For example, 9% complained about not being protected from the offender: "I'm scared now; he may be out for revenge," and "I wanted to proceed further with this case but the D.A. told me it might then be thrown out. I fear for my children because these guys are out on the street." Some victims (7%) were dissatisfied at not having been kept abreast of their case, such as: "At least they should have let me know something about the case," and "I wasn't even notified about the case to appear," and "I thought the case was completed but I saw him walking around two weeks ago." Still others (5%) were angered that the dispute had not been resolved, including: "Nobody cares about what is going on," and "He just keeps doing it over and over again."

On the other hand, some (4%) respondents actually were unhappy because the defendant was punished at all, or at least too severely, such as those indicating: "I didn't really want it to go this far, and I told the D.A.," and "I think he was punished harder than he deserved; he just needs a lesson." The remaining respondents, however, were generally less generous toward the offender. Among the miscellaneous (4%) dissatisfactions were comments such as: "He told the cops I drew a knife on him. I had to drop charges to avoid a record for myself," and "The reason he got off was because he was white. If I had been the one who

had stolen a revolver and had shot at him, I'd probably be doing fifteen years."
And finally, among the malcontents were those (1%) who regretted the offender's not having been given treatment, such as: "My husband is not getting any help that he needs because of his drinking. They should keep him and help him with his mental and drinking problem."

The differences in dissatisfaction among the separate samples were statistically significant (.02), but the relationship was fairly weak (V=.21) (Table 6.3). The biggest variations involved the level of dissatisfaction with the offender's lack of punishment (with Newark claimants the least discontent and Newark non-claimants the most), and whether victims felt their case was a waste of time (with Brooklyn claimants the most dissatisfied and Brooklyn non-claimants the least). And, Brooklyn claimants also were more likely to complain about not being informed adequately about their case. Victims also were asked their relative satisfaction with one specific outcome, guilty pleas, which were the leading means by which the criminal cases in this study were resolved. Only respondents whose cases ended in this manner were asked the question (N=168), but nearly one-half (49%) indicated their clear disapproval, perhaps reflecting the high number of cases where victims felt pleas were taken to lesser charges than the actual crime committed. Almost three in ten (29%) victims did approve of the guilty pleas, while 13% did not care, and 9% did not seem to understand what it meant (Table C.23). The individual samples were consistent with these averages.

Attitudes Toward Offender Treatment. Other measures of satisfaction with one's case may derive from the victim's view of how offenders (including their own) are treated in court. When asked how they felt prosecutors treat criminals, 60% of the victims believed they were too lenient, while 36% felt they were fair, and 4% even said they were too severe (Table 6.4). The differences among the individual samples were statistically significant (.01), but the relationship was not very strong (V=.23). In particular, claimants were considerably more critical of prosecutors' lenience than non-claimants, in both cities.

Likewise, respondents also were asked how they felt judges treat criminals. Even higher numbers accused judges of lenience, including 62% claiming treatment was too easy, while only one-third said treatment was fair, and 5% indicated it was too hard (Table 6.5). Once again, significant (.01) differences occurred among the separate samples, but the relationship was not very strong (V=.23). As with prosecutors, claimants were considerably more critical of judges' lenience toward assailants than were non-claimants, in both cities.

To assess respondents' overall view of how offenders fare in court, victims' foregoing views about prosecutorial and judicial treatment were combined to produce an average rating[12]. The results are similar to when the questions were asked separately. That is, in combination, over one-half (53%) of the respondents believed that prosecutorial and judicial treatment of offenders was too lenient, while 45% rated it as fair, and only 7% called it harsh (Table 6.6). The same

TABLE 6.3 WHY DISSATISFIED WITH CASE OUTCOME

	ALL	Claimants		Non-Claimants	
		BKLN	NEWK	BKLN	NEWK
NA/BL	140 (41)	20 (24)	30 (38)	50 (51)	40 (50)
	%	%	%	%	%
UNPUN	87 (25) 43	27 (32) 41	20 (25) 31	22 (22) 42	18 (23) 45
TREAT	2 (01) 01	0	0	1 (01) 02	1 (01) 02
TOO PUN	8 (02) 04	0	4 (05) 06	3 (03) 06	1 (01) 02
UNRES	11 (03) 05	4 (05) 06	0	3 (03) 06	4 (05) 08
UNPROT	18 (05) 09	5 (06) 08	5 (06) 08	4 (04) 08	4 (05) 08
UNREST	30 (09) 15	9 (11) 14	8 (10) 12	7 (07) 15	6 (08) 13
NO INF	15 (04) 07	7 (08) 11	4 (05) 06	2 (02) 04	2 (03) 04
WASTE	22 (06) 11	10 (12) 15	7 (09) 11	1 (01) 02	4 (05) 08
OTHER	9 (03) 04	3 (04) 05	1 (01) 02	5 (05) 10	0
	342	85	79	98	80

(S=.02) (V=.21)

pattern of differences between claimants and non-claimants arose again, with the former significantly (.01) more likely (V=.24) to chastize both prosecutors and judges for their easy handling of the defendant.

Attitudes Toward Officials. Another measure of case handling was the question of how the judge treated the victims themselves in the case. Among those responding (N=304), less than one-half (45%) felt that the judge had treated them fairly, while 39% felt he had not, and 15% had no opinion (Table 6.7). The

TABLE 6.4 PROSECUTOR TREATMENT OF CRIMINALS

	ALL	Claimants		Non-Claimants	
		BKLN	NEWK	BKLN	NEWK
	%	%	%	%	%
EASY	205 (60)	56 (66)	54 (68)	50 (51)	45 (56)
FAIR	124 (36)	29 (34)	25 (32)	40 (41)	30 (38)
HARD	13 (04)	0	0	8 (08)	5 (06)
	342	85	79	98	80

(S=.01) (V=.23)

TABLE 6.5 JUDICIAL TREATMENT OF CRIMINALS

		Claimants		Non-Claimants	
	ALL	BKLN	NEWK	BKLN	NEWK
	%	%	%	%	%
EASY	212 (62)	60 (71)	53 (67)	57 (58)	42 (53)
FAIR	113 (33)	25 (29)	25 (32)	31 (32)	32 (40)
HARD	17 (05)	0	1 (01)	10 (10)	6 (08)
	342	85	79	98	80

(S=.01) (V=.23)

differences among the separate samples were statistically significant (.05), but the relationship was fairly weak (V=.19). In particular, Brooklyn claimants were considerably less likely to believe that the judge had been fair to them.

Apart from the particular role of the various law-enforcement personnel in each victim's case, respondents also were questioned more broadly about their feelings about these officials. For example, victims were asked their impression of the prosecutor(s) in their case. Despite their frequent, adverse feelings about prosecutors' lenience, one-half the respondents had a favorable view of district attorneys, but almost one-half (43%) were unfavorable, as well, while 7% did not know (Table 6.8). The differences among the samples were again statistically significant (.05), but the relationship was not very strong (V=.20). In particular, claimants (especially those from Brooklyn) were considerably more inclined to give a less positive view of prosecutors than non-claimants.

TABLE 6.6 TREATMENT OF CRIMINALS (RECODED)

		Claimants		Non-Claimants	
	ALL	BKLN	NEWK	BKLN	NEWK
	%	%	%	%	%
EASY	181 (53)	51 (60)	48 (61)	45 (46)	37 (46)
FAIR	154 (45)	34 (40)	31 (39)	47 (48)	42 (53)
HARD	7 (02)	0	0	6 (06)	1 (01)
	342	85	79	98	80

(S=.01) (V=.24)

TABLE 6.7 JUDGE FAIR TO VICTIM

	ALL %	Claimants		Non-Claimants	
		BKLN %	NEWK %	BKLN %	NEWK %
YES	137 (40) 45	26 (31) 35	30 (38) 43	46 (47) 53	35 (44) 49
NO	119 (35) 39	39 (46) 52	23 (29) 33	30 (31) 35	27 (34) 38
OTHER	45 (13) 15	10 (12) 13	14 (18) 20	11 (11) 13	10 (13) 14
NA	38 (11)	10 (12)	9 (11)	11 (11)	8 (10)
	342	85	79	98	80

(S=.05) (V=.19)

Respondents also were asked their impression of the judge(s) in their case. Judges were less supported (only 38% favorable) than prosecutors, while almost one-half (47%) of the respondents rated the judge unfavorably, and 15% did not know (Table 6.9). Some statistically significant (.05) differences emerged from the separate samples, but the relationship was not particularly strong (V=.20). Again, however, it was Brooklyn claimants who were the most dissatisfied.

To complete this view of law-enforcement officials, respondents were asked their impression of the police officer(s) in their case[13]. These officials were much more highly supported, receiving an average of two-thirds favorable ratings, as compared to 27% unfavorable and 6% undecided (Table 6.10). Brooklyn claimants expressed considerably less support for the police, however, than the other samples, and the differences were statistically significant (.05), although the relationship was again fairly weak (V=.20).

TABLE 6.8 HOW FEEL ABOUT PROSECUTOR

	ALL %	Claimants		Non-Claimants	
		BKLN %	NEWK %	BKLN %	NEWK %
FAVOR	170 (49) 50	36 (42) 43	39 (49) 53	55 (56) 57	40 (50) 51
UNFAV	144 (42) 43	44 (52) 53	35 (44) 47	35 (36) 36	30 (38) 37
DK	23 (07) 07	3 (04) 04	0	6 (06) 06	9 (11) 11
NA	5 (02	2 (02)	5 (06)	2 (02)	1 (01)
	342	85	79	98	80

(S=.05) (V=.20)

TABLE 6.9 HOW FEEL ABOUT JUDGE

	ALL	Claimants		Non-Claimants	
		BKLN	NEWK	BKLN	NEWK
	%	%	%	%	%
FAVOR	126(36) 38	24 (28) 29	29(37) 38	41 (42) 45	32 (40) 40
UNFAV	155(45) 47	48 (56) 59	32 (41) 42	40 (41) 44	35 (44) 44
DK	48(14) 15	10 (12) 12	15 (19) 20	10 (10) 11	13 (16) 16
NA	13 (04)	3 (04)	3 (04)	7 (07)	0
	342	85	79	98	80

(S=.05) (V=.20)

When one looks collectively to determine an overall level of support for criminal-justice officials by combining respondents' impressions about prosecutors, judges, and police officers[14], it is not surprising (based on the foregoing discussion) to discover that claimants (average 24% favorable), and especially those from Brooklyn, voice considerably less support than non-claimants (average 35% favorable) (Table 6.11). The differences are statistically significant (.05) but the relationship is not very strong (V=.20). What can be concluded more strongly, however, is that among all victims, the level of support for law-enforcement officials is particularly weak, despite the fact that respondents' comparatively favorable view of police officers did prevent the attitudes from being worse than they could have been.

Attitudes Toward Judicial Process. The relationship between a victim's expectations about his case involvement and his actual participation might be another

TABLE 6.10 HOW FEEL ABOUT POLICE

	ALL	Claimants		Non-Claimants	
		BKLN	NEWK	BKLN	NEWK
	%	%	%	%	%
FAVOR	224(66) 65	48 (56) 56	52 (66) 66	69 (70) 71	55 (69) 69
UNFAV	93 (27) 27	31 (37) 37	20 (25) 25	22 (22) 24	20 (25) 25
DK	20 (06) 06	6 (07) 07	7 (09) 09	2 (02) 02	5 (06) 06
NA	5 (01)	0	0	5 (05)	0
	342	85	79	98	80

(S=.05) (V=.20)

TABLE 6.11 VIEW OF JUSTICE OFFICIALS (RECODED)

	ALL	Claimants		Non-Claimants	
		BKLN	NEWK	BKLN	NEWK
	%	%	%	%	%
FAVOR	96 (28) 29	16 (19) 20	22 (28) 30	33 (34) 38	25 (31) 32
UNFAV	57 (17) 18	19 (22) 24	15 (19) 20	8 (08) 09	15 (19) 19
DK	169 (49) 53	45 (53) 56	39 (49) 51	46 (47) 53	39 (49) 49
	20 (06)	5 (06)	3 (04)	11 (11)	1 (01)
	342	85	79	98	80

(S=.05) (V=.20)

determinant of a victim's relative satisfaction. Respondents were asked whether what they had to do was what they had expected. Over one-half (51%) indicated that their involvement was more than expected, while 28% said it was about as much as expected, and 20% claimed it was less than expected (Table C.24). No significant differences emerged among the separate samples.

These general findings would seem to contradict an earlier discovery (in the previous chapter) that victims felt they were not very involved in their cases. These apparently conflicting findings can be distinguished, however, by considering the quality of participation as opposed to the quantity. In other words, many respondents felt that their cases lasted longer than expected, and thus they were on call for an extended period of time, and may have arrived in court several times. But, what the average victim actually was able to contribute to his case during that period of time apparently was minimal, and disappointing.

Perhaps one of the best indicators of a victim's satisfaction in the criminal process would be whether he felt it was worth coming to court. Only 40% indicated it was worth it, while 43% said it was not, and 17% were not sure (Table 6.12). Among the individual samples, Brooklyn claimants were significantly (.05) less favorable toward their court experience than the other samples, especially Brooklyn non-claimants, although the relationship was fairly weak (V=.20).

To what extent does the victim's court experience affect his willingness to participate again? To begin to answer that question, respondents were asked, simply, whether they would get involved again in the criminal-justice system. Almost one-half (49%) said they would get involved again, while 32% indicated they would not, and 19% were not sure (Table C.25). No significant differences emerged from the separate samples, but the overall finding that so many victims shun future participation is significant itself.

TABLE 6.12 WORTHWHILE CCMING TC COURT

	ALL	Claimants BKLN	NEWK	Non-Claimants BKLN	NEWK
	%	%	%	%	%
YES	119(35) 40	21(25) 29	27(34) 39	43 (44) 4ς	28 (35) 40
NO	129 (38) 43	38 (45) 53	29 (37) 42	32 (33) 36	30 (38) 43
DK	51 (15) 17	13 (15) 18	13 (16) 19	13 (13) 15	12 (15) 17
NA	43 (13)	13 (15)	10 (13)	10 (10)	10 (13)
	342	85	79	98	80

(S=.05) (V=.20)

If respondents are not willing to participate in the formal criminal process (or even if they are), would they be receptive to some alternative means of resolving their case? One possible substitute would be using mediation, whereby the victim and the offender come together with non-court personnel to attempt to resolve their dispute. Since such a practice was already beginning in Brooklyn and being planned in Newark, respondents were asked whether they would consider substituting mediation for participating in the criminal process. The largest group (43%) said they would be willing, but almost as many (41%) said they would not, and 16% were not sure (Table C.26). No significant differences emerged among the separate samples.

Attitudes Toward Victim Services. Thus far, it is clear that respondents are far from satisfied with the criminal process. They were questioned further, however, to assess their feelings about some of the services allied with the court system. For example, as indicated previously (see chapter five), 84% of the respondents claimed to have had contact with either the Victim/Witness Assistance Project in Brooklyn, or the Victim Service Center in Newark—both of which are designed to provide assistance and services to crime victims. To assess respondents' attitudes toward these agencies, they were asked whether they were satisfied with the services rendered. Almost one-half (43%) indicated they were somewhat satisfied, while 38% said they were satisfied, and 18% claimed they were dissatisfied (Table C.27). Although no significant differences emerged among the separate samples, the high amount of ambivalence or dissatisfaction toward these agencies is important when one considers how much more foreboding and frustrating the court experience would be without them, especially since such programs were, at the time, relatively rare. It indicates how very far the court experience must be altered to accommodate the victim.

Another possible source of assistance after victimization might be the various other social-service agencies available in both cities. As previously discussed (see chapter five), however, only 19% of the respondents indicated that they had used various kinds of social agencies after victimization. Those who did use such services (N=65) also were asked about their experience. One-half the respondents were dissatisfied with the results, while only 27% were satisfied, and 23% were somewhat pleased (Table C.28). No significant differences were found among the individual samples.

Attitudes Toward Overall Victimization Experience. To acquire a kind of summary of each respondent's victimization and court experience, respondents were asked to indicate its major impact (Table C.29)[15]. The largest category of responses (20% each) stressed an emotional disruption of the victim's life, or negative feelings toward the system. Among the former responses were comments such as: "I was so shook that I am still shaking. I felt it was the end, and I still feel that way when I'm in a bad neighborhood," and "Everyone who walks into the store is a potential thief; I feel paranoid," and "If I had the money, I would leave New York right now. I don't trust anybody. I lost weight and have trouble with my stomach because of my nerves." And, among those negative toward the system were complaints such as: "I was dissatisfied with the justice system and will handle disagreements myself instead of calling the police and going to court in the future," and "The law doesn't protect the citizen," and "I'm frustrated. I won't deal with the fuckin' system anymore. Next time I'll just kill him and when they take me to court I'm going to tell the judge that I want the same treatment as this guy got!"

Other effects of victimization mentioned included almost as many who were still injured (19%), including: "My head hurts and I can't sleep," and "I'm suffering from pain and trauma." Others (15%) felt embarassed by the incident, such as: "I am very embarassed because of the stigma of having these injuries all my life. I think people will think negatively of me," and "It brought shame on me since the cops have been coming around, and people see things," and "I didn't want anyone to know that I was arrested, too."

The next largest group (13%) indicated no lingering effects, but 8% did cite impaired relationships, including: "I never thought I would have to go to court with a family member," and "It shows that it doesn't pay to trust people and be nice to them." Another 5% indicated financial difficulties, such as: "I have no money and was evicted; I only get a small amount of money from him (the offender) since he's now unemployed, and the kids are hungry, and I have to move in with those dirty Puerto Ricans." And finally, 1% indicated miscellaneous effects of being victimized, of which the least profound was: "The only thing that happened was that I got a haircut." No statistically significant differences emerged among the separate samples.

Respondents also were asked to suggest ways to improve the situation for future crime victims (Table C.30). Almost one in five (19%) indicated the need for better law enforcement, including: "The laws should be changed and judges should be stricter," and "You have to start from the bottom and improve the judicial system," and "Drastic measures must be taken before something more serious occurs. More protection should be offered to all." Other victims (17%) each) either sought greater court concern or better court scheduling. The former group included: "The court should be more concerned about the victim and not treat him as being stupid," and "The victim should be kept informed with the process," and "The victim should be given more dignity instead of making you feel like the criminal." And, the latter group (suggesting better scheduling) included responses such as: "It was a simple case, yet it took all day to resolve," and "Both lawyers should go over their material before the proceedings so that the case is ready on time."

Others (12%) offered miscellaneous suggestions to improve the victim's circumstances, including: "You're so close to them (the offenders) in court, you don't know what they'll do," and "There wouldn't be crime if people had an opportunity to get things they need," and "Be careful who you marry and walk out if he beats you," and "Take care of the situation yourself," and "Victim compensation should be better publicized." Still others (9%) suggested changes in police work, including: "Police should look into cases more thoroughly," and "Police shouldn't beat up suspects."

And finally, it is significant that the largest category of responses as to how to improve a crime victim's situation was no suggestion at all (26%), including comments such as: "I was very satisfied with the courts the way they are," and "Bear with the courts since they have a lot of work." Overall, no significant differences emerged among the individual samples.

Economic Incentives of Crime Victims

Clearly, one of victim compensation's major purposes is to provide monetary payments to crime victims. These payments are not designed merely to help the victim absorb his losses, but rather to also produce a positive effect on victim attitudes and cooperation, and ultimately on law enforcement. Assessing victim compensation's impact on attitudes and cooperation constitutes one of this study's major goals. But, compensation-board payments are not the only possible source of economic recovery available to victims.

In the previous chapter, it was observed that personal motives dominated victims' reasons for pursuing court cases. These concerns included a desire for protection, but also a desire for restitution, or property recovery, or some other form of financial recovery, as well. The present chapter has indicated that one may add witness fees, blood money, and various public and private payments to restitution and property recovery as the major, potential sources of economic assistance.

Although it has been observed that these various alternatives to victim compensation are not, in fact, very reliable sources of recovery, one must assess whether victims believe that some form of economic reward is appropriate, if not a prerequisite for their involvement. And, one must assess whether victims feel those incentives should be provided by government. The results of this inquiry will provide us with a set of attitudes that might indicate to what extent economic incentives, such as those provided by victim compensation, can be relied upon to motivate a victim's participation and cooperation in the criminal-justice process[16].

The subsequent pages will show that victims are, in fact, largely responsive to economic incentives. Witness fees were widely supported as a basis for increased cooperation[17]. And, the prospect of government paying crime victims after the crime also was advocated strongly, and agreement was widespread that it would contribute to increased cooperation, as well. Victims also supported quite liberal eligibility requirements for receiving government assistance, including payments for classes besides the poor, and for property losses. On the other hand, some opposition clearly did emerge to payments in relationship cases, although some significant differences in the other direction also occurred. Overall, victim compensation, as a general assistance program, was very widely accepted among all respondents.

More specifically, among those few (N=6) who did receive witness fees, virtually all of them indicated that the payments were at least somewhat (50%), if not very (50%) important for continuing their court cases (Table C.31). The samples for this inquiry were too small to draw any conclusions from the differences among them.

Furthermore, respondents (including those not actually paid a fee by the prosecutor) were asked whether getting paid would affect their cooperation in the criminal process. An overwhelming number (95%) indicated that it would, while only 5% said it would not (Table C.32). This was consistent among the separate samples as well.

When asked why getting paid would affect their cooperation, all respondents indicated the need for the money, but some more blatantly than others. Forty-one percent, for example, indicated that they plainly needed the money, while 31% said the fee would help defray their expenses, and 29% claimed that receiving the payment would make their participation in the case worthwhile (Table C.33). Once again, the individual samples were consistent with the averages.

And finally, when those few respondents (N=26) who indicated that payments would not affect their cooperation were asked why, a little over one-half (54%) said that a fee would not make pursuing the case worth it. A little over one-third (35%) indicated that payments would not induce them to pursue the case because they believed the defendant was not guilty afterall, while only 12% said that taking payments in exchange for their participation would not be right (Table

C.34). The low number of respondents once again made it impossible to assess the significance of the differences among the samples.

Respondents also were asked whether the government should pay the crime victim after the crime. The overwhelming majority (92%) indicated that such payments were warranted, while only 8% disagreed (Table C.35). Among those supporting government payments to crime victims (N=316), several follow-up inquiries were made. For example, respondents were asked whether government payments would increase their cooperation with law-enforcement officials. Again, a substantial majority (76%) indicated that payments would increase their cooperation, while 24% said they would not (Table C.36). The differences among the separate samples were again insignificant. Respondents also were asked about who should be compensated, and for what kind of losses. The vast majority (96%) indicated that government payments should be made to everyone and not merely to the poor, while 4% disagreed (Table C.37). The individual samples were consistent with these findings.

Most victims (58%) opposed payments being made in the case of any past or present victim-offender relationship, but a sizable number (42%) disagreed (Table 6.13). Significant differences (.001) emerged between claimants and non-claimants, and the relationship (V=.49) was fairly strong. In particular, claimants were considerably more likely to advocate restrictions on relationship cases, as compared to non-claimants.

This divergence, however, might be misleading since it might be due to differences inherent in being either a claimant or non-claimant in the first place. Violent crime victims, in general (and including those in this study), are highly susceptible to cases involving a relationship. But, since applicants for victim compensation are informed that relationship cases are excluded, eventual claimants probably will include mostly victims who do not have such a relationship. Comparatively speaking, therefore, non-claimants should include many more

TABLE 6.13 PAY ONLY NCN-RELATICNSHIP CASES

	ALL	Claimants		Non-Claimants	
		BKLN	NEWK	BKLN	NEWK
	%	%	%	%	%
YES	184(54) 58	63(74) 81	59(75) 79	19(19) 22	45(54) 57
NO	132(39) 42	15(18) 19	16(20) 21	69(70) 78	32(40) 43
BLANK	26(08)	7(08)	4(05)	10(10)	5(06)
	342	85	79	98	80

(S.001) (V=.49)

relationship cases, and thus non-claimants naturally would be more sympathetic to compensating those kinds of cases than would be claimants. This is reflected in Table 6.13.

Victims also were asked about compensating for property loss, and not merely for personal injuries due to the victimization. Almost three-quarters (74%) favored payments for property loss, while 26% were opposed (Table C.38). No significant differences emerged among the separate samples.

Those few (N=28, 8%) who opposed paying crime victims were asked why. The largest category of responses (39%) included those who opposed the welfare state. Almost one-third (32%) preferred private solutions for crime losses, while one-quarter felt that such payments were unnecessary, and 4% claimed that government was too inefficient to perform such a service (Table C.39). Some differences among the individual samples emerged, but the number of respondents (N=28) was too small to assess their significance.

Finally, respondents were asked directly about victim compensation itself. That is, victims were told (some of whom already knew) about the existing programs and then were asked how the programs made them feel. A large majority (81%) favored such programs, while only 10% disapproved, and 9% did not care (Table 6.14). The differences among the separate samples were statistically significant (.01), but the relationship was not very strong (V=.23). In particular, the crucial finding here is that claimants, who obviously have had contact with a compensation board, are considerably less favorable toward victim compensation than non-claimants!

Conclusion

The foregoing pages have examined the various outcomes of the criminal process for the victim, then attempted to assess respondents' specific attitudes toward criminal justice and future involvement in the process, and finally reviewed what clearly appear to be the economic incentives for victims' participation in the court system.

Obviously, most victims were less than happy with the results of their criminal-justice involvement, and with good reason when one considers the specific outcomes. This is especially understandable when one adds to these outcomes victims' unsatisfactory post-victimization experiences in the court system, which were examined in the previous chapter. The displeasure is abundantly reflected in victims' attitudes about the justice system and its officials[18]. And, obviously these negative views will have, at least in the minds of most respondents, a restraining effect on their future willingness to become involved in the criminal process.

It is difficult for us, and for victims themselves, to predict what actual criminal-justice participation they will really undertake in the future. Many who

TABLE 6.14 HOW FEEL AECUT CCMPENSATION PLAN

	ALL	Claimants		Non-Claimants	
		BKLN	NEWK	BKLN	NEWK
	%	%	%	%	%
APPROVE	227 (81)	57 (67)	59 (75)	91 (93)	70 (88)
NO CARE	30 (09)	12 (14)	10 (13)	3 (03)	5 (06)
DISAPP	33 (10)	16 (19)	10 (13)	2 (02)	5 (06)
	342	85	79	98	80

(S=.01) (V=.23)

have claimed that they will stay away might change their minds when the opportunity arises again, perhaps simply based on citizen's duty, or on the momentum of the situation. In fact, with the very high degree of dissatisfaction with the system, one wonders why even more victims did not disavow any future involvement in the system. Perhaps citizen's duty has an impact even on people's attitudes now, since it is hard to imagine what tangible results from participating most victims could hope to achieve, based on their past experience.

This attitude can hardly be the basis for involvement sought by those, including victim compensation's supporters, who seek greater victim participation and cooperation. Although victims do seem quite susceptible to economic incentives for participating in the criminal process, the idea of "buying" victim cooperation might grind on the sensitivities of some observers. Under present circumstances, however, the question is only hypothetical since so few sources of payment actually exist. These include victim compensation, as we shall examine in chapter nine. Perhaps initial victim cooperation or participation can be maintained by holding out the prospect of financial assistance, but when participants (and whoever they tell) discover a largely empty promise, it will not be surprising when their attitudes turn to anger, and they refuse to ever cooperate again.

The present, adverse attitudes of this study's victims toward criminal justice and its officials are especially alarming since much ill-will comes from victims who had applied for compensation. These claimant victims were supposed to have been induced by victim compensation toward more positive attitudes about the system, and toward greater cooperation. What is worse, however, is that not only are claimants poorly disposed toward the court system, but they are often actually significantly *more negative* than non-claimants, and this is especially true among Brooklyn claimants.

Whereas previous chapters have indicated a great similarity between claimants and non-claimants in their backgrounds, in their victimization and post-victimization experiences, and in the outcomes for them from the criminal process, considerable differences between these two groups did emerge in their attitudes toward the criminal-justice system and its personnel. Whether these attitudinal variations can be attributed to their few statistically significant differences in background and experience, or rather to the differences in their exposure and relative success before the compensation boards, must be assessed in the following pages. First, however, it is necessary to take a closer look at the New York and New Jersey compensation boards and their officials, and then at the victims' actual experience in the compensation process itself.

Notes

1. Due to the practice of "overcharging," which exists in many jurisdictions and which is characterized by either police officers or prosecutors filing charges that are higher than the offense for which the suspects should have been arrested, plea bargaining often only negotiates down to the actual crime itself. Thus, victims might not always feel deprived by plea bargaining. See Isaac Balbus, *Dialectics of Legal Repression* (New Brunswick: Transaction, 1973), 21.

2. See numbered tables, all of which show no statistically significant differences, in Appendix C.

3. See Malcolm Feeley, *The Process is the Punishment: Handling Cases in a Lower Court* (New York: Russell Sage, 1979) which, as the title indicates, concludes that psychological, social and economic costs stemming from pre-trial detention, seeking legal counsel, and withstanding repeated continuances are a greater punishment than actual, formal sanctions. Even if offenders are being punished more severely than is apparent, however, this is not likely to be perceived by victims who presumably evaluate the assailant's punishment as a measure of their satisfaction with the criminal process.

4. See Kristen Williams, "Effects of Victim Characteristics on the Disposition of Violent Crimes," in William McDonald (ed.), *Criminal Justice and the Victim* (Beverly Hills: Sage, 1976), 177; Dan Bein, "The Impact of the Victim's Behavior on the Severity of the Offender's Sentence," in Israel Drapkin & Emilio Viano (eds.), *Victimology: Crimes, Victims and Justice* (Lexington: D.C. Heath, 1976), 49; Hugh Barlow, "Crime Victims and the Sentencing Process," unpublished paper presented at 2nd International Symposium on Victimology, Boston, 1976; Jack Kress, "The Role of the Victim at Sentencing," unpublished paper presented at 2nd International Symposium on Victimology, Boston, 1976; David Caudy & Elliott Ennson, "The Influence of the Characteristics of the Criminal and His Victim on the Decisions of Simulated Jurors," *J. Exper. Soc. Psych.*, 5(1969), 141; Martha Meyers, "Determinants of Conviction: The Prosecutorial Roles of the Victim and Defendant," unpublished paper presented at 2nd International Symposium on Victimology, Boston, 1976; for views as to the victim's effect on case dispositions, and thus, ultimately on the degree of punishment sustained by the offender.

5. The measure of statistical significance(s) used is chi square.

6. The measure of strength of relationship is Cramer's V.

7. See Michael Ash, "On Witnesses: A Radical Critique of Criminal Court Procedures," *Notre Dame Lawyer* (46(1972), 386; Doreen J. Barnett, "Victim in the Witness Box—Confronting the Stereotype," unpublished paper presented at 2nd International Symposium on Victimology, Boston, 1976.

8. See, for comparison, Richard J. Richardson, et al., *Perspectives on the Legal Justice System: Public Attitudes and Criminal Victimization* (Chapel Hill: Inst. Res. Soc. Sci., 1972).

9. See Klaus P. Fink, "Ambivalence of Former Victims Toward Their Persecutors at the Petition for Indemnification," in Drapkin & Viano, note 4 *supra,* 107.

10. This composite index of attitudes was comprised of the questions about the victim's level of anger toward the defendant, anger towards himself, fear of the offender's revenge, desire for revenge against the offender, guilt about pursuing the crime, and safety in one's neighborhood. Some of the answers were recoded so that values of each variable would range in order from negative to positive. When combined into a single index, a range of eleven numeric values resulted: the lowest three values being labelled negative attitudes, the next five values being labelled neutral values, and the highest three values being labelled positive values.

11. This victim was a cross complainant; i.e., someone whose alleged assailant also is bringing charges against him.

12. This composite index of offender treatment was comprised of the questions about how the victim felt about the prosecutors' treatment of the offender, and about the judge's treatment of the offender. When combined, a range of five numeric values resulted: the lowest one being labelled easy treatment, the next three being labelled fair treatment, and the highest being labelled hard treatment.

13. See, for comparison, Darlene Walker & Richard J. Richardson, *Public Attitudes Toward the Police* (Chapel Hill: Inst. Res. Soc. Sci., 1972); David R. Bolin, "Police-Victim Interactions: Observations from the Police Foundation," in *Evaluation and Change: Services for Victims* (Minneapolis: Minneap. Medical Res. Found., 1980), 110; E.W. Ostrom, et al., *The Effect of Institutional Arrangements on Citizen Evaluation of Police Performance* (Bloomington: Univ. Indiana Press, 1977); D. Block & A. Reiss, *Patterns of Behavior in Police-Citizen Transactions* (Washington: U.S. Gov't. Printing Ofc., 1967); P.E. Smith, "Victimization: Types of Citizen-Police Contacts and Attitudes Toward the Police," *Law & Soc. R.,* 8(1973), 135; Sacramento Police Department, *Seven Part Program to Improve Manner in Which Crime Victims are Handled by Police and Other Agencies of Criminal Justice System and Health Care Communities* (Washington: Police Foundation, 1974); Fremont Police Department, *Proposal to Conduct Program to Improve and Standardize Police Treatment of Victims and Witnesses* (Washington: Police Found., 1974).

14. This composite index of attitudes toward law-enforcement officials was comprised of the questions about how the victim felt about the prosecutor, the judge, and the police. Some of the answers were recoded so that values of each variable would range in order from favorable to unfavorable. When combined into a single index, a range of seven numeric values resulted: the lowest being labelled favorable attitude, the next three being labelled as neutral, and the highest two being labelled negative attitude.

15. See David L. Smith, "The Aftermath of Victimization: Fear and Suspicion," in Emilio Viano (ed.), *Victims and Society* (Washington: Visage Press, 1976).

16. Although the victim has largely been left out of the calculations, a sizable literature on the economic approach to understanding criminal justice has emerged. See, for example, Lee McPheters & William Strange, *The Economics of Crime and Law Enforcement* (Springfield: Chas. Thomas, 1976); John Harris, "On the Economics of Law and Order," *J. Pol. Econ.* (1970), 165; Robert Hann, "Crime and the Cost of Crime: An Economic Approach," *J. Res. Crime & Delinq.* (1972), 12; Gordon Tullock, "An Economic Approach to Crime" *Soc. Sci. Q.,* 50(1969), 59; David Sjoquist, "Property Crime and Economic Behavior: Some Empirical Results," *Amer. Econ. R.* (1973), 439; Israel Pressman & Carol Arthur, "Crime as a Diseconomy of Scale," *R. Soc. Econ.* (1971), 227; John Allison, "Economic Factors and the Rate of Crime," *Land Econ.* (1972), 193; Carl S. Shoup, "Standards for Distributing a Free Governmental Service: Crime Prevention," *Pub. Finance,* 19(1964), 383; John Weicher, "Allocation of Police Protection by Income

Class," *Urban Stud.* (1971), 207; Norman Walzer, "Economies of Scale and Municipal Police Services: The Illinois Experience," *R. Econ. & Stat.* (1972), 431; Lee McPheters & William Strange, "Law Enforcement Expenditures and Urban Crime," *Nat. Tax J.* (1974), 24; Llad Phillips & Harold Votey, "Economic Analysis of the Deterrent Effect of Law Enforcement on Criminal Activity," *J. Crim. L., Criminol., & Police Sci.* (1972), 330; Kenneth Avio, "Economic Analysis of Criminal Corrections: The Canadian Case," *Canad. J. Econ.,* 6(1973).

17. See William McDonald, "Criminal Justice and the Victim: An Introduction," in *Criminal Justice and the Victim* (Beverly Hills: Sage, 1976), 36 for reference to similar desires voiced by respondents in a study of crime victims conducted by the Philadelphia District Attorney's Office. It was, in fact, their victims' most frequent request.

18. See Mary Knutden, et al., *Crime Victims and Witnesses as Victims of the Administration of Justice* (Milwaukee: Ctr. Crim. Justice & Soc. Policy, 1975); Herbert Maisch, "The Victim in Judicial Proceedings," *Intl. J. Crime & Penol.,* 3(1975), 63; "Treatment of Victims and Witnesses," *Crime & Delinq.,* 21(1975), 190; Richard Knutden, et al., *Victims and Witnesses: Impact of Crime and Their Experiences with the Criminal Justice System* (Milwaukee: Ctr. Crim. Justice & Soc. Policy, 1976); Mary Knutden, "Will Anybody Be Left To Testify? Disenchantment with the Criminal Justice System," unpublished paper presented at American Sociological Association convention, San Francisco, 1975.

CHAPTER SEVEN
The Victim-Compensation Boards

Many crime victims suffer serious losses from their victimization. Some of these losses perhaps cannot be measured in financial terms, but many of them do have a money value. The availability of compensation boards in states such as New York and New Jersey provide victims the potential for financial recovery after their losses. How these boards operate, and their guiding rules and regulations, have a crucial effect on whether these victims actually receive compensation. Thus, it is appropriate to describe the boards' administration.

Initiating the Compensation Boards

New York

Of the two boards, New York's[1] was established first, and was, in fact, one of the first in the world. New York's plan was created, as is the case with so many governmental policies, after a tragedy. Arthur Collins was fatally stabbed on a New York City subway after trying to rescue two women from being harassed by another rider. The case, and its results for the Collins' family, received much publicity.

Consequently, a special police patrol for the subways was established, and shortly thereafter, the New York City Council passed a "Good Samaritan" Act which allowed compensation (at the Council's discretion) to persons (or their survivors) who were injured or killed trying to prevent a crime[2]. Besides providing financial assistance, the Act's purpose included a desire to encourage citizens to aid in law enforcement. The Council's action was supplemented by a resolution asking New York's Governor Rockefeller to launch a study of a more comprehensive approach to victim compensation.

In the meantime, several private groups[3] issued reports on the problem, told of the inadequate remedies currently available to crime victims, and proposed the creation of a compensation program. And, among the mountain of business on the New York State Legislature's agenda the opening day of the 1966 session, bill number one in each house was a compensation measure. The earliest proposals were crude, but initially they would have housed the programs in the Department of Public Welfare. Several committees were formed, which took

143

testimony from many individuals and groups, including Collins' widow, and the state's Trial Lawyer's Association, which (apparently eyeing a potential source of new business) argued enthusiastically for compensation decisions by hearings where victims would be represented[4].

The governor also created a three-man committee to study the problem, which also held hearings, open to the public. Although these sessions produced much support for compensation, at least some objected. For example, one former Manhattan assistant district attorney argued that the money would be better spent on crime prevention, that it was unjust to single out only crime victims for assistance among all possible victims in society requiring help, and that lawyers would probably absorb in their fees as much as one-third of the money appropriated for compensation[5]. He suggested that what victims wanted more than money was consideration and a sense of usefulness in the criminal process. Other witnesses suggested that compensation might, in fact, encourage crime by guaranteeing the offender that his victim would be able to recover.

Despite this opposition, the committee became convinced of compensation's necessity, began drafting legislation, and eventually submitted it to the Legislature for consideration. One of the major objections the committee attempted to appease was the program's potentially large cost. This fear was lessened by including a "means test" that required the victim to show "serious financial hardship" before being eligible for an award.

Even this compromise did not ensure easy passage of the bill. While the New York Assembly was controlled by Democrats, the Senate was controlled by Republicans. It was not until the Republican governor permitted the Assembly's Democratic majority leader to sponsor the Rockefeller committee's bill that the obstacles to the measure's passage began to dissolve[6]. Thereafter, the bill received widespread, bipartisan support. In fact, it was reported that "there must have been fifty guys who wanted to co-sponsor the bill."[7] And, some legislators were even accused of telling their constituents that "they (the legislators) introduced the bill" in the first place.

But, the Republican administration and Senate in New York actually opposed appropriating money for the program after the plan was authorized. The appropriations finally did pass, however, overwhelmingly in the Assembly, but only barely in the Senate, after the Assembly's majority leader exerted pressure. The funded program was signed into law on 1 August 1966.

Despite the recalcitrance of some officials, the bill's passage was quicker than one might have expected, considering the new financial burden it potentially created[8]. It also was speedy considering the general lack of other similar programs from which to seek guidance in establishing the Board's administrative traits. On the other hand, it was an election year, and the obvious public appeal of such a program might have accounted substantially for the idea's quick passage[9].

New Jersey

Since New Jersey's compensation program[10] was adopted several years after New York's, its proponents benefitted more from the experience of others. The idea in New Jersey had, however, been around at least as long as its initial consideration in New York. The first proposals arose from the state's attorney general, and from then Governor Hughes, who advocated such a program as a part of his re-election campaign. An initial bill was proposed in the New Jersey Senate in 1966, and included payments for pain and suffering but no means test. Although it was supported by many, including the police (who argued that it would promote public cooperation), the bill did not succeed.

The major obstacle to passing the New Jersey program again was fear about its costs[11]. But, when the plan was finally adopted in 1971, this problem was not "solved," as it had been in New York, by imposing a means test to limit the number of applicants. Instead, New Jersey's law required no show of "serious financial hardship," but rather limited its appropriations to one-half of those budgeted by New York five years earlier[12]. Thus, even if a person was granted an award by the New Jersey board, his actual recovery would depend on the revenue available. Or, conversely, New Jersey's board officials would not make awards if they knew that appropriations were insufficient to cover payments.

The adoption of compensation programs in both states was dominated by a balancing of fears about costs with the political value of enacting such a policy. In addition, both plans were passed in the "law-and-order" atmosphere of the period, and thus amidst cries about coddling criminals. If, in fact, such a bias really existed, it is nevertheless uncertain whether adopting these plans actually served to significantly diminish it in favor of the victim.

Theories of Compensation

Many reasons for adopting compensation programs have been suggested[13]. The policymakers in New York and New Jersey have chosen among them to provide a basis for their own programs. Clearly, these two states, like many others, did not rely on a single justification for their plans but rather acted based on multiple theories.

Neither state adopted the "strict-liability" theory. This approach would require the government to admit its failure to prevent crime, and permit itself to be subject to a legal claim by those victimized as a result of this failure. Likewise, both states avoided the "government-negligence" rationale by again admitting no liability, and by adopting programs that made eligible more than only those victims who might hold specific law-enforcement officials accountable for their victimization.

Furthermore, neither state positively associated itself with either the "equal protection" or "humanitarian" theories. But, by implication, it can be assumed that these rationales are imbedded in the states' policies. Policymakers in both states, for example, were anxious to adopt compensation to help redress the supposed unequal treatment of victims and offenders. And, at least some policymakers in each state had humanitarian motives in mind when promoting compensation.

More overt evidence exists, however, to attach the New York and New Jersey plans to several of the remaining rationales. First, although it does not appear directly in the enabling legislation, it is clear that political considerations (or the "political motives" theory) influenced legislators in both states. Many politicians, especially those concerned with re-election, favored the at least symbolic satisfaction the public (hopefully in their districts) would feel from adopting such a program. And, some were content with providing that psychological effect and not necessarily a working program, since many voting for authorization actually voted against funding, or for only very limited appropriations.

Apparently, both states also were motivated by the "crime prevention" theory[14]. Supporters frequently made claims about the program's potential for aiding law enforcement through increased victim cooperation as a result of being (or hoping to be) compensated, or even just knowing that compensation was there[15]. And, this basis remains prominent in the programs' actual operations according to the comments of board officials[16].

But, on the most fundamental philosophical basis of each state's program, the two jurisdictions do differ significantly. While both states recognize the desirability (but not legal liability) of satisfying a person's need after victimization, New York does so based on the "social welfare" theory, while New Jersey relies on the "social obligation" approach. Thus, New York awards compensation based only on need or on demonstrating "serious financial hardship." This serves to characterize the New York plan as essentially a welfare program. On the other hand, New Jersey grants payments regardless of the victim's financial circumstances. New York attempts to apply assistance where it feels the aid is most needed, while New Jersey recognizes that victimization losses can have profound effects on the more well-off, as well as on the poor.

In sum, both states rejected any notions of government liability or negligence as a basis for compensation. Instead, to some extent they have acted on egalitarian and humanitarian grounds. But, most clearly, they have acted also for political and crime-prevention motives, as well. The only differences in rationale lies in New York's awarding compensation as welfare as compared to New Jersey's awarding it by right. But, of course, this is a crucial difference, and one that was hypothesized in this study to have a significant effect on each board's outcomes and impact.

Organization of Compensation Boards

Administrative Structures

The structural characteristics and operating procedures of the two compensation boards have undergone some alterations in the time since each board's creation. It is most useful here, however, to describe as accurately as possible the administrative traits characterizing the boards at the time the victims analyzed in this study had contact with them.

Both compensation programs, especially New York's, have become more decentralized over the years. While New Jersey has expanded to two offices (Newark and Trenton), New York had offices in Buffalo, Manhattan, and Albany at the time of this study[17], despite its original location only in the latter city. The center of New Jersey's operations is in Newark, where most of the staff and the board members are located. The administrative center of New York's plan has migrated from Albany to Manhattan because the vast majority of the claims derive from there and the six other counties (including Brooklyn) it coordinates. Each of the cities selected for this study constituted a significant number of the claims filed in each state.

Each of the two compensation plans is financed basically through general revenue collected from taxes. But, as previously indicated, New Jersey's awards are made contingent upon the availability of funds, and thus that state's board members must consider appropriations limits when making awards[18].

In 1977, New York instituted the so-called "Son of Sam" law, named after the New York City mass murderer who had just been caught. In effect, it created a restitution program (and thus a limited, but alternative source of funding) that allowed the board to collect any profits made by an offender's publicizing (such as by writing a book or screenplay) his crime, and which could be used to pay the crime's victims[19]. In fact, the law already has been used to help pay the real-life victims depicted in the motion picture "Dog Day Afternoon."[20] Policymakers in New Jersey also have expressed interest in partially financing their program through earmarked fines on offenders, as is practiced in some other states[21]. Both states, however, are anxiously awaiting the passage of a national program, which will lighten their financial burdens by providing matching funds.

Each of the state's programs operate through specialized administrative agencies. Although the New Jersey board is technically a division of the state's Department of Law and Safety, it is almost completely independent of external controls[22], similar to the New York program. Neither program employs the judicial approach of awarding compensation through the courts, nor the dependent board approach (of being governed by a pre-existing agency).

As some evidence of each program's comparatively professional character, all the board members are full-time employees. Board members in each state are appointed by the governor. New York has five members who serve for seven years, while New Jersey has three members who serve for five years. The terms are staggered in both states to ensure experienced members at all times. This is perhaps a wise decision since the turnover on the boards has been considerable, even before the normal end of terms. Each board has one chairman who is equal in authority to the other members but receives a higher salary because of his extra admininstrative responsibilities. So burdensome are they in New York that the chairman there has devoted himself exclusively to those duties and ended (except for appeals) his consideration of awards[23].

In each of the states, members must be divided in their party affiliation, and since both boards have an uneven number of members, one party always predominates. In New Jersey, two of the members must be lawyers, while all the members in New York must be from that profession. Although apparently no quotas exist for sex, only one woman has served (in New York) on the boards.

The board members in each state divide up the workload for purposes of efficiency, but the division is made on another basis as well. In New Jersey, for example, most of the claims come to the Newark office, and thus the chairman and one other board member divide those cases. The third board member has primary control over the cases arriving in the state's other office in Trenton[24].

In New York, the work is divided among the board members, most of whom are located in Manhattan[25]. Those not in Manhattan handle cases from outside the New York City area through the Albany office, while the rest divide up the Manhattan area (including the Bronx, Staten Island, Brooklyn, Nassau, Suffolk, Queens, and Manhattan itself).

Despite personnel changes and administrative shifts (especially in New York), it was still possible to distinguish Brooklyn and Newark claimants from the others in their respective states, and possible to isolate the board members in each state who considered cases from these two groups of claimants during the time covered by this study.

Processing Claims

Each of the programs requires that claimants either mail or personally deliver to the boards standard claims forms. While New York's form comes attached to a four-page brochure briefly describing the program, eligibility requirements, and procedures, New Jersey's form is separate from that state's brochure, but contains similar information. New Jersey claimants are sent or given different forms depending on whether the claim was for personal injury or death, while New York's one form accommodates both kinds of claims.

New Jersey's forms require noticably more information from the claimant than does New York's, although ultimately, the latter accumulates more total information from applicants throughout the process. New York initially used much more complicated application forms but soon abandoned them for (supposedly) very simple forms so that people would be less reluctant to make a claim.

In the end, both boards ask the victim for similar kinds of information. They are asked their address, phone number, birthdate, marital status, sex, and family circumstances. They also are questioned about their victimization (including the crime and their injuries), their knowledge of (or relationship with) the victim, and whether the crime was reported. Inquiries are made about the victim's losses from the crime, including medical expenses, lost earnings, and loss of support. Victims also are asked about their incomes, assets, liabilities, other expenses, and about other possible sources of recovery for which they might be eligible or have applied.

As previously indicated, board members in each state divide the workload. Thus, each claim is essentially decided by one member of each board. But, board members are assisted by a supporting staff. Each state has clerical assistance and a team of investigators. The size of these staffs differs significantly, however. While New York's secretarial and clerical help is moderately sized, New Jersey's is very small. The clerks in both program have a role in initially screening eligible and ineligible claims. And, while New York has one supervising investigator, two senior investigators, fourteen staff investigators, six claims examiners[26], several financial personnel, a medical fee specialist, and a staff attorney, New Jersey has only three investigators and one financial clerk altogether[27]. New York also has the services of an administrative assistant in Albany and an executive secretary in Manhattan, while no such personnel exist in New Jersey[28].

When a board member receives a claim, he reviews it and then assigns it to one of the investigators. An investigation determines the accuracy and validity of the information included on the claim form and of that requested from the victim thereafter[29]. The claimant bears the burden of initially submitting the required medical records and bills, income and tax (in New York only) information, and any other required affadavits. This allows investigators time to verify information instead of burdening them with collecting it in the first place[30]. But, this procedure also potentially limits the claimant's ability to file a successful case because of the complications of securing that kind of information.

For this and other reasons, each board allows claimants to be represented by attorneys, and much of the board's communication with the claimant often will occur through his counsel, if the victim has secured one[31]. On the other hand, attorneys are not encouraged[32] in either state as each board seeks to reduce the formalities brought into the process by legal technicalities[33].

After the claimant is given a reasonable time to submit all required information, and after the investigation (which verifies the victimization and the information submitted) is complete, a single board member in each state will make a unilateral decision. In all cases, the claimant must cooperate fully with the board and provide all necessary information in order to be considered for an award, even in a worthy claim[34]. Sometimes the board member will order a hearing before making a decision. In that case, the claimant is told when and where to appear, and may arrive with his lawyer to argue his case. Strict common-law rules are eliminated, but testimony is under oath and the claimant may bring or subpeona witnesses on his behalf. But, the burden of proof is on the claimant. Hearings are open to the public except in special circumstances such as a claim for an alleged sexual crime.

Before or after the hearing, the board member in each state may, at his discretion, order that the claimant undergo a medical examination to verify the injuries claimed. New Jersey initially employed a special panel of medical experts and a detailed scheme for examinations, but prohibitive costs forced the abandoning of that approach in favor of private physicians[35].

When the board member has accumulated all the information he desires, he makes a decision[36], and informs the claimant in writing of the outcome, the reasons, and if appropriate, the particulars of the award. A claimant may request a hearing in New Jersey within twenty days of the decision if he was denied an award without benefit of a previous hearing. After this hearing, the decision is reconsidered by the board member and a final decision is rendered.

In New York, a claimant may not request an initial hearing, but can, within thirty days after the single board-member's decision, request a review[37] by the full board. The decision on review actually is made by three members of the board, not including the member issuing the original decision[38], and is final in most cases. The single board member, in both states, may decide on his own or in response to a claimant's request[39], to reopen a case later on. Also, in protracted cases, the New York board reviews its decision every six months automatically, to verify a continuing need[40].

Otherwise, the decision is for all intents and purposes final in both states. That is, in New York no judicial review of the board's decision is allowed unless it is brought by the Attorney General (not the claimant)[41] when he feels that an award has been unjustly granted[42]. In New Jersey, although a claimant can appeal in the courts, judicial decisions clearly have indicated that board rulings will be overturned only in the most blatant cases of a board member's abusing his discretion[43].

Both boards do have some leeway in exercising discretion. Although the rules are fairly specific in both states in many areas of board authority, other areas are more general, and discretion is understood[44]. Thus, for example, the New York board decides what to include in determining whether the claimant faces "serious financial hardship[45]." And, sometimes the boards can go even beyond what appears to be authorized, such as when New Jersey occasionally awards emergency payments[46].

Both boards are interested in maintaining close connections with other criminal-justice agencies. First of all, they rely at least in part on law-enforcement personnel to inform victims about the compensation programs. And, furthermore, board members want to contribute to law-enforcement efforts through the cooperation they induce claimants to give to criminal-justice officials.

But, perhaps most of all, the boards are interested in the corresponding assistance and cooperation they might receive from these officials to help investigate and resolve individual claims. Obviously, board members must make crucial decisions about whether a crime really was committed and whether it was reported, which may rely substantially on information provided by law-enforcement personnel. To promote this assistance, each of the boards will agree to delay a claim's consideration if its outcome might prejudice or otherwise influence an ongoing investigation or prosecution[47].

Unfortunately, this practice is not the only cause of delays. The great number of claims made (although miniscule compared to actual victimizations) and the small staff available in each state to handle the cases cause tremendous backlogs. Although the denials might come as soon as six months after filing a claim, awards regularly take eighteen months to two years in New York[48], and even longer in New Jersey.

The backlogs would be even more extensive if more victims knew the boards existed[49]. Although each board has launched publicity campaigns to increase public awareness of the programs, the efforts have been limited[50]. Each state (although this seems somewhat less so among actual board members) still fears the financial burden that might result if the programs were well-publicized. In New Jersey, in particular, publicity efforts were specifically discontinued because of already excessive financial demands[51].

The publicity campaigns that have existed include the publishing of reports, issuing press releases, radio and television discussions, and distributing brochures to service centers, welfare organizations, hospitals, and physicians. These apparently have produced less than abundant results[52]. More important perhaps have been the boards' efforts to distribute brochures and other information to law-enforcement personnel, especially to the police[53]. In fact, New York state police officers are now formally required[54] to read (in either English or Spanish) victims (from a Miranda-like card) their eligibility to receive compensation[55]. The card does not specify the many restrictions, however, that might jeopardize one's claim.

When awards are made, they are either lump-sum payments[56] or periodic[57]. The former approach is used most frequently, with the latter reserved to installments given to victims with protracted disabilities or to dependents awarded support payments. Emergency awards are formally allowed only in New York[58]. These payments may be requested back from the claimant if his claim is denied, or may be subtracted from a successful claim. Both states also exercise "subrogation'' rights whereby any successful suit brought by the victim against the offender would be paid directly to the board to help cover the compensation award granted to the victim.

Board Financing

Clearly, financing the programs is the dominant administrative consideration for each of the boards[59]. Unfortunately, the financial figures available in each state are not exactly parallel. While New York specifies yearly administrative costs[60] and a running total of expenditures[61] since the program's creation, New Jersey does not. Also, New York's fiscal year runs from 1 April to 31 March, while New Jersey's runs from 1 January to 31 December. Thus, only comparisons of annual disbursements can be made.

During the last five fiscal years, New York (with payments of over $15.2 million) has exceeded New Jersey (with payments of over $4.3 million, including lawyer's fees) by almost four times. New York's payments have steadily increased over those years to a most recent annual figure of $4.3 million[62] (as much as New Jersey's expenditures over the last five years!), while New Jersey's payments actually declined for both 1976 and 1977, and its most recent level ($946,500) actually is less than the 1975 total, which was the program's most expensive year[63]. The state's payments to attorneys have varied correspondingly except for the most recent year, which was the second lowest disbursement the state made for that item in the five-year period.

New York obviously is spending much more money than New Jersey on reimbursing claimants, but then again, New York does have more victims and does run a bigger program. New Jersey actually has granted higher average payments, however. For example, during the two years of concern to this study, New Jersey's payments averaged $3519 and $3486[64], while New York's awards averaged $2922[65] and $2138[66]. Thus, although New Jersey is helping less victims, they are being provided with more lucrative awards[67].

Payments in New Jersey also include attorney's fees since that state pays counsel directly. An attorney can receive no more than 15% of a successful claim[68]. No such limit exists in New York but that state does not provide separate payments to lawyers. Instead, it considers the reasonable costs of counsel for each successful case, the actual amount of work, the claimant's financial situation, and the type of award made. Based on these criteria, the board incorporates a fee into the claimant's award[69]. In New Jersey, an attorney cannot seek more than the 15% ceiling from the victim on his own, while in New York, no such protection or limit exists to restrain attorneys[70]. And, furthermore, in both states the claimant is liable to pay his lawyer completely on his own if his claim is denied by the board. It is unclear how many victims hire lawyers on a contingency-fee basis.

In sum, although some differences exist between the administrative characteristics of the New York and New Jersey compensation boards, a remarkable number of similarities dominate. Comparing the two programs further according to their eligibility requirements shows additional differences, however.

Eligibility for Victim Compensation

Of crucial importance for victims seeking to recover their losses are the requirements they must satisfy to qualify for compensation. The limitations in both state's programs are quite extensive and formidable.

Both states compensate only for losses due to violent crimes that are actually demonstrated to have occurred. Pain and suffering are not reimbursable but mental and nervous shock is sometimes recoverable in New Jersey[71] and also in New York if it accompanies physical injuries[72]. Neither state compensates for property losses. Automobile injuries also are excluded except if a motor vehicle was used as a weapon or used to commit the crime[73]. The eligible violent crimes are not specified in New York, but are listed in New Jersey[74] (although it also compensates for other, unlisted crimes involving violence, as well).

Each of the programs requires that the claimant report the victimization to the police, within 48 hours[75] in New York, and within 30 days in New Jersey. The boards, especially in New York, also give claimants a strong incentive to prosecute their cases and to otherwise cooperate with law-enforcement officials by leaving the impression that failing to do so would reflect poorly on their chances for compensation (which invariably is decided after the criminal case, if any, is completed).

Furthermore, the board requires that the victim make a claim within 90 days of the victimization in New York[76], and within one year in New Jersey. Both boards also require the claimant to cooperate continually and to provide necessary information throughout the case. Violating these rules is grounds for a person's disqualification for an award, although obviously New Jersey was more willing to grant leeway in its reporting requirments.

Although neither state requires that a claimant be a citizen[77], other characteristics did disqualify applicants. Both programs reflect a considerable fear of fraudulent claims[78]. Consequently, among other safeguards, each program eliminates claimants having a past or present relationship with the offender. Thus, both states exclude victims if they are a relative of the offender, live in the same household, or have had a sexual relationship with the offender.

Furthermore, each program also excludes victims found to have been an accomplice or conspirator in the crime committed. And, although provoking a crime against oneself is not automatic grounds for disqualification, it can be used to ultimately deny or reduce an award.

In addition, each state[79] requires that the claimant have a minimum amount of loss (at least $100 worth) in order to be considered for compensation. In a personal injury case, losses must have resulted from out-of-pocket expenses, which include medical costs. And, lost income also is reimbursed in both states but only if at least two weeks of work is missed as a result of the victimization. No formal ceiling appears to constrict New Jersey's reimbursements per week for lost earnings, but New York's limit was $135 per week[80]. Each board also has established maximum limits on overall payments to each claimant. New Jersey's maximum is $10,000, while New York's was $15,000 at the time of this study[81]. But, no limit exists in New York for protracted medical payments. In death cases, each state makes a crime victim's dependents eligible. Support payments (and in New Jersey, pension payments, as well) are authorized as high as the aforementioned state maximums. Funeral expenses of $750 in New Jersey and $1500 in New York also are available.

All awards are reduced by the amount the victim receives from any "collateral" sources, such as workman's compensation, insurance, or criminal restitution. Unfortunately, many decisions are delayed even beyond their normal slowness by the boards' practice of waiting until a victim's other claims have been decided, before making an award[82].

In sum, these eligibility requirements reveal some additional differences between New York's and New Jersey's programs[83]. Although many of the crime reporting, cooperation and fraud characteristics are similar, New York does seem somewhat more generous in its apparent willingness to grant payments (although this must be qualified by the fact that New Jersey has less victims and actually compensates with a higher average payment than in New York) overall.

But, this difference is most severely compromised when one remembers that in New York a claimant is eligible for assistance only after he satisfies all of the eligibility requirements *and* demonstrates "serious financial hardship." Overall, therefore, both states are extremely stringent in their requirements, and thus considerable barriers stand between most claimants and an award.

Now that each of the compensation programs have been described, and their rules, procedures, administration, and requirements compared in a formal sense, it is next necessary to consider some insight into each board's actual operations. This can be best achieved through the eyes of board members themselves. Consequently, the following chapter will examine the results of detailed interviews with these officials, which will, among other things, allow us to further distinguish between the compensation programs in New York and New Jersey.

Notes

1. The most detailed description of the characteristics and development of this state's program can be found in Herbert Edelhertz & Gilbert Geis, *Public Compensation to Victims of Crime* (New York: Praeger, 1974), 21-75.

2. Gilbert Geis, et al., Public Compensation of Victims of Crime: A Survey of the New York Experience," *Crim. L. Bull.*, 9(1973), 9.

3. *Ibid.*, 11, 13.

4. Edelhertz & Geis, note 1 *supra*, 26.

5. Geis, note 2 *supra*, 17.

6. Edelhertz & Geis, note 1 *supra*, 34.

7. Geis, note 2 *supra*, 34.

8. Nevertheless, the program has since become a popular target for criticism and re-form, including many bills proposed to amend the program. See Barbara Campbell, "More Money and Fast Action Asked for Crime Victims," *N.Y. Times*, 26 April 1975, 31.

Some have even accused the Board of being overly strict in applying the law, and thus disqualifying deserving victims. See Geis, note 2 *supra*, 39.

9. Note, "New York Crime Victims Compensation Board: Four Years Later," *Columb. J. Law & Soc. Prob.*, 7(1971), 27.

10. The most detailed description of the characteristics and development of this state's program can be found in Edelhertz & Geis, note 1 *supra*, 154-182.

11. Notes, "New Jersey Criminal Injuries Compensation Act," *Rutgers L.R.*, 27(1974), 728.

12. Edelhertz & Geis, note 1 *supra*, 154.

13. See chapter two for the dominant theories.

14. Geis, note 2 *supra*, 103.

15. Although cooperation with law-enforcement personnel was not legislatively re-quired in order to be considered for an award, claimants were strongly motivated to provide such assistance, in both states. Ironically, the government might thus receive cooperation, while the victim discovers, only later, that he has been denied an award.

16. See chapter 8.

17. The New York program has since added offices in upper Manhattan, Syracuse, and Mineola. See Crime Victims Compensation Board, *1977-78 Annual Report* (Albany: State of New York, 1977), 13.

18. Winsor C. Schmidt, *Legal Issues in Compensating Victims of Crime* (Raleigh: Nat. Assn. Attnys. Gen., 1976), 22.

19. Legislative Committee on Expenditure Review, *Crime Victims Compensation Board* (Albany: State of New York, 1979), 61.

20. Crime Victims Compensation Board, *1977-78 Annual Report* (Albany: State of New York, 1978), 31.

21. Virginia and Florida, for example.

22. Edelhertz & Geis, note 1 *supra,* 155.

23. Legislative Committee on Expenditure Review, note 19 *supra*, 43.

24. Violent Crimes Compensation Board, *Annual Report 1977* (Newark: State of New Jersey, 1978), 7.

25. Legislative Committee on Expenditure Review, note 19 *supra*, 6.

26. Added after the time of this study to make initial assessment of eligibility, to contact claimants for affadavits, and then to pass them to senior investigator for verification.

27. This not only reflects an obvious difference in size and scope between the two programs, but also apparently, to some extent, the greater staff needed by a program that must verify each claimant's "financial hardship."

28. New York's staff was somewhat small at the time of this study.

29. Note, note 9 *supra*, 31.

30. William Doerner, "State Victim Compensation Programs in Action," *Victimology*, 3(1977), 106.

31. Although one report claims that one in five claimants have a lawyer in New York (see Roger Meiners, *Victim Compensation: Economic, Legal, and Political Aspects* (Lex-

ington: D.C. Heath, 1978), 27), the actual figure appears to be 14% for both 1975-76 and 1976-77 (see Crime Victims Compensation Board, note 17 *supra*, 22). But, 56% of the victims before the New Jersey board in its first year of operation had attorneys (see Edelhertz & Geis, note 1 *supra*, 162).

32. But, with the advent of less work for lawyers through the adoption of no-fault automobile insurance in both states, the presence of lawyers in compensation cases may well increase.

33. Edelhertz & Geis, note 1 *supra*, 56.

34. Geis, note 2 *supra*, 113.

35. Edelhertz & Geis, note 1 *supra*, 161.

36. Medical expenses in both states are determined apart from fixed schedules. In fact, a New York board experiment showed that it was paying higher medical payments than a claimant would receive under a fixed rate such as that used in workman's compensation. But, the New York board also has a medical fee specialist who sets limits on fees charged by doctors and hospitals (see Legislative Committee on Expenditure Review, note 19 *supra*, 24).

37. In 1977-78, 14 of the 113 (2% of the total cases decided) cases reviewed in New York were changed to awards (see Crime Victims Compensation Board, note 20 *supra*, 14).

38. Stanley L. Van Rensselaer, "Compensation for Victims of Crime: The New York Experience," *State Gov't.* (1974), 15.

39. LeRoy Lamborn, "The Scope of Programs for Governmental Compensation of Victims of Crime," *U. Ill. L. Forum* (1973), 59.

40. *Ibid.,* 62; Also, this board also will entertain requests for amended decisions to increase a previous award, and in 1977-78, it approved 274 of 375 requests.

41. Since the time of this study, claimants have been granted the right to a judicial appeal (see Legislative Committee on Expenditure Review, note 19 *supra*, 2).

42. Schmidt, note 18 *supra*, 16.

43. *In re Hollywood,* 124 NJ Super. 50, 304 A.2nd 747(1973).

44. Edelhertz & Geis, note 1 *supra*, 156.

45. Stanley L. Van Rensselaer, "A Compensation Board at Work," *Trial,* 8(1972), 21.

46. Notes, note 11 *supra*, 735.

47. Violent Crimes Compensation Board, "Rules and Regulations of the Violent Crimes Compensation Board," (Trenton: State of New Jersey, n.d.), 5; Crime Victims Compensation Board, "Rules Governing Practice and Procedure," (Albany: State of New York, 1976), 3.

48. Kitty Hanson, "Billions on Criminals—How About Victims," *New York Daily News,* 4 October 1977, 33.

49. U.S. House of Representatives, Committee on Judiciary, "Crime Victim Compensation," Hearings, 94th Cong. (Washington: U.S. Gov't. Printing Ofc., 1975-76), serial no. 39, 1274.

50. Wayne King, "If You Are Maimed by a Criminal You Can Be Compensated (Maybe)," *New York Times Magazine,* 26 March 1972, 122; Note, note 9 *supra*, 35 (quotes a board member as saying that the board was not advocating saturation publicity for fear that it is not equipped to handle the deluge of claims that would follow).

51. Department of Law & Public Safety, "Violent Crimes Compensation Board," *1975 Annual Report* (Trenton: State of New Jersey, 1976), 56.

52. But, see extensive new efforts made recently in New York (Crime Victims Compensation Board, note 20 *supra*, 30).

53. LeRoy Lamborn, "The Methods of Governmental Compensation of Crime," *U. Ill. L. Forum* (1971), 669.

54. This policy supposedly began at the time of this study, but apparently it was frequently ignored, or was poorly understood by claimants. In 1978, the New York City Police Department began a new program of notifying by mail or telephone, and this apparently has caused a rise in applications (see Crime Victims Compensation Board, note 17 *supra*, 55).

55. *Ibid.*, iii.

56. In New York, these payments take an average of 52 days from the day of the decision until received by the claimant (see *Ibid.*, 8).

57. Note, note 9 *supra*, 32.

58. Crime Victims Compensation Board, note 20 *supra*, 11.

59. A comparison of several state plans, including New York and New Jersey, shows that program costs may vary according to staff size and renumeration, crime incidence, amount of award per claim, and eligibility requirements (see Schmidt, note 18 *supra*, 12).

60. Roughly 16% of total budget (disbursements 84%), down from higher amounts (e.g., 19% in 1972) in earlier years (see Robert Reiff, *The Invisible Victim* (New York: Basic, 1979), 170). But, for 1977-78, New Jersey spent 17% on administration (disbursements 83%), down from higher amounts (e.g., 18% in 1974) in earlier years (see Legislative Committee on Expenditure Review, *Financial Aid to Victims* (Albany: State of New York, 1975), s-5).

61. $20.8 million on disbursements, $4.9 million on administration, for a $25.7 million total since its creation.

62. Crime Victims Compensation Board, note 20 *supra*, 6.

63. Violent Crimes Compensation Board, *Annual Report 1978* (Newark: State of New Jersey, 1979), 10.

64. Computed from board records (see Violent Crimes Compensation Board, note 24 *supra*, 9.

65. Computed from board records but another source indicates that $1810 was actually the average award (see Crime Victims Compensation Board, note 20 *supra*, 61.

66. *Ibid.*, 62.

67. Gerald Astor, "Crime Doesn't Pay Its Victims Very Well Either," *New York Times*, 30 May 1976, E6.

68. Violent Crimes Compensation Board, note 47 *supra*, 6.

69. Geis, note 2 *supra*, 108.

70. L. Paul Sutton, "Compensation to Victims of Violent Crime in New York State," (Seattle: Battelle Law & Justice Study Ctr., 1972), 4.

71. Lamborn, note 39 *supra*, 38.

72. *Ibid.*, 39.

73. Schmidt, note 18 *supra*, 33.

74. Lamborn, note 39 *supra*, 23.

75. After the time of this study, the time was extended to one week.

76. After the time of this study, the time was extended to one year.

77. Lamborn, note 39 *supra*, 43.

78. Although the boards have made complaints about padded claims from hospitals, doctors, and claimants, fraud has not, in fact, proved to be a legitimate fear (see Geis, note 2 *supra*, 102).

79. Since the time of this study, New York has deleted this requirement.

80. Since the time of this study, this has been increased to $250.

81. Since the time of this study, this has been increased to $20,000.

82. Lamborn, note 53 *supra*, 674.

83. Overall, however, the differences are minor except for the means test, which is required in New York, but not in New Jersey.

CHAPTER EIGHT
Officials in the Compensation Process

Examining the role of those officials administering compensation plans is important for better understanding and evaluating these programs' impact. Board members and investigators occupy the crucial position of translating legislative intent into actual policy outputs and outcomes. Official perspectives about victim compensation's purpose and goals, as well as official backgrounds, attitudes, and decision-making influences, will affect the outcomes of the compensation process and its impact on victims and the criminal-justice process. To provide a close analysis of the role and influence of board administrators, three officials (two members and one investigator) were questioned at both the New York Crime Victims Compensation Board and the New Jersey Violent Crimes Compensation Board[1].

Board officials were asked a wide range of questions designed to illuminate broad aspects of their attitudes and work. Inquiries were made about official backgrounds and career paths, about attitudes, about criminal justice and government, about compensation's goals and purposes, about decision-making influences, and about the program's impact. Many of these questions are comparable to those asked of crime victims themselves, and thus frequent comparisons can be made. And finally, it will be useful to distinguish, whenever possible, between the board members in New York and New Jersey, as well[2].

Official Roles

Despite the many similarities among board administrators, the following pages will illustrate different kinds of board administrators. That is, two different approaches and perspectives as to the role of victim compensation and board administrators emerge. The role distinctions derive largely from whether administrators are "political" in executing, and in thinking about, their functions, as well as from their relative "energy" in promoting the cause of crime victims. The Board officials observed in this study thus can be labelled as either "advocates," or "neutrals."[3]

Advocates

Although none of the officials could be identified as unconcerned or unsympathetic to victims' needs, a couple (one board member in each state) were more activist in their attitudes and apparent behavior. These officials more vigorously criticized legislative policies and other officials connected to victim compensation's goals and operations. They also were more "political" in their backgrounds, attitudes, behavior, and aspirations. That is, they acted with more awareness of victim compensation's role in a broader political and party system. These administrators had much broader visions than their fellow officials of what impact compensation had at present, and what goals it could hope to accomplish in the future. They viewed their agency as an important and integral part of the criminal-justice process. And finally, these officials wanted to champion the victim's cause beyond merely providing some limited recovery to claimants. They were, in other words, "advocates" for victims and victim compensation.

Neutrals

Other board officials (evenly dispersed between the two boards) took a more low-key approach toward their activities. Their attitudes showed concern about victims' needs and their compensation programs, but they were not very "activist," or politically motivated—either for themselves, victims or their programs. These officials (both members and investigators alike) acted more like bureaucrats who wanted to do a good job, but seemed restrained either by their own personalities and backgrounds, or by what they perceived as the limitations of their work. They sometimes criticized these limitations but were nevertheless sympathetic to many of the reasons why they were imposed. These officials did not hold broad perceptions of their roles or their programs. They largely felt that victim compensation had a limited impact, and that compensating at least some victims was the most that could be achieved (but nevertheless valued) under the circumstances. In other words, these officials were "neutrals."

Backgrounds and Career Paths of Board Officials

To begin a more specific characterization of "advocates" and "neutrals," one must examine official backgrounds. Isolating these traits is important not only for categorizing administrators into these two roles, but also because an official's social characteristics may affect his attitudes and decision-making.

Overall, board officials have similar social and economic backgrounds—what might be viewed as typically middle class—although some differences did emerge in race, occupation, education, and political party. All the officials had served in government before, primarily as administrators, but some were more political than others.

More specifically, all of the board officials were male, married, and aged in their forties and fifties. All respondents had resided in their respective states for most, if not all, of their lives, and all had considerable community ties. Also, the administrators were similar in their financial situations. They were middle income, with members somewhat more financially secure than investigators. Board officials worked full-time and thus had little opportunity to supplement their incomes from the programs.

These official characteristics might be usefully compared to the traits of the victims (at least those examined in this study) served by the boards. Although victims also were primarily male and married, they were considerably younger, had few community ties, and were considerably less financially secure—a large portion being unemployed. The contrast between the representatives and the represented is striking.

The background differences that did occur among officials included their race, occupation, education, and political party, but the variance was usually minor. The officials ranged in their education from high school graduates to law school graduates, with a couple in between. Board members are not all lawyers, although New Jersey requires two of its three members to be from that profession. New York's rules apparently require that all members be lawyers yet one of those interviewed was not. Other than lawyers, the officials were either administrators or businessmen by profession. Again, despite some official differences, their contrast with crime victims was even more notable since most of the latter had not gone beyond high school and many others had not even graduated.

All officials were caucasian except for one investigator who was black. All respondents also were Democrats except for one who was Republican. Once again, board rules affected the party affiliation of members, if not investigators. Each board must have a mixture of party ties. Nevertheless, all but one (a Democrat) described their political views as conservative, and this was later confirmed by their stated attitudes. A contrast between administrators and victims emerges here as well, since minority victims outnumbered whites, and since the most victims were members of neither of the major political parties—partly because they belonged to no party at all.

The position of board member is clearly a patronage slot in both states. Each member's party affiliation reflects his ties to the governor who selected him. Only one member apparently had "graduated" into his position based on his earlier work as an investigator. This member admitted that his appointment was "not as political as they usually are." His position was owed partly to another member's lobbying.

Virtually all officials held some prior state administrative or elective post, including positions with the health department, liquor or real-estate commissions, or tax and banking investigations. One official had been a mayor and another had been a state legislator. Other posts had been held with private business and industry, as well as with the Defense Department. Several also had held positions with their respective political parties. In sum, board officials were active politically in their communities and their states, and owed their appointments to their party work and affiliations.

Most of the officials questioned expressed no desire to move on to other political or non-political positions, although some were apparently somewhat frustrated in their work. A couple of officials were not far away from retirement, and indicated they would remain with their board until then. One apparently contented member did, nevertheless, indicate that he might consider a federal appointment if it came along. The only member interested in leaving his board was campaigning for a local civil-court judgeship.

In sum, board administrators are a rather homogeneous group, despite some minor differences in their backgrounds and prior experience. These few variations, however, might have contributed to the different official roles that emerged. And, the differences in social characteristics between the officials and the victims they serve are considerable, in any case.

Official Attitudes

Board administrators were questioned about their general attitudes toward government and criminal justice to better understand their possible effects on official behavior. It was discovered that most officials blame poor upbringing for causing crime, regard crime as a major problem, cite the young as most susceptible to crime, and avoid blaming criminal-justice officials for ineffectiveness. More specifically, when asked what causes crime, officials gave a variety of answers, but family and peer influences predominated. Most officials also mentioned social and economic considerations, and yet they were often the same ones who blamed poor law-enforcement and crime prevention, and who urged increased punishments. Nobody blamed the government (nor the ineffectiveness of law-enforcement officials) for crime, and nobody believed in "born" criminals. In contrast, although the victims in this study joined officials in blaming family upbringing (or general permissiveness, as victims called it) and poor law-enforcement for crime, the former were much more likely to criticize particular criminal-justice officials, and economic and social considerations than were administrators.

Although board officials did recognize some economic causes of crime, the responses had a largely conservative tone. One official complained about living in an "offender-oriented" society, while another claimed that "the police know all the criminals but cannot touch them," and yet a third stressed that "victims have no lobby."

Only one official, the self-described liberal, stressed economic causes to a larger extent, including the role of unemployment and limited skills for young people. He also argued that crime derived from our cities' hostile environments and from rapid social change that was not "representative of certain segments of the populace." He also stressed the conflict between "white cops and minorities." This member's perspective may have been shaped by his previous work as a criminal lawyer.

All but one of the board officials felt that their respective cities had a genuine crime problem. A few indicated that the media and criminal-justice officials had underestimated its seriousness. One investigator, however, argued that, in fact, the media exaggerated the problem, including television shows and sensational press coverage. On the other hand, he believed that this exposure, although overstated, might encourage more crime. Clearly, most crime victims would have agreed with most officials about the crime problems' seriousness.

Each board official had his own favorite as to who was most susceptible to victimization. Some claimed it was the elderly, while others felt that youth were hardest hit. Only a couple admitted that most victims were minority group members. As a matter of fact, studies indicate that the elderly are not among the most likely crime victims, and that those officials emphasizing younger victims were correct. The predominance of non-whites also has been widely observed, including in this study itself.

None of the members, perhaps from a desire to maintain good working relations, accused criminal-justice officials of ineffectiveness, but they all cited various inadequacies in the overall process. Some complained about lenient penalties, and about the inattention to recidivists. Nobody supported rehabilitation, and several expressly indicated its failure and lack of merits. One official cited law-enforcement personnel as overburdened and underpaid. A couple of others cited the legal barriers imposed on criminal-justice personnel, and the negative influence of "liberal" tendencies, such as the "American 'Criminal' Liberties Union," as one official put it.

Although officials criticized law enforcement and crime prevention efforts, none blamed government directly, and all generally supported government's role in society. The "conservatives" were quick to note the limits of government involvement. None, however, blamed government for crime, such as for possibly producing policies creating a climate of criminality. In fact, a couple of officials specifically rejected the idea. Many of the victims in this study were not as generous.

The foregoing general attitudes allow us to begin to separate "advocate" and "neutrals." Some of the officials questioned emerged as more outspokenly political, and more willing to challenge legislators and criminal-justice officials on behalf of victims, while others were more cautious and content with voicing the common government and criminal-justice cliches. A deeper comparison will distinguish the roles even more.

Purposes and Goals of Victim Compensation

Since board members stand to affect victim compensation's impact the most, we must better understand their view of compensation's objectives. Thus, officials were asked about their programs' purposes and goals. Most emphasized reimbursing victims' losses and demonstrating some concern to victims and the public. Virtually all the administrators denied that their programs were "welfare," and supported them as the only alternative to the other, inadequate sources of compensation. And, officials agreed that more revenue and publicity were essential to achieving their program's goals.

In particular, although board officials mentioned several different program goals, several were agreed upon. All mentioned supplying financial relief to crime victims. And, all officials also claimed that their program was designed to recognize a "social problem," and to show concern for the crime's effect on the victim.

Other views as to compensation's purpose varied, however, and were even, to some extent, contradictory. A couple of officials, for example, pushed the board's role as an "advocate" for crime victims, while a couple of others expressly disavowed that function. Other disagreements occurred over whether compensation plans were designed to "appease" victims and the general public against growing disenchantment with government and criminal justice. One official described victim compensation's initiation as "very political." Another mentioned the desire for "social stability," and also indicated that victim compensation in his state (New York) was adopted partially as a favorable "public relations technique" for legislators, and to "calm people down about the crime problem."

A final difference among some officials derived from whether or not to view claimants as "welfare cases." Clearly, New Jersey's plan is not a welfare program, since victims need not demonstrate financial hardship to qualify for compensation, and since claimants from varying economic classes have recovered under the program. But, in New York, the question of welfare is considerably less clear. Claimants must satisfy a "needs test" in order to qualify, which largely reduces those eligible to persons who would qualify for welfare. Apparently, at least one New York board member agrees, but the other claimed it was not a welfare program because many claimants were employed, and only needed the assistance because of the victimization. He claimed that applicants were mainly "working stiffs," but ignored the fact that many of our welfare programs require recipients to work.

Some officials also claimed that ineffective law enforcement helped produce the compensation programs. In fact, one went so far as to argue that government had violated its "contract" with the public by failing to provide reliable crime prevention. A difference of opinion arose, however, about what effect compensation should or could have on law enforcement.

A couple of administrators, for example, indicated that compensation was a "swing away" from crime prevention. That is, they claimed that policymakers had decided to divert resources from the beginning of the criminal process to the end, and thus "compensate" for crime prevention's failure. Others, however, indicated that compensation was provided not to divert attention away from law-enforcement, nor to merely "patch up" unprevented harms with "band-aids," but rather to actually help in law enforcement. They considered victim compensation to be a part of the criminal process, and argued that granting compensation would cause victims to cooperate more with law-enforcement officials, which in turn would enhance crime prevention and criminal apprehension. Thus, victim compensation would help decrease crime, and allow "people to be able to walk around without fear." Another official did not deny that such a goal was in policymakers' minds, but doubted that it was actually being accomplished.

Board members' views of victim compensation's goals and functions are instructive when compared to those mentioned by the lawmakers who created the programs. Whereas policymakers in both states apparently avoided basing compensation on government liability or negligence, at least one board official disagreed. Lawmakers also apparently acted on humanitarian grounds at least to some extent, and this was widely seconded by board officials. Although policymakers imposed extensive monetary restrictions on their programs, one of their objectives was to allow financial recovery for at least some victims, and this also was echoed by board officials.

In sum, the greatest differences of opinion between lawmakers and board administrators existed over the programs' political and crime-prevention goals, as well as over their welfare basis. The welfare issue was only appropriate to New York's "serious financial hardship" test, but whereas lawmakers and at least one board member were unwilling to call their program "welfare," at least one official was. Disagreement on both boards also centered around the political and law-enforcement motives for victim compensation. Lawmakers also were split on the law-enforcement issue, although most championed this goal. As for political intentions, few were expressed clearly by lawmakers, but in this case, actions (indicating the desire to gain votes and curb disenchantment) seemed to speak louder than words.

All officials, for reasons that might be related to their positions, favored government disbursement of compensation instead of alternative methods. Although a couple memtioned the government's responsibility, the others merely saw government involvement as more practical than the alternatives. One administrator claimed that private agencies were "too paternalistic." Several officials felt that insurance would burden the victim, and that many victims could not afford coverage. One official argued for compensation combined with court-ordered restitution from the criminal to the victim, but another found this too impractical and too focused on the criminal instead of on the victim.

A couple of officials cited civil suits as an ineffective alternative as well. And, one final, interesting view was that private sources of compensation would regard their task as merely "a job," and would not approach their work "with enough zeal" as would government officials. Clearly, board officials considered victim compensation as providing an "effective" means of relief for crime victims.

Board officials also were questioned about the government's real level of commitment to the programs, and their publicity. All the officials claimed, not unnaturally, that their program was underfinanced. They admitted the limited commitment by lawmakers to the range and effectiveness of their programs. At least one official from each board also indicated that limited publicity was designed to forestall a "flood" of applications. This was feared, however, not because it might give victims expectations that could not be fulfilled[4], but rather because legislators wanted to restrict budgets, and board administrators wanted to avoid case backlogs.

Despite much caution about publicizing each program, board officials indicated that eventually each board did attempt to make its activities more visible. The programs were advertised through the media, on radio, television, and in the press. Brochures were distributed to social agencies and medical facilities. Attempts also were made to induce law-enforcement officials to inform victims about compensation. In fact, in New York City, police officers finally were required by law to tell victims about their possible eligibility for compensation.

These publicity campaigns, however, produced mixed reactions among board administrators. New Jersey officials agreed that the publicity produced a tremendous increase in claims, but while two of that state's administrators criticized its adverse effects on case backlogs, one official welcomed the flood of cases with the hope that it would induce legislators to increase appropriations and expand the program. In New York, however, the consensus was that the publicity had not increased the caseload that significantly. One official in that state complained that police officers were not actually informing victims about compensation, and indicated that the board had complained to the mayor.

The concern about publicity's effect on the boards' work was mixed, but all respondents admitted that workloads were overwhelming and that backlogs were extensive. One official also noted that many successful applicants had not yet been paid. Despite increased publicity, each state's commitment to victim compensation clearly was limited in the eyes of board officials.

The foregoing differences among board officials over compensation's purposes and goals further distinguishes the "advocate" and "neutral" roles. The advocate seeks an activist stance for the board on the victim's behalf, emphasizes public relations as legislators' major motive for instituting compensation, disavows a limited, welfare approach for the board, claims that compensation actually helps control crime, argues that government owes victims payments for crime, and seeks more program publicity. The neutral official, however, supports a limited, non-activist board, cites victim needs as having produced compensation programs, comes closer to admitting a welfare basis for compensation, claims little effect for compensation on crime, argues that government does not owe victims compensation, and questions more publicity for an already overburdened program.

Influences on Board Decision-Making

Although the foregoing official backgrounds and attitudes may influence board decisions, it is difficult to test that theory directly in this study. Officials were asked, however, to describe the influences on their behavior, and were questioned further about possible pressures, in particular. Not surprisingly, none of those questioned admitted the effect of their backgrounds or attitudes on decision-making, but several other influences were admitted.

Among them were eligibility requirements (some of which officials disagreed with), financial constraints, claimant characteristics, quality of evidence, board investigations, criminal-justice officials, fellow board-members, and administrative problems. Other possible influences on decision-making were belittled, such as the media, judicial review, hearings, legal counsel, and politicians.

Eligibility Requirements

Each of the compensation programs has rather stringent eligibility requirements that are at least formally mandated. The importance of these rules for affecting decision-making was acknowledged by all officials. Board administrators differed, however, about each requirement's influence on outcomes, and in their support for the various rules.

Little disagreement existed over the validity of certain eligibility requirements[5]. All administrators agreed that reporting the crime to the police within a reasonable period of time[6] was appropriate. A consensus also was reached on having a reasonable time limit for making a compensation claim[7], and on requiring claimants to cooperate fully[8] with the board and with law-enforcement officials. And, all agreed that outside payments should be applied against the final award, with one official claiming (apparently in reference to workman's compensation) that the "difference is usually paid by employers." Finally, nobody disagreed with preventing recovery for victims who provoked, or who were otherwise involved in, the crimes committed against them, including one administrator who cited the case of a person who "tried to get himself stabbed" in order to recover. Another officials noted the case of the victims who were beaten in a tavern holdup when the reason they were there was to rob it themselves.

Most officials favored maintaining the property-loss exclusion, not out of insensitivity to this kind of loss but rather in recognition of the potential validation, administrative, and financial costs of property coverage. Less sympathy was felt toward possible claims of pain and suffering (losses for which also are excluded), but again, the main objections to such coverage were financial and administrative. These two factors were not universally offered to justify present eligibility requirements, but some disagreements existed as to when they might be overlooked during the decision-making process itself.

Board officials, for example, disagreed over minimum-loss and maximum-award limitations. Some felt they were justified, while others sought either liberalizing or totally eliminating the restrictions (despite the added costs). Opponents cited victims who were unjustifiably excluded because they lacked a minimum loss, and yet were poor enough so that their actual loss was nevertheless severe for them. Likewise, the critics of maximum awards noted their special severity in death cases. Some board officials supported the rule for a minimum time lost from work for fiscal reasons, while others claimed it imposed an unwarranted burden for some deserving claimants.

A final disagreement evoked some of the strongest responses. Some officials favored the rule excluding victims having a relationship with the offender, while others wanted to liberalize the restriction, or eliminate it entirely. Supporters of the relationship exclusion backed it either to curb fraud or, again, for financial reasons. One official claimed that the board should "steer clear of passionate crimes." Others disagreed, however, and one argued, for example, for waving the requirement in death cases, suggesting that such cases take the fraud argument (and the collusion between victim and offender which it implies) too far. One official, however, went even further, and very strongly indicated his displeasure with the relationship exclusion altogether.

Those favoring the relationship exclusion's liberalization indicated that the board's discretion allowed it to get around some of the "unjust" elimination of claims. Discretion also was mentioned for applying the most crucial eligibility requirement, the "needs test." Although only New York has this test, respondents from both states argued against this requirement. Interestingly, not one official in New Jersey felt that the lack of a "needs test" had any considerable effect on the board's financial or administrative burdens.

The New York administrators had expressed to legislators their opposition to the test (including statements in at least three of the board's annual reports), without any success. A continuing fear persisted about the potential costs of allowing all victims, regardless of means, to qualify. Some would suggest a lack of commitment as perhaps an even greater barrier to changing the policy. In any case, New York's administrators were apparently frustrated by the rule, but again admitted to using their discretion to try to bend the requirements when appropriate. For example, the board had agreed to exempt some objects of value, such as one's home or one year's salary, from its calculation of each claimant's need. This would allow a few more applicants to demonstrate financial hardship, but clearly it was not enough for more than one official.

Perhaps the most significant observation about eligibility requirements was the discretion used in applying at least some of the rules. Board members were conservative in estimating its potential effect on who is actually covered by compensation, but were nevertheless forthright in admitting to a "bending" of the rules.

The conservative estimate of discretion's effects may be justified in at least one area for the New York board. That is, when asked what were the leading causes of claims denials, New York administrators mentioned the failure to meet the "needs test" as a major reason. Apparently, "bending" the rules did not prevent this requirement from being one of the dominant obstacles to a New York victim's successful recovery.

The other major reason for being denied an award occurred in both programs. All officials agreed that many cases were discontinued because of the victim's lack of cooperation. Whether these claimants would have been disqualified (and perhaps knew so) on other grounds anyway is uncertain. With board officials hampered by large workloads, victims often are left with major burdens in promoting their cases, and one administrator admitted that it was "likely to be discouraging in sustaining one's claim."

Curiously, none of the officials mentioned financial or administrative considerations directly as a cause of denials. That is, although they universally lamented their case backlogs and financial limitations, none suggested their effect on claimants. The possibility that some vicitms gave up on their case because of the long wait was not mentioned by administrators. And, the undoubted effect of limited resources on determining awards and denials also was not mentioned.

Finally, only one official advocated adding eligibility requirements. He suggested a ban on covering victims of "rub outs." That is, he felt that some claimants were victims of their own participation in organized crime, and although perhaps not directly causing the crime against them, they were nevertheless undeserving applicants. How one differentiates between "rub outs" and "contract killings" (also apparently committed by organized crime) was not addressed.

Other Decision-Making Influences

Officials also were asked about other factors affecting their decisions, and some of the responses were quite illuminating for understanding board decision-making. Some factors were not considered influential. For example, officials discounted the media's effect and how it might report their activities. Also, the general public was not considered a restriction since so few knew about the board's daily activities. One official, however, claimed that the general public did support the restrictions on eligibility[9]. The threat of judicial review also was not considered as a crucial influence, perhaps because relatively few cases are appealed, or because most judicial reversals favor claimants.

Two more likely decision-making influences would appear to be hearings and legal counsel. But, officials clearly disputed this assumption. Hearings were admittedly influential when they occurred because they allowed the gathering of information that might "make" or "break" a case. But, administrators indicated that they occurred so infrequently[10] that they were only a minor factor in overall decision-making[11].

The impact of lawyers also was widely belittled. Many victims do not have counsel in the first place. For those who do, officials indicated that they were not very effective. One administrator noted that compensation cases were "too rare for lawyers to be really good at it." Another official indicated that many victims with counsel lost their cases, while other administrators discounted the influence of lawyers and legal arguments even in successful cases. Clearly, officials downplayed the effects of formal, legal reasoning, but were less clear on whether lawyers might not be more persuasive, nevertheless, than victims acting alone. At the very least, some question remains as to how effective counsel could be if compensation cases became a significant portion of their workload[12]. Only one official admitted the advantage of having counsel, and he advocated providing an attorney to claimants who needed one.

Despite frequently mentioning financial constraints in other contexts, they were not stressed as a decision-making influence. This was apparently due to the substantial limit that budgetary considerations already had imposed by narrowing the group of victims who would be eligible before each board. Officials could thus make their decisions knowing that they were already within accepted financial limitations. One administrator, for example, claimed that little budgetary oversight occurred, and that legislators were more concerned with the board's backlogs than with finances. This might be the case, but it does seem somewhat contrary (at least in New York) to the frequent expenditure reviews of the board conducted by that state's legislature.

Politicians, including legislators, were not stressed as influences outside of the budgetary restrictions they imposed. One member claimed that "politicians are insignificant." Party influences appeared to have little influence on a board member's decisions, as well. The governor, who appoints board members, also was not mentioned specifically. Currying favor with politicians seems to be important for receiving an appointment, but less so (in board officials' minds) for maintaining one's position on each board. But, to facilitate binding decisions, New York board officials also admitted to having to consider the Attorney General's and Comptroller's responses, both of whom can reopen cases and overrule decisions, and thus potentially can upset compensation awards. One of the members called it a "political contest."

The claimant's characteristics constitute another obvious decision-making influence. Obviously, they help determine whether an applicant satisfies the eligibility requirements. But, it is important to reiterate the importance board officials placed on satisfying one particular eligibility requirement: cooperation with the compensation board. Most administrators indicated the importance of receiving applicant's assistance, perhaps differentiating, therefore, the case outcomes for victims who merely met the bare minimum eligibility and cooperation requirements, and those whose efforts were more extensive.

Equally as obvious an influence on a victim's meeting the eligibility requirements is the kind and quality of evidence received by board members in each case. But, this relies on more than merely the case's actual merits and on the victim's cooperation. It hinges very strongly on investigators' work as well. Board members, especially in New York, admitted the strong influence of investigators, and examiners, as well. A considerable amount of "screening" occurs that limits the board members' caseloads. One official indicated that almost one-half the cases submitted to the board are screened by examiners who isolate obvious eligibility violations.

But, in those cases that are not obviously disqualified, investigators also are credited by board members as being important for determining what evidence is received by the board. Since members frequently decide cases based predominantly on this information, the investigator's influence on shaping evidence cannot be ignored. Board officials also indicated the possible influence of criminal-justice personnel. Although some official disagreement existed about whether victim compensation itself was a part of the criminal-justice process, at least several administrators admitted the need of police cooperation. An important part of a claims decision, for example, might rely on victim or offender characteristics that are found only in police records. Thus, diplomatic relations with the police department, and with the prosecutor's office as well, might be important for the quality of board decision-making.

Board officials also are influenced by each other. In addition to working closely with investigators, members also interact with other members. In New Jersey, decisions often are made after consultation, thus necessitating close official contact and communication. One administrator indicated that major differences were rare, and that minor ones were always "ironed out." In New York, although the decision-making is much more unilateral, the board members apparently still interact extensively, including discussing decision-making standards and criteria. Each board's chairman appears to have no more influence on decision guidelines than other members, and thus appears distinguished only by his extra administrative duties. Apparently, these extra duties are not perceived as influencing the chairman's decision to grant or deny awards.

The aforementioned decision guidelines provide, in themselves, important influences on compensation-board outcomes. They determine how statutory requirements actually are to be implemented. Interpreting the requirement, or even the aforementioned "bending" of the rules, potentially can affect the grant or denial of awards. In other words, the board officials' use of discretion allows the creation of, as one administrator called them, "informal guidelines" that go beyond legislative mandates.

Administrative Problems

Board officials cited several factors impeding program efficiency and effectiveness. Clearly, case backlogs and delay were great problems. New Jersey officials complained especially about insufficient staff. Some indications of inadequate pay advancements for staff also were evident.

Most administrative obstacles, however, apparently derived from having to depend on others outside each board. The frequent lack of victim cooperation caused frustration and considerable needless work (according to board members), such as when an investigation occurred but the case was dropped later because the claimant failed to keep in contact with the board. Another outside obstacle, of course, were financial constraints imposed by legislators.

The remaining external impediments to board effectiveness, however, were largely other criminal-justice officials. Although it was not cited as a frequent obstacle, sometimes the prosecutor's office would withhold important information from the board, or would request a processing delay pending the outcome of the court case. More frequently, at least in New York, obstacles were imposed by the Attorney General, who could veto board decisions.

And finally, board officials in both states were concerned about their relationship with the police. Officials on both boards, but especially in New Jersey, felt that police officers often impeded a case's processing because the compensation board relied on police records that frequently were withheld from board examination. One investigator cited his difficulties despite having interacted with the same police department for over six years.

Furthermore, in New York, board officials were concerned about how police officers' failure to tell victims about compensation was preventing more claims. Reduced claims do help the board's backlogs, but also subvert the program's goal of compensating, in the first place. And, although one official discounted the relationship between victim compensation and the criminal-justice process, most others welcomed the chance for more visibility in other areas of law enforcement, as well as the chance to become a part of the system.

Overall, board officials were willing to admit to few decision-making influences outside the formal rules, although board investigators, fellow board-members, and claimant characteristics provide some notable exceptions. The willingness of officials to admit to other influences was divided, and this helps to further define the differing roles adopted by board administrators.

That is, "advocates" were more willing to view victim compensation as a part of the political process, as compared to "neutrals" who were more likely to talk about impartial, administrative principles. Advocates also were more likely to pressure for increased expenditures to reduce the board's financial constraints, while neutrals were more content to work within existing budgets. And finally, advocates also were more willing to admit using discretion to manipulate the formal rules to some extent, expecially when not doing so would produce apparent injustices. Neutrals, on the other hand, while not unsympathetic to victims, were more likely to remain within the boundaries of the formal rules.

Impact of Victim Compensation

Finally, respondents were asked about the overall effect of their programs. Because of their strategic location, understanding the board members' perspectives about compensation's impact on victims, offenders, politicians, the general public, law-enforcement officials, and criminal justice generally, is worthwhile. Victim compensation is intended to have particular effects on these groups and institutions, and thus assessing administrators' views of its actual impact will be useful in beginning to evaluate such programs.

Overall, much disagreement exists among board officials over how well compensation is achieving its goals. In particular, board officials were asked their opinions of compensation's effect on crime victims. The answers showed some disagreement. Some officials, including the three from New Jersey, claimed that compensation had a positive impact on victims. They felt that the program improved victim attitudes and induced victims to get involved and cooperate, when otherwise they probably would not have done so. This, of course, is exactly what legislators hoped would occur. One official admitted that the awards were not enough, but that the property exclusion was not widely resented, and that claimants were aware of what they could hope to get when applying[13]. He went on to state that most complaints emphasized the problem of "not getting the award back quickly enough." Another official sharing this perspective claimed that applicants are "so amazed to get anything, that it is not important if it is inadequate." As we shall begin to see in the next chapter, victims often disagreed with this viewpoint.

A couple of administrators (including two from New York) also disagreed. They indicated that compensation was unsatisfactory for many victims who did receive awards, and non-existent for many victims who (many times unjustifiably) failed to quality. In their minds, these results could hardly produce positive attitudes and future cooperation. One of these officials cited victims' frequent disappointment in discovering they could not qualify; particularly "middle class applicants who failed to meet the needs test."

Board administrators also were asked how they felt victim compensation affected the community in general. Victim compensation's advocates often claim that such programs will appease the general public, even if they are never victimized and never receive compensation benefits. Although board officials agreed that this was possible if the public was aware of victim compensation, most questioned how well informed people were. One official claimed that even if it was known, "people don't care until victimized." Only one board member disagreed, claiming that recent publicity had made the public aware of victim compensation, and that people were grateful.

Victim compensation's supporters claim that the combination of appeasing or comforting the public and of improving the attitudes of actual victims, will cause more people to back law-enforcement efforts. The result should thus be less crime and better criminal justice. Board officials were questioned about these theories, but their opinions were mixed.

More than one-half the officials questioned did not believe that victim compensation was actually helping criminal justice. A couple indicated that whatever hopes had existed for such a goal had been dispelled by reality: "victim compensation is primarily here to make some awards, and that's the end of it." Another described it as "limited aid and comfort."

Since compensation's effects on offenders also might affect criminal justice, board officials also were questioned about them. All but one administrator disclaimed any effect on offenders, largely concluding that offenders also were unaware of victim compensation. A couple specifically rejected the contention of compensation's detractors that it might induce offenders' complacency about crime since victims would now be able to recover their losses. One of these two members argued that in fact "criminals are more apt to commit crime if the victim is ignored."

One other official disagreed, however, claiming that some offenders were aware of compensation but that rather than producing complacency, it would signal instead a new concern for victims that might bode increasing opposition to criminal activities in other ways. This official also was joined by another administrator (both from New Jersey) in disagreeing with doubts about compensation's effects on criminal justice. These officials felt that it did have an impact on crime in their state, and that the effects would increase. One of them also offered his view that compensation might reduce crime by dissuading victims from taking revenge, or by making crime unnecessary for financial survival after being victimized. Both agreed that their program was geared "toward better apprehension of criminals, and toward encouraging the report of crime."

Few officials commented very extensively on victim compensation's effects on politicians. But, one did claim that a part of the reason for the program's creation in the first place was to produce favorable political publicity. "Now," indicated another official, "money is the big thing," apparently alluding to the political problems of adequately financing the program without spending too much money. Another official defended legislators by denying their complacency toward crime, or lack of good intentions.

Most officials felt that their program had become a legitimate and important government unit, despite its limitations and problems. It often was felt to have a positive effect, even if not as extensively as officials would have liked. Less agreement, however, existed over whether compensation programs actually had become a part of the criminal-justice process in each state. Some officials felt strongly that their program contributed to law enforcement and had developed linkages with other criminal-justice personnel and offices, but other board officials had their doubts, such as one who complained that most policemen "don't even know about the program."

Finally, board officials were questioned about any unanticipated impacts or consequences of victim compensation. Most respondents could think of none. One official, however, felt that policymakers had misjudged the likelihood of fraud, and thus perhaps were too restrictive in some of their eligibility requirements. This had the adverse effect of denying awards to some deserving victims. This official also indicated that although the program was underfinanced, policymakers nevertheless created obstacles to recovery (such as deadlines and eligibility requirements) to save money when the actual costs of each claim were not as expensive as anticipated. The boards' complaints about budgetary restrictions derived from not being financed sufficiently to cover the number of claims, not the cost of each claim.

As one possibly negative impact of compensation plans (as they currently operate), board officials were asked about the possibly adverse attitudes created among victims denied awards. One administrator called the idea "hogwash," while most of the others were unsure. Only one official (in New York) was really receptive to the possibility. In fact, he argued that claimants denied an award might be even more disenchanted (if not now "bitter") about government and criminal justice than had the possibility of getting compensation never existed in the first place. He indicated that he had "had contact with many victims who were infuriated at not being able to meet the eligibility requirements." He claimed that he "wondered sometimes whether the program was making things worse" for some victims.

In sum, although some officials were reserved in assessing compensation's actual impact and achievement of its objectives, most credited their programs with having a clear and positive effect. The attitudinal difference about compensation's impact helps us complete the picture of official roles. Quite simply, "advocates" claim a far greater and widespread impact for their programs (and seek to expand it further) than do the "neutrals," who are more content with viewing victim compensation as a limited purpose program.

Conclusion

This chapter has examined the views and traits of victim-compensation officials so as to illuminate the effect of their backgrounds and attitudes on board decision-making and behavior, to assess their contribution to the programs' impact, to contrast board officials, lawmakers and crime victims, to characterize different official roles, and to make any distinctions possible between the two state's plans.

Gaining board membership is largely a matter of party patronage, and the officials promoted to the boards possess the middle class backgrounds common to most state bureaucrats. Their attitudes on criminal justice and government are predominantly conservative. They believe strongly in victim compensation but often are realistic about some of its limitations. They admit to some other influences on their decision-making, but stress the primary importance of board rules and regulations as determining case outcomes. And, they clearly believe that compensation is working and having a favorable impact.

Despite this composite description of official traits and attitudes, some notable distinctions can be made, and they largely define the separation between "advocates" and "neutrals." Advocates approach their work much more politically, challenge government and law-enforcement officials to do more for victims, adopt a broader view of what victim compensation is and can be, and generally are more activist on behalf of victims and their programs. Neutrals, on the other hand, are more bureaucratic and accept a more limited, but no less important, role for themselves and their programs on behalf of victims.

If some differences among board administrators exist, the distinctions between them and the crime victims they serve are even more striking, both in backgrounds and in attitudes. While the social and economic status of board officials is primarily white, middle class, and middle aged, most crime victims are minorities, working or lower class, and young. In attitudes, although both officials and victims lash out at criminals and inadequate law enforcement, the similarity ends there. Whereas administrators hold mainstream political viewpoints, are conservative, and believe in the system, many victims are alienated, and tend to place the blame more specifically on particular government and criminal-justice officials, as well as on the economic and social foundations of the society itself.

The next chapter will facilitate a further comparison between officials and victims since it will describe the latter's view of compensation's impact to contrast with the official perspectives that have been examined in this chapter. One will see how the gap between officials and victims widens.

One also can contrast administrators' views with those of lawmakers, upon which board officials must rely for cues as to how to run the programs. If we clearly and correctly have labelled board officials as conservative, then lawmakers are even moreso. That is, although many legislators have argued vigorously the merits of victim compensation, their fiscal and eligibility policies reflect very limited visions and programs. Most board officials, on the other hand, were at least somewhat (neutrals), and sometimes very much (advocates), more expansive in their views of compensation's goals and potential.

Although most differences among board officials did not divide neatly between the New Jersey and New York boards, some distinctions between the two programs' officials might be made. For example, various New York board officials were willing to challenge conventional wisdom in areas such as the causes of crime, and the motivations of legislators. In addition, New York administrators were more willing to admit the dissatisfaction of unsuccessful claimants. New Jersey officials were much more convinced that the public and victims understood their program's limits, and appreciated whatever help could be given.

And, a final difference between the two boards consists of each program's "atmosphere" as reflected in official responses about their work and attitudes, and in the author's observations of their work situation. New Jersey's board, partly because of its smaller size, appeared to be more low-keyed (despite the presence of a strong "advocate"), almost like a "family" operation. New Jersey administrators seems to fit together better, both temperamentally and psychologically, as a unit. New York's program, however, had more of a bureaucratic atmosphere, with more specialization, more personnel, more hierarchy, and clearly more diverging points of view about politics, criminal justice, and victim compensation.

What are the effects of the foregoing differences among officials, lawmakers, crime victims, and compensation programs? The impact is not entirely clear. But, one can observe that victim compensation's success might depend in the long run on who wins the battle between officials and lawmakers over the programs' proper scope. The success of board officials in broadening victim compensation may depend substantially on who dominates the boards: advocates or neutrals. The successful impact of compensation also might depend, in part, on whether background and attitudinal differences between victims and officials are reduced. And, all other things being equal, victims might find more satisfaction in the atmosphere existing at the New Jersey board than at the New York program.

The next chapter discusses the crime victim's overall experience and level of satisfaction with compensation. The foregoing pages have described in detail the administrative characteristics of the two compensation boards and then the backgrounds, attitudes, and decision-making context of the board officials. And now, finally, we must examine the victim's actual role in the compensation process, and the outcomes and attitudes it produces.

Notes

1. See questionnaire in Appendix E at end of text.

2. Since so many similarities exist between the members and investigators in both programs, they will be described together except where significant differences emerge. These officials are being described not necessarily as respresentative of all board administrators in the two states. Those actually questioned are being examined in particular

because they were the officials who made the decision in the cases involving the victims in this study.

3. All of the board officials in this study seemed to embody either the "advocate" or "neutral" role, but it is conceivable that yet a third kind of administrator exists or could exist. Although it would be illogical to assume that a person who was against victim compensation would ever be appointed as a board member (although people who are against constitutional rights often are appointed as judges), it is possible that an appointment might be made to counterbalance the activist views of other members. That is, especially in times of budgetary constraints, a governor might think it wise to place someone on the board who can restrain the board's spending or its expansion. This kind of appointee might be no less political than an "advocate," but his efforts would be devoted more toward checking instead of promoting the board's activities under conditions of financial restraint or reduced commitment. This kind of official necessarily would have a limited vision of the board's goals. He also would be appropriate if policymakers wanted to create a program, but purposely limit its tangible impact (although they have already done a good job of that despite the advocates and neutrals in New York and New Jersey), perhaps content merely with the symbolic effect of creating the program in the first place. Board officials appointed to help enact this kind of strategy might be called "reluctants."

4. As indicated in chapter three, it was hypothesized in this study that these unfulfilled expectations and their negative effects might be an unanticipated consequence of the programs.

5. These official views will be compared to victim attitudes in chapter nine.

6. New York had recently increased the amount of time to report the crime from 48 hours (which existed for the respondents in this study at the time of their victimization) to one week.

7. New York had recently increased the amount of time for making a claim from 90 days (which existed for the respondents in this study at the time of their victimization) to one year.

8. The amount of cooperation required from the victim with the compensation board and with the criminal-justice system was discretionary and within the power of board members to determine.

9. As will be noted in chapter nine, this view is not supported by the vast majority of victims (as one segment of the general public) questioned in this study.

10. This is confirmed by board reports which show that hearings occur in less 10% of the cases.

11. See, however, the impressions of those hearing as recorded by another observer (of the New York program), especially about the exercise of discretion, which is consistent with the present study's observations of both the New York and New Jersey boards. Herbert Edelhertz & Gilbert Geis, *Public Compensation to Victims of Crime* (New York: Praeger, 1974), 64-65.

12. This is despite the fact that both states have requirements mandating that at least two-thirds of the members be lawyers themselves, presumably so as to provide officials who can understand legal arguments.

13. This and several other positive views of compensation's effect will be disputed by attitudes expressed by the victims themselves, in chapter nine.

CHAPTER NINE
Victims in the Compensation Process

Thus far, this study has examined the characteristics of violent-crime victims, their victimization and post-victimization experiences in the system, and the impact of the criminal process on them and their attitudes. That examination has included both crime victims who did and did not use the compensation programs in their respective states. Evaluating victim compensation would be incomplete, however, without further describing the actual experiences of the crime victims who did make compensation claims. That is, in addition to understanding victims' role in earlier stages of the criminal process, and to understanding program officials and compensation-board operations, we also must examine the victim's involvement and attitudes in the compensation process itself.

Consequently, many inquiries were made about the compensation-board experience. But, they were asked of only about one-half of this study's victims since obviously the rest had been purposely selected because they lacked any contact with their state's compensation board. As a matter of fact, although this goal was largely realized in the control group of so-called "non-claimants," actually a couple of victims in each city had made a compensation claim. This miniscule number of exceptions, however, makes it impossible to draw any meaningful conclusions from their responses, but the small number does, fortunately, preserve the control group's validity for comparative purposes. These exceptions will be ignored, and instead, the emphasis will be on analyzing those victims who have been identified as "claimants."

In order to assess the compensation experience for claimant victims, respondents were asked about why they applied, about the problems and inconveniences they incurred pursuing their claims, about their case involvement, about their attitudes toward board members and requirements, about their ability to get an award, about their satisfaction with their case's outcome, and about compensation's effect on their past and future cooperation with the justice system. Through these inquiries, it is possible to not only assess victim-compensation's effects on actual victims, but also to compare victim perceptions with those of legislators and board officials.

Applying for Victim Compensation

As previously discussed (see chapter five), it appears that a victim's likelihood of discovering victim compensation is left purely to chance. Program publicity (at least about the actual application process) is quite scarce, with police officers and brochures constituting the dominant sources of what little announcement does exist. Thus, limits already restrict who can benefit from the programs. Clearly, the eligibility requirements constitute a further impediment to making claims, and also discourage at least some of those who learn about the programs. But, some victims hear about victim compensation and do actually apply, and thus we must examine why they do so.

Since prior experience might affect a person's future use of a service, respondents were asked[1] whether they had ever used their state's compensation program in the past. Predictably, only one victim in each city had applied before. And, when asked whether they were satisfied before, both indicated their dissatisfaction. Both claimed their displeasure derived from not having been granted an award. This result seems hardly an incentive for reapplying, but both victims did so nevertheless.

Respondents also were asked what caused them to apply for victim compensation in their most recent case (Table D.1)[2]. The largest category of victims (20%) claimed that they had done so because they felt they had a right to such benefits, such as those who said: "I pay my taxes, and I expect something in return for it," and "Criminals have rights, and so do I." This claim to compensation as a matter of right (especially since it constituted the largest group of responses) is significant because it indicates that victims feel they are not applying for (what is often considered demeaning) welfare. But, such a belief obviously clashes directly with the premise (the welfare approach) of the New York program.

Other reasons why victims used the compensation programs indicated the desire for financial aid (19%), such as "I lost a lot in the incident, and needed someway to get it back," and "It's about time they provided some help for victims." Many other respondents simply voiced the particular losses they sought to recompense, including medical (17%), property (14%), lost income (10%), and out-of-pocket (7%) losses.

In contrast to those viewing compensation as a right, some others (9%) did appear to regard it as a form of welfare, such as: "I am very poor, and I needed help," and "My unemployment ran out and so I applied (for compensation)." And finally, some victims (4%) applied for compensation because they sought restitution from the offender, obviously misunderstanding the source of these programs' funds. Overall, no statistically significant differences emerged between the Brooklyn and Newark samples in their reasons for making a compensation claim.

Respondents also were asked whether they had hesitated using the compensation programs. Almost one-third (32%) said they had hesitated, while over two-thirds (68%) had not (Table D.2).

When those who hesitated applying were asked why, a wide variety of responses were given (Table D.3). Clearly, the most dominant answer (42%) was that the victim thought the application was futile, such as those who indicated: "I can never win in these things," and "I didn't think they'd ever give me an award," and "I thought it was hopeless and I was right." The second source of hesitation derived from victims having been unsure how to proceed with a compensation claim (11%), such as: "I didn't know where to go, or what I would have to do."

Still others (9% each) either thought they were ineligible for an award or did not want to be put through another government bureaucracy. Adherents of the former view made comments such as: "I thought I would be eliminated by the rules," or "I didn't think my application would be on time," or "They hadn't caught the guy (offender) yet," Those complaining about the process, on the other hand, indicated: "I applied to these (kind of) agencies before, and it's ridiculous what you have to go through," and "It was just a hassle, like all the rest of them."

Respondents gave miscellaneous other reasons for their hesitancy, as well, including the time and bother of pursuing a case (7%), their desire to either forget the crime or their initial view of compensation as inappropriate (5% each), their fear about the application's cost or difficult forms (4% each), and their desire to avoid an investigation (2%). No significant differences in reasons for hesitating to apply emerged among the victims in the two samples.

Pursuing the Compensation Case

Board Hearings

Despite the hesitancy of some, obviously all of these "claimants" did eventually apply for compensation. It is important next to understand what respondents had to do to press their claim upon the compensation board. The most obvious vehicle of involvement in one's case would seem to be an appearance at a formal hearing about the case. But, only 13% of the respondents actually had such a hearing (Table D.4). This figure clearly is low, but nevertheless typical when compared to the average of 10% hearings held yearly by the two compensation boards. No significant differences occurred between the two samples, but the general lack of hearings in which to pursue one's case is important in itself.

Board Inconveniences

Whether or not the victim had an actual hearing, a wide variety of inconveniences potentially could hinder the pursuit of his case. Forty percent of the respondents cited problems taking time off from work (Table D.5), while 27%

mentioned transportation (Table D.6), and only 10% indicated child or elderly care (Table D.7). Although the inconveniences were not major, they affected victims who had no hearing as well as those who did, since evidence must be gathered by all claimants, whether it is presented formally at a hearing or not, and these interferences could prevent the collection of that information.

Those having had a formal hearing indicated other inconveniences including trouble locating the compensation board (Table D.8) or no place to wait (Table D.9) when they arrived (19% each), as well as those (57%) experiencing a poor hearing time (Table D.10). Again, no significant differences emerged between the separate samples on these problems.

Victims also were asked whether they had any problems with the compensation process in general, and almost one-half (45%) said they had (Table D.11). In particular, 16% of the respondents complained about completing the forms (Table D.12) (and, in fact, some victims had hesitated applying for this reason in the first place).

Three final difficulties might have had the most crucial influence on a claimant's success. Two-thirds of the respondents, for example, cited a difficulty getting witnesses for their case (Table 9.1). Brooklyn claimants (75%) were significantly (.05)[3] more inconvenienced by this problem than Newark claimants (57%), although the relationship (V=.21)[4] was not very strong[5].

Seventy-one percent of the victims also had problems gathering evidence for their cases (Table D.13) and 88% had difficulties getting a lawyer (Table D.14). These problems clearly were serious, but they apparently affected victims equally in both samples since no significant differences between the two groups emerged.

TABLE 9.1 INCONVENIENCE GETTING WITNESSES IN CASE

	ALL	Claimants		Non-Claimants	
		BKLN	NEWK	BKLN	NEWK
	%	%	%	%	%
YES	112 (33) 67	64 (75) 75	45 (57) 57	2 (02) 100	1 (01) 50
NO	56 (16) 33	21 (25) 25	34 (43) 43	0	1 (01) 50
NA	174 (51)	0	0	96 (98)	78 (98)
	342	85	79	98	80
(S=.05) (V=.21)					

Participation in the Compensation Case

Case Involvement

If their desire to become substantively or meaningfully involved in the criminal case (see chapter six) indicates their desire to participate in their compensation case, then the victims in this study would be expected to want a great deal of involvement. But, when asked whether they were satisfied with their involvement in their compensation claim, only a very small number (14%) were content, while 18% were somewhat satisfied, and over two-thirds (68%) were dissatisfied (Table 9.2). Newark victims were significantly (.05) less discontent with their involvement than Brooklyn victims, although the relationship was fairly weak (V = .19).

When those victims who were at least somewhat satisfied with their involvement were asked why, most mentioned the compensation board's responsiveness during the case (70%), while the remainder cited the board's informing them about their case (30%) (Table D.15).

Those dissatisfied with their involvement mostly were discontent because they felt the process was too difficult (35%). The second group complained about not being able to get an attorney (24%), followed by not being kept informed about their case (17%), the board's lack of concern (16%), and their inability to get a hearing (9%) (Table D.16). No significant differences emerged between the samples in victims' reasons either for satisfaction or dissatisfaction with their case involvement.

The amount of information the victim had about his case already appears to strongly affect his relative satisfaction with his case, but respondents were asked directly about the matter, as well. Only 23% indicated their satisfaction with their information about their case and its progress, while 29% were somewhat satisfied, and almost one-half (48%) were dissatisfied (Table D.17). Again, no significant differences occurred between the separate samples.

TABLE 9.2 SATISFIED COMPENSATICN CASE INVOLVEMENT

	ALL	Claimants BKLN	Claimants NEWK	Non-Claimants BKLN	Non-Claimants NEWK
	%	%	%	%	%
SATIS	24 (07) 14	9 (11) 11	14 (18) 18	0	1 (01) 01
SOME	30 (09) 18	11 (13) 13	18 (23) 23	1 (01) 50	0
UNSAT	1 14 (33) 68	65 (77) 77	47 (60) 60	1 (01) 50	0
NA	174 (51)	0	0	96 (98)	78 (98)
(S=.05) (V=.19)					

Length of Case

Victims might conceivably be concerned not only with this information, but also with how quickly their claim is being processed. Since one of the board administrators' major complaints was their backlog of cases, it was no surprise to find so little victim satisfaction (11%) with their case's speed. Some other victims were somewhat satisfied (21%), but the vast majority (67%) clearly were dissatisfied with their case's length (Table D.18). The responses of victims to this inquiry showed no significant differences between the samples.

When one examines actually how long the compensation cases for these victims took, it is no mystery why the dissatisfaction is so pronounced. Almost one-half (47%) of the cases lasted between 12 and 18 months, followed by 37% lasting between 18 and 24 months, 12% lasting between 24 and 30 months, 3% lasting between 6 and 12 months, and 1% taking less than six months (Table 9.3). It is also not surprising (but nevertheless important), based on each board's reported case backlogs, that the claims of Brooklyn victims (most of whose cases took between 12 and 18 months) were processed significantly (.01) faster than those of Newark victims (most of whose cases took between 18 and 24 months), and the relationship (V=.58) was considerably strong.

Assessing Board Members and Requirements

Board Members

As with criminal-justice officials, it was important to have victims evaluate board administrators to help understand what kind of job these personnel have been doing, and what kinds of attitudes the compensation experience is produc-

TABLE 9.3 LENGTH COMPENSATION CASE (MONTHS)

		Claimants		Non-Claimants	
	ALL	BKLN	NEWK	BKLN	NEWK
	%	%	%	%	%
NA	175 (51)	0	1	96 (98)	78 (97)
0 - 6	2 (01) 01	1 (01) 01	1 (01) 01	0	0
6-12	5 (02) 03	4 (05) 05	1 (01) 01	0	0
12-18	78 (23) 47	50 (59) 59	27 (34) 34	1 (01) 50	0
18-24	62 (18) 37	20 (24) 24	39 (49) 49	1 (01) 50	2 (3) 100
24-30	20 (06) 12	10 (12)	10 (3)	0	0
	342	85	79	98	80
(S=.01) (V=.58)					

ing among the victims who use such programs. Respondents were asked their impressions of the board officials, and only 20% were favorable, while another 20% were unsure, and a considerable number (60%) were unfavorable (Table 9.4). Newark claimants (27% favorable) were significantly (.05) less negative toward board members than Brooklyn claimants (14% favorable), however, although the relationship was not very strong (V=.20).

Respondents also were asked more specifically about the board and its members. First, they were asked if the board had been fair in their case, but only 20% said they thought so, while 5% did not know, and 75% denied the board's fairness (Table 9.5). Newark claimants were significantly (.01) more convinced of their board's fairness than Brooklyn claimants, but again the relationship was not very strong (V=.24).

Second, victims were asked whether they thought the board really was concerned about crime victims. Only 16% felt that their board was very concerned, while 24% felt it was somewhat concerned, and a clear majority (60%) denied any such concern (Table D.18). No significant differences emerged between the samples on this inquiry.

When victims' impressions of board officials, their fairness, and their concern are examined collectively[6], one can assess their overall attitudes toward administrators. One in five respondents indicated a favorable view of board officials, while 15% had mixed feelings, and 65% regarded administrators unfavorably (Table D.20). No significant differences arose between the two samples.

Eligibility Requirements

A victim's attitudes toward the compensation experience also might be reflected in his views of the major eligibility requirements imposed by each state's legislature, and enforced by each state's compensation board. Respondents were

TABLE 9.4 IMPRESSICN COMPENSATICN BOARD MEMBERS

		Claimants		Non-Claimants	
	ALL	BKLN	NEWK	BKLN	NEWK
	%	%	%	%	%
FAVOR	33 (10) 20	12 (14) 14	21 (27) 27	0	0
MIXED	33 (10) 20	18 (21) 21	13 (17) 17	1 (01) 50	1 (01) 50
UNFAV	102 (30) 60	55 (65) 65	45 (57) 57	1 (01) 50	1 (01) 50
NA	174 (51)	0	0	96 (98)	78 (98)
	342	85	79	98	80
(S=.05) (V=.20)					

TABLE 9.5 COMPENSATION BOARD FAIR

	ALL	Claimants		Non-Claimants	
		BKLN	NEWK	BKLN	NEWK
	%	%	%	%	%
YES	34 (10) 20	14 (16) 16	20 (25) 25	0	0
NO	125 (37) 75	68 (80) 80	55 (70) 70	1 (01) 50	1 (01) 50
DK	9 (03) 05	3 (04) 04	4 (05) 05	1 (01) 01	1 (01) 01
NA	174 (51)	0	0	96 (98)	78 (98)
	342	85	79	98	80

(S=.01) (V=.24)

asked about the need to report the crime to the police (with 48 hours in New York, and 30 days in New Jersey, at the time of this study) and the overwhelming majority (91%) agreed with this rule, with only 5% undecided, and 4% disapproving (Table D.21). And, claimants also were asked about the need to cooperate with law-enforcement officials. Somewhat fewer victims clearly approved (73%) this requirement, while 20% were undecided, and 7% disapproved (Table D.22). No significant differences emerged between the separate samples on these questions.

Victims also were asked about the ban on provoking the crime as a condition of being eligible for compensation. Almost all (97%) victims agreed with this condition, except 3% who were undecided, perhaps reflecting the uncertainties of relationship cases where the true instigator is often considerably unclear (Table D.23).

In addition, respondents were asked their views about the requirements that imposed financial limitations on making claims. For example, they were asked about the rule requiring a mimimum loss (at least $100 worth in each state at the time of this study), and practically all respondents (92%) were opposed, with 8% undecided, and less than 1% in agreement (Table D.24). And, respondents were asked about the maximum-award amount ($15,000 in New York and $10,000 in New Jersey at the time of this study) and again the disapproval was high, with well over one-half (62%) opposed, while 32% were undecided, and only 6% approved (Table D.25). Again, no significant differences occurred between the samples on these questions.

Finally, respondents were asked about two further financial requirements, beginning with the rule requiring that outside awards be subtracted from board payments. About 60% approved, 21% were undecided, and 19% disagreed (Table D.26). And second, victims were asked how they felt about the rule requiring at least two week of missed work in order to qualify for lost-income payments.

Practically nobody (2%) agreed with this rule, while 3% were undecided, and 95% disapproved (Table D.27). Again, the separate samples were consistent with these averages.

When one examines these rules collectively[7] to assess their overall support by victims, the responses are very indecisive. While an equal amount (4% each) either clearly supported or opposed the rules, the vast majority (92%) were uncertain (Table D.28), although the tone of their comments about the rules was clearly negative. No significant differences characterized the two samples, however.

The Compensation Decision and Its Impact

Case Outcome

Beyond a victim's satisfaction with his compensation-case involvement, and with the board and its regulations, a claimant is presumably most interested in receiving an award. Thus, this ultimate decision would seem to be greatly important to a victim's welfare, as well as to his attitudes toward the compensation process. And, if one of this study's theses is correct, the case outcome will affect his general attitudes toward criminal justice and government, as well.

To assess the compensation decision and its impact, victims were asked initially simply whether they had gotten an award. Only 38% of the applicants were given an award, while 62% had their claims denied (Table D.29). These figures corresponded to the average percentage of awards for all claims considered by the compensation boards in the years surrounding this study. No significant differences emerged between the two samples. Each of the compensation boards lists in its annual report a summary of the reasons for denying awards. For the year of this study, New York's report indicates that more than one-half (52%) of the denials were caused by insufficient information and cooperation having been supplied by the claimant, followed by numerous miscellaneous reasons (18%), no minimum eligibility (6%), workman's compensation pending (5%), withdrawn applications or no serious financial hardship or no cooperation with the police or unable to locate claimant or the claimant's provocation or the claimant's ineligibility (3% each), and a victim-offender relationship or no crime or an ineligible auto claim or no physical injury (1%) (Table D.30)[8].

When those New York (Brooklyn) victims whose claims were denied were asked why they thought they were rejected, the answers differed considerably from the board report. The largest category of responses (28%) claimed that the board's unfairness produced the denial, followed by no lost earnings (17%), no minimum loss (13%), either a victim-offender relationship or an insufficient loss or no serious financial hardship (11% each), and no cooperation with law-enforcement officials (6%), and withdrawn applications (2%) (Table D.31).

For the same year, New Jersey's report indicated that failing to meet the minimum requirements (33%) was the main reason for a claim's denial, followed by insufficient cooperation (17%), provocation (14%), no police report (9%), no compensable loss (7%), an untimely claim (6%), miscellaneous reasons (4%), a victim-offender relationship (3%), and a withdrawn application (2%) (Table D.32)[9].

In comparison, however, the New Jersey (Newark) victims in this study claimed they were denied compensation for the following reasons: the board's unfairness (34%), a victim-offender relationship (17%), no lost earnings (13%), no reimbursable loss (11%), no minimum loss (9%), no financial need (6%), no cooperation with law-enforcement officials (4%), and either a late claim or provocation or the receipt of other payments (2% each) (Table D.31). Although the victims reasons for their claims denials differed noticeably from their respective state's official version, no significant differences emerged between the two cities in the reasons given. In fact, the responses were remarkably similar. It is also interesting to note that the major reason (the board's unfairness) mentioned by victims in both samples was subjective, instead of objectively attributing it to failing to satisfy particular requirements.

Respondents also were asked whether they actually expected an award when they applied. Almost two-thirds (64%) said they had, while only 36% claimed they had not (Table D.33). When those victims who had expected an award (N=106) were asked why, almost one-third (32%) claimed that granting awards was the government's duty, followed by either trusting the government to deliver or because they were told they would get an award (26% each), and finally, because they believed they had legitimate losses (22%) (Table D.34). Again, no significant differences emerged between the victims in the two samples.

Fewer respondents (N=63) had not expected an award when they applied. When asked why, almost one-half (48%) believed that government was unfair, followed by either feeling they were ineligible or having heard that practically no awards were granted (14% each), feeling fatalistic (13%), and believing that the government's inefficiency would deny them an award (11%) (Table D.35). No meaningful differences appeared between the two groups of claimants.

Case Satisfaction

Since victims can appeal their denials, respondents were asked whether they had done so. Only 3% sought review of their case, however, while 97% had not (Table D.36). And, none of the cases (N=5) was appealed successfully (Table D.37). No significant differences emerged between the two samples of victims.

To help assess the victims' overall impressions of the compensation experience (presumably including their view of their involvement, the board members, requirements, and decisions) respondents were asked simply whether they were satisfied with the outcome of their case. Only 14% (less than one-third of those who even managed to get an award) expressed their satisfaction, while 18% were somewhat satisfied, but over two-thirds (68%) were dissatisfied (Table 9.6)! This level of dissatisfaction constitutes a strong blow to the idea of compensation's improving victim attitudes. But, Newark claimants were significantly (.05) more satisfied (20%) than Brooklyn claimants (8%), with a fairly strong relationship (V=.43) emerging.

Those claiming they were at least somewhat satisfied with their case's outcome (N=56) were asked why. The largest category of responses (38%) included victims who were happy that they gotten at least some award. Almost as many (36%) were pleased with having received "an" award, presumably one they felt they deserved, followed by being gratified to receive "some" government assistance (18%), and satisfied with the board's concern (9%) (Table D.38). The reasons for being satisfied were consistent between the two samples.

Most claimants, however, were dissatisfied with their claim's outcome (N=112), and when asked why, they indicated their disappointment ("I really thought I would be reimbursed but ended up with nothing"), if not anger ("It's the same old story; nobody gives a damn about us; we just get screwed") about not getting an award (45%) (Table D.39). Others complained that the board was unfair (25%), such as: "I knew I wouldn't get a fair shake with those people; they didn't really care about what happened," or "They say I didn't qualify; it's just another injustice." It is significant that some victims received an award and yet were dissatisfied because they believed they got less than they deserved (14%), such as: "This is just a pittance of what I lost to that guy," and "How do they expect me to pay my bills with what they gave me?"

Other dissatisfied respondents indicated those angered by their case's delay (5%), such as: "I waited forever, and got nothing," and "It took over a year of hassles, and it just wasn't worth it." An equal number (5%) were dissatisfied with the board's procedures, such as: "I had to hire a lawyer because I couldn't

TABLE 9.6 SATISFIED CCMFENSATICN CASE OUTCCME

	ALL	Claimants		Non-Claimants	
		BKLN	NEWK	BKLN	NEWK
	%	%	%	%	%
SATIS	24 (07) 14	8 (09) 09	16 (20) 20	0	0
SOME	32 (09) 19	14 (16) 16	16 (20) 20	1 (01) 50	1 (01) 50
UNSAT	112 (32) 67	63 (74) 74	47 (60) 60	1 (01) 50	1 (01) 50
NA	174 (51)	0	0	96 (98)	78 (98)
	342	85	79	98	80
(S=.05) (V=.43)					

figure out what to do," and "They just wouldn't stop asking me for information just like I was on trial." And finally, another 5% complained about the cost of making their claim, such as: "I wasted a lot of money pursuing the thing and where did it get me?" and "My award just covered the costs of making a claim; it was ridiculous." As with those satisfied with their case's outcome, no significant differences between the two samples occurred for dissatisfied victims.

Effects of Compensation Process

Victim compensation's advocates often have claimed that such programs will produce the benefit of inducing at least victims, if not citizens generally, to cooperate with law-enforcement officials. To help test this theory, respondents were asked simply whether their desire for compensation influenced their cooperation with the criminal-justice personnel in their case. Although it may not have been the only reason they decided to cooperate, a large majority (79%) admitted that an award was one of their motivations, while only 21% claimed it had no effect (Table D.40). No significant differences emerged between the two groups of victims in their motivation.

Since victim compensation's supporters also have claimed that such programs will induce a claimant's future cooperation, respondents were asked just that (Table D.41). Presumably influenced not only by the program's mere existence, but also by their recent involvement, the largest category of responses (36%) were all anti-criminal justice in one way or another. Some of the comments included: "The whole system stinks; I'm clearing out as soon as I can," and "The police don't protect us and the judges let the criminals go and then we don't get paid like we're supposed to," and "Their all a bunch of crooked crooks," and "The hassles of that program, and the tiny payment show that they don't care, so why should I," and "Compensation is a joke and so is the whole process."

Almost as many (31%) disgruntled victims indicated more specifically their intention not to cooperate in the future. Responses included: "What incentive have I got when I am not given money to make up my losses," and "If I'm ever victimized again, and I wouldn't be surprised if I was with police protection what it is, then I won't set foot near a court, and even then, I'll take care of it myself in the future," and "Why should I cooperate; nobody cares about me," and "Getting no payment was just another lie; I've had enough of them."

A few respondents, however, were more positive about victim compensation's effect on their future participation in the criminal process. That is, 13% supported law-enforcement officials and the system generally, such as: "Well, the police did a real good job, and the payments help, too," and "These officials are trying to do their best, and the money shows that they at least care a little." An equal number of respondents (13%) were supportive by more specifically expressing their intention to cooperate, such as: "I think the program shows that victims are beginning to get a fair shake, and so I want to do my part," and "Well, I hope I'm not victimized again, but I would go along if it meant getting back my losses."

And finally, some (7%) indicated that victim compensation would have no effect on their willingness to cooperate. Some of these respondents were willing to cooperate anyway, such as: "I don't need money to get me to do what is right against these guys." But, most victims who denied compensation's influence were not willing to cooperate, including: "Even if I had gotten an award, I want no part of this again; I never should have pursued it in the first place," and "The money doesn't impress me; it's the least they could do but it won't get me back to court again." Among these responses, once again no significant differences occurred between the two samples.

Respondents also were asked whether or not they would ever apply for victim compensation again. Among those certain of their response, only one-quarter of the respondents predicted that they would, while three-quarters said they would not (Table D.42)! When those (N=47) who were either unsure or willing to reapply for compensation were asked why, only 45 responded, but the vast majority (76%) of them simply indicated their wish for an award, while 24% somehow attributed it to citizen's duty (Table D.43). No significant differences emerged between the separate samples.

A large majority of victims expressed their intention not to apply again, and thus they were asked why not (Table D.44). The largest category of responses (39%) mentioned their inability to get an award, including: "I got shafted the last time, so why will it be any different?" and "These kinds of things never pay for me." Almost one-third (32%) also complained about being unable to get an award, but specifically tied it to being ineligible, such as: "The rules make it impossible," and "I don't know how you can possibly qualify for that thing."

Others justified not reapplying by indicating the award's insufficiency (18%), including: "The amount they give you isn't related to the losses, so you get gyped," and "This little bit cannot make up for the loss." Still others complained about processing delays (6%), such as: "I can't wait forever again for a decision," and "Why should I wait for nothing." Some respondents claimed that the board was just not concerned with victims (3%), while a few (2%) others were angered by meagre involvement in their cases. Once again, no significant differences emerged between the two samples.

Finally, respondents were asked how to improve victim compensation. Most victims (29%) said that providing more or larger awards would be the best improvement. Almost as many others (26%), however, argued for easing the eligibility requirements, followed by more victim involvement (21%), less processing delays (13%), more board concern for victims (10%), and simplified procedures (2%) (Table D.45). No meaningful differences emerged between Brooklyn and Newark claimants.

Summary and Conclusion

Much has been claimed by compensation's advocates and by legislators who create such programs about their supposed effects on victims. Although somewhat more realistic in their expectations, board officials also share in attributing largely positive results for such programs. This chapter has provided some insight, however, into compensation's effects in the eyes of the victims themselves. These perceptions create a fairly coherent image of the compensation experience, and it must be compared to the official version. Doing so will help us to evaluate whether compensation achieves its intended goals, and consequently, whether the programs have been successful.

Practically no victims ever used a compensation program prior to the claim for which they were interviewed, and that small use was uniformly disappointing. A considerable number also hesitated before actually using their state's program, largely believing it to be futile, or failing to understand the procedures. And, when claimants did apply, they did so primarily because they regarded reimbursement as a right, and because they wanted aid. That most victims considered compensation a right is extremely significant, especially when contrasted to the welfare basis and "needs test" of the New York program. It also indicates how simply offering assistance can quickly transform a program into something to which people feel entitled.

Few victims were given a hearing, but contrary to official views that they are not that important for decision-making, they were very much regarded as the opposite by crime victims. Respondents specified various difficulties in pursuing their claims, some of which related to those few who were granted hearings. Thus, although finding the board's location and a place to wait were not significant problems, getting an inconvenient hearing time clearly was.

Other minor difficulties in pursuing one's case included child or elderly care, transportation, and filling out the forms. But, some considerable problems emerged in other areas, such as (in increasing prevalence) taking time off from work, the compensation process, being unable to get witnesses and evidence, and most prominently, finding it difficult to get a lawyer.

Many, if not all, of these difficulties were not mentioned by board members in their interviews, and yet were very significant for the victims. These problems would seem to be especially important in New York, whose board decided several years ago that because of extensive workloads, promoting one's case (and providing the requisite evidence and so on) would have to be placed more in the hands of the claimants themselves, instead of with the board. Also, it is important to note that while most board officials shunned the value of lawyers in pursuing one's case, victims very much believed otherwise, largely because they felt that lawyers could guide them through what often was perceived as a difficult process.

Another measure of a victim's satisfaction with his case, his direct involvement, also was ignored in official interviews. But, not only were victims very dissatisfied with their involvement when asked directly about it, but they also often volunteered that complaint independently. Those few who were satisfied with their involvement claimed the board was responsive, but the vast majority of malcontents again complained about the process' difficulty and the problem of securing a lawyer to help them. Few were satisfied with the information they received about their case either.

Crime victims echoed the complaints of board administrators, however, about processing delays, since only a small number were satisfied with their case's speed. The fact that the average case lasted between 12 and 18 months, and often longer (up to 30 months), made this complaint easy to understand.

The respondents view of board members was lukewarm, and their fairness and concern for victims was even less respected. Although board members did not dwell much in their interviews on their image in the eyes of claimants, it is obviously not a very positive one.

The claimants' views of board regulations and requirements were mixed. Victims strongly agreed with board administrators (and obviously with the legislators who created the requirements) about the rules requiring the crime be reported to the police and forbidding victim provocation. Agreement was somewhat less pronounced (but nevertheless clear) about the need to cooperate with the board and law-enforcement officials, and the need to subtract other benefits from the compensation award.

Victims clearly disagreed, often severely, with legislators and sometimes with board administrators, however, about the financial requirements surrounding a successful claim. Respondents rejected the maximum-award limitation, and strongly disputed both the minimum-loss and minimum time-lost-at-work requirements. But, at least some board members agreed with these complaints, including some administrators who have been trying to convince their legislators to change the rules.

As indicated in chapter six, respondents (claimants as well as non-claimants) were asked about some other, important rules governing claims in New York and New Jersey. In these cases, almost all the respondents, including those claimants analyzed in this chapter, strongly indicated that payments should be made to all, and not just to the poor, and that property loss should be reimbursed as well as physical injury. Both of these views conflict with New York's rules, and the latter conflicts with one of New Jersey's restrictions.

The view that compensation should not be dispensed as welfare strikes at the heart of New York's "needs" approach. As with some of the other requirements, some New York board officials agreed with the victims' complaints. For example, some board administrators strongly attacked the "needs test," and in fact the board actually has been formally petitioning against the rule for several years.

New Jersey board officials also uniformly opposed the welfare approach, which they obviously do not have to cope with themselves since their state grants compensation by right. One of that state's board officials also shared the victims' and some New York administrators' opposition to the property exclusion.

The validity of the relationship exclusion was the final rule disputed. While most claimants agreed with this limit, they are undoubtedly a poor gauge of this rule's validity since more than any other regulation, this exclusion is made perfectly clear to prospective applicants. Thus, claimants are probably victims who survived an initial period of self-selection and exclusion among would-be applicants. A better gauge of victims' support for the relationship rule might be found among non-claimants, a majority of whom opposed the exclusion. And, once again, they were not alone since some of the board administrators from each state rejected the requirement as well. In sum, remarkable agreement about appropriate rules exists between a strong majority of victims, and at least some of the two board's officials, and yet although many more rules are opposed than supported, they nevertheless persist.

The number of victims in the study receiving awards was just about average for the two boards, but this level was meagre considering that almost two-thirds of all claims were rejected. The reasons given by the victims differed considerably from official reasons, since the board reports emphasized a lack of cooperation and failing to meet minimum requirements as the major causes of denials, while the board's unfairness was blamed largely among the victims themselves. The respondents' conclusions were obviously subjective, but perhaps not much less so than the official reasons, since the amount of cooperation (the reports' major reason for denial) sufficient to pursue one's claim has never been defined.

The vast majority of claimants expected an award, obviously only to be disappointed in the end. Those expecting an award again emphasized the government's obligation (ie., their right), or the fact that they were told they would be reimbursed. Those who did not expect an award largely prejudged the government as being unfair.

It is not surprising that very few victims were satisfied with their case's outcome, including somewhat less than even those who did manage to get at least some award. Those few who were satisfied were happy to get an award, or at least some award, while those who were dissatisfied complained about no award and the board's unfairness.

The vast majority of claimants had been induced to cooperate with law-enforcement officials and to pursue their cases at least partially by the prospect of receiving compensation. This seems to indicate that most of those who eventually apply for compensation hear about the program, if at all, early in their case, and thus may, in fact, be influenced by a possible award. This coincides with the earlier finding that the police were the victims' primary source of information about victim compensation. Some board members expressed considerable concern that the police had not been informing victims about compensation at the crime scene despite being either required (in New York) or requested (in New Jersey) to do so. And yet, despite that undoubtedly well-grounded concern, police officers still outpaced several other sources of compensation-board publicity.

Undoubtedly affected by their recent compensation experience, respondents advanced a markedly different indication about their likely future cooperation when compared to their past enthusiasm. The vast majority berated the criminal process or vowed to avoid the justice system in the future, despite possibly getting compensated. And, once again, those willing to apply again numbered considerably less than even those who managed to get at least some award. Their desire to get an award motivated most of the potential reapplicants, while a perceived inability to get an award preoccupied those unlikely to reapply in the future.

Other reasons for future avoidance included justifications that undoubtedly were not anticipated by administrators or legislators, such as delay, insufficient awards, insufficient case involvement, and the board's inadequate concern for them as crime victims. The improvements suggested by claimants were dominated by the desire for more or higher awards and lowered eligibility requirements, followed by increased victim involvement, reduced delay, greater board concern for victims, and easier procedures. These suggestions, the various sources of victim dissatisfaction with their case outcomes, and their reasons for declining future crimnal-justice cooperation and compensation-board applications, indicate some crucial difficulties with the programs that are important for both administrators and legislators to heed.

Some of the practices, for example, opposed by at least some board officials, also were criticized by the claimants, and thus provide important backing for those administrators seeking legislative change. On the other hand, these complaints include many which have been ignored by administrators and legislators alike, including the desire for more case involvement, and the board's inadequate concern for victims. A final example is the frequently negative effect of only a partial award, which was a potential attitude wrongly dismissed by at least one administrator (in the official interviews) as "hogwash," Numerous comments indicate just the opposite, perhaps further demonstrating that victims will come to expect awards when a program is created, even if it is new. And, these victims will resent not receiving what they feel they deserve.

Victim compensation's advocates, the legislators who created such programs, and most board officials attribute to such plans certain positive effects, including paying a victim's losses, improving his attitudes toward law-enforcement officials and criminal justice, producing fuller victim cooperation with the justice system, and generally improving his attitudes toward government. These are the major goals of victim compensation as they have been stated repeatedly.

Unfortunately, these objectives have not been well achieved by New York's and New Jersey's compensation programs thusfar. First of all, only a very small proportion of all violent-crime victims apply for compensation in the first place, due in part to purposely restricted program publicity. And then, among those who do apply, only a very small number actually get an award, and many of them believe it is insufficient.

Second, with this record, it is not surprising that victims' attitudes (about compensation, and about criminal justice and government for that matter) among those having had contact with a compensation board are no better, and in many cases often worse, than those of victims with no such contact. And, it is possible that claimants have worse attitudes than non-claimants because of their elevated, but ultimately frustrated, expectations about getting an award.

Third, it is also no mystery that if such a poor compensation record does little to improve victim attitudes, it is also not likely to inspire a victim's future cooperation with the justice system. Thus, the goal of increased participation apparently has not been realized either. This also lends considerable doubt to the claim that increased involvement will help crime prevention.

And fourth, a more favorable impression of government generally hardly seems to have been generated among most claimants (see chapter six). Victims' frequent references to the unfairness of government, law enforcement, and the compensation boards, and victims' general unwillingness to participate any longer in a major governmental process such as the criminal-justice system, all seem to verify a failure in achieving pro-government attitudes and involvement.

These results obviously present a dismal picture of the attitudes of those who have applied for victim compensation. And yet, the underlying rationale of such programs may, in fact, be sound. That is, some victims were satisfactorily reimbursed and seem (see chapter ten) not to have been alienated by any other aspect of the compensation process. Thus, their attitudes toward law-enforcement officials, the compensation board, and criminal justice seem very positive. Furthermore, we already know that many victims were, in fact, induced by possible compensation to at least cooperate more readily in pursuing their cases against the offender. These are the major goals of victim compensation, but if such programs are producing some positive results, then unfortunately (for the plans' supporters), the programs are positively affecting only a very miniscule number of crime victims. But, at least it may indicate that it can be done.

New York vs. New Jersey Boards

The two compensation boards in question in this study, the one in New York and the one in New Jersey, have thusfar been presented almost as one. The fact that these programs are similar in so many ways justifies this treatment. But, some important, if not statistically significant, differences do exist between the outcomes and attitudes characterizing the victims using these boards.

First, Newark claimants were frequently more positive in their attitudes than

Brooklyn claimants. The former showed less hesitancy in applying for compensation, less difficulty in accumulating the necessary evidence for their case, less trouble in finding or needing a lawyer, less restrictions on information about their case, less criticism of the board's fairness and concern, less opposition to the board's requirements, less unwillingness to reapply for compensation or cooperate with law-enforcement officials in the future, and even less inclination to view victim compensation as a right, as compared to Brooklyn victims.

Some of the differences between the two samples were even more pronounced. Brooklyn claimants were significantly more troubled in getting witnesses for their case, and they also were considerably less satisfied with crucial aspects of their claim, including their involvement, their impression of board members, and their satisfaction with their case's outcome. Only about their case's speed were Brooklyn claimants significantly more positive than Newark claimants. Overall, these tendencies lend some credence to the hypothesis (made in this study) that New Jersey's program, despite its many similarities to the New York program, is producing more positive attitudes (or at least less negative ones) among its users. Exactly why these differences are occurring, and why, generally, claimant attitudes and cooperation are so uninspiring, must be examined in the next chapter. That is, although clearly differences between the two samples of claimants exist, and although it is obvious that the sentiments and motivations of many of the victims in both groups are poor, one must examine whether the victim-compensation programs themselves, as compared to the various other influences on crime victims examined in previous chapters, explain these differences and disincentives. In other words, now that the crime victims, their characteristics and attitudes, their victimization and post-victimization experiences, and their role in the compensation process have been described, it is necessary to look ahead, in this study's evaluation of victim-compensation programs, to the overall impact of such plans.

Notes

1. See questionnaire in Appendix E.
2. See numbered tables, all of which show no statistically significant differences, in Appendix D.
3. The test of statistical significance (S) used is chi square.
4. The test of strength of relationship used is Cramer's V.
5. Although all tables in this chapter show the results for the non-claimant samples, only the claimant samples were considered when statistical tests were performed.
6. This composite index of feelings toward board officials was comprised of the questions about the victim's impression of board administrators, his view of board fairness, and his estimate of the board's concern for victims. Some of the answers were recoded so that the values of each variable would range in order from favorable to unfavorable. When combined into a single index, a range of seven numeric values resulted: the lowest two

being labelled favorable, the next three being labelled mixed feelings, and the highest two being labelled unfavorable.

7. This composite index of support for board regulations was comprised of the questions inquiring about the victim's support for the need to report crime and cooperate with law-enforcement officials, to have a minimum loss and minimum time off from work, to limit maximum award requested, to subtract other payments, and to avoid provoking the crime, as prerequisites for receiving an award. Some of the answers were recoded so that the values of each variable would range in order from approval to disapproval. When combined into a single index, a range of fifteen numeric values resulted: the lowest four being labelled approval, the next seven being labelled uncertain, and the highest four being labelled disapproval.

8. Crime Victims Compensation Board, *1977-78 Annual Report* (Albany: State of New York, 1978), 8-9.

9. Violent Crimes Compensation Board, *1977 Annual Report* (Newark: State of New Jersey, 1978), 9.

CHAPTER TEN
Impact of Victim Compensation

The foregoing chapters have been devoted largely to describing, from the victims' perspective, their general attitudes and backgrounds, their victimization, and their post-victimization experiences, outcomes, and attitudes, including the role for some in the compensation process. This description has shown considerable discontent among crime victims, and a reluctance to participate in the criminal process in the future.

It has been a major purpose of this study to analyze the claim made by victim compensation's supporters that such programs will have an important positive impact on a victim's attitudes toward criminal justice and government, and on his likely future cooperation and participation. It is now appropriate, therefore, to test more systematically this theory. In doing so, we must first examine who applied for compensation and who did not, and what determined whether or not a claim was made. Next, we must determine who received an award and who did not, and what contributed to that outcome. Then, we must analyze the various, dominant measures of a victim's attitudes toward government, criminal justice, and the compensation process to determine what factors in each respondent's experience are associated with either his satisfaction or dissatisfaction with the system. And finally, we must study the major indicators of a victim's likely future participation in government, criminal justice, and the compensation process, and assess the determinants of that level of cooperation, as well.

It is possible that these attitudes could be best explained by aspects of a victim's background and criminal-justice experience instead of by his compensation experience. Obviously, for those victims not exposed to victim compensation, their attitudes would necessarily have to be associated with influences other than their contact with the compensation boards. But, if victim compensation's advocates are correct, then the compensation experience and its outcomes should be prominent among the various determinants of victim attitudes for those respondents who have had contact with a compensation board. Furthermore, any similarities among the four, separate samples in those factors that explain victim attitudes will presumably be reduced when key indicators of the compensation experience are added to the analysis.

In other words, the results of examining what contributes most to explaining victim attitudes should indicate some clear differences among the samples, largely related to whether or not the victims in the sample were exposed to the compensation process. Looking for these differences will help us assess compensation's impact. Unfortunately for victim-compensation's supporters, however, the previous chapters clearly have indicated that victim attitudes are predominantly negative, even among claimants, and thus if compensation can be shown to have an effect, it will be essentially that of contributing to that dissatifaction.

As a part of analyzing victim compensation's effect, this chapter will necessarily examine the determinants of who is applying for compensation and who is getting awards. In other words, it will assess who gets what from the compensation process, and attempt to explain why. It is already clear that only a miniscule number of those who potentially qualify for victim compensation are doing so, and thus we must examine why some apply and are beneficiaries, while others are not. Then, we can assess compensation's impact for those few who have had some experience before their state's compensation board.

Methodology of the Quantitative Analysis

In order to assess more systematically the determinants of who applies for compensation, who gets an award, and what impact (as compared to other possible influences) the compensation process and its outcomes have on victim attitudes, this chapter will show the results of a series of multivariate analyses of relevant dependent and independent variables. The dependent variables consist of those measures that best capture both the tangible and attitudinal outcomes of the victimization and post-victimization experiences, including the compensation process in particular. These dependent variables are:

1) whether or not the victim applied for compensation
2) whether or not a compensation award was received
3) whether or not the victim was paid by any other sources
4) whether or not the victim was satisfied with his compensation-case involvement
5) whether or not the victim approved of the compensation-board officials in his case
6) whether or not the victim was satisfied with his compensation-case outcome
7) whether or not the victim felt it was worthwhile coming to court
8) whether or not the victim approved of the criminal-justice officials in his case
9) whether or not the victim was satisfied with the criminal-case outcome
10) whether or not the victim felt that criminal-justice officials were doing all they could to cope with crime
11) whether or not the victim felt that government was responsive
12) whether or not the victim intended to apply to the compensation board in the future
13) whether or not the victim intended to get involved in the criminal process in the future
14) whether or not the victim intended to participate in government in the future

These variables can best be understood as measuring who gets paid after being victimized (variables 1-3), what are a victim's attitudes toward victim compensation, law-enforcement, and government (variables 4-11), and the extent to which victims are likely to participate in the compensation process, in the criminal-justice system, and in government generally in the future (variables 12-14).

What are the determinants of these outcomes and attitudes? Finding the answer lies in examining a series of independent variables that might, when combined, explain or predict a victim's responses on the dependent variables. To do so, multivariate analysis was used. In particular, discriminant function analysis was chosen as the statistical technique appropriate for the data in this study[1]. This kind of analysis is most suitable for studying noncontinuous dependent variables whose values are divided into two or three categories, such as apply/no apply (for compensation), award/no award (from compensation), government responsive/unresponsive, and so on. Discriminant analysis relies on a computer routine that separates cases into the appropriate categories (e.g., award/no award) with the help of the information contained in the independent variables. The independent variables are selected based on their hypothesized relationship with the dependent variable in question.

More specifically, the first group of independent variables selected for analysis included those indicators identified (in chapter three) as being theoretically linked with victim attitudes. For example, it was hypothesized that a victim's compensation-board experience would affect his attitudes not only about victim compensation, but also about criminal justice and government generally. Thus, for example, any inconveniences mentioned by victims in applying for compensation were isolated as being among the important independent variables that might affect victims' responses on the dependent variables.

In different stages of the analysis, some of the dependent variables also were considered, temporarily, as independent variables. For example, when analyzing what contributed to the responses on the dependent variable measuring whether or not the victim was satisfied with his compensation case, other dependent variables (see previous list), such as the victim's level of satisfaction with his compensation-case involvement, were used as independent predictors for that analysis, along with several other independent variables.

The rest of the independent variables were selected based on the results of a series of bivariate analyses that sought to identify, on a one-to-one basis, those variables that were the most highly correlated with the major dependent variables.

When all these independent variables were combined, they were then used in the discriminant analyses to seek the best prediction of each dependent variable, or the best separation of the categories (or values) for each of these variables. The predictive capability of the independent variables is measured by a canonical correlation coefficient, which indicates the strength of relationship. When the correlation is squared, it produces a value that indicates the percentage of variance in the dependent variable explained by the combination of independent variables used in each analysis.

In addition, discriminant analysis also allows one to assess the contribution made by each of the independent variables separately[2], which can then be converted into individual percentages. These percentages are derived from a statistic that indicates the change in Rao's V, which corresponds to the distance which a particular independent variable "moves" cases toward one category or another on the dependent variable. Finally, discriminant analysis also produces an additional statistic that indicates the percentage of cases in which the combination of independent variables correctly predicts the values of the dependent variable, and thus provides a further measure of the explanatory value of the independent variables selected for use in the analysis.

The final independent variables selected for each discriminant analysis result from a trial and error process that chooses among those variables that already have been identified as theoretically important. The process continues until the best "fit" occurs to account for the greatest variance in the dependent variable. Besides a process of inclusion and exclusion based on the main hypotheses of this study, some other independent variables also were eliminated because they were too highly interrelated with the other independent variables in the analysis. In other words, the variables were tested for multicollinearity[3], the presence of which would have jeopardized the validity of the analysis because it would have produced a measure of the predictive capacities of the independent variables that would have been artificially high.

The quantitative analysis used in this study is not statistically pure. The difficulties of conducting research in this area of criminal justice made sampling, for example, imperfect (see chapter three). Ideally, discriminant analysis requires completely random samples. The samples used in this study did not always meet that standard, but at the very worst were stratified, random samples. In other words, despite the imperfections, the statistical analysis was still well within the bounds of acceptable social-science research[4].

To guard against misleading findings, discriminant analysis also provides several tests of statistical significance. That is, using probability theory, a discriminant computer routine indicates the likelihood of relationships having emerged by chance, and only correlations that were significant at the .05 level or lower have been reported.

How each multivariate analysis is presented in this chapter depends on the question being addressed. Some questions (such as what determined who applied for compensation and who had not) are relevant to all the victims in the study considered together. Other questions (such as whether victims were satisfied with the criminal-case outcome) focus on all the victims but warrant a more specific breakdown of respondents into their respective samples for purposes of comparison. And, still other questions (such as whether victims were satisfied with their compensation-case outcomes) are relevant only to the two claimant samples.

Although it is often desirable to separate and contrast the individual samples, all the samples were uniform in the independent variables used to attempt to predict the dependent variable in each discriminant analysis. In other words, comparisons across samples will be among the relative contribution of the same combination of independent variables in each analysis, and not among independent variables that are selected uniquely for each sample to predict the dependent variable being examined. The tables will thus present the relative (in percentages) contribution of each set of independent variables for each sample listed separately, and then present the contributions for the claimant samples combined.

A major purpose of this chapter is to assess the impact of various measures of the compensation experience on dependent variables that reflect a victim's level of satisfaction with victim compensation, criminal justice, and government generally. Since the questions about victim compensation obviously were asked of only two (claimants) of the four samples in this study, it is necessary to engage in two separate, discriminant analyses of each dependent variable for these two samples.

That is, when considering what independent variables should be examined to assess their ability to predict each victim's responses to any given dependent variable, the victims in the claimant samples will (if we really want to consider the impact of victim compensation) necessarily possess a set of explanatory variables not available to non-claimants. Thus, for example, when we are examining the dependent variable that reflects a victim's level of satisfaction with criminal-justice officials, the number of independent variables that might affect this outcome will be larger among claimants than among non-claimants since in the case of the former we might also want to test the contribution of whether or not the victim received a compensation award as a result of his claim, or the effects of other indicators of his compensation experience.

Consequently, when appropriate, it is necessary first to conduct a discriminant analysis of each of the four samples using a set of independent variables that does not include any measures of the compensation experience. Then, a second discriminant analysis of the same dependent variable must be conducted only for the claimant samples using the same set of independent variables as in the first analysis plus an additional group of variables relevant to these victims' compensation experience. The two analyses will then be compared (including the comparative contributions for all claimants combined) to assess the extent to which the compensation variables add to explaining each dependent variable.

A uniform set of compensation variables has been selected which captures the essence of the compensation process and its outcomes. These variables include the following five measures:

1) the extent to which a victim was inconvenienced in pursuing his compensation case
2) the victim's relative satisfaction with compensation-board officials
3) the victim's relative satisfaction with his compensation-case outcome
4) the victim's relative satisfaction with his compensation-case involvement
5) whether or not the victim was given a compensation award

These will be the variables that are consistently used to help perform the second discriminant analysis when appropriate on each dependent variable for the claimant samples, as described above.

Similarly, two other major purposes of this chapter include assessing the impact of what city a victim comes from and whether or not a compensation claim is brought in the first place. These distinctions are important because it has been suggested by victim compensation's supporters that contact with the compensation programs will be associated with positive attitudes toward the plans as well as toward criminal justice and government generally. Furthermore, it has been hypothesized in this study that whichever state's compensation program victims encounter (and therefore which city victims are from) will be important for their attitudes as well. That is, it was predicted that contact with New Jersey's plan would produce more positive (or at least less negative) sentiments.

Using the distinction between claimants and non-claimants and between Brooklyn and Newark victims as independent variables in the following discriminant analyses will allow these hypotheses to be further tested. These variables, however, will be presented in a somewhat different fashion from the other independent variables being considered in this chapter. Since the following tables often divide this study's victims into the separate samples according to city and to the victim's claim status (either claimants or non-claimants), it would be inappropriate to consider these independent variables for these sub-analyses. But, each table also presents the results of a disciminant analysis for all victims, and thus it is in this calculation that the Brooklyn/Newark and claimant/non-claimant variables will be considered, when they are appropriate to the analysis[5].

The following pages will show the results of the multivariate analyses. Beginning with who gets what payments after being victimized, those factors associated with who applies for compensation, who receives an award, and who receives payments from alternative sources will be examined. Then, the analysis will examine victim attitudes. in particular, attitudes toward victim compensation will be studied by examining the factors associated with the victims' view of their court involvement, the law-enforcement officials in their case, the criminal-case outcome, and the work of criminal-justice personnel generally. And, attitudes toward government will be studied by examining the measures associated with the victims' faith in government's responsiveness.

Finally, the chapter will end with an explanation of the victims' willingness to participate in victim compensation, criminal justice, and government in the future. These levels of cooperation will be analyzed by examining the factors associated with a victims' relative willingness to use the compensation program again, to cooperate in the criminal-justice process again, and to participate in government in the future.

Who Gets Compensated After Victimization?

Obviously, the most prominent and immediate goal of compensation programs is to provide financial assistance to victims to help them recover their losses. Clearly, the foregoing chapters have indicated that this objective has not been realized since many victims never receive compensation awards. Some victims do recover some of their losses through other kinds of payments but they, too, are vastly insufficient. In fact, the inadequacy of these payments was one of the primary reasons for creating compensation programs in the first place.

Some victims, however, do come much closer to receiving an award (and some do successfully receive an award) than others. It is important to try to characterize the differences, therefore, between those victims who apply and those who do not apply for victim compensation, between those who receive an award and those who do not, and between those who receive some other kind of payments and those who do not.

Who Applies for Victim Compensation?

The number of victims in this study who applied for victim compensation almost equals the number who did not. What are the differences between these two groups, and what traits characterize victims who do apply for compensation and those who do not? Table 10.1 indicates the results of a discriminant analysis of those who applied for compensation. It shows a combination of variables that explains almost two-thirds (64%) of the decision whether or not to apply for compensation, and also correctly predicts this decision for the vast majority (82%) of the cases in the study.

The table also indicates that the greatest determinant of whether an application is made is whether the victim had ever heard of the program. Lack of awareness is a major problem since application information is so scarce. One way of discovering a compensation program, however, is through being helped by a victim-service center, and thus it is no surprise that this was highly correlated with making a claim, as well.

When a victim is aware of the program, what determines whether he will then apply? Initially, one might assume that a victim considers how his circumstances square with what he knows about the board's eligibility requirements. Table 10.1 indicates, therefore, that making a claim was related to being injured, to lacking a victim-offender relationship, and to being unemployed. Other board rules, however, did not apparently have an effect.

TABLE 10.1 APPLY FOR VICTIM COMPENSATION?

CANONICAL CORRELATION SQUARED		.64

% Explained Variance Acct. For By:

(+)	EVER HEARD OF VICTIM COMPENSATION	45
(+)	EVER HELPED BY VICTIM SERVICE CENTER	13
(+)	INJURED BY CRIME	8
(+)	HOW FEEL ABOUT HAVING COMPENSATION PROGRAM	7
(+)	RECEIVE OTHER PAYMENTS	5
(+)	HOW FEEL ABOUT CJS OFFICIALS IN CASE	4
(+)	EVER TRY AFFECT CITY COUNCIL BEFORE	4
(+)	POLITICAL EFFICACY	4
(+)	FEEL GOVERNMENT RESPONSIVE	3
(−)	VICTIM-OFFENDER RELATIONSHIP	3
(+)	PRIOR COURT INVOLVEMENT	2
(−)	OWN SOLUTION FOR VICTIMIZATION	2
(−)	EMPLOYED	1

% Cases Correctly Predicted	82
NUMBER OF CASES	333

Other factors contributing to making a claim include measures of a person's relative confidence in becoming involved in government activities. That is, applying for compensation was positively related to a victim's having tried to influence government before, to his desire to participate in government in the future, and to his belief in government's responsiveness. And, since a victim's impressions about the criminal-justice officials in his case also are associated with making a compensation claim, we can conclude perhaps that the victim decides, in part, whether government can help based on whether officials have helped him in his criminal case. Also related was whether a victim had been involved in the court system before, perhaps providing an extra opportunity to have heard about victim compensation.

Finally, but no less importantly, the decision to apply for compensation also seems related to a victim's experience with the alternatives. For example, a victim's decision to seek his own solution, usually as a result of his dissatisfaction with the criminal process, was positively related to his decision not to seek compensation. On the other hand, while one could perhaps expect that getting payments from other sources would also lessen a victim's tendency to apply, in fact, the opposite occurred.

Who Gets Compensation Awards?

Since only about one-half the victims in this study applied for compensation, our understanding of who actually received an award will be based on the chacteristics of only the Brooklyn and Newark claimant samples. These two samples were selected purposely to include recipients and non-recipients proportional to the overall board averages around the time of the study. Consequently, the comparisons are between the average of two-fifths of each sample who received an award and three-fifths who did not.

What characterizes those victims who fall into each category, and what factors are associated with getting or not getting an award? Table 10.2 provides some answers. First, it shows that the combination of variables it contains explains a considerable amount (68%) of the variance in whether or not a victim receives an award, and also correctly predicts either of these two outcomes for the vast majority (90%) of the cases in the two samples.

In particular, the most important determinant of receiving an award was not having collected payments from other sources. But, many other factors associated with getting an award relate to board regulations and economic status. Receiving an award was negatively associated with being related to the offender, or failing to sustain an injury. And, it is also negatively related to having higher

TABLE 10.2 COMPENSATION AWARD GRANTED?

		Bk Claim	Nk Claim	All
CANONICAL CORRELATION SQUARED		.77	.88	.68
% Explained Variance Acct. By:				
(-)	RECEIVE OTHER PAYMENTS	26	9	19
(+)	INJURED BY CRIME	6	27	18
(+)	CRIMINAL CASE OUTCOME	6	21	11
(-)	VICTIM-OFFENDER RELATIONSHIP	8	18	10
(-)	COMP. CASE INCONVENIENCE	13	3	10
(-)	INCOME	5	8	6
(-)	HOW INVOLVED COURT BEFORE	7	6	5
(+)	EMPLOYED	9	2	5
(-)	DROP CHARGES	6	5	5
(+)	APPEAR IN COURT	9	1	4
(-)	RACIAL BACKGROUND	3	0	1
(+)	NUMBER OF DEPENDENTS	2	0	1
% Cases Correctly Predicted		92	98	90
NUMBER OF CASES		85	79	164

incomes and few dependents to support. Ironically, unemployed victims also were less likely to get compensated than those who were employed (but not earning too much), perhaps reflecting both boards' rules about needing to miss at least two weeks work before recovering.

Finally, receiving an award also was associated with cooperating with law-enforcement officials, with the victim's innocence, and with miscellaneous other reasons. Awards were more likely to be denied if victims had never been to court, or if they had decided to drop charges, or if the criminal case ended in a dismissal or acquittal, or if the victim had been involved previously in the court system. And, getting an award was less likely when a victim was inconvenienced by the compensation board, such as in getting a lawyer, gathering evidence, providing information, and so on. Also, whites were proportionally more successful than non-whites in getting compensated.

Table 10.2 also indicates some important differences between the Brooklyn and Newark samples, and thus between the award decisions of the New York and New Jersey compensation boards. Receiving other payments and being inconvenienced by the compensation process had the greatest impact in Brooklyn, while injury, case outcome, and the victim-offender relationship had the greatest effect in Newark.

Who Gets Payments besides Victim Compensation?

This study has considered the availability of other kinds of payments, besides copensation awards, that might help victims recoup their losses. These alternatives include private and public insurance or other assistance, offender restitution, witness fees, "blood money" from the defendant or his counsel, and other forms of payment. Although these sources have been discussed as being quite inadequate in their assistance, it is nevertheless important to examine the characteristics of those victims who either did or did not recover from one of these alternatives.

After recoding to eliminate those few mentioning victim compensation, a discriminant function analysis was performed to analyze those factors contributing to a victim's financial recovery from sources other than victim compensation. Table 10.3 shows a combination of variables that explains between 32% and 84% of the variance in each sample, and which also correctly predicts whether or not a victim was paid in at least 87% of the cases in each sample.

More specifically, Table 10.3 reveals that receiving outside payments was related to the criminal-case outcome, to pursuing one's case against the assailant, to the crime's characteristics, and to the victim's background. That is, getting paid was positively associated with a criminal conviction (perhaps validating the legitimacy of the claim), and with the victim's arriving in court, making it to court each time he was asked, and not dropping charges.

In addition, experiencing one-on-one crimes of robbery, when the victim was

TABLE 10.3 RECEIVE PAYMENTS BESIDES VICTIM COMPENSATION?

CANON. CORREL. SQUARED	.58	.84	.32	.41	.49
% Explained Variance Acct. For By:	Bkln Claim	Bkln Non-Cl	Newk Claim	Newk Non-Cl	All Claim
(+) CRIM.CASE OUTCOME	9	9	35	7	17
(+) MAKE COURT EACH TIME	8	8	14	18	10
(-) KIND OF CRIME	8	23	7	8	12
(-) PROPERTY STOLEN	3	8	11	13	6
(+) USE SOC. SERVICES	9	5	19	0	9
(-) VICTIM-OFFEND. REL.	10	7	0	15	9
(+) NUMBER OF DEFENDANTS	6	7	7	11	8
(+) NUMBER OF DEPENDANTS	11	8	0	10	8
(+) APPEAR IN COURT	4	13	0	11	8
(+) INJURED FROM CRIME	12	11	0	0	7
(-) DROP CHARGES	7	0	6	7	4
(-) RACIAL BACKGROUND	12	0	0	0	2
% Cases Correct. Predict.	89	94	87	88	87
NUMBER OF CASES	98	74	80	66	318

less likely to get injured but more likely to lose property, relegated victims to a status that made financial recovery more difficult than for assault victims who were attacked, and injured, especially by more than one assailant. And, finally, victims who were white and who had more than one dependent were more likely to recover, as well as those using social-science agencies after their victimization.

Some notable differences exist among the separate samples in what contributes to whether or not a victim receives a payment. First, the combination of variables in Table 10.3 explains much less of the variance among Newark victims than among Brooklyn victims, although the predictive power of these variables is uniform, and strong, among all the samples. Second, each sample contains at least one independent variable which stands out among the others. Among Brooklyn non-claimants, a victim's racial background and injuries explains most of the variance, while for Newark non-claimants, the criminal-case outcome is most important. And, while the kind of crime was most crucial for Brooklyn claimants, the victim's ability to make it to court each time he was asked explains most of the variance among Newark claimants.

As indicated in this chapter's introduction, some of the potentially important, explanatory variables in this study derived from questions asked of only about one-half the victims. Those variables include various measures of the victim's compensation experience, since only claimants could provide answers to those kind of inquiries. It is important to examine whether these variables, when added to the analysis, might improve our ability to predict who receives payments aside from victim compensation. In this case, only one of the variables (see previous list of independent variables) could conceivably have an effect. Since the other compensation variables largely measure only a victim's own attitudes about the process, only the question of whether or not the victim received a compensation award could theoretically affect the receipt of other payments. In addition, we also are concerned with the contributions of a victim's city (Brooklyn vs. Newark), and his claim status (claimant vs. non-claimant). Table 10.4 presents the claimant samples, showing the effects of adding these variables as compared to their absence in Table 10.3.

The results of this second discriminant analysis indicate that these new variables have an important effect. First, when added to the analysis, the overall

TABLE 10.4 RECEIVE PAYMENTS BESIDES VICTIM COMPENSATION?

CANON. CORREL. SQUARED	.87	.68	.65
% Explained Variance Acct. For By:	Brooklyn Claimants	Newark Claimants	All
(-) VICTIM'S CITY	NA	NA	2
(+) APPLY COMPENSATION	NA	NA	5
(-) GET COMPENS. AWARD	11	10	12
(+) INJURED FROM CRIME	19	13	13
(+) CRIM. CASE OUTCOME	14	18	18
(-) VICTIM-OFFEND. REL.	3	16	7
(-) PROPERTY STOLEN	6	9	6
(+) USE SOCIAL SERVICES	5	8	7
(+) MAKE COURT EACH TIME	6	7	8
(+) NUMBER OF DEFENDANTS	6	6	6
(-) KIND OF CRIME	10	2	7
(+) NUMBER OF DEPENDENTS	12	0	4
(-) DROP CHARGES	0	9	3
(+) APPEAR IN COURT	7	2	2
% Cases Correct. Predict.	96	95	92 --
NUMBER OF CASES	85	79	164

amount of explained variance in the dependent variable for all claimants increases from 49% to 65%, and the predictive capacity of the independent variables increases from 87% to 90% (with corresponding increases in the two samples considered separately). And second, these new variables, in combination, explain almost one-fifth (19%) of the variance in the dependent variable when added to the analysis.

Obviously, this illustrates the impact of these variables on getting outside payments. A victim's ability to get a compensation award appears to be particularly influential on preventing outside payments, while being from Newark and failing to make a compensation claim in the first place contributes to a similar result.

Summary

Overall, the question of who gets compensated after victimization requires a somewhat complicated answer. But, in its briefest form, applying for compensation depends most prominently on discovering the program in the first place, and then on having some faith in government participation.

Getting a compensation award depends most clearly on simply satisfying the eligibility requirements (which, of course, already reflect certain biases). To actually meet these regulations, however, is not such a simple matter. A victim can do little to change the victimization's circumstances to satisfy the stringent regulations, although his cooperation in the criminal process many help afterwards. In addition, a victim will usually fare better in getting an award if he has not received payments from other sources.

And, whether a victim will be paid by these other sources largely seems to depend on his cooperation in the criminal process, on the defendant's conviction, and on failing to receive a compensation award.

In sum, the victim seems to have only limited control over getting compensated, from any source, after being victimized. Other officials, including law-enforcement personnel, government bureaucrats, and board members in particular, hold most of the power over granting awards, but despite some minor evidence of racial preference in the payments granted, no other irregularities in compensating could be detected in this study.

Victim Attitudes

Victim compensation's second major goal is to create favorable public attitudes, especially among victims, toward not only the compensation process and the criminal-justice system, but also toward government generally. The foregoing pages indicate, however, that the level of victim satisfaction is quite low. And, the dissatisfaction has been shown to be present equally among both claimants and non-claimants, if not more among the former. Thus, it is necessary to analyze the factors, including the influence of the compensation experience, associated with this disenchantment.

A series of analyses were completed to discover these influences on victim attitudes. In so doing, a victim's attitudes were measured in several ways. First, his views of the compensation process were gauged by his relative satisfaction with his case involvement, with his case outcome, and with board officials. Second, a victim's views of the criminal process were measured by his relative satisfaction with coming to court, with the criminal-case outcome, with the law-enforcement officials in his case, and with their general activities to cope with the crime problem. And third, a victim's attitudes toward government were indicated by his view of government's responsiveness to the public.

Attitudes Toward Victim Compensation

Case Involvement. To understand what contributes to a victim's attitudes toward victim compensation, the analysis began by focusing on one way of measuring those attitudes: the victim's relative satisfaction with his compensation-case involvement. Table 10.5 presents the results of a discriminant analysis of this variable, and shows a combination of independent variables that explain the vast majority (83%) of the variance in the dependent variable, and that correctly predicts the responses of over 90% of the cases in the two samples (of claimants) relevant to this inquiry.

More specifically, Table 10.5 shows that the major determinants of a victim's satisfaction with his involvement either relate to victim compensation's internal workings or they derive from a victim's outside experiences. Beginning with the former, clearly the greatest determinant is the victim's relative satisfaction with his compensation-case outcome[6]. Having favorable impressions of board officials, sufficient case information, limited processing delays, favorable attitudes toward board regulations, and a successful claim were all additional compensation experiences positively associated with being satisfied with one's compensation-case involvement.

Among the influences outside the compensation process, the victim's ability to get other payments was most strongly correlated with being satisfied with his compensation-case involvement. Other apparent determinations included a victim's satisfaction with the criminal-justice officials in his case, with the case outcome, and with law-enforcement officials in general.

Table 10.5 also indicates the differences between Brooklyn and Newark in the contributions of the independent variables to explaining a victim's satisfaction with his compensation-case involvement. The most notable variations included the impact of being informed about one's case (more important in Newark) and one's impression of board officials (more important in Brooklyn). Also, it seems clear not only that Newark victims are happier, but that the city in which one is

TABLE 10.5 SATISFIED WITH COMPENSATION-CASE INVOLVEMENT?

CANON. CORREL. SQUARED	.92	.88	.83
% Explained Variance Acct. For By:	Brooklyn Claimants	Newark Claimants	All
(+) VICTIM'S CITY	NA	NA	10
(+) SATIS.COMP.CASE OUT.	42	33	28
(+) RECEIVED OTHER PAYMT	21	11	14
(+) INFORM COMP. CASE	0	24	12
(+) CJS OFFIC.DOING ALL	10	9	7
(+) VIEW BOARD OFFICIALS	17	2	8
(+) SATIS.COMP.SPEED	10	5	8
(+) GET COMPENS. AWARD	0	5	7
(+) SATIS. CJS OFFIC.	0	4	2
(+) APPROVE CCMP. RULES	0	3	5
(-) LENGTH COMP. CASE	1	2	1
(+) SATIS.CJ CASE OUT.	1	2	1
% Cases Correct.Predict.	94	91	90
NUMBER OF CASES	85	79	164

victimized makes an important contribution (10%) to one's relative satisfaction with this aspect of their compensation experience.

Impression of Board Officials. A second measure of satisfaction with the compensation experience is a victim's impressions of board officials. Table 10.6 presents the results of a discriminant analysis of this variable[7], and shows a combination of independent variables that explains a considerable majority (78%) of the variance in the dependent variable, and that correctly predicts the responses of 87% of the cases in the two samples (of claimants) relevant to this inquiry.

More specifically, Table 10.6 shows that once again the major variables associated with a victim's impressions of board officials derive from factors both inside and outside the compensation process. The internal determinants contributing to positive views of these officials were again dominated by the victim's satisfaction with his case outcome, but also by being satisfied with his case involvement, speed, information, and regulations, being successfully granted an award, and being free of difficulties in pursuing the case.

External influences producing positive feelings towards board officials were

TABLE 10.6 IMPRESSION OF BOARD OFFICIALS?

CANON. CORREL. SQUARED	.78		.91	.78
% Explained Variance Acct. For By:		Brooklyn Claimants	Newark Claimants	All
(+) VICTIM'S CITY		NA	NA	10
(+) SATIS.COMP.CASE OUT.		53	38	35
(+) SATIS.COMP. INVOLVE.		16	6	11
(+) RECEIVED OTHER PAYMT		7	15	11
(−) RACIAL BACKGROUND		3	17	8
(+) INFORM. COMP. CASE		6	8	9
(+) GET COMPENS. AWARD		0	10	5
(+) SATIS.CRIM.CASE OUT.		4	6	4
(+) APPROVE COMP. RULES		6	0	3
(−) COMP.CASE INCONVEN.		4	0	2
(+) SATIS.COMP. SPEED		0	1	1
% Cases Correct. Predict.		89	89	87
NUMBER OF CASES		85	79	164

led by a victim's ability to receive outside payments and by being white instead of non-white, as well as by being satisfied with the criminal-case outcome.

Table 10.6 also indicates the differences between Brooklyn and Newark claimants on this variable. The amount of variance explained by the aforementioned variables was more evenly distributed in Newark than in Brooklyn. The biggest differences between the samples were in the influence of race and whether a victim received an award, with Newark victims much more likely to be influenced in their views of board officials by these factors. And, once again, not only were Newark victims happier overall, but in general the city where one is victimized makes an important contribution (10%) to one's relative satisfaction with board officials.

Outcome of the Compensation Case. A final measure of the compensation experience is the most comprehensive: to what extent was the victim satisfied with his compensation-case outcome? Table 10.7 presents the results of a discriminant analysis of this variable, and shows a combination of independent variables that explains the vast majority (82%) of the variance in the dependent variable, and that correctly predicts the responses of 91% of the cases in the two samples (of claimants) relevant to this inquiry.

TABLE 10.7 SATISFIED COMPEnSATICN-CASE CUTCOME?

CANON. CORREL. SQUARED	.84	.90	.82
% Explained Variance Acct. For By:	Brooklyn Claimants	Newark Claimants	All
(+) VICTIM'S CITY	NA	NA	11
(+) SATIS.CCMP. INVOLVE.	19	17	16
(+) VIEW BOARD OFFICIALS	20	14	15
(+) GET COMPENS. AWARD	20	9	13
(-) RACIAL EACKGROUND	10	15	10
(+) RECEIVE OTHER PAYMT	14	5	8
(+) SATIS.COMP. SPEED	3	14	10
(-) LENGTH COMP. CASE	10	3	4
(-) COMP.CASE INCONVEN.	5	6	5
(+) APPROVE COMP. RULES	0	8	3
(+) SATIS.CRIM.CASE OUT.	0	5	3
(+) INFORMED COMP. CASE	0	4	2
% Cases Correct.Predict.	93	94	91
NUMBER OF CASES	85	79	164

As with the previous two analyses, the various factors associated with this level of satisfaction were both internal and external to the compensation process. Beginning with the former, a victim's satisfaction with his compensation case is positively related to getting an award, and to his satisfaction with board officials and case involvement. Positive attitudes also resulted from having speedy decisions, and few difficulties in pursuing one's case, as well as from being satisfied with board regulations and one's case information.

Among the external influences, being white and receiving outside payments after victimization were associated with positive attitudes, as well as being satisfied with one's criminal-case outcome.

Table 10.7 indicates the differences among Brooklyn and Newark victims in their satisfaction with their compensation case. Few variations stood out, but at the very least getting a compensation award clearly contributed more to positive attitudes in Brooklyn than in Newark. Again, however, Newark victims were the happiest overall, and in general the city where one is victimized makes an important contribution (11%) to one's relative satisfaction overall with one's compensation-case outcome.

Summary. In sum, among the foregoing three measures of a victim's attitudes toward the compensation experience, factors internal to that process dominate in explaining the level of satisfaction. It is not surprising that receiving compensation was an important influence, but victims also were concerned about board regulations, board officials, being kept informed about their case, the case's speed, and their ability to participate in the compensation process. Having largely negative views on these measures contributes as much to the existing dissatisfaction with the program as simply not receiving an award.

And, among the external influences on satisfaction, being white and able to recover losses from alternative sources were additional, important predictors of a victim's satisfaction with the compensation plans.

The previous chapter already has indicated a greater degree of satisfaction with victim compensation among Newark claimants than among Brooklyn claimants. One can add to this difference that (among the other relatively minor variations between the two samples) Newark victims seem to be much more affected by how well informed they are kept about their cases and by how much they are able to participate, both of which are greater in practice for them than for Brooklyn claimants. Perhaps this greater contact is a function of the smaller, non-bureaucratic scale of the New Jersey program.

Attitudes Toward Criminal Justice

Worthwhile Appearing in Court? To understand what contributes to a victim's attitudes toward criminal justice, the analysis began by focusing on one way of measuring those attitudes: whether the victim felt it was worthwhile coming to court. Table 10.8 presents the results of a discriminant analysis of this variable, and shows a combination of independent variables that explains between 40% and 79% of the variance in the dependent variable, and that correctly predicts the responses of at least 72% of the cases in each sample.

In particular, Table 10.8 shows that measures[8] of a victim's attitudes toward criminal justice, when considered together, predict most of his relative satisfaction with his court involvement. Thus, that satisfaction is positively associated with a victim's support of the criminal-case outcome, the work of criminal-justice officials generally, the offender's treatment, and the law-enforcement personnel involved in his case.

Believing it was worthwhile coming to court also was linked to a victim's case involvement, and its outcomes, as well as to certain elements of a victim's background characteristics. A positive view of his court involvement was indicated by infrequent court appearances, and by being able to testify, as well as by receiving outside payments after victimization, by denying the defendant bail, and by the offender's ultimate punishment. And, positive attitudes also were more likely to come from whites who were not closely related to the assailant.

Table 10.8 also indicates the differences among the four samples. The most

TABLE 10.8 WORTHWHILE APPEARING IN COURT?

CANON. CORREL. SQUARED	.40	.72	.79	.74	.66
% Explained Variance Acct. For By:	Bkln Claim	Bkln Non-Cl	Newk Claim	Newk Non-Cl	All
(+) SATIS.CRIM.CASE OUT.	16	20	8	19	18
(+) SATIS. CJS OFFIC.	11	22	17	10	13
(+) CJS OFFIC. DCING ALL	29	0	9	0	11
(+) ASKED TO TESTIFY	9	10	7	11	12
(+) OFFENDER TREATMENT	8	12	4	8	9
(+) CRIM. CASE OUTCOME	0	16	8	8	6
(-) OFFENDER BAILED	10	8	6	4	8
(-) MAXIMUM TIME COURT	5	0	16	7	5
(+) RECEIVE OTHER PAYMT	7	12	0	8	4
(-) RACIAL BACKGROUND	10	0	9	8	7
(-) VICTIM-OFFENC. REL.	0	0	10	13	4
(-) NUMBER TIMES COURT	0	0	5	4	3
% Cases Correct. Predict.	72	92	84	93	75
NUMBER OF CASES	98	85	80	79	342

important variation is undoubtedly in the overall amount of explanation provided by the independent variables examined. They obviously explain a lot less of the variance in whether victims felt coming to court was worthwhile among Brooklyn non-claimants than among the other samples. While the former were most influenced by their general estimation of criminal-justice officials, Brooklyn claimants and Newark non-claimants were most affected by their views of the actual law-enforcement personnel in their cases, and Newark claimants were mostly influenced by the criminal-case outcome.

The foregoing indicators of a victim's satisfaction with his court involvement included only factors external to the compensation experience, since only Brooklyn and Newark claimants would have had any such experience. To test the impact of the compensation process on whether victims felt it was worthwhile coming to court, however, these two samples must be examined separately. Doing so also will allow us to assess the contribution of whichever city's criminal-justice system was encountered and whether a compensation claim was made in the first place.

Table 10.9 presents the claimant samples and shows the effects of adding these new variables (including all five of the key measures of the compensation experience—see previous list) as compared to their absence in Table 10.8. The results indicate that these variables had an important impact. In combination, they explain 39% of the variance in the dependent variable for all claimants,

TABLE 10.9 WORTHWHILE APPEARING IN COURT?

	CANON. CORREL. SQUARED	.89	.87	.86
	% Explained Variance Acct. For By:	Brooklyn Claimants	Newark Claimants	All
(+)	VICTIM'S CITY	NA	NA	2
(+)	APPLY COMPENSATION	NA	NA	6
(+)	SATIS.COMP. INVOLVE.	13	7	10
(+)	VIEW BOARD OFFICIALS	6	12	9
(+)	SATIS.COMP.CASE OUT.	12	3	5
(+)	GET COMPENS. AWARD	3	5	3
(-)	COMP.CASE INCONVEN.	4	2	4
(-)	VICTIM-OFFEND. REL.	10	10	11
(+)	CRIM. CASE OUTCOME	12	4	6
(+)	OFFENDER BAILED	3	12	8
(+)	RECEIVE OTHER PAYMT	2	9	6
(+)	ASKED TO TESTIFY	8	3	7
(-)	NUMBER TIMES COURT	11	0	3
(+)	CJS OFFIC. DOING ALL	3	7	4
(+)	SATIS.CRIM.CASE OUT.	5	4	5
(+)	SATIS. CJS OFFIC.	4	5	6
(-)	CASE WHAT EXPECTED	3	6	2
(-)	MAXIMUM TIME COURT	0	8	0
(+)	OFFENDER TREATMENT	2	3	1
	% Cases Correct.Predict.	92	94	90
	NUMBER OF CASES	85	79	164

when added to the analysis. And, these variables also increase the overall amount of explained variance from 66% to 86%, and improve the predictive capacity of the independent variables from 75% to 90% (with corresponding increases in the two samples considered separately). Although the amount of contribution provided by these variables is not exactly the same in each sample, the difference is not significant.

Impression of Officials in Criminal Case. A second measure of criminal-justice attitudes is a victim's view of the particular officials he confronted after his victimization and when he appeared in court. Table 10.10 presents the results of a discriminant analysis of this variable[9], and shows a combination of independent variables that explains between 32% and 76% of the variance in the dependent variable, and that correctly predicts the responses of at least 74% of the cases in each sample.

TABLE 10.10 IMPRESSICN OF CJS OFFICIALS IN CRIMINAL CASE?

	Bkln Claim	Bkln Non-Cl	Newk Claim	Newk Non-Cl	All
CANON. CORREL. SQUARED	.36	.70	.72	.65	.57
% Explained Variance Acct. For By:					
(+) OFFENDER TREATMENT	19	19	22	10	20
(+) RECEIVE OTHER PAYMT	8	48	0	15	14
(+) FEEL GOV'T RESPONSIVE	9	0	20	19	13
(-) PRIOR COURT INVOLVE.	9	15	7	6	10
(-) NUMBER TIMES COURT	17	0	4	15	11
(+) ASKED TO TESTIFY	6	5	10	14	8
(-) VICTIM-OFFFEND. REL.	0	0	22	15	11
(+) CRIM. CASE OUTCOMF	11	3	3	7	4
(+) SATIS.CRIM.CASE OUT.	9	5	7	0	8
(-) RACIAL BACKGROUND	11	5	5	0	3
% Cases Correct.Predict.	69	74	84	80	70
NUMBER OF CASES	98	85	80	79	342

More specifically, Table 10.10 indicates results similar to the preceding analysis, but with some important differences. A victim's impressions of law-enforcement personnel once again are predicted by positive attitudes about the court process, its outcomes, and criminal justice generally, as well as by certain victim characteristics. But, the relative contributions are different and some new factors have an impact.

Being white and not closely related to the offender, for example, contribute to a victim's positive attitudes toward criminal-justice officials, as does not having been involved in court previously. A victim also was more positive when he had some faith in government's responsiveness. And finally, a victim's support of these officials was enhanced by infrequent court appearances, being able to testify, convicting the offender, and collecting outside payments after victimization.

Table 10.10 also indicates the differing contributions made by those factors influencing a victim's view of criminal-justice officials among the four samples. Again, the most important variation lies in the overall amount of explanation provided by the independent variables examined, since once again, they account for much less explanation among Brooklyn non-claimants. And, while these victims were most affected by the offender's treatment and by their frequency in court, Brooklyn claimants were most influenced by whether outside payments were received, and Newark claimants and non-claimants were most affected by the victims' views of government's responsiveness, and by the victim-offender relationship, respectively.

As in the previous analysis, a second discriminant analysis was completed to test the impact of the compensation process on explaining a victim's view of the criminal-justice officials in his case, as compared to the influence of the variables already considered. In addition, we are once again concerned about the contribution made by which city's criminal-justice system a victim encounters and whether or not a compensation claim is made in the first place. Table 10.11 presents the claimant samples and shows the effects of adding these variables (including all five key measures of the compensation experience) as compared to their absence in Table 10.10. The significant effect of these variables is again evident when the second discriminant analysis is examined.

In combination, these new variables explain almost one-half (47%) of the variance in the dependent variable for all claimants when added to the analysis. And, these variables also increase the overall amount of explained variance from 57% to 85%, and improve the predictive capacity of the independent variables from 70% to 88% (with corresponding increases in the two samples considered separately). Although the differences are not extensive, the amount of contribution provided by these variables is greater among Newark claimants than among Brooklyn claimants.

TABLE 10.11 IMPRESSION OF CJS OFFICIALS IN CRIMINAL CASE?

CANON. CORREL. SQUARED	.89	.87	.85
% Explained Variance Acct. For By:	Brooklyn Claimants	Newark Claimants	All
(+) VICTIM'S CITY	NA	NA	5
(+) APPLY COMPENSATION	NA	NA	7
(+) SATIS.COMP. INVOLVE.	19	25	15
(−) COMP.CASE INVOLVE.	9	7	7
(+) GET COMPENS. AWARD	6	9	5
(+) SATIS.COMP.CASE OUT.	2	8	6
(+) VIEW BOARD OFFICIALS	2	4	2
(+) RECEIVE OTHER PAYMT	16	28	15
(+) ASKED TO TESTIFY	17	5	11
(+) CRIM.CASE OUTCOME	6	5	6
(+) OFFENDER TREATMENT	7	4	4
(+) SATIS.CRIM.CASE OUT.	11	0	3
(−) RACIAL BACKGROUND	4	0	4
(+) GOVT. RESPONSIVE	1	1	2
(−) PRIOR COURT INVOLVE.	1	1	1
(−) CASE WHAT EXPECTED	0	2	1
(−) VICTIM−OFFEND. REL.	0	1	1
% Cases Correct.Predict.	90	92	88
NUMBER OF CASES	85	79	164

Satisfaction with Criminal-Case Outcome. A third measure of criminal-justice attitudes is a victim's relative satisfaction with the criminal-case outcome. Table 10.12 presents the results of a discriminant analysis of this variable, and shows a combination of independent variables that explains between 51% and 89% of the variance in the dependent variable, and that correctly predicts the responses of at least 80% of the cases in each sample.

In particular, Table 10.12 shows that, as with the previous two dependent variables analyzed, the indicators fall into several categories. A victim's other criminal-justice attitudes are most associated with criminal-case satisfaction, such as feeling it was worthwhile coming to court, that the offender was properly handled, and that criminal-justice officials were doing everything possible. One new influence, however, was a victim's attitudes toward the offender. When one controls for the particular case outcome, one discovers that victims with negative attitudes toward the offender will be more satisfied with the case outcome as the assailant's punishment increases, and vice versa.

The characteristics of one's court involvement (including frequent and long court appearances, prior court involvement, and being unable to testify) and the criminal-justice outcomes (including being unable to recover losses, and the of-

TABLE 10.12 SATISFIED WITH CRIMINAL-CASE OUTCOME?

CANON. CORREL. SQUARED		.51	.72	.70	.89	.72
% Explained Variance Acct. For By:		Bkln Claim	Bkln Non-Cl	Newk Claim	Newk Non-Cl	All
(+) VIEW OF OFFENDER		15	6	8	33	19
(-) EVER THREATENED		13	12	21	13	13
(-) NUMBER TIMES COURT		19	8	15	5	10
(+) ASKED TO TESTIFY		0	17	10	7	12
(+) WORTHWHILE COURT		5	8	8	9	8
(+) OFFENDER TREATMENT		4	11	0	4	4
(+) RECEIVE OTHER PAYMT		10	15	0	3	8
(-) RACIAL BACKGROUND		9	0	19	0	8
(+) CJS OFFIC. DOING ALL		0	6	13	6	5
(+) CRIM. CASE OUTCOME		6	8	5	0	6
(-) PRIOR COURT INVOLVE.		8	6	0	4	2
(-) MAXIMUM TIME COURT		0	4	0	14	2
(-) OFFENDER BAILED		10	0	0	4	3
% Cases Correct. Predict.		80	88	81	89	80
NUMBER OF CASES		98	85	80	79	342

fender's getting bail or lenience) were associated with negative feelings among victims about the criminal-case outcome. Also, for the first time, being threatened by the offender also was related to a victim's dissatisfaction. And finally, more positive attitudes were again produced by being white.

Table 10.12 also indicates the differences among the four samples in the factors that influence a victim's responses to this question. Again, these measures explain the least amount of variance in the dependent variable for Brooklyn non-claimants. And, while the independent variables were dominated among these victims by their frequency in court, Brooklyn claimants were most affected by their ability to testify. Newark claimants and non-claimants were mostly influenced by their attitudes toward the offender, and by the offender's threats or by their own race, respectively.

The results of the second discriminant analysis for this variable are presented in Table 10.13. The findings are consistent with a developing pattern whereby the compensation variables and those measures distinguishing the two cities and claimants from non-claimants make an important contribution in explaining the dependent variable when added to the analysis.

In combination, these indicators explain 39% of the variance in the dependent variable among claimants. And, these variables also increase the overall amount of explained variance from 72% to 84%, and improve the predictive capacity of the independent variables from 80% to 92% (with corresponding increases in the two samples when considered separately). These additional variables especially dominate among Brooklyn claimants.

Justice Officials Doing All They Can? The final measure of a victim's criminal-justice attitudes is his view of whether law-enforcement personnel, in general, are doing everything possible to cope with crime. Table 10.14 presents the results of a discriminant analysis of this variable, and shows a combination of independent variables that explains between 44% and 78% of the variance in the dependent variable, and that correctly predicts the responses of at least 81% of the cases in each sample.

More specifically, Table 10.14 indicates that among the categories identified in the previous three analyses, other criminal-justice attitudes (such as being satisfied with the offender's treatment, the criminal-case outcome, and the criminal-justice officials in one's case) are highly associated with a positive view of law-enforcement officials generally.

Positive attitudes also were associated with various aspects of a victim's involvement in the criminal process (including infrequent and short court appearances), the outcomes of that process (such as getting payments after being victimized, and severely punishing the offender and denying him bail). And finally, being white was again associated with more positive feelings.

Table 10.14 also indicates the differences among the four samples. The fact that these measures are less able to predict a victim's response among Brooklyn

TABLE 10.13 SATISFIED WITH CRIMINAL-CASE OUTCOME?

CANON. CORREL. SQUARED	.83	.94	.84
% Explained Variance Acct. For By:	Brooklyn Claimants	Newark Claimants	All
(+) VICTIM'S CITY	NA	NA	4
(+) APPLY COMPENSATION	NA	NA	6
(+) SATIS.COMP. INVOLVE.	19	4	9
(+) VIEW BOARD OFFICIALS	11	9	7
(--) COMP.CASE INCONVEN.	13	4	6
(+) GET COMPENS. AWARD	8	4	4
(+) SATIS.COMP.CASE OUT.	3	3	3
(+) VIEW OF OFFENDER	5	17	12
(+) RECEIVE OTHER PAYMT	9	6	9
(--) EVER THREATENED	6	6	8
(+) ASKED TO TESTIFY	6	4	7
(--) NUMBER TIMES COURT	4	6	6
(+) CJS OFFIC. DOING ALL	3	7	8
(+) OFFENDER TREATMENT	3	6	3
(-) OFFENDER BAILED	5	4	2
(--) PRIOR COURT INVOLVE.	3	4	4
(-) MAXIMUM TIME COURT	0	6	2
% Cases Correct.Predict.	94	96	92
NUMBER OF CASES	85	79	164

non-claimants (as compared to the other samples) completes a perfectly consistent pattern among the four indicators of criminal-justice attitudes that have been considered in this section. While Brooklyn non-claimants were dominated here by the frequency and length of their court appearances, Brooklyn claimants were most influenced by their ability to receive outside payments. Newark non-claimants were most affected by their particular feelings towards the criminal-justice officials in their case, while Newark claimants shared with their Brooklyn counterparts being most influenced by their ability to receive payments.

The results of the second discriminant analysis for this variable are presented in Table 10.15. The findings complete another consistent pattern of the compensation variables and those measures distinguishing the two cities and claimants from non-claimants having an important influence in explaining the dependent variable. In combination, these indicators explain an average of 49% of the variance in the dependent variable for all claimants when added to the analysis. And,

TABLE 10.14 CJS OFFICIALS DCING ALL THEY CAN?

CANON. CORREL. SQUARED	.44	.72	.78	.70	.57
% Explained Variance Acct. For By:	Bkln Claim	Bkln Non-Cl	Newk Claim	Newk Non-Cl	All
(+) SATIS. CJS OFFIC.	22	5	33	23	17
(-) MAXIMUM TIME COURT	30	17	5	10	19
(+) RECEIVE CTHEF PAYMT	6	17	2	26	15
(-) NUMBER TIMES COURT	32	11	7	0	11
(+) OFFENDER TREATMENT	7	8	22	9	12
(-) OFFENDER EAILED	0	14	14	16	9
(-) RACIAL BACKGROUND	4	8	7	11	11
(+) CRIM. CASE OUTCOME	0	14	2	6	4
(+) SATIS.CRIM.CASE OUT.	0	6	7	0	2
% Cases Correct.Predict.	81	92	94	94	84
NUMBER OF CASES	98	85	80	79	342

these variables also increase the overall amount of explained variance from 57% to 77%, and improve the predictive capacity of the independent variables from 84% to 91% (with corresponding increases in the two samples considered separately).

Once again, some differences between the samples emerged, including Brooklyn claimants being more influenced in evaluating law enforcement generally by their satisfaction with their compensation-case outcome, as compared to Newark claimants being more concerned about their compensation-case involvement.

Summary. Overall, among the foregoing four measures of a victim's attitudes toward the criminal process, positive responses derive from literally all the positive responses on other measures of criminal-justice attitudes, as well as from infrequent court appearances, more severe penalties for the offender, receiving outside payments, having no victim-offender relationship and no prior court involvement, and being white.

Chapter six already has indicated much dissatisfaction among most of the victims in this study with criminal justice. It also has been demonstrated that the disenchantment is no less among claimants than among non-claimants, and is, in fact, sometimes worse. This section's discussion of criminal-justice attitudes further indicates that compensation variables contribute significantly to explaining

TABLE 10.15 CJS OFFICIALS DOING ALL THEY CAN?

		Brooklyn Claimants	Newark Claimants	All
CANON. CORREL. SQUARED		.78	.83	.77
% Explained Variance Acct. For By:				
(+)	VICTIM'S CITY	NA	NA	3
(+)	APPLY COMPENSATION	NA	NA	8
(+)	GET COMPENS. AWARD	19	11	12
(+)	SATIS.COMP. INVOLVE.	5	22	14
(+)	SATIS.COMP.CASE OUT.	19	0	9
(+)	VIEW BOARD MEMBERS	4	6	3
(−)	COMP.CASE INCONVEN.	0	0	0
(−)	RACIAL BACKGROUND	7	19	14
(+)	OFFENDER TREATMENT	5	14	10
(+)	RECEIVE OTHER PAYMT	7	11	11
(−)	OFFENDER BAILED	6	9	5
(−)	NUMBER TIMES COURT	9	2	2
(+)	CRIM. CASE OUTCOME	9	0	3
(+)	SATIS. CJS OFFICIALS	3	6	5
(−)	MAXIMUM TIME COURT	5	0	1
% Cases Correct.Predict.		95	96	91
NUMBER OF CASES		85	79	164

victims' feelings. That means, therefore, that the low level of satisfaction is explained largely by the effects of the compensation experience. In addition, this discussion has highlighted the importance of whether or not one applies for compensation in the first place, and the city in which one is victimized. Both variables consistently contributed to a victim's relative satisfaction or dissatisfaction. And finally, this analysis of criminal-justice attitudes also has indicated a difference between Brooklyn and Newark claimants in the impact of the compensation variables. While the compensation measures contribute an average of 45% to explaining the four dependent variables among Brooklyn claimants, they only contribute 36% among Newark claimants. Thus, if the previous chapter's findings, which showed that victim sentiments toward victim compensation are more negative in Brooklyn than in Newark, are combined with the results of this chapter's multivariate analysis, one is tempted to conclude that both compensation plans are alienating most victims from the programs themselves and from criminal justice, and that New York's plan is producing more alienation and negative feelings in particular, compared to New Jersey's program.

Attitudes Toward Government Generally

Government Responsiveness. To understand what contributes to yet a third, broad measure of a victim's attitudes—his general sentiments toward government—attention was paid to the major indicator of those feelings: a victim's view of government's responsiveness. Table 10.16 presents the results of a discriminant analysis of this variable, and shows a combination of independent variables that explains between 44% and 88% of the variance in the dependent variable, and that correctly predicts the responses of at least 69% of the cases in each sample.

In particular, Table 10.16 indicates that influences similar to those affecting a victim's criminal-justice attitudes were dominant. Positive attitudes about government's responsiveness were associated with a victim's satisfaction with the law-enforcement officials in his case, with the criminal-case outcome, with criminal-justice personnel generally, and with the offender's treatment. Believing that government should not be held responsible for crime also was positively related to faith in government. A victim's belief in the government's responsiveness also was positively related to his court involvement (including infrequent and short court appearances), to criminal-case outcomes (including severely punishing the offender and receiving outside payments), and to a victim's background charactertistics (such as being white and having no prior court involvement).

TABLE 10.16 GOVERNMENT RESPONSIVE?

CANON. CORREL. SQUARED	.44	.70	.69	.88	.63
% Explained Variance Acct. For By:	Bkln Claim	Bkln Non-Cl	Newk Claim	Newk Non-Cl	All
(+) RECEIVE OTHER PAYMT	55	5	6	18	17
(+) OFFENDER TREATMENT	4	30	10	10	18
(-) PRIOR COURT INVOLVE.	6	18	9	13	10
(+) CJS OFFIC. DOING ALL	5	0	28	13	10
(-) NUMBER TIMES COURT	10	6	12	13	9
(+) SATIS.CRIM.CASE OUT.	18	3	9	3	9
(-) MAXIMUM TIME COURT	0	12	15	7	10
(-) GOVT RESPONS. CRIME	6	6	5	7	4
(+) SATIS. CJS OFFICIALS	0	12	3	7	5
(+) CRIM. CASE OUTCOME	0	6	0	6	4
(-) RACIAL BACKGROUND	0	4	3	4	4
% Cases Correct. Predict.	69	81	78	82	76
NUMBER OF CASES	98	85	80	79	342

Table 10.16 also indicates the differences among the four samples. It shows, to continue a pattern already established, that the independent variables again explain less of the variance among Brooklyn non-claimants than among the other samples. Furthermore, this sample was particularly influenced by whether victims had received payments after being victimized, while Brooklyn claimants were most affected by the offender's treatment. Newark claimants and non-claimants were most influenced by whether payments were received, and by whether victims felt criminal-justice officials were doing all they could, respectively.

To assess the impact of the respective cities, whether or not a compensation claim was made, and if so, the compensation experience itself on a victim's view of government's responsiveness, a second discriminant analysis was completed. Table 10.17 presents the claimant samples, showing the effects of adding these variables as compared to their absence in Table 10.16.

TABLE 10.17 GOVERNMENT RESPONSIVE?

CANON. CORREL. SQUARED		.87	.89	.84
% Explained Variance Acct. For By:		Brooklyn Claimants	Newark Claimants	All
(+) VICTIM'S CITY		NA	NA	3
(+) APPLY COMPENSATION		NA	NA	6
(+) SATIS.COMP. INVOLVE.		22	13	15
(+) VIEW BOARD OFFICIALS		17	15	14
(+) GET COMPENS. AWARD		2	13	6
(+) SATIS.COMP.CASE OUT.		4	9	4
(−) COMP.CASE INCONVEN.		6	0	1
(+) CRIM. CASE OUTCOME		10	13	12
(+) OFFENDER TREATMENT		16	5	9
(−) MAXIMUM TIME COURT		10	5	10
(−) PRIOR COURT INVOLVE.		4	3	4
(+) SATIS. CJS OFFICIALS		1	6	4
(+) CJS OFFIC. DOING ALL		2	5	4
(−) GOVT RESPONS. CRIME		0	4	3
(−) NUMBER TIMES COURT		2	2	4
(+) SATIS.CRIM.CASE OUT.		0	4	1
(+) RECEIVE OTHER PAYMT		1	3	1
(−) RACIAL BACKGROUND		2	0	4
% Cases Correct.Predict.		94	96	92
NUMBER OF CASES		85	79	164

In combination, these measures explain 48% of the variance in the dependent variable for all claimants when added to the analysis. And, these variables also increase the overall amount of explained variance from 63% to 84%, and improve the predictive capacity of the independent variables from 76% to 92%. The amount of variance explained by these new variables is fairly equal in the two samples.

Summary. Overall, the factors associated with a victim's view of government's responsiveness are similar to those affecting his view of criminal justice. Criminal-justice involvement, outcomes, and attitudes, and certain victim backgrounds are the predominant influences. That is, they dominate until one takes the victim's claimant status, city, and compensation experience into consideration. Thereafter, predicting a victim's faith and good will toward government is overtaken by these variables.

As with victim attitudes toward criminal justice, the results of the multivariate analysis can be combined with findings (in chapter six) indicating little satisfaction generally with government, to demonstrate an overall disenchantment, whereby claimant victims are no more content than non-claimants, and sometimes less so. Since a victim's city, claim status, and compensation experience contribute so extensively to explaining a victim's relative satisfaction with government's responsiveness, these variables are apparently intensifying the discontentment. No clear distinctions can be made between Brooklyn and Newark claimants, however, since the experimental variables explain the same amount of variance in this dependent variable for both samples. Consequently, no meaningful differences can be identified between the New York and New Jersey compensation board either.

Victim Cooperation

A third major goal, after allowing victims to recoup their victimization losses and improving their attitudes, of compensation is to increase a victim's cooperation not only with the compensation board, but more importantly, with criminal-justice officials, and with government and government officials generally. This increased cooperation allegedly will contribute not only to smoother board operations, but also to better crime prevention and law enforcement, as well as to more effective public participation, and thus to better government.

As with previous analyses, it already has been demonstrated (see chapter six) that most victims' desire to cooperate with criminal justice and government is quite low. Thus, this section's purpose is to assess what contributes to this unwillingness to cooperate. It is important to note the extent to which the victim's city, claim status, and the various measures of his compensation experience contribute to a victim's relative cooperation. But first, we want to examine what effects the compensation process has had on victims' willingness simply to apply for an award again.

Willingness to Use Compensation Program Again

To understand a victim's relative willingness to participate in the compensation process in the future, respondents in the Brooklyn and Newark claimant samples were asked simply whether or not they would ever apply again. Table 10.18 presents the results of a discriminant analysis of this variable, and shows a combination of independent variables that explains the vast majority (87%) of the variance in the dependent variable, and that correctly predicts the responses for 91% of the cases in the two samples.

More specifically, Table 10.18 shows that the major determinants of a victim's willingness to reapply for compensation either relate to victim compensation's internal workings, or to a victim's outside experiences. Beginning with the former, the most prominent indicator of a victim's future claim was receiving an award from his last claim. The victim's satisfaction with his compensation case outcome, with his case involvement, with board officials, with case information and speed, and with overcoming inconveniences in pursuing his claim also were associated with reapplying.

TABLE 10.18 APPLY FOR VICTIM COMPENSATION AGAIN?

CANON. CORREL. SQUARED	.90	.91	.87
% Explained Variance Acct. For By:	Brooklyn Claimants	Newark Claimants	All
(+) VICTIM'S CITY	NA	NA	15
(+) GET COMPENS. AWARD	20	58	27
(+) SATIS.COMP.CASE OUT.	29	5	20
(+) VIEW BOARD OFFICIALS	22	3	13
(+) POLITICAL EFFICACY	5	8	4
(+) WORTHWHILE COURT	8	4	4
(-) RACIAL BACKGROUND	5	4	3
(+) SATIS.COMP. INVOLVE.	0	9	5
(+) INFORMED COMP. CASE	6	0	2
(-) LENGTH COMP. CASE	0	6	4
(+) CJS OFFIC. DOING ALL	3	3	1
(-) COME. CASE INCONVEN.	4	0	2
% Cases Correct.Predict.	96	93	91
NUMBER OF CASES	85	79	164

External factors positively influencing reapplication included a victim's approving generally of criminal-justice officials, having arrived in court, and his viability in his government activities. These responses partly reflect a faith in the system and perception of duty that might induce a victim's participation in the compensation process even if an award was denied on the previous application. And finally, whites again were more likely to indicate their intention to reapply than were non-whites.

Table 10.18 also indicates the differences between Brooklyn and Newark claimants. While Brooklyn claimants were most influenced by their relative satisfaction with their compensation-case outcome, Newark claimants were overwhelmingly predominated by whether or not they received an award. Both samples, however, were clearly more affected by compensation variables than by other influences. And finally, it can be observed that not only are Newark claimants more likely to reapply than Brooklyn claimants, but that a victim's city contributes substantially (15%) to the overall explanation of whether victim compensation will be applied for again.

Willingness to Get Involved in the Criminal Process Again

To understand what contributes to a victim's willingness to participate in the criminal process in the future, respondents were asked exactly that. Table 10.19 presents the results of a discriminant analysis of this variable, and shows a combination of independent variables that explains between 41% and 86% of the variance in the dependent variable, and that correctly predicts the responses of at least 67% of the cases in each sample.

In particular, Table 10.19 shows that influences similar to those explaining victim attitudes toward criminal justice emerged once again. The major variables positively associated with a victim's willingness to become involved in the criminal process in the future derive, in fact, from his view of criminal justice, including being satisfied with the offender's treatment, with the law-enforcement officials in his case, with the criminal-case outcome, and with the work of criminal-justice personnel generally. Likewise, victims also were positively influenced by their belief that government is not responsible for causing crime.

A victim's desire to cooperate in the criminal process again also was positively associated with some of his background characteristics (such as being white, unrelated to the offender, and lacking prior court involvement), with his criminal-justice experience (such as infrequent and short court appearances, and being asked to testify), and with criminal-justice outcomes (such as receiving outside payments, avoiding the offender's threats, and denying the defendant bail).

Table 10.19 also indicates the differences among the four samples. It shows that the independent variables again explain far less of the variance among Brooklyn non-claimants than among the other samples. And, these victims were

TABLE 10.19 GET INVOLVED IN JUSTICE SYSTEM AGAIN?

		Bkln Claim	Bkln Non-Cl	Newk Claim	Newk Ncn-Cl	All
CANON. CORREL. SQUARED		.41	.79	.86	.83	.70
% Explained Variance Acct. For By:						
(+)	CJS OFFIC. DCING ALL	14	10	18	20	14
(−)	RACIAL BACKGROUND	5	10	22	7	13
(−)	GOVT RESPONS. CRIME	5	19	9	8	11
(+)	ASKED TO TESTIFY	16	6	4	14	8
(−)	VICTIM-OFFEND. REL.	16	7	7	7	10
(+)	SATIS.CJS OFFICIALS	13	4	2	10	7
(−)	OFFENDER FAILED	10	10	5	3	8
(−)	NUMBER TIMES COURT	9	7	3	2	6
(−)	HOW PRIOR CT INVOLVE	5	0	10	4	5
(−)	MAXIMUM TIME COURT	4	8	0	6	3
(+)	RECEIVE OTHER PAYMT	4	6	7	0	6
(+)	OFFENDER TREATMENT	0	5	6	5	3
(−)	EVER THREATENED	0	0	7	8	4
(+)	SATIS.CRIM.CASE OUT.	0	7	0	5	2
% Cases Correct. Predict.		67	94	95	95	82
NUMBER OF CASES		98	85	80	79	342

particularly influenced by the victim-offender relationship, and the victim's ability to testify, while Brooklyn non-claimants were most affected by their assessment of government's responsibility for crime. Newark claimants and non-claimants were most influenced by their general view of criminal-justice officials and by their racial backgrounds, respectively.

To contrast the foregoing variables (and to assess their relative contribution) with those reflecting the victim's city, claim status, and his compensation experience, a second discriminant analysis of a victim's future willingness to participate in the criminal process was completed. Table 10.20 presents the claimant samples, showing the effects of adding these new variables as compared to their absence in Table 10.19.

In combination, these measures exlain 33% of the variance in the dependent variable for all claimants when added to the analysis. And, these variables also increase the overall amount of explained variance from 70% to 85%, and improve the predictive capacity of the independent variables from 82% to 90%.

TABLE 10.20 GET INVOLVED IN JUSTICE SYSTEM AGAIN?

CANON. CORREL. SQUARED % Explained Variance Acct. For By:	.87 Brooklyn Claimants	.94 Newark Claimants	.85 All
(+) VICTIM'S CITY	NA	NA	4
(+) APPLY COMPENSATION	NA	NA	7
(+) GET COMPENS. AWARD	16	4	8
(+) SATIS.COMP. INVOLVE.	3	12	5
(+) VIEW BOARD OFFICIALS	4	3	3
(+) SATIS.COMP.CASE OUT.	4	2	4
(-) COMP.CASE INVOLVE.	0	3	2
(--) VICTIM-OFFEND. REL.	5	22	13
(-) OFFENDER BAILED	7	11	12
(--) GOVT RESPONS. CRIME	12	3	8
(--) MAXIMUM TIME COURT	10	4	5
(+) SATIS. CJS OFFICIALS	5	9	6
(--) RACIAL BACKGROUND	10	3	4
(+) CJS OFFIC. DOING ALL	7	4	4
(+) ASKED TO TESTIFY	5	4	5
(+) OFFENDER TREATMENT	5	2	2
(+) SATIS.CRIM.CASE OUT.	0	6	4
(-) HOW PRIOR CT INVOLVE	0	5	2
(+) RECEIVE OTHER PAYMT	0	3	1
(-) NUMBER TIMES COURT	0	2	1
% Cases Correct.Predict.	95	98	90
NUMBER OF CASES	85	79	164

The amount of variance explained by the compensation variables is practically the same in each of the samples.

Future Willingness to Participate in Government

To understand what contributes to a victim's willingness to participate in government in the future, this analysis examined the results of a series of inquiries which were combined into a composite measure of a victim's political efficacy[10]. Table 10.21 presents the results of a discriminant analysis of this variable, and shows a combination of independent variables that explains between 46% and 55% of the variance in the dependent variable, and that correctly predicts the responses of at least 78% of the cases in each sample.

More specifically, Table 10.21 shows that the major influences again fell into the same categories as in previous analyses. The factors contributing most positively were a victim's attitudes toward criminal justice, such as having favorable

TABLE 10.21 POLITICAL EFFICACY

CANON. CORREL. SQUARED	.46	.48	.53	.55	.47
% Explained Variance Acct. For By:	Bkln Claim	Bkln Non-Cl	Newk Claim	Newk Non-Cl	All
(+) CJS OFFIC. DCING ALL	22	20	48	21	26
(+) WORTHWHILE COURT	4	43	0	30	17
(-) GOVT RESPONS. CRIME	10	8	7	8	12
(+) SATIS.CRIM.CASE OUT.	0	4	17	5	8
(-) VICTIM-OFFEND. REL.	9	5	6	5	4
(--) NUMBER TIMES COURT	25	0	0	0	7
(-) RACIAL BACKGROUND	8	5	5	6	5
(+) RECEIVE OTHER PAYMT	6	5	5	8	3
(+) GOVT RESPONSIVE	7	6	5	5	7
(+) CRIM. CASE OUTCOME	5	0	3	9	4
(+) SATIS CJS OFFICIALS	5	0	0	3	2
(--) MAXIMUM TIME COURT	0	4	0	0	3
(-) PRIOR COURT INVOLVE.	0	3	3	0	2
% Cases Correct. Predict.	80	78	80	83	79
NUMBER OF CASES	98	85	80	79	342

views of the criminal-justice officials in his case, of the compensation-case outcome, of having appeared in court, and of law-enforcement officials generally.

A victim's attitudes toward government (including his belief in its responsiveness and innocence in producing crime) also were positively related to his future willingness to become involved in government. Also positively associated were certain victim characteristics (such as having no victim-offender relationship and no prior court experience, and being white), certain aspects of his criminal-justice involvement (including infrequent and short court appearances) and certain criminal-justice outcomes (such as receiving payments after victimization, and having the offender receive some punishment).

Table 10.21 indicates the differences among the four samples. It shows that for the first time among the various discriminant analyses completed in this chapter, the independent variables did not explain significantly less of the variance in the dependent variable among Brooklyn non-claimants than among the other samples. This analysis also shows some great inconsistencies among the separate samples in the contributions made by each independent variables.

Brooklyn non-claimants were most influenced in their future willingness to participate in government by their frequency of court appearances, while Brooklyn claimants were most affected by their general view of criminal-justice officials. And, while Newark non-claimants also were most influenced by their view of law-enforcement officials, Newark claimants were most affected by whether it had been worthwhile appearing in court.

To contrast the foregoing variables with those that reflect the victim's city, claim status, and compensation experience, a second discriminant analysis of the victims' future willingness to participate in government was completed. Table 10.22 presents the claimant samples, showing the effects of adding the new variables as compared to their absence in Table 10.21.

In combination, these measures explain 44% of the variance in the dependent variable among claimants when added to the analysis. And, these variables also increase the overall amount of explained variance from 47% to 69%, and improve the predictive capacity of the independent variables from 79% to 85%. The amount of variance explained by these variables is considerably greater among Brooklyn claimants than among Newark claimants, and the difference is most accounted for by the victim's ability to receive compensation and by his difficulties in pursuing his compensation case.

TABLE 10.22 POLITCAL EFFICACY

CANON. CORREL. SQUARED	.64	.82	.69
% Explained Variance Acct. For By:	Brooklyn Claimants	Newark Claimants	All
(+) VICTIM'S CITY	NA	NA	6
(+) APPLY COMPENSATION	NA	NA	4
(+) GET COMPENS. AWARD	29	12	15
(+) SATIS.COMP. INVOLVE.	7	9	6
(+) VIEW BOARD OFFICIALS	6	8	7
(--) COMP. CASE INCONVEN.	7	0	4
(+) SATIS.COMP.CASE OUT.	2	4	2
(+) WORTHWHILE CCURT	14	10	13
(+) CJS OFFIC. DCING ALL	12	0	8
(+) CRIM. CASE OUTCOME	6	5	5
(+) SATIS. CJS OFFICIALS	0	10	6
(−) GOVT RESPONS. CRIME	3	6	2
(--) RACIAL BACKGROUND	4	4	5
(+) GOVT RESPONSIVE	5	3	3
(+) SATIS.CRIM.CASE OUT.	3	5	4
(−) MAXIMUM TIME COURT	0	8	3
(--) VICTIM-OFFENE. REL.	3	4	3
(+) RECEIVE CTHER PAYMT	0	6	2
(−) PRIOR COURT INVOLVE.	0	6	2
% Cases Correct.Predict.	88	89	85
NUMBER OF CASES	85	79	164

Summary

Overall, the factors associated with a victim's future willingness to participate in the compensation, criminal justice, and government processes are similar to those affecting his attitudes towards those processes. The same measures of criminal-justice involvement, outcomes, and attitudes, and background characteristics dominate in explaining a victim's willingness to cooperate until the victim's city, claim status, and compensation experience are taken into account. Thereafter, those variables explain a large amount of the variance in the dependent variable.

And, as with victim attitudes, the results of the multivariate analyses in this section can be combined with chapter six's findings that indicated victims' strong reluctance to participate in government, criminal-justice, and victim compensation, and that claimant victims were no more willing than non-claimants, and oftentimes less so. Since a victim's city, claim status, and compensation experience contribute so extensively to explaining this relative willingness to cooperate, the apparently low level of that cooperation can be attributed to those variables in particular.

Finally, Brooklyn and Newark claimants can again be distinguished by the amount of variance the compensation variables explain in each of the samples. While they explain an average of over 50% among Brooklyn claimants, they explain an average of only 44% among Newark claimants. Although the difference is smaller than in previous analyses, it still indicates that since victims are largely uncooperative, the influence of the New York compensation program explains more of that alienation in Brooklyn than the New Jersey plan explains in Newark.

Conclusion

This chapter has examined closely the three most prominent goals of victim-compensation programs. Those objectives include granting awards, producing more favorable attitudes toward victim compensation, criminal justice, and government, and inducing greater cooperation with the same institutions. Although this study cannot directly test[11] the program's success in achieving yet a fourth goal, better crime prevention, this chapter has at least provided some statistical evidence for evaluating the first three objectives.

Previous chapters began to demonstrate victim compensation's failure to achieve these goals by indicating that most victims did not apply for compensation; those who did apply were unable to get an award; those who sought alternative payments were unsuccessful; attitudes toward victim compensation, criminal justice, and government were poor; and victims were unwilling to participate in those processes in the future. Furthermore, previous chapters also indicated that victims who had contact with their state's compensation program were just as dissatisfied as victims who had no such contact, and sometime moreso.

This chapter has carried that analysis one step further. By employing a series of discriminant function analyses, it was possible to examine what contributed the most to explaining the largely negative attitudes and outcomes discussed in earlier chapters. It was discovered that much interaction and relationship exists among the attitudes and experiences a victim accumulates from government, criminal justice, and victim compensation. Dissatisfaction with any one is almost always associated with disenchantment with the other two.

Consequently, victim compensation's advocates are correct in assuming that a victim's compensation experience can have an impact on his other attitudes and behavior. Unfortunately for these proponents, the actual impact appears to be exactly the opposite from what was intended. That is, victim compensation does have an effect, but its influence, at least among the New York and New Jersey applicants, is largely negative. As measured by the many dependent variables analyzed in this chapter, victims' dissatisfaction with government, criminal justice, and victim compensation itself, is explained substantially by the victims' city, his status as either a claimant or non-claimant, and especially by the compensation experience itself.

The logic of victim compensation is valid. In fact, those few victims who are compensated adequately[12] do have favorable attitudes toward the compensation programs, as well as toward government and criminal justice. The reason why these results are not more widespread in New York and in New Jersey is due to some very severe flaws in these states' programs. Specific information about the compensation plans is not well publicized and thus practically nobody (compared to all those victimized) ever finds out about how to apply to the programs. When informed about the plans, victims are strongly discouraged from applying by the stringent eligibility requirements. And, when some victims do actually apply, most of them are denied awards largely because of those same restrictive regulations.

Furthermore, although getting an award is probably the single most important outcome for victims from the compensation process, their case length, involvement, difficulties, and information, and their impression of board officials are other important things evaluated by victims. From the responses given by this study's claimants, victims are just as dissatisfied with these aspects of the compensation experience. In sum, these flaws have resulted in victims who are not more favorably disposed toward criminal justice and government at all.

In fact, some evidence exists to indicate that in many instances claimants are even more dissatisfied than non-claimants, despite what one would have guessed (prior to this study) to be the greater satisfaction resulting from their compensation experience. In other words, policymakers and other victim-compensation supporters failed to anticipate the negative attitudes that would result from victims being informed about compensation and frequently developing the impression on their own[13] that they would receive an award, only to later discover that they would rather consistently fail to qualify and thus fail to get compensated. If one can put trust in this study's research design, which sought to compare claimants and non-claimants to assess victim's feelings when exposed or not exposed to a compensation program, then it is clear that attitudes toward criminal justice and government among most claimants would have been better if victim compensation had never existed at all. But, of course, the number of victims having contact with a compensation board is miniscule when compared to all victims, and to all citizens, and thus the positive, symbolic, and psychological effect of the program for most people might still be intact.

In addition to both programs' generally not achieving their intended goals, New York's plan seems to have done an even worse job, in victims' eyes, than the New Jersey plan. Previous chapters have indicated that Brooklyn claimants are quite regularly more dissatisfied than Newark claimants, and less likely to cooperate in the future. In addition, much of this dissatisfaction is explained by the compensation experience (and not by the victims' other characteristics and experiences), and is even better explained by those measures among Brooklyn claimants than among Newark claimants. In other words, the New York program seems to contribute more to a victim's dissatisfaction with victim compensation, criminal justice, and government than does the New Jersey program.

It is unclear what accounts for this difference between the two programs. It was hypothesized in this study that New York's welfare philosophy in granting awards would produce more dissatisfaction than New Jersey's rights approach. Although substantial opposition to New York's "means test" was indicated by respondents, no statistical verification of that as the entire problem can be offered, and thus only the author's impressions (formed from actually talking to the victims in the interviews) about that test's repercussions can be suggested. As discussed in chapter eight, the two boards also have contrasting working environments that make New York's plan more bureaucratic and New Jersey's program more personal, and thus this difference provides the only apparent competition to the boards' contrasting award philosophies for explaining the lower dissatisfaction among Newark claimants than among Brooklyn claimants.

In sum, the impact of victim compensation is both favorable and unfavorable. For a very few victims, it produces financial benefits and improved attitudes. For most other victims, it apparently has the potential to achieve the same results. But, due to the largely intentional characteristics of compensation programs, most victims (including most of those in Brooklyn and Newark, and even most of those actually applying to the New York and New Jersey plans) do not receive financial benefits, nor are their attitudes improved, and in fact, they might be worsened. Whether or not policymakers ever really intended victim compensation to achieve its supposed goals, it is clear that those objectives are not being realized in either case.

Notes

1. For a further description of discriminant analysis, see William W. Cooley & Paul R. Lohnes, *Multivariate Data Analysis* (New York: John Wiley, 1971); William Klecka, *Discriminant Analysis* (Beverly Hills: Sage, 1980); Maurice Tatsuoka, *Multivariate Analysis* (New York: John Wiley, 1971); Norman Nie, et al., *Statistical Package for the Social Sciences* (New York: McGraw Hill, 1975); John Van de Geer, *Introduction to Multivariate Analysis for the Social Sciences* (San Francisco: W.H. Freeman, 1971); J. Aldrich & C.F. Cnudde, "Probing the Bounds of Conventional Wisdom: A Comparison of Regression, Probit, and Discriminant Analysis," *Amer. J. Pol. Sci.*, 29(1975), 571; Fred Kort, "Regression Analysis and Discriminant Analysis: An Application of R.A. Fisher's Theorem to Data in Political Science," *Amer. Pol. Sci. R.*, 67(1973), 555.

2. Discriminant analysis allows a comparison of independent variables that is not possible by simply comparing the results of bivariate correlations.

3. In testing for multicollinearity, variables having a correlation of .60 or higher were excluded from the analysis.

4. For a study showing the "robustness" of discriminant analysis, and thus the extent to which one can be confident in one's conclusions despite not satisfying the textbook requirements of the technique, see P.A. Lachenbruch, *Discriminant Analysis* (New York: Hafner, 1975).

5. They would be inappropriate, for example, in Table 10.1. Obviously, whether or not a compensation award was sought separates claimants and non-claimants by definition, and thus that variable is inappropriate. Also, although the city a victim comes from might, under other circumstances, determine whether or not an award is sought, it would be misleading to consider its effects in this study because the research design purposely rigged the samples to include a desired (and roughly equal) number of victims from each city.

6. This interrelationship is the first of several that arise in the following pages where cause and effect are unclear. That is, the major measures of the compensation experience (whether an award was received, satisfaction with case involvement, satisfaction with case outcome, inconvenience of the compensation process, and impression of board officials) are related to each other. When any one of these variables is examined as a dependent variable in a discriminant analysis, the other four variables will usually explain, in combination with the other independent variables considered, some of the variance. Establishing cause and effect under these circumstances is difficult. For example, is a victim's impressions of board officials "caused" by his level of satisfaction with the outcome of his case, or is it vice versa? The same ambiguity of direction will occur among certain other variables in this chapter as well. Although no firm conclusions can be drawn in these instances, the associations will be noted nevertheless.

7. As discussed in chapter nine, this composite index of feelings toward board officials was comprised of the questions about the victim's impression of board administrators, his view of board fairness, and his estimate of the board's concern for victims. Some of the answers were recoded so that the values of each variable would range in order from favorable to unfavorable. When combined into a single index, a range of seven numeric

values resulted: the lowest two being labelled favorable, the next three being labelled mixed feelings, and the highest two being labelled unfavorable.

8. See note 6.

9. As discussed in chapter six, this composite index of attitudes toward the law-enforcement officials in the criminal case was comprised of the questions about how the victim felt about the prosecutor, the judge, and the police. Some of the answers were recoded so that the values of each variable would range in order from favorable to unfavorable. When combined into a single index, a range of seven numeric values resulted: the lowest two being labelled favorable attitude, the next three being labelled as neutral, and the highest two being labelled negative attitude.

10. As discussed in chapter four, this composite index of a victim's political efficacy was comprised of the questions about whether he felt he would have an effect on city council, whether he would ever try to exert such influence, and whether he felt he would receive fair treatment from government officials. Some of the answers were recoded so that the values of each variable would range in order from good to poor. When combined into a single index, a range of four numeric values resulted: the lowest two being labelled as good efficacy, and the highest two being labelled as poor efficacy.

11. A couple of studies described in chapter two, however, have attempted to test the ability of victim compensation to achieve this goal. See William Doerner, "A Quasi-Experimental Analysis of Selected Victim Compensation Programs," *Canad. J. Crim.*, 20(1978), 239; Susan Stelzenmuller Silverman & William Doerner, "The Effect of Victim Compensation Programs Upon Conviction Rates," *Sociol. Symposium,* 25(1979), 40.

Also, the research herein provides circumstantial evidence against victim compensation's effect on crime since the plans fail to generate the tangible public support for law enforcement that criminal-justice officials claim is necessary for better crime control.

12. The importance of economic motivations to crime victims in helping to determine their cooperation, and the influence of financial reward on improving attitudes are considerable, and their effects can be seen not only in the receipt of victim compensation, but also in a victim's recovery of payments from alternative sources.

13. See chapter nine for evidence that a victim's expectations of receiving compensation are often elevated, and then disappointed.

CHAPTER ELEVEN
Conclusion: The Politics of Victim Compensation

Professor Heinrich Applebaum is a criminologist who feels that unless the police start cracking down on the victims of criminal acts, the crime rate in this country will continue to rise.

"The people who are responsible for crime in this country are the victims. If they didn't allow themselves to be robbed, the problem of crime in this country would be solved." Applebaum said.

"That makes sense, Professor. Why do you think the courts are soft on victims of crime?"

"We're living in a permissive society and anything goes," Applebaum replied. "Victims of crimes don't seem to be concerned about the consequences of their acts. They walk down a street after dark, or they display jewelry in their store window, or they have their cash registers right out where everyone can see them. They seem to think that they can do this in the United States and get away with it."[1]

Art Buchwald's wry humor can be taken several ways. By drawing upon the cliches that usually are directed toward our society's supposedly "soft" treatment of criminals, we can understand his words as a critique of those easy explanations for continued crime. When taken at its face value, however, Buchwald's fun can be seen as a serious poke at the extent to which victims actually do precipitate crimes against them, and in some cases they do. But, his satire's most likely purpose is to defend victims by showing how ridiculous we look "blaming" them, and by how little we have done to assist them in handling victimization or in preventing it in the first place.

Since 1969, when Buchwald wrote, much apparently has been done for the crime victim. Chapter one provides a broad summary of the wide variety of activities promoted on the victim's behalf in the last fifteen years, from victim-service centers to trying to involve the victim more productively as a witness at

241

trial. The crime victim has received wide attention not only from policymakers but also from academics: thus, the creation of the field of "victimology."

One of the most important steps taken in the United States to assist the victim has been the efforts of some of our states to follow the lead of several other nations in establishing victim compensation programs. It has been this study's purpose to evaluate two such programs as they exist in New York and New Jersey, and to assess in particular the extent to which they are achieving their goals, and what kind of impact they are having on crime victims, criminal justice, and government.

Summary of Findings

Chapter one has introduced the question of victim compensation's effectiveness. The discussion suggested that compensation should be viewed within the context not only of a wider group of victim services, but also within a broader perspective that examines the victim's general role in the criminal-justice process. That role cannot be considered apart from the incentives of criminal-justice officials nor separate from offenders and the basic causes of the crime that produces victimization in the first place. Victim compensation appears to provide a clear benefit for crime victims, but the actual results of such programs, as well as the actual motives and degree of commitment behind them, are important areas of consideration.

Chapter two has surveyed the extensive literature comprising one portion (the area of victim compensation) of the field of victimology. That review emphasized both the importance of the existing research, and its fundamental limitations. Most of the literature has been formalistically descriptive, prescriptive, and speculative in discussing victim compensation. Practically no research has attempted to evaluate such programs in action, by observing their activities and by intensively questioning the administrators and applicants. This study has attempted to fill that gap.

Chapter three has described the research design devised to conduct this study and the difficulties of completing such a project. An attempt to assess victim compensation's impact was made through a detailed and extensive questioning of board officials and crime victims. Although surveying the former required only a straight-forward interviewing of the board members and investigators who decided the cases of those who applied to the New York and New Jersey compensation boards, questioning the crime victims themselves was a considerably more complicated matter.

Since a longitudinal study of crime victims was not economically or practically feasible, a comparative design was adopted that provided for both an experimental and control group of victims in each state. Since Brooklyn and Newark are large cities in each of the two states, and since they possessed numerous similarities in their characteristics, environments, and plentiful supply of violent-crime victims, the samples were chosen from these localities. The "experiment" consisted of exposing (or, more correctly, of locating victims who had been exposed) one group of victims in each city to victim compensation, while the control group was chosen deliberately so that its members would lack any such exposure.

The basic research question asked was: what impact did victim compensation have and how could applicants be distinguished from non-applicants in their attitudes and willingness to cooperate with criminal justice and government generally. To answer this question was to test substantially the goals of victim compensation. That is, to what extent were crime victims being compensated? Did compensation produce the supposed improvement in attitudes? And, could it be associated with improving crime prevention by encouraging the kind of victim cooperation and participation that might assist law-enforcement efforts?

Distinguishing the control group of "non-claimants" from the experimental group of "claimants" required not merely examining the compensation experience and its outcomes. To differentiate properly the attitudes held by victims in the two groups, and to contrast adequately the two separate compensation programs as well, it was necessary to examine any differences existing in the victims general backgrounds and characteristics, as well as to follow their journey through the criminal process from the moment of victimization onward.

Chapter four begins to describe that process by examining victims' backgrounds and characteristics, including their social traits, their community ties, and their general attitudes toward government and criminal justice. The results indicate that most victims were young, married, non-white males with a low socioeconomic status, few community attachments, and poor attitudes toward government institutions, including the criminal-justice system. These characteristics are consistent with other studies of violent crime. The separate samples of victims also did not differ significantly from each other, and thus these background characteristics did not contribute very much to the ultimate differences in victim attitudes and behavior.

Chapter five starts a victim's journey through the criminal process. We begin understanding what it is to be victimized, and what motivates a victim to pursue his case in the justice system. We see, through the victim's perspective, how the court looks from within to those who get involved in it. And, we discover a crime victim's frustrations when he actively seeks to pursue his case only to discover the obstacles to his effective participation, beginning with his first appearance in the court to make a complaint through the various arraignment and post-arraignment stages of the process. In sum, we see that a victim's goals in participating in the process in the first place are rarely realized, and this experience is common in both cities and thus to all the samples examined in this study. Thus, criminal-justice experiences also do not account very much for the differences among victims in attitudes and behavior.

Chapter six examines the impact of the criminal process, particularly to discover what are the system's actual outcomes for the victim, and what attitudes are associated with those results. One discovers that the outcomes are as discouraging for the victims as were the barriers to his effective participation in the process. Consequently, negative attitudes toward criminal justice and its personnel are not surprising, nor is the widespread unwillingness to cooperate in the future which is associated with those sentiments.

Examining the court system's impact also makes clear the actual and potential economic motivations of crime victims. Such attitudes seem strong enough to induce increased cooperation if the monetary rewards for doing so are forthcoming. In practice, they are not.

Finally, in this chapter we discover for the first time some significant differences among the samples in victims' specific attitudes toward the officials in their case and toward their general criminal-justice experience. Brooklyn claimants were almost uniformly less satisfied with their case outcome, with judges and prosecutors and their specific treatment of offenders, with their own treatment in court, and with appearing in court in the first place. Victims differ in these attitudes despite the fact that their backgrounds, characteristics, victimizations, motivations, and court experiences and outcomes were quite similar. What then accounts for these attitudinal variations?

Chapter seven begins to examine directly the hypothesized answer to that question. That is, this chapter begins to consider victim compensation's role and its possible effects on shaping victim attitudes toward the criminal process and the government generally. Initially, we discover the particular characteristics of the New York and New Jersey compensation boards and programs. It is clear how similar the two plans are, including their administration, procedures, structures, eligibility requirements, and the politics of their adoption.

The major differences emerging between the programs lies in their underlying philosophies for granting compensation: New York's based on a "welfare approach" that requies a showing of financial need, and New Jersey's based on a "rights approach" that makes one's economic status irrelevant. It was hypothesized in this study that this difference would be important to the comparative effectiveness of each program.

Chapter eight describes actual board members and investigators in the two programs, including their backgrounds, careers, attitudes toward government and criminal justice, perspectives on victim compensation, and decision-making influences. We discover two different official "roles," including "advocates" who take an activist and broad view of victim compensation's purposes and potential, and "neutrals" who take a moderate and limited view of the programs' activities.

This chapter also clearly presents a contrast between board officials and the victims they serve in their backgrounds, and frequently in their attitudes, as well.

Moreover, we learn that board officials often feel constrained in their activities by the preferences and budgets provided by policymakers. The tendency is to restrict publicity so as to limit the number of applicants, but at least some board members try to use their limited discretion to extend coverage to a few more victims than the strict rules might permit. Board officials' views of compensation's impact vary from "considerable" to "very limited." And finally, we discover perhaps another element distinguishing the two state's programs: the tendency of New Jersey's board to be a more like-minded, cohesive, and personal organization as compared to New York's diverse, bureaucratic atmosphere.

Chapter nine finally brings us to the compensation process in action, and allows us to examine the experience of at least those victims in this study who applied for an award in either of the two states. That experience includes the application process, the requirements and difficulties of pursuing a case, the victim's ability to participate in his case, the outcomes of the process, and the victim's assessment of the results.

Clearly, most victims, including some who actually were given awards, were much more negative toward compensation than were board officials. Respondents were dissatisfied with delays, inconveniences, poor information, inability to participate, and the restrictive eligibility requirements. These sentiments, coupled with the large number of award applications that were denied, produced strongly negative attitudes among victims toward victim compensation. And, to add some credence to the belief that New Jersey's program would be more favorably perceived than New York's, victims responded exactly that way, often significantly so.

Since victim compensation's major goals are to recompense victims and to improve their attitudes and cooperation, the two programs can be regarded as nothing short of failures, at least in the eyes of the victims who the programs are designed to serve, not to mention all those victims who are not served by the plans because they never learn about how to apply to the programs, or fail to apply because of the eligibility requirements, or are denied an award because of the same rules. The dissatisfaction of victims extends not only to displeasure with victim compensation itself (and for reasons, such as board insensitivity, case delays, and inadequate participation that go beyond merely being denied an award), but also to disenchantment with the broader institutions of criminal justice and government. Can we blame this broader dissatisfaction on victim compensation?

Chapter ten attempts to answer this question. It is clear that victim displeasure with compensation, the court system, and the political system is very extensive among most of this study's respondents. It is also evident that those attitudes are no better among victims who applied for compensation than among those who had not, and that often the attitudes are worse. Victim compensation's supporters, however, have predicted exactly the opposite results for those victims using compensation programs. Are the plans responsible for producing a result that directly contradicts the one intended?

Early chapters showed that differences among the victims in this study in their backgrounds, motivations, involvement, and the other possible repercussions of their victimization and post-victimization experiences were almost non-existent. The only clear and major differences among the samples were based on whether or not victims had applied for compensation and on whether they had contact with the New York program as opposed to the New Jersey plan. The emerging differences in victim attitudes toward government and the court system, there-fore, would appear to be attributable to differences in the compensation, and not the criminal-justice, experience.

Unfortunately for victim compensation's advocates, victims having applied to the compensation programs were more discontent than those who had not, thus causing one to wonder whether attitudes would not have been better overall if victim compensation had never existed. And, victims having contact with New York's program expressed more displeasure, about criminal justice and govern-ment, as well as about victim compensation, than those applying to New Jersey's plan. Whether one wants to attribute this divergence to these boards' differing scale and work atmosphere (as observed in chapter eight), or to their differing philosophies in granting awards (as described in chapter seven), the distinction neverthless remains.

Clearly, not all victims applying for victim compensation were unhappy. Many, but not all, of those few who did receive awards expressed considerable satisfaction (at least compared to other victims) not only with the programs but also with criminal justice and government as well. But, most claimants were very dissatisfied. To assess the extent to which victim compensation might be "responsible" not merely for the differences in attitudes among all the samples, but also for a general dissatisfaction among the victims using the plans, chapter ten presented a series of multivariate analyses to compare the various, potential influences.

Using discriminant function analysis in particular, it was discovered that when one compares the apparent "contributions" of the variables in this study to pro-ducing the extensive victim dissatisfaction with compensation, criminal justice, and government, the influence of the compensation experience is considerable. Compensation does have an impact just as supporters of such programs claim, but thusfar it is a largely negative and unintended one.

Implications of the Study

Figure 11.1 shows what has become a popular representation of the "criminal injustice system." Appearing in places such as the annual report of New York's compensation board, it purports to show the criminal's advantages and the victim's disadvantages as a reflection of this injustice. While the overall conclusion (the injustice) about the criminal process is clearly accurate, it hardly derives from the criminal's supposed advantages. In other words, at least one-half of Figure 11.1 (i.e., that part referring to the offender) is based on gross distortion, exaggeration, and misinformation.

In particular, Figure 11.1 is laden with values and misconceptions about criminals that are as harmful to the victim's interest as they are to the offender's. First, contrary to our supposed practice of assuming innocence until proven guilty, the description of the "criminal's" path through the system already pre-establishes his culpability. Next, it assumes that the "criminal" has a choice, and implies a rationality about common crime that is almost completely contradicted by past research[2]. What evidence we do have, however, on the sources of crime (in particular, social and economic conditions) renders the "criminal's" supposed "choice" very questionnable.

It is further assumed that the "criminal" continues to live a life of crime, when it is unclear that any such thing exists among the vast majority of those who break the law, much less that we can assume that those who are not apprehended will lead such a life. A long list of the "criminal's" supposed rights appears despite the notable evidence that in practice these liberties are regularly ignored[3]. Pre-trial detention is portrayed as a kind of country club for "criminals," presumably as a warmup for the even bigger country club called state prison. These "paradises" are, in fact, completely dispelled by the actual conditions of our prisons, not the least of which is the practical non-existence of all the rehabilitation programs Figure 11.1 suggests are available[4].

Actually, one could challenge almost every presumption and statement about criminals and their treatment in the criminal process listed on Figure 11.1. Unfortunately, the fallacious contrast between the criminal's "paradise" and the victim's "hell" can only be counterproductive for the crime victim's interests.

More specifically, the now long-term trend toward considering the "plight" of the victim has been associated almost exclusively (especially in the media, in government, and among those outside government who seem to most influence public officials) with a hard-line approach toward criminals and criminal justice. Largely abandoned has been any attempt to seek out and eradicate what the President's Commission on Law Enforcement and the Administration of Justice identified fifteen years ago as the "root causes" (i.e., social and economic conditions) of crime. Instead, what has arisen is a "law-and-order" perspective, or what one writer calls the "new conservative criminology,"[5] which seeks to "combat" crime by what might be called the "vietnamization of criminal justice," or the application of more men, more hardware, more weapons, more offensives, and swifter and more severe punishments to deter another largely non-white enemy[6]. Although it is clear that some segments of the society would clearly have no interest in (and everything to lose from) ending this militarization

FIGURE 11.1: CRIMINAL INJUSTICE SYSTEM

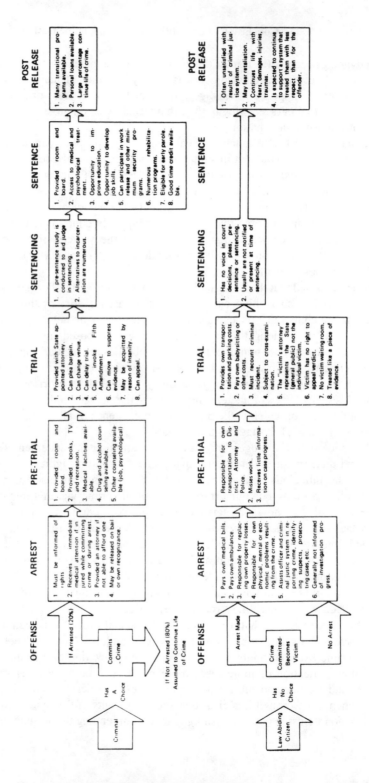

of law enforcement in favor of addressing these "root causes," those who suffer are not only those who violate the law, but also the crime victims themselves[7].

In other words, a hard-line approach to law enforcement has not shown any results, undoubtedly due to the inadequacy of the process to handle all the crime (even among those criminals who are apprehended) in our society, and due to the questionnable deterrent or preventive effect of beefed-up police forces and stricter penalties in the first place. In fact, the only "deterrent" that creating such an atmosphere might produce would be for those people who normally do not commit common crimes, since invariably their freedom and sense of security are reduced in the process[8].

The major point, however, is that even if the "law-and-order" approach was more effective in checking the increase in crime or even in reducing it to some extent, the "root causes" of crime would still remain. If policymakers really are concerned about crime victims, then the "conservative" mentality is certainly not the best approach.

But, are policymakers really concerned, and does a "law-and-order" approach purposely perpetuate crime, causing a continued susceptibility for people to become victims as well as criminals? When one learns about victim-compensation programs and other such victim services, one is tempted to conclude that the concern for victims is genuine. But, although some of the people who actually administer the programs, and some of those who established the plans in the first place are, in fact, concerned, one's faith is undermined by a number of other considerations. That is, when one looks more closely at a program such as victim compensation (as this study has done), one discovers vastly differing levels of commitment to victim needs, and an overall sense of limited concern emerges.

Similar to the motives of many who argue for the victim's role in the criminal process, many of victim compensation's advocates emphasize the goal of "using" the victim in the criminal process. The stress is on how to induce (apparently by buying their participation) victims to be more cooperative, as if to admit that little presently characterizes the justice system to encourage participation on its own. Although some genuinely want to compensate victims for its value alone, many others, including some politicians and board officials, apparently view awards as a means to an end. And, that end includes not merely creating favorable attitudes among victims toward criminal justice, but also favorable views among victims and the broader public toward government generally.

When one tries to decide whether victim compensation was legislated with the interests of crime victims as most prominent, or rather as a "political placebo," the evidence seems to support the latter. The programs seem to constitute a "symbolic" benefit of the system, but not a concrete, tangible one[9].

First, we know that in both states examined in this study, the rush to authorize a compensation program found legislators and executives tripping over one another, but when it came time to appropriating money to actually make the plans run, it apparently took some time to round policymakers up. Sponsoring and supporting and establishing victim-compensation programs are very popular activities for representatives who care about their constitutents' views, but actually committing the resources necesary to make the plans operate involved considerable reluctance, and apparently even some opposition among some of those who had voted to authorize the programs in the first place[10].

When appropriations finally came for these programs, the apparent lack of real commitment was bolstered further by the meagre revenue provided, which gave the plans little chance of achieving their stated goals. Victim compensation remains a popular program, undoubtedly improving public opinion about the extent to which victims and law-abiding citizens are finally being considered, even if almost nobody in the general public receives its benefits. The perception is presumably that "the program is there if it is needed, but with luck I will never need it." The reality is that if it is needed, the program is not actually there.

In other words, although many people, including many of the victims in this study, have heard of victim compensation, they are largely lacking in the information needed to apply when they are actually victimized and have cause to use the program. Many other victims in this study had not even heard of the programs, and thus had no chance to apply either. Actual publicity about how the programs can be used is not widespread, largely due to policymakers' efforts to forestall a flood of applications. Although some board members have sought to further publicize the plans and get increased appropriations, their hands usually are tied, as much as they like to suggest their independence from political controls. Not getting the cooperation of police officers, which is only a reflection of the larger inability of compensation programs to really integrate themselves into the criminal-justice system, who are supposed (at least in New York) to tell victims about the plans, is a further impediment.

When victims do hear about compensation and find out specifically how to apply, most are little better off than if they had never known about the programs in the first place. That is, the eligibility requirements are so stringent and restrictive that most applicants are disqualified before they even apply. Again, the genuine commitment to victims, even to violent-crime victims alone much less other kinds, is questioned by these narrow rules.

Why is the commitment apparently so limited? Is it because victims just cannot compete with more important priorities in the society, or because of a variety of practical reasons offered by policymakers? Or, is it something more? One might argue that it is the latter. To start, we know that violent crimes are the offenses that most frighten Americans. Thus, it is logical to focus public policy on these crimes, not only in restricting victim compensation to only these offenses, but also in simultaneously stressing a "get tough" approach with perpetrators of the most "serious"[11] crimes.

Most Americans have been led to widely fear these kinds of crimes, and thus to accept a "militarized" law enforcement to combat it, despite the fact that much of that fear is experienced by those people in our society (i.e., middle classes) who actually have much less reason to fear violent crimes. That is, most violent crimes are committed by lower-class people against other lower-class people[12].

Jeffrey Reiman suggests that this level of fear among the wrong segment of the society is no accident, but in fact performs a particular, ideological function[13]. Specifically, Reiman claims that middle classes are induced to think of lower classes as the "enemy," and to seek hard-line measures to combat it, even if it means a reduction in middle class freedom in the process. The argument claims that this result deflects attention away from the real "enemy" or source of crime, which he argues is our particular social and economic system as it is shaped largely by the upper classes. One need not fully accept this theory to find it difficult, nevertheless, to avoid viewing victim compensation as merely a symbolic gesture aimed primarily at "potential" and not actual crime victims. Actual crime victims almost never get an award.

Why else would victim compensation be useful? One might further argue that policymakers are fully aware of lower-class fears of crime as well, which in fact are the most justified fears of all since these people are predominantly the victims. Why would these people not be just as pleased to have victim compensation as anyone else? Since violent-crime victims, many of whom are poor, do get compensated, can we not recognize at least some beneficial results for the lower classes of society?

Perhaps, but maybe not if one accepts the thesis of Piven and Cloward. After completing an extensive study of the effects of the "welfare state" since the 1930's and through the 1970's, these scholars conclude that welfare programs have had very limited results for their intended recipients, and that such programs have arisen and declined, both in numbers of programs and in the appropriations given to support them, directly proportional to periods of unrest in society, including the economic failures of the depression and the riots of the 1960's and 1970's. Their conclusion is that welfare has been used to buy and regulate the poor both to diffuse their justifiable discontent and to induce their acceptance and cooperation with the economic and political systems[14].

As essentially welfare programs themselves, if for no other reason than the economic class the programs largely serve (especially in New York), victim compensation might be correctly viewed as a palliative in a period of unrest. In a time when extensive crime was coupled with anti-war demonstrations and civil-rights protest, it is perhaps not surprising that such a program might surface, just as other welfare programs did. That the programs achieved much less than what was promised is not surprising either when compared to the failures, for example, of most Great Society programs, and if one accepts Piven and Cloward's perspective that such programs were adopted for their symbolic (for middle and lower classes alike), and only minimal tangible (for largely lower classes), appeal.

Just as Reiman, and Piven and Cloward do not assume that the state of our criminal-justice system or our welfare programs is necessarily a conspiracy perpetrated by the "powers that be,"[15] neither must we necessarily draw that conclusion about the purpose and status of victim compensation. It might, instead, be seen merely as what Bachrach and Baratz have called the "mobilization of bias,"[16] in government policy, or a reflection of those values (including those presently dominating our social and economic systems) most widely accepted and believed among those who make government decisions. The criminal-justice system reflects the configuration, including the social conditions and the distribution of material goods, of the broader society in which it is located[17].

Indicting victim compensation is not meant to place all the responsibility for a victim's dilemma on these programs. Certainly, the victm's treatment after being victimized, and his experience in the criminal process, provide strong competition to victim compensation for producing negative attitudes. Victims often are treated callously by police officers, and then no better in subsequent stages of the court system. Their desires are almost completely ignored, and their involvement (if any) is almost always related to when and how they can be "used," instead of to when and how they could be served, or free to choose to get involved in the prosecution.

As Eduard Ziegenhagen has observed:

> The claims of victims who are poor or can be recognized as persons of low status . . . are not perceived as being entirely legitimate or compelling to most criminal justice professionals. . . The likelihood that the claims of lower strata victims will be discounted or at best receive perfunctory attention in combination with the relative invulnerabilitiy of criminal-justice professionals to challenges of their performance, contributes to the treatment crime victims receive.[18]

Our society pays little concern to crime victims, whether it be in the criminal process or even through most victim-service programs such as victim compensation, because most victims are lower-class people who have interests and characteristics that are almost totally unrepresented in the political system. Criminals, or those likely to turn to crime, suffer the same fate.

The response of criminal-justice officials to crime victims, however, is not completely without rationalization. The goals and incentives of law-enforcment personnel have long operated without the need to consider the crime victim. Arresting, prosecuting, and sentencing have been pursued predominantly against suspects, defendants, and criminals on behalf of the entire society and not for the particular benefit of the victims.

In fact, other than to "use" the victim to pursue their goals of arrests, convictions, and disposing cases, it might well be appropriate to understand why any greater role for the victim would constitute an interference for criminal justice officials in what Eisenstein and Jacob have called the "courtroom workgroups" that keep the system running[19]. In other words, law enforcement personnel have not been given an incentive in their work to take victims widely into consideration. Thus, "it is not surprising that victims are viewed as a resource to be drawn upon in the pursuit of organizational objectives, most of which are incidental to the satisfaction of victims' individual interests."[20]

Furthermore, one also might understand the callous view of law-enforcement officials toward most victims, especially those of violent crimes. First, as largely lower class, poor blacks and hispanics, most victims are like most criminals, but they are both perceived to be different in backgrounds and values from most of our law-enforcement personnel. Second, besides this apparent "cultural" gap, it is widely perceived that victims are often just as guilty as the offenders. Although this perception is exaggerated, it contains at least a grain of truth.

Many violent crimes are characterized by a relationship of some kind between the two parties in the criminal event. In other words, they are frequently not strangers. Existing as they do in what has been called the "subculture of violence,"[21] it becomes almost a matter of chance as to who will be the victim and who will be the offender for any particular crime, almost a matter of who strikes first. Consequently, it is difficult to clearly attribute guilt, especially since some crime victims have criminal records themselves. And, when it comes to pursuing cases in court, some cases are discontinued because of this relationship, either because the two parties have "made up," or because it is possible for a defendant to threaten a victim into dropping charges for fear of retaliation afterwards.

But, do these concessions really justify the limited commitment to crime victims? These admissions might explain the logic of some official court behavior under the present circumstances, but they hardly justify perpetuating the system and the atmosphere that creates it. Unfortunately, that is exactly what the new concern for crime victims has done. It has paid lip-service to the problems of victims and yet has done little to eradicate those forces that produce the crime victim in the first place, or that give law-enforcement officials the incentives they pursue. And, just as the system has failed to rehabilitate the offender, so too has it failed to rehabilitate the victim[22].

This research has attempted to evaluate victim compensation as one major approach to assisting crime victims. It has sought to evaluate both the process and the impact of such programs, and in both instances the plans have come up lacking.

First, the victim-compensation process is troublesome. From the perspective of board officials, the process is largely determined by the rules and constraints imposed by the legislators who have created and perpetuated the programs. Except for a small degree of discretion that board officials might use to slightly expand the eligibility requirements to cover a few more victims, the administrators are largely constricted. In particular, they are restrained by narrow budgetary limits. And, from the victim's perspective, the process is inadequate not only because it most frequently disqualifies them from coverage, but also due to long delays, inadequate participation, difficulties in pursuing one's case, and insufficient information about the case's progress.

Second, victim compensation's impact is equally inadequate. It has been stated repeatedly in this study that the programs have produced adverse consequences. To relate them specifically to the programs' goals, this means that victims are not being adequately compensated, that their attitudes toward criminal justice are not being improved, and that their willingness to cooperate is low[23]. Consequently, it also unlikely that the programs have achieved their other intended (but not directly tested in this research) objective of helping to prevent crime[24], and unclear whether the plans have had a general positive effect on those elements of the general public who have not become crime victims but nevertheless know of the program's existence.

It was hypothesized in this study that these goals would not be met, and thus it appears that the theory has been borne out, not only by the statistics compiled and formal questioning, but also by the author's general observations in conducting the research. Three other hypotheses guided this study, as well, however, and they seem almost equally realized.

First, it was theorized that victim compensation might produce the unanticipated consequence of raising expectations among crime victims, only to have them rather consistently frustrated by the board regulations, and thus produce not only negative attitudes, but perhaps even more dissatisfaction than would have existed if victim compensation had never been adopted at all. Comparing the claimant and non-claimant samples in this study seems to verify that hypothesis.

Second, it was also hypothesized that victim compensation would have the positive effect (claimed for it by its supporters) for those who received an award, and also (but less so) for those who at least received some award, even if not regarded as full payment. In fact, this theory was only partially correct, since although some fully reimbursed victims were satisfied, others were not (not to mention many who were only partly reimbursed). In conjunction with this theory, it also was suggested that a victim's motives for compensation might reflect only a portion of his general economic incentives (or susceptibilities) for participating in the court system, and for thinking about his future willingness to cooperate again. Examining a victim's response to other forms of payments besides compensation, it is apparent that although monetary reward was certainly not a victim's only goal, it certainly was an important one, and thus seems to verify this economic contention.

And third, it was theorized in this study that New Jersey claimants would be more content than New York claimants because the former's program took a rights approach, while the latter's practiced a welfare philosophy. Although the level of victim satisfaction with compensation, criminal justice, and government was generally higher in New Jersey than in New York, it is unclear whether underlying philosophy was the decisive reason. Few alternative explanations besides the differing working atmospheres of each board provide any effective challenge to the hypothesis, however.

Policy Recommendations

If it is unavoidable to assess victim compensation as at worst a failure and at best a disappointment, then what course should policymakers take with regard to the programs in the future? Recommendations can be made on two levels, one more realistic than the other under the present circumstances.

One would be well justified in suggesting change on a fundamental level, but it would require much more than merely altering compensation programs themselves. Such basic change requires, instead, no less than a complete transformation of the criminal-justice system into a process that is actually the adversarial system that we are supposed to have in the first place. Such a change, however, would require extensive alterations in the broader society that supports the criminal process we now have. Real change would mean that we would have to get really serious about wanting to eliminate crime, and put forth the kinds of policies and resources our society can well afford, not for the purpose of overwhelming crime with force and firepower, but rather to undercut the real sources of crime, most of which are completely known to us.

For example, we could reduce the extensive drain on our justice system caused by an unnecessary and massive overcriminalization, drastically reduce our use of prisons, change our economic incentives, and extensively redistribute wealth and benefits in our society. The consequence of these changes would be considerably less crime committed in the first place. Then, victim compensation and offender restitution could be tailored to fit whatever crime problem and victim needs (and they would be considerably reduced) that remained, and do so with a real commitment in mind (without having to "buy" a victim's support for the system) both to seriously helping victims and criminals, and to seriously reducing the crime rate even further.

As LeRoy Lamborn has observed:

> A renewed concern for a victim orientation in criminal theory does not mean desire for a retreat from interest in the criminal, rather, the hope is that a substantial interest in the perspective of the victim will supplement the traditional criminal orientation and that the two together will increase the success of efforts to prevent crime, and to understand more fully the criminal justice process.[25] (Emphasis mine.)

Although it is very unclear, based on its past track record of largely ignoring the most fundamental sources of crime, whether the "traditional" orientation is desirable, a coordinated concern for both the criminal and the victim (linked to the proposed eliminating of the sources of crime) would be a big step in the right direction.

But, "action and research on victims cannot divorce itself from the political (and I would add, economic) context which frames and uses it."[26] Since it is not likely that the aforementioned changes will be immediately forthcoming, it is tempting to advocate the plans' abolishment. Even politicians might be wondering whether the symbolic advantages of such programs outweigh the alienation they cause most victims who actually use them. More importantly, the programs are providing very little assistance for victims, and are perpetuating the myth that you can cope with the crime problem by putting "bandaids" on the problem after the fact.

Clearly, the decision whether or not to eliminate the programs involves trade-offs since despite the obviously and predominantly negative effects of such plans, at least some victims do get some compensation, which they would not otherwise receive. Thus, if policymakers decide to continue these programs and want to improve them (keeping in mind that doing so will do nothing to lead to a long-term solution for crime or crime victims), they might begin with the following kinds of piecemeal reforms:

1) Push for a national compensation program that provides the already proposed seventy-five percent of the funding for state programs, and which will give an incentive for those states not having a program to adopt one.
2) All compensation plans should be based on a "rights" approach, and the "means test" should be eliminated.
3) The burden of proof in pursuing one's compensation claim should be reduced as long as lawyers are not made available to victims.
4) The following eligibility requirements should be eliminated: victim-offender relationship, minimum missed work time, minimum loss and maximum award limitations.
5) Publicity about victim compensation, and how to actually apply for it, should be vastly expanded.
6) Compensation boards should seek new means to better integrate themselves into the criminal-justice system, especially to seek a way to give law-enforcement officials an incentive to consider the victim in their work.
7) Beyond maintaining the requirement that the crime should be reported to the police, the victim should not be compelled, as a condition for an award, to cooperate with law-enforcement officials.
8) Board funding should be significantly increased to help pay for these changes, and to pay for the increased staff (which should also be decentralized) that will be necessary to accomodate the vastly greater amount of victims that will apply.
9) Boards should reduce their goals to solely providing full compensation, and eliminate all other objectives.

In sum, although these changes would require considerable resources, a society that produces so much crime and thus provides such a large reservoir of victims, and a society whose policymakers continue to perpetuate the circumstances that make a reduction of crime impossible, must be willing to pay for the results. They might be added to what one writer has called the "social expenses" of maintaining the system and its adverse consequences[27]. These are the reforms that piecemeal change is made of, and clearly, without them, the plans should be discontinued.

For the broader criminal process, the needs of victims are great but changes are likely to be few under the present system and under the present course of events. For the short run, however, a continued effort to provide and direct victims towards various social services should be maintained and expanded. In addition, it is necessary to find a basis for giving criminal-justice officials more incentive to consider the needs and desires of victims in their work.

Furthermore, giving victims legal counsel to match that of the defendant and to add to that of the prosecution should be avoided since what is most important to the victim is not that the criminal be punished (and there already exists considerable state power to rather consistently ensure that outcome without another lawyer anyway), but rather that he (the victim) have his other needs attended to by organizations, other than the courts, trained to do so. And finally, mediation (which is the informal settling of a case between the offender and the victim, and which was regarded with some favor by the victims in this study) and other alternatives to the formal court system, should be vastly expanded to promote a resolution of the conflict that avoids the pitfalls that the criminal process produces for both the criminal and the victim.

This study of victim compensation has had as its purpose the desire to evaluate victim-compensation programs in action, not only to add to the research in the field, but more importantly to add to our knowledge of these plans and how they are working. As a piece of research, the study seems to help the overall literature into the next stage of inquiry: it moves us beyond considering victim compensation abstractly or normatively or formalistically, and allows actual contact with the people who administer, and with those who are "served" by, the programs.

And, as a policy evaluation, it provides insights into why compensation is not working, and what are, as much as we might not like to admit them, the underlying sources of this failure, including the characteristics not only of the programs, but also of the broader criminal-justice, political, and economic systems in our society. Policymakers can choose to make piecemeal or fundamental changes accordingly. Future research should dwell not on how to make victim compensation better so much as on how to make victim compensation unnecessary in the first place.

If it is true that "the criminal is at war with society not the victim,"[28] then it is also the case that the victim is at war with society and not the offender. Although "war" is an unfortunate metaphor, the society, more than each other, is the real enemy.

Notes

1. Art Buchwald, "Solving the Crime Problem," *Washington Post,* 5 February 1969, 37.

2. See, for example, Burton Leiser, *Liberty, Justice and Morals* (New York: MacMillan, 1979); Erik Wright, *Politics of Punishment* (New York: Harper & Row, 1973); Ted Honderick, *Punishment: The Supposed Justifications* (London: Penguin, 1971); Jack Douglas (ed.), *Crime and Justice in American Society* (New York: Bobbs Merrill, 1971).

3. See, for example, Richard Quinney (ed.) *Criminal Justice in America* (Boston: Little, Brown, 1974); Richard Quinney (ed.) *Crime and Justice in Society* (Boston: Little, Brown, 1969); William Chambliss (ed.), *Crime and the Legal Process* (New York: McGraw, 1969); Howard James, *Crisis in the Courts* (New York: McKay, 1971); Lois Forer, *The Death of the Law* (New York: McKay, 1975); Jonathan Casper, *American Criminal Justice* (Englewood Cliffs: Prentice Hall, 1972); Leonard Downie, *Justice Denied* (Baltimore: Penguin, 1971).

4. Jessica Mitford, *Kind and Usual Punishment* (New York: Knopf, 1973); Ronald Goldfarb, *Jails* (New York: Simon & Schuster, 1973); Ronald Goldfarb & Linda Singer, *After Conviction* (New York: Touchstone, 1973); Karl Menninger, *The Crime of Punishment* (New York: Viking, 1971).

5. Lynn A. Curtis, "Victims, Policy, and the Dangers of a Conservative Mentality," unpublished paper delivered at the 2nd International Symposium on Victimology, Boston, 1976.

6. Center for Research on Criminal Justice, *The Iron Fist and the Velvet Glove: An Analysis of U.S. Police* (Berkeley: Garrett, 1977).

7. William Chambliss, *Whose Law? Whose Order?* (New York: John Wiley, 1974); Isaac Balbus, *The Dialectics of Legal Repression* (New Brunswick: Transaction, 1977); Barry Krisberg, *Crime and Punishment* (Englewood Cliffs: Prentice Hall, 1975); James Inciardi (ed.), *Radical Criminology* (Beverly Hills: Sage, 1980); Ted Gurr, *Rogues, Rebels, and Reformers* (Beverly Hills: Sage, 1976).

8. Alan Wolfe, The Seamy Side of Democracy (New York: Longman, 1978); American Friends Services Committee, *Struggle for Justice* (New York: Hill & Wang, 1971).

9. Murray Edelman, *The Symbolic Uses of Politics* (Urbana: U. Ill. Press, 1967).

10. Herbert Edelhertz & Gilbert Geis, *Public Compensation for Victims of Crime* (New York: Praeger, 1976).

11. Some argue that, in fact, by emphasizing common varieties of violent crime we actually are not isolating the most serious threats (or at least only the tip of the iceberg) at all. Wide areas of activity, heretofore largely not even defined as crime, are much more life threatening even than murder. For example, in 1972, one murder occurred every twenty-six minutes, while one industrial death due to accidents and diseases, most of which are totally preventable, occurred every four minutes. In that same year, the Uniform Crime Reports indicated that 10,000 people were the victims of homicide, surely an exorbitant amount. But, it pales compared to the deaths caused annually by industrial disease (100,000), industrial accidents (14,200), unnecessary prescriptions (2000-10,000), unnecessary surgery (16,000), improper emergency medical care (20,000), and environmentally produced cancer (210,000-315,000). See Jeffrey Reiman, *The Rich Get Richer and the Poor Get Prison* (New York: Wiley, 1979), 65. Since most of these deaths are produced by persons who know death will occur, and who could prevent it, one might

argue that they should be held criminally liable, not to mention countless others such as manufacturers who knowingly sell lethal gas tanks, tampons, and so on. See also, John Conklin, *Illegal But Not Criminal* (Englewood Cliffs: Prentice Hall, 1977); Edwin Schur, *Our Criminal Society* (Englewood Cliffs: Prentice Hall, 1969).

12. Herbert Jacob, *Crime and Justice in Urban America* (Englewood Cliffs: Prentice Hall, 1980).

13. Reiman, note 12 *supra*, 76.

14. Frances Fox Piven & Richard A. Cloward, *Regulating the Poor: The Functions of Public Welfare* (New York: Vintage, 1971).

15. Although at least one writer has concluded exactly that. See Richard Quinney, *Critique of Legal Order* (Boston: Little, Brown, 1974); Richard Quinney, *Class, State and Crime* (New York: Longman, 1980).

16. Peter Bachrach & Morton Baratz, *Power and Poverty: Theory and Practice* (New York: Oxford U. Press, 1970), 43.

17. Isadore Silver (ed.), *The Crime Control Establishment* (Englewood Cliffs: Prentice Hall, 1974); William Chambliss & Robert Seidman, *Law, Order and Power* (Reading, MA.: Addison-Wesley, 1971).

18. Eduard Ziegenhagen, *Victims, Crime and Social Control* (New York: Praeger, 1977), 85.

19. James Eisenstein & Herbert Jacob, *Felony Justice* (Boston: Little, Brown, 1977).

20. Ziegenhagen, note 18 *supra*, 87.

21. Marvin Wolfgang & Franco Ferracuti, *Subculture of Violence* (London: Soc. Sci. Paperbacks, 1967).

22. Lois Forer, *Criminals and Victims: A Trial Judge Reflects on Crime and Punishment* (New York: Norton, 1980).

23. It must be admitted that the question of willingness to cooperate only measures an attitude and not necessarily a victim's actual, future performance. "Questions of this kind are not always correctly answered, since we often do not know why we behave as we do." See, B.F. Skinner, *About Behaviorism* (New York: Vintage, 1974), 34. In practice, a person may actually be either more or less willing to participate than he indicates here. Greater cooperation, for example, might be induced by citizen's duty, which may not have been considered by victims when questioned. On the other hand, some of those who said they would participate, might not actually do so when the opportunity presents itself.

24. What evidence we do have on the victim compensation's impact, although offered tentatively by the authors, seems to contradict this study since their research shows some positive effect on law enforcement. See Susan Stelzenmuller Silverman & William Doerner, "The Effect of Victim Compensation Programs Upon Conviction Rates," *Sociol. Symposium*, 25(1979), 40.

25. LeRoy Lamborn, "Toward a Victim Orientation in Criminal Theory," *Rutgers L.R.*, 22(1968), 735.

26. Curtis, note 5 *supra*, 13.

27. Quinney, note 15 *supra*.

28. Forer, note 22 *supra*.

Chapter Four Tables

TABLE A.1 MARITAL STATUS

	ALL	Claimants BKLN	Claimants NEWK	Non-Claimants BKLN	Non-Claimants NEWK
	%	%	%	%	%
SINGLE	106(31) 32)	28(33) 33)	23(29) 29)	27(28) 29)	28(35) 35)
MARRIED	153(45) 46)	39(46) 46)	31(39) 39)	53(54) 57)	30(38) 38)
SEP/DIV	55(16) 16)	11(13) 13)	18(23) 23)	11(11) 12)	15(19) 19)
WIDOW	22 (6) (6)	7 (8) (8)	7 (9) (9)	2 (2) (2)	6 (8) (8)
REFUSE	6 (2)	0	0	5 (5)	1 (1)
	342	85	79	98	80

TABLE A.2 RACIAL BACKGROUND

	ALL	Claimants BKLN	Claimants NEWK	Non-Claimants BKLN	Non-Claimants NEWK
	%	%	%	%	%
WHITE	146 (43)	43(51)	33(42)	36(37)	34(43)
BLACK	135 (40)	30(35)	31(39)	42(43)	32(40)
HISPANIC	52 (15)	9(11)	14(18)	18(18)	11(14)
ORIENTAL	4 (1)	1 (1)	0	1 (1)	2 (3)
OTHER	5 (1)	2 (2)	1 (1)	1 (1)	1 (1)
	342	85	79	98	80

TABLE A.3 IMPORTANCE OF RELIGION

	ALL	Claimants BKLN	Claimants NEWK	Non-Claimants BKLN	Non-Claimants NEWK
	%	%	%	%	%
VERY	72(21) 23)	20(24) 25)	16(20) 22)	20(20) 22)	16(20) 21)
SOMEWHAT	197(58) 62)	50(59) 63)	45(57) 61)	57(58) 63)	45(56) 60)
NONE	49(14) 15)	9(11) 11)	13(17) 18)	13(13) 14)	14(18) 19)
REFUSE	23 (7)	6 (7)	5 (6)	7 (7)	5 (6)
	342	85	79	98	80

TABLE A.4 EDUCATION

	ALL	Claimants BKLN	Claimants NEWK	Non-Claimants BKLN	Non-Claimants NEWK
	%	%	%	%	%
8 OR LESS	40(12) 12)	7 (8) (8)	9(11) 12)	14(14) 14)	10(13) 13)
SOME HS	140(41) 41)	27(32) 33)	32(41) 41)	45(46) 46)	36(45) 46)
HS GRAD	102(30) 30)	30(35) 36)	25(32) 32)	23(24) 24)	24(30) 30)
COLLEGE	35(10) 10)	11(13) 13)	8(10) 10)	10(10) 10)	6 (8) (8)
COLL GRAD	11 (3) (3)	5 (6) (6)	2 (3) (3)	3 (2) (2)	2 (3) (3)
POSTGRAD	9 (3) (3)	3 (4) (6)	2 (3) (3)	3 (3) (3)	1 (1) (1)
DK	1 (0)	0	0	1 (1)	0
REFUSE	4 (1)	1 (2)	1 (2)	0	1 (1)
	342	85	79	98	80

TABLE A.5 EMPLOYMENT STATUS

	ALL %	Claimants		Non-Claimants	
		BKLN %	NEWK %	BKLN %	NEWK %
FULLTIME	119 (35) 35)	35 (41) 41)	28 (35) 35)	30 (31) 31)	26 (33) 33)
PARTTIME	34 (10) 10)	12 (14) 14)	9 (11) 11)	5 (5) (5)	8 (10) 10)
SELF-EMPL.	28 (8) (8)	5 (6) (6)	6 (8) (8)	12 (12) 13)	5 (6) (6)
STUDENT	18 (5) (5)	2 (2) (2)	2 (3) (3)	11 (11) 12)	3 (4) (4)
UNEMPLOY	141 (41) 42)	31 (31) 37)	34 (43) 43)	38 (39) 40)	38 (48) 48)
BLANK	1 (0)	0	0	1 (1)	0
REFUSE	1 (0)	0	0	1 (1)	0
	342	85	79	98	80

TABLE A.6 OCCUPATION

	ALL %	Claimants		Non-Claimants	
		BKLN %	NEWK %	BKLN %	NEWK %
BLANK	130 (38)	26 (31)	31 (39)	37 (38)	36 (45)
PROFESSNL	15 (4) (7)	5 (6) (8)	3 (4) (6)	3 (3) (5)	4 (5) (9)
MANAGER	19 (6) (9)	6 (7) 10)	5 (6) 10)	5 (5) (8)	3 (4) (7)
CLERICAL	28 (7) 11)	12 (14) 20)	7 (9) 15)	7 (7) 11)	2 (3) (5)
SALES	23 (7) 11)	7 (8) 12)	5 (6) 10)	8 (8) 13)	3 (4) (7)
CRAFT	7 (2) (3)	2 (2) (3)	1 (1) (2)	4 (4) (7)	0
SKILLED	26 (7) 12)	5 (6) (8)	7 (9) 15)	8 (8) 13)	6 (8) 14)
LABORER	20 (6) (9)	4 (5) (7)	4 (5) (8)	3 (3) (5)	9 (11) 20)
SERVICE	41 (12) 19)	11 (13) 19)	11 (14) 23)	9 (9) 15)	10 (13) 23)
STUDENT	18 (5) (8)	2 (2) (3)	2 (3) (4)	11 (14) 18)	3 (4) (7)
RETIRED	15 (4) (7)	5 (6) (8)	3 (4) (6)	3 (3) (5)	4 (5) (9)
	342	85	79	98	80

TABLE A.7 INCOME

	ALL %	Claimants		Non-Claimants	
		BKLN %	NEWK %	BKLN %	NEWK %
WELFARE	111 (33) 41)	23 (27) 36)	26 (33) 42)	33 (34) 40)	29 (36) 47)
$0-4999	22 (6) (8)	4 (5) (6)	5 (6) (8)	9 (9) 11)	4 (5) (7)
$5G-7400	23 (7) (8)	4 (5) (6)	5 (6) (8)	6 (6) (7)	8 (10) 13)
$7500-9999	34 (10) 13)	8 (9) 13)	7 (9) 11)	12 (12) 15)	7 (9) 11)
$10G-14999	55 (16) 20)	16 (19) 25)	13 (17) 21)	17 (17) 21)	9 (11) 15)
$15G-24999	18 (5) (7)	7 (8) 11)	4 (5) (7)	4 (4) (5)	3 (4) (5)
$25G+	8 (2) (3)	2 (2) (3)	2 (3) (3)	2 (2) (2)	2 (3) (3)
BLANK	20 (6)	5 (6)	4 (5)	6 (6)	5 (6)
REFUSE	51 (15)	16 (19)	13 (17)	9 (9)	13 (16)
	342	85	79	85	80

TABLE A.8 NUMBER OF DEPENDENTS

		Claimants		Non-Claimants	
	ALL	BKLN	NEWK	BKLN	NEWK
	%	%	%	%	%
0	36 (11)	8 (9)	6 (8)	15 (15)	7 (9)
1	109 (32)	28 (33)	25 (32)	30 (31)	26 (33)
2	58 (17)	18 (21)	13 (17)	17 (17)	10 (13)
3	44 (13)	12 (14)	10 (13)	11 (11)	11 (11)
4	41 (12)	10 (12)	11 (14)	8 (8)	12 (15)
5	37 (11)	4 (5)	10 (13)	12 (12)	11 (14)
6	10 (3)	3 (4)	3 (4)	2 (2)	2 (3)
7	3 (1)	1 (1)	1 (1)	1 (1)	0
8	4 (1)	1 (1)	0	2 (2)	1 (1)
	342	85	79	98	80

TABLE A.9 TIME AT PRESENT ADDRESS

		Claimants		Non-Claimants	
	ALL	BKLN	NEWK	BKLN	NEWK
	%	%	%	%	%
LESS 6 MO.	26 (7)	5 (6)	6 (7)	9 (9)	6 (8)
6 MO-2 YR	94 (28)	20 (24)	21 (27)	31 (32)	22 (28)
2 - 5 YR	102 (30)	22 (26)	25 (32)	29 (30)	26 (33)
5 - 10 YR	65 (19)	20 (24)	16 (20)	17 (17)	12 (15)
10 - 20 YR	37 (11)	12 (14)	7 (9)	8 (8)	10 (13)
20+ YR	18 (5)	6 (7)	4 (5)	4 (4)	4 (5)
	342	85	79	98	80

TABLE A.10 TIME IN BROOKLYN/NEWARK

		Claimants		Non-Claimants	
	ALL	BKLN	NEWK	BKLN	NEWK
	%	%	%	%	%
NON-RESIDENT	1 (0)	0	1 (1)	0	0
LESS 6 MO	9 (3)	0	1 (1)	6 (6)	2 (3)
6 MO-2 YR	88 (26)	20 (24)	20 (25)	27 (28)	21 (26)
2 - 5 YR	95 (28)	25 (29)	25 (32)	20 (20)	25 (31)
5 - 10 YR	69 (20)	17 (20)	15 (19)	22 (22)	15 (19)
10 - 20 YR	50 (15)	14 (17)	9 (11)	17 (17)	10 (13)
20+ YR	30 (9)	9 (11)	8 (10)	6 (6)	7 (9)
	342	85	79	98	80

TABLE A.11 MEMBERSHIP IN COMMUNITY GROUPS

		Claimants		Non-Claimants	
	ALL	BKLN	NEWK	BKLN	NEWK
	%	%	%	%	%
YES	133 (39)	37 (44)	31 (39)	37 (39)	28 (35)
NO	209 (61)	48 (56)	48 (61)	61 (61)	52 (65)
	342	85	79	98	85

TABLE A.12 USE SOCIAL SERVICE AGENCIES

	ALL %	Claimants		Non-Claimants	
	ALL %	BKLN %	NEWK %	BKLN %	NEWK %
YES	218 (64)	50 (59)	49 (62)	68 (69)	52 (64)
NO	123 (36)	35 (41)	30 (38)	30 (31)	28 (35)
	342	85	79	98	80

TABLE A.13 WHICH SOCIAL SERVICES USED

	ALL %	Claimants		Non-Claimants	
	ALL %	BKLN %	NEWK %	BKLN %	NEWK %
LEGAL AID	6 (2) (3)	2 (2) (4)	2 (3) (4)	2 (2) (3)	0
WELFARE	47 (14) 22	9 (11) 18	9 (11) 18	15 (15) 22	14 (18) 28
DAYCARE	48 (14) 22	9 (11) 18	9 (11) 18	15 (15) 22	15 (19) 30
COMM.CTR	16 (5) (7)	5 (6) 10	3 (4) (6)	5 (5) (7)	3 (4) (6)
COUNSELING	2 (1) (1)	0	1 (1) (2)	1 (1) (1)	0
MEDICAL	57 (17) 26	17 (20) 34	13 (17) 27	16 (16) 23	11 (14) 22
SOC.WORKER	39 (11) 18	8 (9) 16	10 (13) 20	14 (14) 20	7 (9) 14
VICTIM SERV	3 (1) (1)	0	2 (3) ($)	1 (1) (1)	0
NA	124 (36)	35 (41)	30 (38)	29 (30)	30 (38)
	342	85	79	98	80

TABLE A.14 POLITICAL PARTY

	ALL %	Claimants		Non-Claimants	
	ALL %	BKLN %	NEWK %	BKLN %	NEWK %
NONE	95 (28) 28	21 (25) 25	23 (29) 29	29 (30) 30	22 (28) 28
REPUBLICAN	63 (18) 19	19 (22) 22	13 (17) 17	19 (19) 19	12 (15) 15
DEMOCRAT	134 (39) 39	34 (40) 40	28 (35) 35	40 (41) 41	32 (40) 41
INDEPEND.	42 (12) 12	8 (9) (9)	14 (18) 18	9 (9) (9)	11 (14) 14
OTHER	6 (2) (2)	3 (4) (4)	1 (1) (1)	1 (1) (1)	1 (1) (1)
REFUSE	2 (1)	0	0	0	2 (2)
	342	85	79	98	80

TABLE A.15 WOULD HAVE EFFECT CN CITY COUNCIL

	ALL %	Claimants		Non-Claimants	
	ALL %	BKLN %	NEWK %	BKLN %	NEWK %
MUCH	5 (2) (2)	0	2 (3) (3)	2 (2) (2)	1 (1) (1)
SOME	117 (34) 36	30 (35) 37	30 (38) 40	27 (28) 29	30 (38) 40
NONE	205 (60) 63	52 (61) 63	44 (56) 58	64 (65) 69	45 (56) 59
DK	15 (4)	3 (4)	3 (4)	5 (5)	4 (5)
	342	85	79	98	80 —

TABLE A.16 WOULD TRY TO AFFECT CITY COUNCIL

	ALL %	Claimants BKLN %	NEWK %	Non-Claimants BKLN %	NEWK %
YES	94 (28)	20 (24)	24 (30)	28 (29)	22 (28)
NO	248 (73)	65 (77)	55 (70)	70 (71)	58 (72)
	342	85	79	98	80

TABLE A.17 REGISTERED TO VOTE

	ALL %	Claimants BKLN %	NEWK %	Non-Claimants BKLN %	NEWK %
YES	156 (46)	37 (44)	38 (48)	42 (42)	40 (50)
NO	186 (54)	48 (56)	41 (52)	57 (58)	40 (50)
	342	85	79	79	80

TABLE A.18 PARTICIPATE IN POLITICAL CAMPAIGN

	ALL %	Claimants BKLN %	NEWK %	Non-Claimants BKLN %	NEWK %
YES	14 (4)	3 (4)	2 (3)	4 (4)	5 (6)
NO	328 (96)	82 (96)	77 (97)	94 (96)	75 (94)
	342	85	79	98	80

TABLE A.19 RECEIVE EQUAL TREATMENT

	ALL %	Claimants BKLN %	NEWK %	Non-Claimants BKLN %	NEWK %
YES	165 (48)	41 (48)	39 (49)	50 (51)	35 (44)
NO	177 (52)	44 (52)	40 (51)	48 (49)	45 (56)
	342	85	79	98	80

TABLE A.20 POLITICAL EFFICACY

	ALL %	Claimants BKLN %	NEWK %	Non-Claimants BKLN %	NEWK %
POOR	189 (55) 58	48 (56) 59	46 (59) 61	54 (55) 58	41 (50) 54
GOOD	138 (40) 42	34 (40) 41	30 (37) 39	39 (40) 42	35 (45) 46
BLANK	15 (5)	3 (4)	3 (4)	5 (5)	4 (5)
	342	85	79	98	80

TABLE A.21 CAUSE OF CRIME

	ALL %	Claimants BKLN %	Claimants NEWK %	Non-Claimants BKLN %	Non-Claimants NEWK %
DK	8 (2)	2 (2)	2 (3)	3 (3)	1 (1)
LENIENCY	40 (12)	12 (14)	9 (11)	11 (11)	8 (10)
POOR LENF	52 (15)	13 (15)	15 (19)	14 (14)	10 (13)
POVERTY	43 (13)	10 (12)	7 (9)	14 (14)	12 (15)
RACISM	18 (5)	6 (7)	2 (3)	5 (5)	5 (6)
PERMISSIVE	77 (23)	17 (20)	17 (22)	24 (25)	19 (24)
SOC DECAY	59 (17)	16 (19)	20 (25)	13 (13)	10 (13)
BORN CRIM.	35 (10)	6 (7)	7 (9)	10 (10)	12 (15)
BOREDOM	7 (2)	1 (1)	0	4 (4)	2 (3)
REPRESSION	3 (1)	2 (2)	0	0	1 (1)
	342	85	79	98	80

TABLE A.22 HOW HIGH CRIME RATE

	ALL %	Claimants BKLN %	Claimants NEWK %	Non-Claimants BKLN %	Non-Claimants NEWK %
HIGH	293 (86) 90)	76 (89) 95)	69 (87) 92)	83 (85) 88)	65 (81) 83)
MODERATE	30 (9) (9)	3 (4) (4)	6 (8) (8)	10 (10) 11)	11 (14) 14)
LOW	4 (1) (1)	1 (1) (1)	0	1 (1) (1)	2 (3) (3)
DK	15 (4)	5 (6)	4 (5)	4 (4)	2 (3)
	342	85	79	98	80

TABLE A.23 FRIEND RECENTLY VICTIMIZED

	ALL %	Claimants BKLN %	Claimants NEWK %	Non-Claimants BKLN %	Non-Claimants NEWK %
YES	130 (38) 41)	36 (42) 43)	29 (37) 40)	35 (36) 39)	30 (38) 40)
NO	189 (55) 59)	47 (55) 57)	43 (54) 60)	54 (55) 60)	45 (56) 60)
BLANK	22 (6)	2 (2)	7 (9)	8 (8)	5 (6)
	342	85	79	98	80

TABLE A.24 WHY GOVERNMENT RESPONSIBLE FOR CRIME

	ALL %	Claimants BKLN %	Claimants NEWK %	Non-Claimants BKLN %	Non-Claimants NEWK %
NO PROTECT	48 (14) 35)	14 (17) 34)	12 (15) 41)	12 (12) 30)	10 (13) 39)
SOC ATMOS	13 (4) 10)	4 (5) 10)	3 (4) 10)	5 (5) 10)	1 (1) (4)
REP/RACISM	5 (2) (4)	2 (2) (5)	1 (1) (3)	2 (2) (5)	0
LENIENCY	42 (12) 31)	11 (13) 27)	8 (10) 28)	13 (13) 33)	10 (13) 39)
UNCONCERN	28 (8) 21)	10 (12) 24)	5 (6) 17)	8 (8) 20)	5 (6) 19)
NA	206 (60)	44 (52)	50 (63)	58 (59)	54 (68)
	342	85	79	98	80

TABLE A.25 WHY GOVERNMENT NOT RESPONSIELE FOR CRIME

	ALL %	Claimants		Non-Claimants	
		BKLN %	NEWK %	BKLN %	NEWK %
NO FAULT	100 (29) 51)	25 (29) 57)	20 (25) 40)	23 (24) 47)	32 (40) 60)
OTHER	97 (28) 49)	19 (22) 43)	30 (38) 60)	26 (27) 53)	22 (28) 41)
BLANK	9 (3)	0	0	9 (9)	0
NA	136 (40)	41 (48)	29 (37)	40 (40)	26 (33)
	342	85	79	98	80

Chapter Five Tables

TABLE B.1 KIND OF CRIME

		Claimants		Non-Claimants	
	ALL	BKLN	NEWK	BKLN	NEWK
	%	%	%	%	%
ASSAULT	265 (64)	55 (65)	49 (62)	65 (66)	50 (62)
ROBBERY	122 (36)	30 (35)	30 (38)	32 (33)	30 (38)
BLANK	1 (0)	0	0	1 (1)	0
	342	85	79	98	80

TABLE B.2 EXTENT OF INJURY

		Claimants		Non-Claimants	
	ALL	BKLN	NEWK	BKLN	NEWK
	%	%	%	%	%
NONE	13 (4)	1 (1)	2 (3)	7 (7)	3 (4)
MINOR	76 (22)	15 (18)	12 (15)	28 (29)	21 (26)
MEDICAL	198 (58)	50 (59)	53 (67)	50 (51)	45 (56)
HOSPITAL	55 (16)	19 (22)	12 (15)	13 (13)	11 (14)
	342	85	79	98	80

TABLE B.3 PROPERTY LOSS

		Claimants		Non-Claimants	
	ALL	BKLN	NEWK	BKLN	NEWK
	%	%	%	%	%
NO	207 (60)	48 (57)	44 (56)	67 (68)	48 (60)
YES	135 (40)	37 (43)	35 (44)	31 (32)	32 (40)
	342	85	79	98	80

TABLE B.4 WHICH PROPERTY STOLEN

		Claimants		Non-Claimants	
	ALL	BKLN	NEWK	BKLN	NEWK
	%	%	%	%	%
BLANK	204 (60)	48 (57)	44 (56)	67 (68)	45 (56)
HOUSEHOLD	3 (1) (2)	0	2 (3) (3)	0	1 (1) (1)
CREDIT	3 (1) (2)	3 (1) (1)	0	0	1 (1) (1)
CASH	60 (18) 43)	15 (18) 18)	15 (19) 19)	15 (15) 15)	15 (19) 15)
JEWELRY	19 (6) 14)	5 (6) (6)	5 (6) (6)	4 (4) (4)	5 (6) (6)
CLOTHING	5 (2) (4)	2 (2) (2)	1 (1) (1)	0	2 (3) (3)
WALLET	28 (8) 20)	8 (9) (9)	9 (11) 11)	4 (4) (4)	7 (9) (9)
ELECTRIC	8 (2) (6)	2 (2) (2)	3 (4) (4)	1 (1) (1)	2 (3) (3)
OFFICE	3 (1) (2)	1 (1) (1)	0	1 (1) (1)	2 (3) (3)
BIKE	6 (2) (4)	1 (1) (1)	0	5 (5) (5)	0
OTHER	3 (1) (2)	1 (1) (1)	0	0	1 (1) (1)
	342	85	79	98	80

TABLE B.5 VICTIM-OFFENDER RELATIONSHIP

	ALL %	Claimants BKLN %	Claimants NEWK %	Non-Claimants BKLN %	Non-Claimants NEWK %
STRANGER	169 (49) 51)	54 (64) 65)	49 (62) 62)	36 (37) 38)	30 (38) 40)
SPOUSE	13 (4) (4)	1 (1) (1)	0	6 (6) (6)	6 (8) (8)
EX-SPOUSE	8 (2) (2)	0	1 (1) (1)	3 (3) (3)	4 (5) (5)
GIRL/BOY	5 (2) (2)	1 (1) (1)	1 (1) (1)	1 (1) (1)	2 (3) (3)
X GIRL BOY	7 (2) (2)	2 (2) (2)	1 (1) (1)	1 (1) (1)	3 (4) (4)
SIS/BROTH	1 (0)	0	0	1 (1) (1)	0
MOTH/FATH	3 (1) (1)	0	0	1 (1) (1)	2 (3) (3)
OTHER REL	4 (1) (1)	0	0	3 (3) (3)	1 (1) (1)
FRIEND	14 (4) (4)	0	0	8 (8) (8)	6 (8) (8)
FRIEND FAM	4 (1) (1)	0	1 (1) (1)	2 (2) (2)	1 (1) (1)
ACQUAINT	30 (9) (9)	10 (12) 12)	6 (8) (8)	5 (5) (5)	9 (11) 12)
INDIR REL	3 (1) (1)	0	0	3 (3) (3)	0
SEEN BEF	38 (11) 11)	8 (9) 10)	11 (14) 14)	13 (13) 14)	6 (8) (8)
CO-WORKER	8 (2) (2)	2 (2) (2)	2 (3) (3)	3 (3) (3)	1 (1) (1)
NEIGHBOR	26 (8) (8)	5 (6) (6)	7 (9) (9)	10 (10) 10)	4 (5) (5)
BLANK	9 (2)	2 (2)	0	2 (2)	5 (6)
	342	85	79	98	80

TABLE B.6 NUMBER OF OFFENDERS

	ALL %	Claimants BKLN %	Claimants NEWK %	Non-Claimants BKLN %	Non-Claimants NEWK %
1	263 (77)	65 (77)	59 (75)	76 (78)	63 (79)
2	53 (16)	13 (15)	10 (13)	20 (20)	10 (13)
3	17 (5)	7 (8)	6 (8)	2 (2)	2 (3)
4	5 (2)	0	2 (3)	0	3 (4)
5	3 (1)	0	1 (1)	0	2 (3)
8	1 (0)	0	1 (1)	0	0
	342	85	79	98	80

TABLE B.7 SEX OF FIRST OFFENDER

	ALL %	Claimants BKLN %	Claimants NEWK %	Non-Claimants BKLN %	Non-Claimants NEWK %
MALE	305 (89)	80 (94)	72 (91)	82 (84)	71 (89)
FEMALE	36 (11)	5 (6)	7 (9)	16 (16)	9 (11)
	342	85	79	98	80

TABLE B.8 SEX OF SECOND OFFENDER

	ALL %	Claimants BKLN %	Claimants NEWK %	Non-Claimants BKLN %	Non-Claimants NEWK %
MALE	76 (22) 92)	20 (23) 95)	19 (24) 95)	20 (20) 80)	17 (21) 100)
FEMALE	6 (2) (7)	1 (1) (5)	1 (1) (5)	4 (4) 16)	0
NA	259 (76)	64 (75)	59 (75)	73 (75)	63 (79)
	342	85	79	98	80

TABLE B.9 SEX OF THIRD OFFENDER

	ALL %	Claimants BKLN %	Claimants NEWK %	Non-Claimants BKLN %	Non-Claimants NEWK %
MALE	32 (9) 97)	7 (8) 100	10 (13) 100	8 (8) 89)	7 (9) 100
FEMALE	0	0	0	0	0
NA	309	78 (92)	69 (87)	89 (91)	73 (91)
	342	85	79	98	80

TABLE B.10 WOULD HAVE CALLED POLICE

	ALL %	Claimants BKLN %	Claimants NEWK %	Non-Claimants BKLN %	Non-Claimants NEWK %
YES	131 (38) 87)	32 (38) 87)	28 (35) 85)	42 (43) 89)	29 (36) 88)
NO	19 (6) 13)	5 (6) 14)	5 (6) 15)	5 (5) 11)	4 (5) 12)
NA	181 (53)	45 (53)	44 (56)	49 (50)	43 (54)
DK	11 (3)	3 (4)	2 (3)	2 (2)	4 (5)
	342	85	79	98	80

TABLE B.11 WHY REPORT CRIME

	ALL %	Claimants BKLN %	Claimants NEWK %	Non-Claimants BKLN %	Non-Claimants NEWK %
NA	173 (51)	42 (49)	37 (47)	53 (54)	41 (51)
BLANK	5 (1) (3)	1 (1) (2)	1 (1) (2)	2 (2) (4)	1 (1) (3)
PROT.SELF	29 (8) 17)	5 (6) 12)	7 (9) 17)	8 (8) 18)	9 (11) 23)
PROT.SOC.	24 (7) 14)	7 (8) 16)	6 (7) 14)	8 (8) 18)	3 (4) (8)
RECUR.SIT.	5 (1) (3)	1 (1) (2)	0	4 (4) (9)	0
PROP.LOSS	28 (8) 17)	10 (12) 23)	9 (11) 21)	3 (3) (7)	6 (8) 15)
PUNISH	21 (6) 12)	6 (7) 14)	5 (6) 12)	5 (5) 12)	5 (6) 13)
DEF.WRONG	32 (9) 19)	8 (8) 19)	7 (9) 17)	9 (9) 20)	8 (10) 21)
INJURY	24 (7) 14)	5 (6) 12)	6 (8) 14)	6 (6) 13)	7 (9) 18)
OTHER	1 (0)	0	1 (1) (2)	0	0
	342	85	79	98	80

TABLE B.12 WHY REPORT CRIME (RECODED)

	ALL %	Claimants BKLN %	NEWK %	Non-Claimants BKLN %	NEWK %
VICTIM	85(25)53)	21(25)50)	22(28)55)	21(21)49)	22(28)50)
SOCIETY	24 (7)15)	7 (8)17)	6 (8)15)	8 (8)19)	9(11)20)
OFFENDER	53(15)33)	14(18)33)	12(15)30)	14(14)33)	13(16)36)
OTHER	179(52)	43(54)	39(49)	55(56)	36(45)
	342	85	79	98	80

TABLE B.13 PRESS CHARGES

	ALL %	Claimants BKLN %	NEWK %	Non-Claimants NEWK %	NEWK %
YES	308(90)94)	80(94)96)	76(96)97)	79(81)90)	73(91)92)
NO	5 (2)(2)	0	0	3 (3)(3)	2 (3)(3)
OTHER	15 (4)(5)	3 (4)(4)	2 (3)(3)	6 (6)(7)	4 (5)(5)
DK	14 (4)	2 (2)	1 (1)	10(10)	1 (1)
	342	85	79	98	80

TABLE B.14 WHY PRESS CHARGES

	ALL %	Claimants BKLN %	NEWK %	Non-Claimants BKLN %	NEWK %
BLANK	28 (8)	5 (6)	3 (4)	15(15)	5 (6)
SOC.INJUS	52(15)17)	12(14)15)	13(17)18)	17(17)20)	10(13)13)
PROT.SELF	51(15)16)	10(12)13)	14(18)19)	15(15)18)	12(15)16)
PROT.SOC.	39(11)13)	10(12)13)	10(13)14)	9 (9)11)	10(13)13)
REST/PROP	32 (9)10)	8 (9)10)	8(10)11)	8 (8)10)	8(10)11)
PUNISH	70(21)23)	20(24)25)	16(20)22)	19(19)23)	15(19)20)
OTHER DEF.	1 (0)	0	0	0	1 (1)(1)
OTHER	14 (4)(5)	4 (5)(5)	3 (4)(4)	4 (4)(5)	3 (4)(4)
TREATMENT	16 (5)(5)	5 (6)(6)	3 (4)(4)	2 (2)(2)	6 (8)(8)
RECUR.SIT.	36(11)11)	10(12)13)	7 (9)(9)	9 (9)11)	10(13)13)
	342	85	79	98	80

TABLE B.15 WHY PRESS CHARGES (RECODED)

	ALL %	Claimants BKLN %	NEWK %	Non-Claimants BKLN %	NEWK %
VICTIM	119(35)40)	28(33)37)	29(37)41)	32(33)41)	30(38)42)
SOCIETY	91(27)31)	22(26)29)	23(29)32)	26(27)33)	20(25)28)
OFFENDER	87(25)29)	25(29)33)	19(24)27)	21(21)27)	21(26)30)
OTHER	45(13)	10(12)	8(10)	19(19)	9(11)
	342	85	79	98	80

TABLE B.16 IMPORTANCE OF RESTITUTION

| | ALL % | Claimants | | Non-Claimants | |
		BKLN %	NEWK %	BKLN %	NEWK %
VERY	156(46)51	37(44)46	39(49)53	37(38)47	43(54)61
SOME	72(21)24	19(22)24	19(24)26	19(19)24	15(19)21
NONE	76(22)25	24(28)30	16(20)22	23(24)29	13(16)18
NA	38(11)	5 (6)	5 (7)	19(19)	9(11)
	342	85	79	98	80

TABLE B.17 IMPORTANCE OF JAILING OFFENDER

| | ALL % | Claimants | | Non-Claimants | |
		BKLN %	NEWK %	BKLN %	NEWK %
VERY	168(49)55	45(53)56	41(52)55	44(45)56	38(48)54
SOME	79(23)26	19(22)24	21(27)28	19(19)24	20(25)28
NONE	58(17)19	16(19)20	13(17)17	16(16)20	13(16)18
NA	37(11)	5 (6)	4 (5)	19(19)	9(11)
	342	85	79	98	80

TABLE B.18 PRIOR COURT INVOLVEMENT

| | ALL % | Claimants | | Non-Claimants | |
		BKLN %	NEWK %	BKLN %	NEWK %
YES	130(38)39	30(35)36	26(33)34	43(44)44	31(39)39
NO	206(60)61	53(62)63	51(65)66	54(55)56	41(60)61
BLANK	6 (2)	2 (2)	2 (3)	1 (1)	1 (1)
	342	85	79	98	80

TABLE B.19 KIND OF PRIOR INVOLVEMENT

| | ALL % | Claimants | | Non-Claimants | |
		BKLN %	NEWK %	BKLN %	NEWK %
WITNESS	13 (4)10	3 (4)10	3 (4)12	5 (5)15	2 (3) (7)
VICTIM	42(12)35	9(11)30	8(10)31	11(11)33	14(18)45
DEFENDANT	43(13)36	11(13)37	8(10)31	15(15)46	9(11)29
VIC & DEF	19 (6)16	5 (6)17	6 (8)23	2 (2) (6)	6 (8)19
OTHER	3 (1) (3)	2 (3) (7)	1 (1) (1)	0	0
NA	212(65)	55(65)	53(67)	65(66)	49(61)
	342	85	79	98	80

TABLE B.20 EVER THREATENED BY OFFENDER

	ALL	Claimants		Non-Claimants	
		BKLN	NEWK	BKLN	NEWK
	%	%	%	%	%
YES	65 (19) 19)	20 (23) 24)	13 (17) 17)	19 (19) 20)	13 (16) 16)
AT CRIME	37 (11) 11)	8 (9) 10)	9 (11) 11)	13 (13) 14)	7 (9) (9)
NO	236 (69) 70)	56 (66) 67)	57 (72) 72)	63 (64) 66)	60 (75) 75)
NA	4 (1)	1 (1)	0	3 (3)	0
	342	85	79	98	80

TABLE B.21 HOW THREATENED BY OFFENDER

	ALL	Claimants		Non-Claimants	
		BKLN	NEWK	EKLN	NEWK
	%	%	%	%	%
VERBAL	63 (18) 62)	13 (15) 47)	10 (13) 50)	30 (31) 79)	10 (13) 63)
PHYSICAL	15 (4) 15)	6 (7) 20)	2 (3) 10)	4 (4) 11)	4 (5) 25)
BY OTHERS	23 (7) 23)	8 (9) 27)	8 (10) 40)	4 (4) 11)	2 (2) 13)
NA	241 (70)	58 (68)	59 (74)	60 (61)	64 (80)
	342	85	79	98	80

TABLE B.22 ARRIVE IN COMPLAINT ROOM

	ALL	Claimants		Non-Claimants	
		BKLN	NEWK	EKLN	NEWK
	%	%	%	%	%
YES	239 (70)	57 (67)	59 (75)	65 (66)	58 (73)
NO	102 (3)	28 (32)	20 (25)	33 (34)	22 (28)
	342	85	79	98	80

TABLE B.23 WHY NOT ARRIVE IN COMPLAINT ROOM

	ALL	Claimants		Non-Claimants	
		BKLN	NEWK	BKLN	NEWK
	%	%	%	%	%
NA	239 (70)	57 (67)	59 (75)	65 (66)	58 (73)
BLANK	1 (0) (1)	0	0	1 (1) (3)	0
TOLD NO	9 (3) (9)	2 (2) (7)	4 (5) 20)	1 (1) (3)	2 (3) (9)
NOT ASKED	41 (12) 39)	13 (15) 48)	5 (6) 25)	14 (14) 42)	9 (11) 41)
CRIME	12 (4) 12)	3 (4) 11)	3 (4) 15)	5 (5) 15)	1 (1) (5)
OTHER	10 (3) 10)	3 (4) 11)	2 (3) 10)	1 (1) (3)	4 (5) 18)
VS PROSEC	6 (2) (6)	1 (1) (4)	2 (3) 10)	2 (2) (6)	1 (1) (5)
CT/ARRAIGN	2 (1) (2)	1 (1) (4)	0	1 (1) (3)	0
X COMPL	12 (4) 12)	1 (1) (4)	2 (3) 10)	6 (6) 18)	3 (4) 14)
THREAT	8 (2) (8)	3 (4) 11)	2 (3) 10)	1 (1) (3)	2 (3) (9)
GOT LOST	1 (0)	0	0	1 (3)	0
	342	85	79	98	80

TABLE B.24 WHAT DONE IN COMPLAINT ROOM

	ALL %	Claimants BKLN %	NEWK %	Non-Claimants BKLN %	NEWK %
PAPERWORK	23 (7) 10)	2 (2) (4)	4 (5) (7)	11 (11) 17)	6 (8) 10)
ARRAIGN	15 (4) (6)	3 (4) (5)	4 (5) (7)	5 (5) (8)	3 (4) (5)
TALKED DA	52 (15) 22)	11 (13) 19)	14 (18) 24)	16 (16) 25)	11 (14) 19)
STAYED PO	116 (34) 48)	33 (39) 58)	32 (41) 54)	21 (21) 32)	30 (38) 52)
NOTHING	18 (5) (8)	5 (6) (9)	2 (3) (3)	5 (5) (8)	6 (8) 10)
OTHER	15 (4) (6)	3 (4) (5)	3 (4) (5)	7 (7) 11)	2 (3) (3)
NA	103 (30)	28 (33)	20 (25)	33 (34)	22 (28)
	342	85	79	98	80

TABLE B.25 PRESENT AT ARRAIGNMENT

	ALL %	Claimants BKLN %	NEWK %	Non-Claimants BKLN %	NEWK %
YES	167 (49) 51)	42 (49) 51)	41 (52) 53)	43 (44) 47)	41 (51) 53)
NO	160 (47) 49)	40 (47) 49)	36 (46) 47)	48 (49) 53)	36 (45) 47)
NA	5 (1)	2 (2)	1 (1)	0	2 (3)
DK	10 (3)	1 (1)	1 (1)	7 (7)	1 (1)
	342	85	79	98	80

TABLE B.26 CASE SETTLED AT ARRAIGNMENT

	ALL %	Claimants BKLN %	NEWK %	Non-Claimants BKLN %	NEWK %
NO	219 (64)	56 (66)	55 (70)	57 (58)	51 (64)
YES	95 (28)	25 (29)	20 (25)	26 (27)	24 (30)
DK	27 (8)	4 (5)	3 (4)	15 (15)	5 (6)
NA	1 (0)	0	1 (1)	0	0
	342	85	79	98	80

TABLE B.27 DEFENDANT GET BAIL

	ALL %	Claimants BKLN %	NEWK %	Non-Claimants BKLN %	NEWK %
JAIL-NO	67 (20) 27)	17 (20) 27)	19 (24) 33)	13 (13) 19)	18 (23) 29)
BAIL-YES	124 (36) 49)	33 (39) 52)	26 (33) 46)	38 (39) 55)	27 (34) 43)
BOTH-YES	62 (18) 25)	14 (17) 22)	12 (15) 21)	18 (18) 26)	18 (23) 29)
NA	1 (0)	0	0	1 (1)	0
DK	88 (26)	21 (25)	22 (28)	28 (29)	17 (21)
	342	85	79	98	80

TABLE B.28 APPROVE OF BAIL

	ALL %	Claimants BKLN %	NEWK %	Non-Claimants BKLN %	NEWK %
APPROVE	13 (4) (7)	5 (6) 11)	2 (3) (5)	4 (4) (7)	2 (3) (4)
DONT CARE	10 (3) (5)	3 (4) (6)	1 (1) (3)	4 (4) (7)	2 (3) (4)
DISAPP	163 (48) 88)	39 (45) 83)	35 (44) 92)	48 (49) 86)	41 (51) 91)
NA	156 (46)	38 (45)	41 (52)	42 (43)	35 (44)
	342	85	79	98	80

TABLE B.29 BAIL AFFECT COURT APPEARANCE

	ALL %	Claimants BKLN %	NEWK %	Non-Claimants BKLN %	NEWK %
YES	32 (9) 18)	8 (9) 18)	7 (9) 19)	11 (11) 20)	6 (8) 14)
NO	147 (43) 81)	37 (44) 81)	29 (37) 80)	45 (44) 79)	38 (48) 86)
DK	7 (2) (1)	2 (2) (1)	2 (3) (1)	2 (2) (1)	1 (1) (1)
	342	85	79	98	80

TABLE B.30 HOW DID BAIL AFFECT COURT APPEARANCE

	ALL %	Claimants BKLN %	NEWK %	Non-Claimants BKLN %	NEWK %
FEAR	18 (5) 45)	5 (6) 50)	3 (4) 30)	8 (8) 62)	2 (3) 29)
AVOIDED	10 (3) 25)	2 (2) 20)	3 (4) 30)	2 (2) 15)	3 (4) 43)
ANGER	11 (3) 28)	3 (4) 30)	3 (4) 30)	3 (3) 23)	2 (3) 29)
NA	302 (88)	75 (88)	69 (87)	85 (87)	73 (91)
	342	85	79	98	80

TABLE B.31 ARRIVE IN COURT

	ALL %	Claimants BKLN %	NEWK %	Non-Claimants BKLN %	NEWK %
YES	296 (87) 88)	71 (84) 85)	69 (87) 89)	86 (88) 88)	70 (88) 90)
NO	42 (12) 12)	13 (15) 16)	9 (11) 12)	12 (12) 12)	8 (10) 10)
NA	4 (1)	1 (1)	1 (1)	0	2 (2)
	342	85	79	98	80

TABLE B.32   TIMES APPEARED IN COURT

	ALL %	Claimants BKLN %	NEWK %	Non-Claimants BKLN %	NEWK %
0	46 (13)	14 (15)	10 (13)	12 (12)	10 (13)
1	78 (23) 26)	14 (17) 20)	18 (23) 26)	24 (25) 28)	22 (28) 31)
2	112 (33) 38)	28 (34) 39)	25 (32) 36)	33 (34) 38)	26 (33) 37)
3	69 (20) 23)	19 (22) 22)	17 (22) 25)	18 (18) 21)	15 (19) 21)
4	23 (7) (8)	7 (8) (8)	5 (6) (7)	8 (8) (9)	3 (4) (4)
5	7 (2) (2)	2 (2) (2)	2 (3) (3)	1 (1) (1)	2 (3) (3)
6	6 (2) (2)	1 (1) (1)	1 (1) (1)	2 (2) (2)	2 (3) (3)
8	1 (0)	0	1 (1) (1)	0	0
	342	85	79	98	80

TABLE B.33 MINIMUM AMOUNT OF TIME IN COURT

	ALL %	Claimants BKLN %	NEWK %	Non-Claimants BKLN %	NEWK %
0	45 (13)	13 (15)	10 (13)	12 (12)	10 (13)
1	48 (14) 16)	10 (13) 14)	12 (15) 17)	13 (13) 15)	13 (16) 19)
2	54 (16) 18)	11 (13) 15)	15 (19) 22)	16 (16) 19)	12 (15) 17)
3	50 (15) 17)	12 (14) 17)	11 (14) 16)	17 (17) 20)	10 (13) 14)
4	40 (12) (13)	11 (13) 15)	11 (14) 16)	6 (6) (7)	12 (15) 17)
5	47 (14) 16)	12 (14) 17)	11 (14) 16)	12 (12) 14)	12 (15) 17)
6	20 (6) (7)	6 (7) (8)	3 (4) (4)	10 (10) 12)	1 (1) (1)
7	24 (7) (8)	9 (8) 10)	3 (4) (4)	7 (7) (8)	7 (9) 10)
8	11 (3) (4)	2 (2) (3)	2 (3) (3)	5 (5) (6)	2 (3) (3)
9	3 (1) (1)	1 (1) (1)	1 (1) (1)	0	1 (1) (1)
	342	85	79	98	80

TABLE B.34 MAXIMUM AMOUNT OF TIME IN COURT

	ALL %	Claimants BKLN %	NEWK %	Non-Claimants BKLN %	NEWK %
0	45 (13)	13 (15)	10 (13)	12 (12)	10 (13)
1	5 (2) (2)	0	0	5 (5) (6)	0
2	12 (4) (4)	0	5 (6) (7)	6 (7) (7)	1 (1) (1)
3	16 (5) (5)	3 (4) (4)	4 (5) (6)	7 (7) (8)	2 (3) (3)
4	25 (7) (8)	5 (6) (7)	7 (9) 10)	6 (6) (7)	7 (9) 10)
5	42 (12) 14)	12 (14) 17)	10 (13) 14)	9 (9) 10)	11 (14) 16)
6	49 (14) 16)	16 (19) 22)	10 (13) 14)	11 (11) 13)	12 (15) 17)
7	44 (13) 15)	14 (17) 19)	6 (8) (9)	12 (12) 14)	12 (15) 17)
8	45 (13) 15)	11 (13) 15)	11 (14) 16)	9 (9) 10)	14 (18) 20)
9	27 (8) (9)	6 (7) (8)	5 (6) (7)	11 (11) 13)	5 (6) (7)
10	10 (3) (3)	3 (4) (4)	2 (3) (3)	2 (2) (2)	3 (4) (4)
11	8 (2) (3)	2 (2) (3)	4 (5) (6)	1 (1) (1)	1 (1) (1)
12	8 (2) (3)	0	3 (4) (4)	3 (3) (3)	2 (3) (3)
13	4 (1) (1)	0	2 (3) (3)	2 (2) (2)	0
14	2 (1) (1)	0	0	2 (2) (2)	0
	342	85	79	98	80

TABLE B.35 MAKE IT TO COURT EACH TIME ASKED

	ALL	Claimants		Non-Claimants	
		BKLN	NEWK	BKLN	NEWK
	%	%	%	%	%
YES	182(53)54)	46(54)54)	42(53)53)	55(56)57)	39(49)49)
NOT ASKED	68(20)20)	16(19)19)	14(18)18)	24(25)25)	14(18)18)
NO	87(25)26)	23(27)27)	23(29)29)	15(15)16)	26(33)33)
OTHER	2 (1)	0	0	2 (2)(2)	0
NA	3 (1)	0	0	2 (2)	1 (1)
	342	85	79	98	80

TABLE B.36 INCONVENIENCED TAKING TIME OFF FROM WORK

	ALL	Claimants		Non-Claimants	
		BKLN	NEWK	BKLN	NEWK
	%	%	%	%	%
YES	89(26)30)	21(25)29)	22(28)32)	26(27)31)	20(25)29)
NO	207(61)70)	51(60)71)	47(60)68)	59(60)69)	50(63)71)
NA	46(14)	13(15)	10(13)	13(13)	10(13)
	342	85	79	98	80

TABLE B.37 INCONVENIENCED BY TRANSPORTATION TO COURT

	ALL	Claimants		Non-Claimants	
		BKLN	NEWK	BKLN	NEWK
	%	%	%	%	%
YES	61(18)20)	13(15)18)	14(18)20)	25(26)29)	9(11)13)
NO	235(69)80)	59(69)82)	55(70)80)	60(61)71)	61(76)87)
NA	46(14)	13(15)	10(13)	13(13)	10(13)
	342	85	79	98	80

TABLE B.38 INCONVENIENCED BY CHILD/ELDERLY CARE

	ALL	Claimants		Non-Claimants	
		BKLN	NEWK	BKLN	NEWK
	%	%	%	%	%
YES	43(13)15)	8 (9)11)	6 (8)(9)	23(24)24)	6 (8)(9)
NO	253(74)85)	64(75)89)	63(80)91)	62(63)63)	64(80)91)
NA	46(14)	13(15)	10(13)	13(13)	10(13)
	342	85	79	98	80

TABLE B.39 INCONVENIENCED FINDING COURT

	ALL	Claimants		Non-Claimants	
		BKLN	NEWK	BKLN	NEWK
	%	%	%	%	%
YES	56(16)19)	13(15)18)	14(18)20)	15(15)17)	14(18)20)
NO	240(70)81)	59(69)82)	54(68)78)	72(73)83)	55(69)79)
NA	44(13)	13(15)	10(13)	11(11)	10(13)
	342	85	79	98	80

TABLE B.40 INCONVENIENCED FINDING A PLACE TO WAIT

| | | Claimants | | Non-Claimants | |
	ALL	BKLN	NEWK	BKLN	NEWK
	%	%	%	%	%
YES	40 (12) 14)	9 (11) 13)	13 (17) 19)	8 (8) (9)	10 (13) 14)
NO	257 (75) 86)	63 (74) 88)	56 (71) 81)	78 (80) 91)	60 (75) 86)
NA	45 (13)	13 (15)	10 (13)	12 (12)	10 (13)
	342	85	79	98	80

TABLE B.41 ASKED TO TESTIFY IN COURT

| | | Claimants | | Non-Claimants | |
	ALL	BKLN	NEWK	BKLN	NEWK
	%	%	%	%	%
YES	91 (27) 30)	20 (24) 28)	23 (29) 33)	27 (28) 32)	21 (26) 30)
NO	204 (60) 70)	52 (61) 72)	46 (58) 67)	57 (58) 68)	49 (61) 70)
NA	47 (14)	13 (15)	10 (13)	14 (14)	11 (13)
	342	85	79	98	80

TABLE B.42 CONSULTED BY PROSECUTOR ABOUT CASE

| | | Claimants | | Non-Claimants | |
	ALL	BKLN	NEWK	BKLN	NEWK
	%	%	%	%	%
YES	40 (12) 12)	8 (9) 10)	6 (8) (8)	14 (14) 15)	12 (15) 15)
NO	290 (85) 88)	75 (88) 90)	72 (91) 92)	77 (79) 85)	66 (83) 85)
NA	10 (3)	2 (2)	1 (1)	6 (6)	1 (1)
DK	2 (1)	0	0	1 (1)	1 (1)
	342	85	79	98	80

TABLE B.43 PROSECUTOR FOLLOW SUGGESTIONS ABOUT CASE

| | | Claimants | | Non-Claimants | |
	ALL	BKLN	NEWK	BKLN	NEWK
	%	%	%	%	%
NA	310 (88)	77 (91)	73 (92)	84 (86)	67 (84)
YES	21 (6) 50)	3 (4) 38)	4 (5) 67)	9 (9) 69)	5 (6) 38)
NO	19 (6) 50)	5 (6) 62)	2 (3) 33)	4 (4) 31)	8 (10) 62)
OTHER	1 (0)	0	0	1 (1)	0
	342	85	79	98	80

TABLE B.44 CONSULT WITH JUDGE ABOUT CASE

| | | Claimants | | Non-Claimants | |
	ALL	BKLN	NEWK	BKLN	NEWK
	%	%	%	%	%
YES	30 (9) 10)	7 (8) (9)	8 (10) 11)	11 (11) 13)	4 (5) (6)
NO	275 (80) 90)	70 (82) 91)	64 (81) 89)	72 (74) 87)	69 (86) 95)
NA	37 (11)	8 (9)	7 (9)	15 (15)	7 (9)
	342	85	79	98	80

TABLE B.45 CCNSULTED ABOUT CASE

| | ALL % | Claimants | | Non-Claimants | |
		BKLN %	NEWK %	BKLN %	NEWK %
YES	57 (17) 20)	13 (15) 18)	14 (18) 21)	15 (15) 19)	15 (19) 22)
NO	231 (68 (80)	59 (69) 79)	53 (67) 79)	66 (67) 82)	53 (66) 78)
NA	54 (16)	13 (15)	12 (15)	17 (17)	12 (15)
	342	85	79	98	80

TABLE B.46 REMAIN WITH CASE UNDER OTHER CIRCUMSTANCES

| | ALL % | Claimants | | Non-Claimants | |
		BKLN %	NEWK %	BKLN %	NEWK %
YES	25 (7) 51)	8 (9) 62)	5 (6) 63)	5 (5) 31)	7 (9) 58)
NO	24 (7) 49)	5 (6) 39)	3 (4) 38)	11 (11) 69)	5 (6) 42)
NA	292 (86)	72 (85)	71 (90)	82 (84)	68 (85)
	342	85	79	98	80

TABLE B.47 EVER HEAR ABOUT VICTIM COMPENSATION

| | ALL % | Claimants | | Non-Claimants | |
		BKLN %	NEWK %	BKLN %	NEWK %
YES	246 (72)	85 (100)	79 (100)	45 (46)	37 (46)
NO	96 (28)	0	0	53 (54)	43 (54)
	342	85	79	98	80

TABLE B.48 HOW HEARD ABOUT VICTIM COMPENSATION

| | ALL % | Claimants | | Non-Claimants | |
		BKLN %	NEWK %	BKLN %	NEWK %
RADIO/TV	46 (14) 19)	15 (18) 18)	10 (13) 13)	13 (13) 28)	8 (10) 22)
BROCHURES	60 (18) 24)	20 (24) 24)	20 (25) 25)	9 (9) 20)	11 (14) 30)
NEWPAPERS	40 (12) 16)	14 (17) 17)	16 (20) 20)	5 (5) 11)	5 (6) 14)
POLICE	61 (18) 25)	21 (25) 25)	19 (24) 24)	16 (16) 35)	5 (6) 14)
PROSECUTOR	5 (2) (2)	2 (2) (2)	1 (1) (1)	1 (1) (2)	1 (1) (3)
FRIEND	10 (3) (4)	3 (4) (4)	4 (5) (5)	1 (1) (2)	2 (3) (5)
VWAP/VSC	25 (7) 10)	10 (12) 12)	9 (11) 11)	1 (1) (2)	5 (6) 14)
NA	95 (28)	0	0	52 (53)	43 (54)
	342	85	79	98	80

TABLE B.49 WHY NEVER USE VICTIM COMPENSATION

	ALL %	Claimants BKLN %	Claimants NEWK %	Non-Claimants BKLN %	Non-Claimants NEWK %
NA(USED)	168 (49)	85 (100)	79 (100)	2 (2)	2 (2)
UNHEARD	90 (26) 52)	0	0	52 (52) 54)	38 (47) 49)
LOST FORM	3 (1) (2)	0	0	1 (1) (1)	1 (3) (3)
BOTHER	3 (1) (2)	0	0	2 (2) (2)	1 (1) (1)
COST	1 (0) (1)	0	0	1 (1) (1)	0
INELIGIBLE	19 (6) 11)	0	0	9 (9) (9)	10 (13) 13)
FORGET	2 (1) (1)	0	0	1 (1) (1)	1 (1) (1)
FUTILE	20 (6) 11)	0	0	11 (11) 12)	9 (11) 11)
OTHER AID	4 (1) (2)	0	0	2 (2) (2)	2 (3) (3)
INVESTIG	3 (1) (2)	0	0	2 (2) (2)	1 (1) (1)
TOO LATE	1 (1) (1)	0	0	1 (1) (1)	0
UNSURE HOW	15 (4) (9)	0	0	8 (8) (8)	7 (9) (9)
HARD FORMS	7 (2) (4)	0	0	3 (3) (3)	4 (5) (5)
DELAY	3 (1) (2)	0	0	3 (3) (3)	4 (5) (5)
UNNEEDED	2 (1) (1)	0	0	1 (1) (1)	1 (1) (1)
INAPPROP.	1 (0) (1)	0	0	1 (1) (1)	0
	342	85	79	98	80

APPENDIX C:
Chapter Six Tables

TABLE C.1 CRIMINAL CASE OUTCOME

	ALL %	Claimants		Non-Claimants	
		BKLN %	NEWK %	BKLN %	NEWK %
DISMISS	107(31)	23(27)	23(29)	37(38)	24(30)
PLEAD GUILTY	160(47)	43(51)	36(46)	40(41)	41(51)
ACQUITTED	7(2)	2(2)	2(3)	0	3(4)
CONVICTED	52(15)	14(17)	13(17)	14(14)	11(14)
CHARGE DROP	4(1)	0	1(1)	3(3)	0
OTHER	12(4)	3(4)	4(5)	4(4)	1(1)
	342	85	79	98	80

TABLE C.2 PROBLEMS FROM VICTIMIZATION

	ALL %	Claimants		Non-Claimants	
		BKLN %	NEWK %	BKLN %	NEWK %
BLANK	11(3)	0	0	10(10)	1(1)
NONE	38(11)	10(12)	9(11)	12(12)	7(9)
PROP.GEN.	22(6)	8(9)	3(4)	6(6)	5(6)
PROP.INCON.	9(3)	3(4)	0	5(5)	1(1)
PROP.FINANC.	48(14)	7(8)	16(20)	10(10)	15(19)
LOST INCOME	37(11)	10(12)	11(14)	6(6)	10(13)
MEDICAL	37(11)	8(9)	12(15)	7(7)	10(13)
EMOTIONAL	53(16)	15(18)	9(11)	18(18)	11(14)
DISTURBANCE	39(11)	10(12)	7(9)	13(13)	9(11)
INJURY	48(14)	14(17)	12(15)	11(11)	11(14)
	342	85	79	98	80

TABLE C.3 WHERE IS PROPERTY NOW

	ALL %	Claimants		Non-Claimants	
		BKLN %	NEWK %	BKLN %	NEWK %
POLICE	10 (3) 35	2 (2) 25	2 (3) 29	5 (5) 46	1 (1) 33
COURT	5 (2) 17	1 (1) 13	1 (1) 14	2 (2) 18	1 (1) 33
VICTIM	13 (4) 45	5 (6) 63	4 (5) 57	3 (3) 27	1 (1) 33
OTHER	1 (0) (3)	0	0	1 (1) (9)	0
NA	313(92)	77(91)	72(91)	87(89)	77(96)
	342	85	79	98	80

TABLE C.4 PAID WITNESS FEES BY PROSECUTOR

	ALL %	Claimants		Non-Claimants	
		BKLN %	NEWK %	BKLN %	NEWK %
YES	6 (2)(2)	1 (1)(1)	2 (3)(3)	2 (2)(2)	1 (1)(1)
NO	292(85)98	71 (84)99	67 (85)97	85 (87)98	69(86)99
NA	44(13)	13(15)	10(13)	11(11)	10(13)
	342	85	79	98	80

TABLE C.5 RECOVER FINANCIAL LOSSES

	ALL %	Claimants		Non-Claimants	
		BKLN %	NEWK %	BKLN %	NEWK %
SOME	73 (21)	21(25)	17(22)	20(20)	15(19)
YES	44 (13)	9(11)	16(20)	9 (9)	10(13)
NO	225 (66)	55 (65)	46 (58)	69 (70)	55 (69)
	342	85	79	98	80

TABLE C.6 WHO PAID FINANCIAL LOSSES

	ALL %	Claimants		Non-Claimants	
		BKLN %	NEWK %	BKLN %	NEWK %
NA	218(64)	55(65)	42(53)	66(67)	55(69)
BLANK	7 (2)	0	4 (5)	3 (3)	0
CVCB-VCCB	24 (7)	11(13)	13(17)	0	0
WELFARE	12 (4)13	2 (2)11	2 (3)10	4 (4)14	4 (5)16
MEDICAID	32 (9)34	5 (6)26	5 (6)25	11(11)38	11(14)44
MEDICARE	11 (3)12	3 (4)16	3 (4)15	4 (11)14	1 (1)(4)
WORK COMP	7 (2)(8)	2 (2)11	2 (2)11	2 (2)(7)	2 (3)(8)
SSI	6 (2)(6)	1 (1)(5)	1 (1)(5)	2 (2)(7)	1 (1)(4)
HEALTH INS	8 (2)(9)	2 (2)11	2 (2)11	2 (2)(7)	2 (3)(8)
PROP INS	4 (1)(4)	1 (1)(5)	1 (1)(5)	1 (1)(3)	0
AUTO INS	1 (0)(1)	0	0	0	0
SS RETIRE	5 (1)(5)	2 (2)11	2 (2)11	0	2 (3)(8)
RESTITUTE	5 (1)(5)	1 (1)(5)	1 (1)(5)	1 (1)(3)	2 (3)(8)
DEF/COUNSEL	2 (1)(2)	0	0	2 (2)(7)	0
	342	85	79	98	80

TABLE C.7 PAID BY PRIVATE INSURANCE

	ALL %	Claimants		Non-Claimants	
		BKLN %	NEWK %	BKLN %	NEWK %
YES	33(10)26	10(12)33	12(15)32	6 (6)19	5 (6)17
NO	91(27)71	20(24)67	25(32)68	26(27)81	20(25)67
NA	218(64)	55(65)	42(53)	66(67)	55(69)
	342	85	79	98	80

TABLE C.8 JUDGE ORDER RESTITUTION

	ALL %	Claimants BKLN %	NEWK %	Non-Claimants BKLN %	NEWK %
YES	9 (3) (7)	1 (1) (3)	2 (3) (7)	3 (3) (9)	3 (4) 11)
NO	112(33) 93)	29(34) 97)	26(33) 93)	32(33) 91)	25(32) 89)
NA	221(65)	55(65)	51(65)	63(64)	52(65)
	342	85	79	98	80

TABLE C.9 RECEIVE RESTITUTION

	ALL %	Claimants BKLN %	NEWK %	Non-Claimants BKLN %	NEWK %
YES	4 (1) 50)	0	2 (3) 100	0	2 (3) 67)
NO	4 (1) 50)	1 (1) 100	0	2 (2) 100	1 (1) 33)
NA	334(98)	84(99)	77(97)	96(98)	77(96)
	342	85	79	98	80

TABLE C.10 SATISFIED WITH RESTITUTION

	ALL %	Claimants BKLN %	NEWK %	Non-Claimants BKLN %	NEWK %
SATIS	0	0	0	0	0
SOME	1 (0) 33)	0	0	0	1 (1) 50)
DISSATIS	2 (1) 67)	0	1 (1) 100	0	1 (1) 50)
NA	339(99)	85(100)	78(99)	98(100)	78(98)
	342	85	79	98	80

TABLE C.11 DEFENDANT OR COUNSEL GIVE PAYMENTS

	ALL %	Claimants BKLN %	NEWK %	Non-Claimants BKLN %	NEWK %
DEFENDANT	26 (8) 57)	7 (8) 64)	7 (9) 58)	6 (6) 46)	6 (8) 60)
COUNSEL	14 (4) 30)	3 (4) 27)	3 (4) 25)	5 (5) 38)	3 (4) 30)
BOTH	6 (2) 13)	1 (1) (9)	2 (3) 17)	2 (2) 15)	1 (1) 10)
NO	296(86)	74(87)	67(85)	85(87)	70(88)
	342	85	79	98	80

TABLE C.12 WHY NOT RECOVER LOSSES

		Claimants		Non-Claimants	
	ALL	BKLN	NEWK	BKLN	NEWK
	%	%	%	%	%
PROP UNRET	15 (4) (7)	4 (5) (7)	2 (3) (4)	4 (4) (6)	5 (6) 10)
NO RESTIT	12 (4) (5)	2 (2) (4)	2 (3) (4)	6 (6) (8)	2 (3) (4)
NO FIN AID	55 (16) 25)	13 (15) 24)	12 (15) 26)	17 (17) 24)	13 (16) 26)
NO ELIGIB	41 (12) 18)	9 (11) 16)	6 (8) 13)	17 (17) 24)	9 (11) 18)
NO INSUR	22 (6) 10)	2 (2) (4)	6 (8) 13)	9 (9) 13)	5 (6) 10)
NO WELFARE	9 (3) (4)	4 (5) (7)	2 (3) (4)	1 (1) (1)	2 (3) (4)
VIC IGNORE	70 (21) 31)	21 (25) 38)	16 (20) 35)	18 (18) 25)	15 (19) 29)
NA	118 (35)	30 (35)	33 (42)	26 (27)	29 (36)
	342	85	79	98	80

TABLE C.13 ANGRY WITH DEFENDANT

		Claimants		Non-Claimants	
	ALL	BKLN	NEWK	BKLN	NEWK
	%	%	%	%	%
VERY	113 (33) 33)	34 (40) 40)	25 (32) 32)	30 (31) 31)	24 (30 (30)
SOME	101 (30) 30)	25 (30 (30)	26 (33) 33)	24 (25) 25)	26 (33) 33)
NONE	126 (37) 37)	26 (31) 31)	28 (35) 35)	42 (43) 44)	30 (38) 38)
NA/BLANK	1 (0)	0	0	1 (1)	0
DK	1 (0)	0	0	1 (1)	0
	342	85	79	98	80

TABLE C.14 ANGRY WITH ONESELF

		Claimants		Non-Claimants	
	ALL	BKLN	NEWK	BKLN	NEWK
	%	%	%	%	%
VERY	43 (13) 13)	8 (9) 10)	9 (11) 12)	16 (16) 17)	10 (13) 13)
SOME	88 (26) 27)	21 (25) 26)	20 (25) 27)	27 (28) 28)	20 (25) 27)
NONE	193 (56) 60)	51 (60) 64)	45 (57) 61)	52 (53) 55)	45 (50) 60)
NA/BLANK	1 (0)	0	0	1 (1)	0
DK	17 (5)	5 (6)	5 (6)	2 (2)	5 (6)
	342	85	79	98	80

TABLE C.15 FEAR OFFENDER'S REVENGE

		Claimants		Non-Claimants	
	ALL	BKLN	NEWK	BKLN	NEWK
	%	%	%	%	%
VERY	86 (25) 25)	21 (25) 25)	19 (24) 24)	21 (21) 22)	25 (31) 31)
SOME	42 (12) 12)	10 (12) 12)	10 (13) 13)	12 (12) 12)	10 (13) 13)
NONE	213 (63) 63)	54 (64) 64)	50 (63) 63)	65 (65) 66)	45 (56) 56)
NA/BLANK	1 (0)	0	0	1 (1)	0
	342	85	79	98	80

TABLE C.16 WANT REVENGE AGAINST OFFENDER

	ALL %	Claimants BKLN %	Claimants NEWK %	Non-Claimants BKLN %	Non-Claimants NEWK %
VERY	49(14)14)	14(17)17)	14(18)18)	13(13)13)	8(10)10)
SOME	35(10)10)	11(13)13)	5 (6)(6)	9 (9)(9)	10(13)13)
NONE	257(75)75)	60(71)71)	60(76)76)	75(77)77)	62(78)78)
NA/BLANK	1 (0)	0	0	1 (1)	0
	342	85	79	98	80

TABLE C.17 FEEL GUILTY ABOUT PURSUING CASE

	ALL %	Claimants BKLN %	Claimants NEWK %	Non-Claimants BKLN %	Non-Claimants NEWK %
VERY	24 (7)	5 (6)	3 (4)	9 (9)	7 (9)
SOME	33 (10)	8 (9)	4 (5)	13(13)	8(10)
NONE	285(83)	72(85)	72(91)	76(78)	65(81)
	342	85	79	98	80

TABLE C.18 FEEL LESS SAFE

	ALL %	Claimants BKLN %	Claimants NEWK %	Non-Claimants BKLN %	Non-Claimants NEWK %
VERY	77(23)23)	20(24)24)	16(20)20)	21(21)22)	20(25)25)
SOME	42(12)12)	9(11)11)	10(13)13)	16(16)17)	7 (9)(9)
NONE	220(64)65)	56(66)66)	53(67)67)	58(59)61)	53(66)66)
NA/BLANK	3 (1)	0	0	3(3)	0
	342	85	79	98	80

TABLE C.19 OVERALL ATTITUDES TOWARD OFFENDER (RECODED)

	ALL %	Claimants BKLN %	Claimants NEWK %	Non-Claimants BKLN %	Non-Claimants NEWK %
NEGATIVE	32 (9)10)	8 (9)10)	5 (6)(7)	9 (9)10)	10(13)13)
NEUTRAL	291(85)90)	72(85)90)	69(87)93)	85(87)90)	65(81)87)
POSITIVE	1 (0)	0	0	1 (1)(1)	0
NA	18 (5)	5 (6)	5 (6)	3 (3)	5 (6)
	342	85	79	98	80

TABLE C.20 KNOW CRIMINAL CASE OUTCOME

	ALL	Claimants		Non-Claimants	
		BKLN	NEWK	BKLN	NEWK
	%	%	%	%	%
YES	301 (88) 90	77 (91) 91	72 (91) 92	84 (86 (88)	68 (85) 87)
NO	35 (10) 10	8 (9)	6 (8) (8)	11 (11) 12)	10 (13) 13)
NA	6 (2)	0	1 (1)	3 (3)	2 (3)
	342	85	79	98	80

TABLE C.21 INTERESTED IN CRIMINAL CASE OUTCOME

	ALL	Claimants		Non-Claimants	
		BKLN	NEWK	BKLN	NEWK
	%	%	%	%	%
YES	26 (8) 76)	7 (8) 88)	5 (6) 83)	6 (6) 56)	8 (10) 80)
NO	7 (2) 21)	1 (1) 13)	1 (1) 17)	4 (4) 36)	1 (1) 10)
OTHER	1 (0) (3)	0	0	0	1 (1) 10)
NA	307 (90)	77 (91)	73 (93)	87 (89)	70 (88)
	342	85	79	98	80

TABLE C.22 WHY SATISFIED WITH CRIMINAL CASE OUTCOME

	ALL	Claimants		Non-Claimants	
		BKLN	NEWK	BKLN	NEWK
	%	%	%	%	%
NA	214 (63)	65 (77)	49 (62)	59 (60)	41 (51)
BLANK	3 (1)	0	0	2 (2)	1 (1)
PUNISH DEF	19 (6) 15)	3 (4) 15)	6 (8) 20)	5 (5) 14)	5 (6) 13)
SOME DONE	49 (15) 38)	9 (11) 45)	10 (13) 33)	15 (15) 41)	15 (19 (39)
DISP RESOL	6 (2) (5)	0	1 (1) (3)	2 (2) (5)	3 (4) (8)
NO PUNISH	9 (3) (7)	0	1 (1) (3)	5 (5) 14)	3 (4) (8)
VIC PROTEC	24 (7) 19)	5 (6) 25)	8 (10) 27)	4 (4) (1)	7 (9) 18)
VIC RESTIT	4 (1) (3)	1 (1) (3)	1 (1) (3)	0	2 (3) (5)
JUST. DONE	11 (3) (9)	2 (2) 10)	3 (4) 10)	3 (3) (8)	3 (4) (8)
OTHER	3 (1) (2)	0	0	3 (3) (8)	0
	342	85	79	98	80

TABLE C.23 APPROVE OF GUILTY PLEA

	ALL	Claimants		Non-Claimants	
		BKLN	NEWK	BKLN	NEWK
	%	%	%	%	%
APPROVE	48 (14) 29)	10 (12) 23)	12 (15) 33)	15 (15) 32)	11 (14) 26)
DISAPP	83 (24) 49)	22 (26) 51)	17 (22) 47)	23 (24) 49)	21 (26) 50)
NO UNDERST	15 (4) (9)	6 (7) (14)	2 (3) (6)	3 (3) (6)	4 (5) 10)
NO OPINION	22 (6) 13)	5 (6) 12)	5 (6) 14)	6 (6) 13)	6 (8) 14)
NA	174 (60)	42 (49)	43 (54)	51 (52)	38 (48)
	342	85	79	98	80

TABLE C.24 AMOUNT OF CASE INVOLVEMENT EXPECTED

	ALL %	Claimants BKLN %	NEWK %	Non-Claimants BKLN %	NEWK %
MORE	175 (51)	47 (55)	40 (51)	49 (50)	39 (49)
AS MUCH	97 (28)	20 (24)	24 (30)	27 (28)	26 (33)
LESS	69 (20)	17 (20)	15 (19)	22 (22)	15 (19)
	342	85	79	98	80

TABLE C.25 GET INVOLVED IN CRIMINAL PROCESS AGAIN

	ALL %	Claimants BKLN %	NEWK %	Non-Claimants BKLN %	NEWK %
YES	166 (49) 60)	40 (47) 58)	39 (49) 61)	47 (48) 59)	40 (50) 64)
NO	110 (32) 40)	29 (34) 42)	25 (32) 39)	33 (34) 41)	23 (29) 37)
DK	66 (19)	16 (19)	15 (19)	18 (18)	17 (21)
	342	85	79	98	80

TABLE C.26 CONSIDER USING MEDIATION

	ALL %	Claimants BKLN %	NEWK %	Non-Claimants BKLN %	NEWK %
YES	147 (43) 43)	31 (37) 37)	33 (42) 42)	47 (48) 50)	36 (45) 45)
NO	139 (41) 41)	41 (48) 48)	32 (41) 41)	36 (37) 38)	30 (38) 38)
OTHER	53 (16) 16)	13 (15) 15)	14 (18) 18)	12 (12) 13)	14 (18) 18)
BLANK	3 (1)	0	0	3 (3)	0
	342	85	79	98	80

TABLE C.27 SATISFIED WITH VICTIM SERVICES

	ALL %	Claimants BKLN %	NEWK %	Non-Claimants BKLN %	NEWK %
NA	56 (16)	22 (26)	15 (19)	5 (5)	14 (18)
SATISFIED	110 (32) 38)	20 (24) 32)	25 (32) 39)	39 (40) 42)	26 (33) 39)
SOMEWHAT	124 (36) 43)	28 (33) 44)	25 (32) 39)	39 (40) 42)	32 (40) 48)
DISSATIS	52 (15) 18)	15 (18) 24)	14 (18) 22)	15 (15) 16)	8 (10) 12)
	342	85	79	98	80

TABLE C.28 SATISFIED WITH SOCIAL SERVICE AGENCIES

	ALL		Claimants		Non-Claimants	
			BKLN	NEWK	BKLN	NEWK
	%		%	%	%	%
SATISFIED	18	(5) 27)	7 (8) 29)	4 (5) 33)	3 (3) 16)	4 (5) 40)
SOMEWHAT	15	(4) 23)	7 (8) 29)	2 (3) 17)	5 (5) 26)	1 (1) 10)
DISSATIS	32	(9) 50)	10 (12 (42)	6 (8) 50)	11 (11) 58)	5 (6) 50)
NA	277	(81)	61 (72)	67 (24)	79 (81)	70 (88)
	342		85	79	98	80

TABLE C.29 EFFECT OF VICTIMIZATION

	ALL	Claimants		Non-Claimants	
		BKLN	NEWK	BKLN	NEWK
	%	%	%	%	%
NONE	45 (13) 13)	13 (15) 16)	12 (15) 15)	11 (11) 12)	9 (11) 11)
EMOTION	67 (20) 20)	14 (17) 17)	15 (19) 19)	21 (21) 22)	17 (21) 21)
NEGATIVE	66 (19) 20)	20 (24) 24)	15 (19) 19)	16 (16) 17)	15 (19) 19)
EMBARASS	51 (15) 15)	16 (19) 19)	10 (13) 13)	12 (12) 13)	13 (16) 16)
RELATIONS	27 (8) (8)	2 (2) (2)	3 (4) (4)	14 (14) (15)	8 (10) 10)
INJURY	63 (18) 19)	16 (19) 19)	19 (24) 24)	17 (17) 18)	11 (14) 14)
FINANCIAL	16 (5) (5)	3 (4) (4)	4 (6) (6)	3 (3) (3)	6 (7) (7)
MISCELLAN	3 (1) (1)	0	1 (1) (1)	1 (1) (1)	1 (1) (1)
BLANK	3 (1)	0	0	3 (3)	0
DK	1 (0)	1 (1)	0	0	0
	342	85	79	98	80

TABLE C.30 SUGGESTIONS TO HELP AFTER VICTIMIZATION

	ALL	Claimants		Non-Claimants	
		BKLN	NEWK	BKLN	NEWK
	%	%	%	%	%
NONE	86 (25) 26)	19 (22) 23)	25 (32) 33)	26 (27) 28)	16 (20) 21)
POLICE	30 (9) (9)	7 (8) (9)	7 (9) (9)	6 (6) (7)	10 (13) 13)
CT SCHED	57 (17) 17)	15 (18) 18)	13 (17) 17)	19 (19) 20)	10 (13) 13)
CT CONCERN	56 (16) 17)	15 (18) 18)	10 (13) 13)	15 (15) 16)	16 (20) 21)
IMPR. LENF	62 (18) 19)	16 (19) 20)	13 (17) 17)	17 (17) 18)	16 (20) 21)
OTHER	39 (11) 12)	10 (12) 12)	9 (11) 12)	10 (10) 11)	10 (13) 13)
BLANK	4 (1)	0	0	4 (4)	0
DK	8 (2)	3 (4)	2 (3)	1 (1)	2 (3)
	342	85	79	98	80

TABLE C.31 PAYMENTS IMPORTANT TO CONTINUING CASE

		Claimants		Non-Claimants	
	ALL	BKLN	NEWK	BKLN	NEWK
	%	%	%	%	%
VERY	3 (1) 50)	1 (1) 100)	1 (1) 50)	0	0
SOME	3 (1) 50)	0	1 (1) 50)	1 (1) 50)	1 (1) 100)
NONE	0	0	0	0	0
NA	336 (98)	84 (99)	77 (98)	96 (98)	79 (99)
	342	85	79	98	80

TABLE C.32 PAYMENTS AFFECT COOPERATION

		Claimants		Non-Claimants	
	ALL	BKLN	NEWK	BKLN	NEWK
	%	%	%	%	%
YES	308 (90) 95)	76 (89) 95)	70 (89) 95)	87 (89) 95)	75 (94) 97)
NO	15 (4) (5)	4 (5) (5)	4 (5) (5)	5 (5) (5)	2 (3) (3)
NA	6 (2)	1 (1)	2 (3)	2 (2)	1 (1)
DK	13 (4)	4 (5)	3 (4)	4 (4)	2 (3)
	342	85	79	98	80

TABLE C.33 WHY COOPERATE AFTER PAYMENTS

		Claimants		Non-Claimants	
	ALL	BKLN	NEWK	BKLN	NEWK
	%	%	%	%	%
NEED $	126 (37) 41)	30 (35) 40)	28 (35) 40)	36 (37) 40)	32 (40) 43)
WORTH IT	89 (26) 29)	23 (27) 30)	23 (29) 33)	26 (27) 29)	17 (21) 23)
EXPENSES	95 (28) 31)	23 (27) 30)	19 (24) 27)	27 (28) 30)	26 (33) 35)
NA	32 (9)	9 (11)	9 (11)	9 (9)	5 (6)
	342	85	79	98	80

TABLE C.34 WHY NOT COOPERATE WITH PAYMENTS

		Claimants		Non-Claimants	
	ALL	BKLN	NEWK	BKLN	NEWK
	%	%	%	%	%
NOT RIGHT	3 (1) 12)	1 (1) 13)	2 (3) 29)	0	0
DEF INNOC.	9 (3) 35)	2 (2) 25)	2 (3) 29)	3 (3) 43)	2 (3) (3)
NOT WORTH	14 (4) 54)	5 (6) 63)	3 (4) 43)	4 (4) 57)	2 (3) (3)
BLANK	316 (92)	77 (91)	72 (91)	91 (93)	76 (95)
	342	85	79	98	80

TABLE C.35 SHOULD GOVERNMENT PAY VICTIM

	Claimants		Non-Claimants	
	ALL	BKLN	NEWK	BKLN	NEWK
	%	%	%	%	%
YES	316 (92)	78 (92)	75 (95)	88 (90)	75 (94)
NO	26 (8)	7 (8)	4 (5)	10 (10)	5 (6)
	342	85	79	98	80

TABLE C.36 WOULD GOVERNMENT PAYMENTS INCREASE COOPERATION

	Claimants		Non-Claimants	
	ALL	BKLN	NEWK	BKLN	NEWK
	%	%	%	%	%
YES	240 (70) 76	56 (66) 72	55 (70) 73	74 (76) 84	55 (69) 73
NO	76 (22) 24	22 (26) 28	20 (25) 27	14 (14) 16	20 (25) 27
NA	26 (7)	7 (8)	4 (5)	10 (10)	5 (6)
	342	85	79	98	80

TABLE C.37 SHOULD PAYMENTS BE TO POOR ONLY

	Claimants		Non-Claimants	
	ALL	BKLN	NEWK	EKLN	NEWK
	%	%	%	%	%
ALL	303 (89) 96	75 (88) 96	72 (91) 96	85 (87) 97	71 (89) 95
POOR ONLY	13 (4) (4)	3 (4) (4)	3 (4) (4)	3 (3) (3)	4 (5) (5)
NA	26 (7)	7 (8)	4 (5)	10 (10)	5 (6)
	342	85	79	98	80

TABLE C.38 SHOULD PROPERTY LOSSES BE REIMBURSED

	Claimants		Non-Claimants	
	ALL	BKLN	NEWK	BKLN	NEWK
	%	%	%	%	%
YES	233 (68) 74	61 (72) 77	51 (65) 68	70 (71) 80	51 (64) 68
NO	84 (25) 26	18 (21) 23	24 (30) 32	18 (18) 21	24 (30) 32
NA	24 (7)	5 (6)	4 (5)	10 (10)	5 (6)
	342	85	79	98	80

TABLE C.39 WHY AGAINST GOVERNMENT PAYMENTS

	Claimants		Non-Claimants	
	ALL	BKIN	NEWK	EKLN	NEWK
	%	%	%	%	%
VS. WELFARE	11 (3) 39	2 (2) (2)	2 (3) 50	5 (5) 39	2 (3) 40
INEFFIC.	1 (0) (4)	0	0	1 (1) (8)	0
UNNECESS.	7 (2) 25	0	1 (1) 25	5 (5) 39	1 (1) 20
PRIV SOLUT	9 (3) 32	4 (5) (5)	1 (1) 25	2 (2) 15	2 (3) 40
NA	314 (92)	79 (93)	75 (95)	85 (87)	75 (95)
	342	85	79	98	80

APPENDIX D:
Chapter Nine Tables

TABLE D.1 WHY APPLY FOR VICTIM COMPENSATION

	ALL %	Claimants BKLN %	Claimants NEWK %	Non-Claimants BKLN %	Non-Claimants NEWK %
GET AID	32 (9) 19)	15 (18) 18)	16 (20) 20)	0	0
MEDICAL	29 (9) 17)	14 (17) 17)	15 (19) 19)	0	0
PROP LOSS	24 (7) 14)	14 (17) 17)	9 (11) 11)	1 (1) 50)	0
RIGHT	33 (10) 20)	16 (19) 19)	16 (20) 20)	1 (1) 50)	0
POOR	15 (4) (9)	7 (8) (8)	7 (9) (9)	0	1 (1) 50)
LOST INCOM	16 (5) 10)	8 (9) (9)	8 (10) 10)	0	0
OUT POCKET	12 (4) (7)	6 (7) (7)	6 (7) (7)	0	0
RESTITUT	7 (2) (4)	5 (6) (6)	2 (3) (3)	0	0
NA	174 (51)	0	0	96 (98)	78 (98)
	342	85	79	98	80

TABLE D.2 HESITATE USING VICTIM COMPENSATION

	ALL %	Claimants BKLN %	Claimants NEWK %	Non-Claimants BKLN %	Non-Claimants NEWK %
YES	54 (16) 32)	33 (39) 39)	20 (25) 25)	1 (1) 50)	0
NO	114 (34) 68)	52 (61) 61)	59 (75) 75)	1 (1) 50)	2 (3) 100)
NA	174 (60)	0	0	96 (98)	78 (97)
	342	85	79	98	80

TABLE D.3 WHY HESITATE USING VICTIM COMPENSATION

	ALL %	Claimants BKLN %	Claimants NEWK %	Non-Claimants BKLN %	Non-Claimants NEWK %
NA	287 (84)	51 (60)	59 (75)	97 (99)	80 (100)
UNSURE HOW	6 (2) 11)	4 (5) 12)	2 (3) 10)	0	0
NO INVEST	1 (0) (2)	1 (1) (3)	0	0	0
INELIGIBLE	5 (2) (9)	3 (4) (9)	2 (3) 10)	0	0
FORGET	3 (1) (5)	1 (1) (3)	2 (3) 10)	0	0
HARD FORM	2 (1) (4)	1 (1) (3)	1 (1) (5)	0	0
INAPPROP	3 (1) (5)	2 (2) (6)	1 (1) (5)	0	0
HASSLE	5 (2) (9)	4 (5) 12)	1 (1) (5)	0	-0
NEED $	1 (0) (2)	1 (1) (3)	0	0	0
FUTILE	23 (5) 42)	12 (14) 35)	10 (13) 50)	1 (1) (1)	0
BOTHER	4 (1) (7)	4 (5) 12)	0	0	0
LOST FORM	2 (1) (4)	1 (1) (3)	1 (1) (5)	0	0
	342	85	79	98	80

TABLE D.4 HAVE A FORMAL HEARING

	ALL %	Claimants BKLN %	NEWK %	Non-Claimants BKLN %	NEWK %
YES	21 (6) 13)	10(12) 12)	10(13) 13)	0	1 (1) 50)
NO	146 (43) 87)	75 (88) 88)	68 (86) 87)	2 (2) 100)	1 (1) 50)
NA	175 (51)	0	1 (1)	96 (98)	78 (98)
	342	85	79	98	80

TABLE D.5 INCONVENIENCED BY TAKING TIME OFF FROM WORK

	ALL %	Claimants BKLN %	NEWK %	Non-Claimants BKLN %	NEWK %
YES	70 (21) 40)	36 (42) 42)	30 (38) 38)	2 (3) 100)	2 (3) 100)
NO	98 (29) 60)	49 (58) 58)	49 (62) 62)	0	0
NA	174 (51)	0	0	96 (98)	78 (97)
	342	85	79	98	80

TABLE D.6 INCONVENIENCED BY TRANSPORTATION DIFFICULTIES

	ALL %	Claimants BKLN %	NEWK %	Non-Claimants BKLN %	NEWK %
YES	46 (14) 27)	23 (27) 27)	20 (25) 25)	1 (1) 50)	2 (3) 100)
NO	122 (36) 73)	62 (73) 73)	59 (75) 75)	1 (1) 50)	0
NA	174 (51)	0	0	96 (98)	78 (97)
	342	85	79	98	80

TABLE D.7 INCONVENIENCED BY CHILD OR ELDERLY CARE

	ALL %	Claimants BKLN %	NEWK %	Non-Claimants BKLN %	NEWK %
YES	17 (5) 10)	8 (9) 9)	8 (10) 10)	0	1 (1) 50)
NO	151 (44) 90)	77 (91) 91)	71 (90) 90)	2 (2) 100)	1 (1) 50)
NA	174 (51)	0	0	96 (98)	78 (98)
	342	85	79	98	80

TABLE D.8 INCONVENIENCED LOCATING COMPENSATION BOARD

	ALL %	Claimants BKLN %	NEWK %	Non-Claimants BKLN %	NEWK %
YES	6 (2) 19)	4 (5) 27)	2 (3) 13)	0	0
NO	25 (7) 81)	11 (13) 73)	13 (17) 87)	0	1 (1) 100)
NA	311 (91)	70 (82)	64 (81)	98 (100)	79 (99)
	342	85	79	98	80

TABLE D.9 INCONVENIENCED FINDING A PLACE TO WAIT

	ALL %	Claimants BKLN %	NEWK %	Non-Claimants BKLN %	NEWK %
YES	4 (1) 19)	3 (4) 30)	1 (1) 10)	0	0
NO	17 (5) 81)	7 (8) 70)	9 (11) 90)	0	1 (1) 100)
NA	321 (94)	75 (88)	69 (87)	98 (100)	79 (99)
	342	85	79	98	80

TABLE D.10 INCONVENIENCED BY HEARING TIME

	ALL %	Claimants BKLN %	NEWK %	Non-Claimants BKLN %	NEWK %
YES	12 (4) 57)	5 (6) 50)	6 (8) 60)	0	1 (1) 100)
NO	9 (3) 43)	5 (6) 50)	4 (5) 40)	0	0
NA	321 (94)	75 (88)	69 (87)	98 (100)	79 (99)
	342	85	79	98	80

TABLE D.11 PROBLEM WITH COMPENSATION PROCESS

	ALL %	Claimants BKLN %	NEWK %	Non-Claimants BKLN %	NEWK %
YES	76 (22) 45)	41 (48) 48)	32 (41) 41)	1 (1) 50)	2 (3) 100)
NO	92 (27) 55)	44 (52) 52)	47 (60) 60)	1 (1) 50)	0
NA	174 (51)	0	0	96 (98)	78 (97)
	342	85	79	98	80

TABLE D.12 PROBLEM WITH COMPENSATION FORMS

	ALL %	Claimants BKLN %	NEWK %	Non-Claimants BKLN %	NEWK %
YES	27 (8) 16)	18 (21) 21)	8 (10) 10)	1 (1) 50)	0
NO	141 (41) 84)	67 (79) 79)	71 (90) 90)	1 (1) 50)	2 (3) 100)
NA	174 (51)	0	0	96 (98)	78 (97)
	342	85	79	98	80

TABLE D.13 PROBLEM GATHERING EVIDENCE

	ALL %	Claimants BKLN %	NEWK %	Non-Claimants BKLN %	NEWK %
YES	119 (35) 71)	64 (75) 75)	51 (65) 65)	2 (2) 100	2 (3) 100)
NO	49 (14) 29)	21 (25) 25)	28 (35) 35)	0	0
NA	174 (51)	0	0	96 (98)	78 (97)
	342	85	79	98	80

TABLE D.14 INCONVENIENCED GETTING A LAWYER

	ALL %	Claimants BKLN %	Claimants NEWK %	Non-Claimants BKLN %	Non-Claimants NEWK %
YES	139 (41) 88	71 (84 (89)	64 (81) 87)	2 (2) 100)	2 (3) 100)
NO	19 (6) 12	9 (11) 11)	10 (13) 14)	0	0
NA	184 (54)	5 (6)	5 (6)	96 (98)	78 (97)
	342	85	79	98	80

TABLE D.15 WHY SATISFIED WITH COMPENSATION INVOLVEMENT

	ALL %	Claimants BKLN %	Claimants NEWK %	Non-Claimants BKLN %	Non-Claimants NEWK %
BD RESPON	37 (11) 70)	17 (20) 85)	19 (24) 59)	0	1 (1) 100
BD INFORM	16 (5) 30)	3 (4) 15)	13 (17) 41)	0	0
NA	289 (85)	65 (77)	47 (60)	98 (100)	79 (99)
	342	85	79	98	80

TABLE D.16 WHY DISSATISFIED WITH COMPENSATION INVOLVEMENT

	ALL %	Claimants BKLN %	Claimants NEWK %	Non-Claimants BKLN %	Non-Claimants NEWK %
NO INFO	20 (6) 17)	11 (13) 17)	8 (10) 17)	0	1 (1) 100)
NO ATTNY	27 (8) 24)	18 (21) 28)	9 (11) 19)	0	0
NO HEAR.	10 (3) (9)	5 (6) (8)	5 (6) 1C)	0	0
TOO HARD	40 (12) 35)	21 (25 (32)	18 (23) 38)	1 (1) 100)	0
UNCONCER	18 (5) 16)	10 (12) 15)	8 (10) 17)	0	0
NA	227 (66)	20 (24)	31 (39)	97 (99)	79 (99)
	342	85	79	98	80

TABLE D.17 INFORMED OF COMPENSATION CASE PROGRESS

	ALL %	Claimants BKLN %	Claimants NEWK %	Non-Claimants BKLN %	Non-Claimants NEWK %
SATISFIED	39 (11) 23)	19 (22) 22)	19 (24) 24)	0	1 (1) 50)
SOMEWHAT	49 (14) 29)	23 (27) 27)	24 (30) 30)	1 (1) 50)	1 (1) 50)
DISSATIS	80 (23) 48)	38 (45) 45)	31 (39) 39)	1 (1) 50)	0
NA	174 (51)	5 (6)	5 (6)	96 (98)	78 (98)
	342	85	79	98	80

TABLE D.18 SATISFIED WITH COMPENSATION CASE SPEED

| | ALL % | Claimants | | Non-Claimants | |
		BKLN %	NEWK %	BKLN %	NEWK %
SATISFIED	19 (6) 11)	11(13) 13)	8(10) 10)	0	0
SOMEWHAT	36 (11) 21)	17 (20) 20)	17 (22) 22)	1 (1) 50)	1 (1) 50)
DISSATIS	113 (33) 67)	57 (67) 67)	54 (68) 68)	1 (1) 50)	1 (1) 50)
NA	174 (51)	0	0	96 (98)	78 (98)
	342	85	79	98	80

TABLE D.19 COMPENSATICN BOARD CONCERNED ABOUT VICTIMS

| | ALL % | Claimants | | Non-Claimants | |
		BKLN %	NEWK %	BKLN %	NEWK %
VERY	26 (8) 16)	14 (17) 17)	12 (15) 15)	0	0
SOME	41 (12) 24)	17 (20) 20)	21 (27) 27)	2 (2) 100)	1 (1) 50)
NONE	101 (30) 60)	54 (64) 64)	46 (58) 58)	0	1 (1) 50)
NA	174 (51)	0	0	96 (98)	78 (98)
	342	85	79	98	80

TABLE D.20 OVERALL VIEW OF BOARD OFFICIALS (RECODED)

| | ALL % | Claimants | | Non-Claimants | |
		BKLN %	NEWK %	BKLN %	NEWK %
FAVOR	33 (10) 20)	13 (15) 15)	20 (25) 25)	0	0
MIXED	26 (8) 16)	12 (14) 14)	12 (15) 15)	1 (1) 50)	1 (1) 50)
UNFAVOR	109 (32) 65)	60 (71) 71)	47 (60) 60)	1 (1) 50)	1 (1) 50)
NA	174 (51)	0	0	96 (98)	78 (98)
	342	85	79	98	80

TABLE D.21 APPROVE OF NEED TO REPORT CRIME

| | ALL % | Claimants | | Non-Claimants | |
		BKLN %	NEWK %	BKLN %	NEWK %
APPROVE	152 (44) 91)	74 (87) 87)	74 (94) 94)	2 (2) 100)	2 (3) 100)
DISAPP	7 (2) (4)	4 (5) (5)	3 (4) (4)	0	0
UNSURE	9 (3) (5)	7 (8) (8)	2 (3) (3)	0	0
NA	174 (51)	0	0	96 (98)	78 (97)
	342	85	79	98	80

TABLE D.22 APPROVE NEED TO COOPERATE W/JUSTICE OFFICIALS

	ALL	Claimants		Non-Claimants	
		BKLN	NEWK	BKLN	NEWK
	%	%	%	%	%
APPROVE	123(36)73)	59(69)69)	61(77)77)	1 (1)100)	2 (3)100)
DISAPP	11 (3)(7)	5 (6)(6)	5 (6)(6)	0	0
UNSURE	34(10)20)	20(24)24)	13(16)16)	1 (1)(1)	0
NA	174(51)	1 (1)	0	96(98)	78(98)
	342	85	79	98	80

TABLE D.23 APPROVE BAN AGAINST PROVOKING CRIME

	ALL	Claimants		Non-Claimants	
		BKLN	NEWK	BKLN	NEWK
	%	%	%	%	%
APPROVE	163(48)97)	82(96)96)	77(97)97)	2 (2)100)	2 (3)100)
DISAPP	0	0	0	0	0
UNSURE	5 (2)(3)	3 (4)(4)	2 (3)(3)	0	0
NA	174(51)	0	0	96(98)	78(98)
	342	85	79	98	80

TABLE D.24 APPROVE OF MINIMUM LOSS REQUIREMENT

	ALL	Claimants		Non-Claimants	
		BKLN	NEWK	BKLN	NEWK
	%	%	%	%	%
APPROVE	1 (0)(1)	0	1 (1)(1)	0	0
DISAPP	153(45)92)	79(93)100)	70(89)99)	2 (2)100)	2 (3)100)
UNSURE	14 (4)(8)	6 (7)(7)	8(10)10)	0	0
NA	174(51)	0	0	96(98)	78(97)
	342	85	79	98	80

TABLE D.25 APPROVE OF COMPENSATION AWARD LIMIT

	ALL	Claimants		Non-Claimants	
		BKLN	NEWK	BKLN	NEWK
	%	%	%	%	%
APPROVE	10 (3)(6)	4 (5)(5)	6 (8)(8)	0	0
DISAPP	104(30)62)	55(65)65)	46(58)58)	2 (2)100)	1 (1)100)
UNSURE	54(16)32)	26(31)31)	27(34)34)	0	1 (1)(1)
NA	174(51)	0	0	96(98)	78(98)
	342	85	79	98	80

TABLE D.26 APPROVE NEED TO SUBTRACT OUTSIDE AWARDS

	ALL %	Claimants BKLN %	NEWK %	Non-Claimants BKLN %	NEWK %
APPROVE	101 (30 (60)	50(59) 59)	48 (61) 61)	1 (1) 99)	2 (3) 100)
DISAPP	32 (9) 19)	16 (19) 19)	16(20) 20)	0	0
UNSURE	35 (10) 21)	19 (22) 22)	15 (19) 19)	1 (1) (1)	0
NA	174 (51)	0	0	96 (98)	78 (97)
	342	85	79	98	80

TABLE D.27 APPROVE NEED TO MISS MINIMUM TIME AT WORK

	ALL %	Claimants BKLN %	NEWK %	Non-Claimants BKLN %	NEWK %
APPROVE	3 (1) (2)	1 (1) (1)	2 (3) (3)	0	0
DISAPP	160 (47) 95)	81 (95) 95)	75 (95) 97)	2 (2) 100)	2 (3) 100)
UNSURE	5 (2) (3)	3 (4) (4)	2 (3) (3)	0	0
NA	174 (51)	0	0	96 (98)	78 (97)
	342	85	79	98	80

TABLE D.28 OVERALL APPROVAL OF COMPENSATION RULES

	ALL %	Claimants BKLN %	NEWK %	Non-Claimants BKLN %	NEWK %
APPROVE	6 (2) (4)	3 (4) (4)	3 (4) (4)	0	0
DISAPP	7 (2) (4)	5 (6) (6)	2 (3) (3)	0	0
UNSURE	155 (45) 92)	77 (91) 91)	74 (94) 94)	2 (2) 100)	2 (3) 100)
NA	174 (51)	0	0	96 (98)	78 (97)
	342	85	79	98	80

TABLE D.29 GET COMPENSATION AWARD

	ALL %	Claimants BKLN %	NEWK %	Non-Claimants BKLN %	NEWK %
YES	64 (19) 38)	32 (38) 38)	32 (41) 41)	0	0
NO	104 (30) 62)	53 (62) 62)	47 (59) 59)	2 (2) 100)	2 (3) 100)
NA	174 (51)	0	0	96 (98)	78 (97)
	342	85	79	98	80

TABLE D.30 OFFICIAL REASONS FCR CLAIMS DENIALS (NEW YORK)

	%
INSUFFICIENT INFORMATICN/CCCEERATION	1580 (52)
MISCELLANEOUS	541 (18)
NO MINIMUM ELIGIBILITY	189 (6)
WORKMANS COMPENSATION PENDING	152 (5)
APPLICATION WITHDRAWN	107 (3)
NO FINANCIAL HARDSHIP	82 (3)
NO COOPERATION WITH POLICE	77 (3)
UNABLE TO LOCATE CLAIMANT	74 (3)
CLAIMANT NOT INNOCENT	85 (3)
CLAIMANT INELIGIBLE	69 (3)
VICTIM-OFFENDER RELATIONSHIP	44 (1)
NO CRIME	34 (1)
INELIGIBLE AUTO CASE	15 (1)
NO INJURY	14 (1)
	3063 (100)

TABLE D.31 WHY WERE YOU DENIEC AN AWARC

	ALL %	Claimants BKLN %	Claimants NEWK %	Non-Claimants BKLN %	Non-Claimants NEWK %
NA	238 (70)	32 (38)	32 (41)	96 (98)	78 (98)
BD UNFAIR	33 (1) 32)	15 (18) 28)	16 (20) 34)	1 (1) 50)	1 (1) 50)
NO COOP	6 (2) (6)	3 (4) (6)	2 (3) (4)	0	0
MIN. LOSS	11 (3) 11)	7 (8) 13)	4 (5) (9)	0	0
MIN. WORK	15 (4) 14)	9 (11) 17)	6 (8) 13)	0	0
DISCONTIN	1 (0) (1)	1 (1) (2)	0	0	0
RELATION	14 (4) 13)	6 (7) 11)	8 (10) 17)	0	0
LATE CLAIM	1 (0) (1)	0	1 (1) (2)	0	0
PROVOKE	1 (0) (1)	0	1 (1) (2)	0	0
LOSS INEL.	12 (4) 12)	6 (7) 11)	5 (6) 11)	1 (1) 50)	0
FIN.NEED	9 (3) (9)	6 (7) 11)	3 (4) (6)	0	0
OTHER PAY	1 (0) (1)	0	1 (1) (2)	0	0
	342	85	79	98	80

TABLE D.32 OFFICIAL REASONS FCR CLAIMS DENIALS (NEW JERSEY)

	%
NO MINIMUM REQUIREMENTS	86 (33)
LACK OF COOPERATION	44 (17)
PROVOCATICN	35 (14)
NO POLICE REPORT	23 (9)
NO COMPENSIBLE LOSS	19 (7)
LATE CLAIM	16 (6)
NO VIOLENT CRIME	12 (5)
MISCELLANEOUS	10 (4)
VICTIM-OFFENDER RELATIONSHIP	8 (3)
CLAIM WITHDRAWN	5 (2)
	258 (100)

TABLE D.33 EXPECT TO GET COMPENSATION AWARD

	ALL %	Claimants BKLN %	NEWK %	Non-Claimants BKLN %	NEWK %
YES	106 (31) 64)	57 (67) 68)	47 (60) 60)	1 (1) 100)	1 (1) 50)
NO	60 (18) 36)	27 (32) 32)	32 (40) 40)	0	1 (1) 50)
NA	176 (51)	1 (1)	0	97 (99)	78 (98)
	342	85	79	98	80

TABLE D.34 WHY EXPECT TO GET COMPENSATION AWARD

	ALL %	Claimants BKLN %	NEWK %	Non-Claimants BKLN %	NEWK %
GOVT DUTY	29 (9) 27)	18 (21) 32)	10 (13) 22)	0	1 (1) 100)
REAL LOSS	23 (7) 22)	12 (14) 21)	11 (14) 24)	0	0
TRUST GOV	27 (8) 26)	15 (18) 26)	10 (13) 22)	2 (2) 100)	0
TOLD SO	27 (8) 26)	12 (14) 21)	15 (19) 33)	0	0
NA/BLANK	236 (69)	28 (33)	33 (42)	96 (98)	79 (99)
	342	85	79	98	80

TABLE D.35 WHY NCT EXPECT TO GET COMPENSATION AWARD

	ALL %	Claimants BKLN %	NEWK %	Non-Claimants BKLN %	NEWK %
UNFAIR	30 (9) 48)	13 (15) 46)	16 (20) 49)	0	1 (1) 100)
INEFFIC	7 (2) 11)	3 (4) 11)	4 (5) 12)	0	0
INELIG	9 (3) 14)	4 (5) 14)	5 (6) 15)	0	0
NO AWARDS	9 (3) 14)	3 (4) 11)	5 (6) 15)	1 (1) 100)	0
FATALIST	8 (2) 13)	5 (6) 18)	3 (4) (9)	0	0
NA	279 (82)	57 (67)	46 (58)	97 (99)	79 (99)
	342	85	79	98	80

TABLE D.36 APPEAL COMPENSATICN BOARD IECISION

	ALL %	Claimants BKLN %	NEWK %	Non-Claimants BKLN %	NEWK %
YES	5 (2) (3)	2 (2) (2)	3 (4) (4)	0	0
NO	163 (48) 97)	83 (98) 98)	76 (96) 96)	2 (2) 100)	2 (3) 100)
NA	174 (51)	0	0	96 (98)	78 (97)
	342	85	79	98	80

TABLE D.37 WHAT HAPPENED WITH APPEAL

	ALL %	Claimants BKLN %	NEWK %	Non-Claimants BKLN %	NEWK %
LOST CASE	5 (1) 100	2 (2) 100)	0	0	0
NA	337 (99)	83 (98)	79 (1000)	98 (100)	80 (100)
	342	85	79	98	80

TABLE D.38 WHY SATISFIED WITH COMPENSATION CASE

	ALL %	Claimants BKLN %	NEWK %	Non-Claimants BKLN %	NEWK %
AWARD	20 (6) 36)	9 (11) 36)	11 (14) 38)	0	0
SOME AWD.	21 (6) 38)	10 (12) 40)	10 (13) 35)	1 (1) 100)	0
HELPED	10 (3) 18)	5 (6) 20)	5 (6) 17)	0	0
CONCERN	5 (2) (9)	1 (1) (4)	3 (4) 10)	0	1 (1) 100)
NA	286 (84)	60 (71)	50 (63)	97 (99)	79 (99)
	342	85	79	98	80

TABLE D.39 WHY DISSATISFIED WITH COMPENSATION CASE

	ALL %	Claimants BKLN %	NEWK %	Non-Claimants BKLN %	NEWK %
PROCED.	6 (2) (5)	4 (5) (7)	2 (3) (4)	0	0
NO AWARD	50 (15) 45)	29 (34) 48)	20 (25) 40)	1 (1) 100)	0
INSUFFIC	16 (5) 14)	9 (11) 15)	7 (9) 14)	0	0
BD UNFAIR	28 (8) 25)	13 (15) 22)	15 (19) 30)	0	0
DELAY	6 (2) (5)	2 (2) (3)	4 (5) (8)	0	0
COST	6 (2) (5)	3 (4) (5)	2 (3) (4)	0	1 (1) 100)
NA	230 (67)	25 (29)	29 (37)	97 (99)	79 (99)
	342	85	79	98	80

TABLE D.40 DESIRE FOR AWARD AFFECT PAST COOPERATION

	ALL %	Claimants BKLN %	NEWK %	Non-Claimants BKLN %	NEWK %
YES	133 (39) 79)	68 (80) 80)	62 (79) 79)	2 (2) 100)	1 (1) 50)
NO	35 (10) 21)	17 (20) 20)	17 (22) 22)	0	1 (1) 50)
NA	174 (51)	0	0	96 (98)	78 (98)
	342	85	79	98	80

TABLE D.41 WILL COMPENSATION AFFECT FUTURE COOPERATION

	ALL %			Claimants BKLN %			NEWK %			Non-Claimants BKLN %			NEWK %		
NO EFFECT	12	(4)	(7)	8	(9)	(9)	4	(5)	(5)	0			0		
COOPERATE	21	(6)	13)	9	(11)	11)	12	(15)	15)	0			0		
PRO-CJS	22	(6)	13)	8	(9)	(9)	14	(18)	18)	0			0		
NO COOP	52	(15)	31)	25	(29)	29)	24	(30)	30)	1	(1)	50)	2	(3)	100)
ANTI-CJS	61	(18)	36)	35	(41)	41)	25	(32)	32)	1	(1)	50)	0		
NA	174	(51)		0			0			96	(98)		78	(97)	
	342			85			79			98			80		

TABLE D.42 WOULD APPLY FOR COMPENSATION AGAIN

	ALL %			Claimants BKLN %			NEWK %			Non-Claimants BKLN %			NEWK %		
YES	42	(12)	25)	20	(24)	23)	22	(28)	28)	0			0		
NO	126	(37)	75)	65	(76)	77)	57	(72)	72)	2	(2)	100)	2	(3)	100)
NA	174	(51)		0			0			96	(98)		78	(97)	
	342			85			79			98			80		

TABLE D.43 WHY APPLY FOR COMPENSATION AGAIN

	ALL %			Claimants BKLN %			NEWK %			Non-Claimants BKLN %			NEWK %		
AWARD	34	(9)	76)	18	(21)	75)	16	(20)	76)	0			0		
DUTY	11	(3)	24)	6	(7)	25)	5	(6)	24)	0			0		
NA	297	(87)		61	(72)		58	(73)		98	(100)		80	(100)	
	342			85			79			98			80		

TABLE D.44 WHY NOT APPLY FOR COMPENSATION AGAIN

	ALL %			Claimants BKLN %			NEWK %			Non-Claimants BKLN %			NEWK %		
NO AWARD	50	(15)	39)	26	(31)	40)	20	(25)	35)	2	(2)	100)	2	(3)	100)
INSUFF	23	(7)	18)	11	(13)	17)	12	(15)	21)	0			0		
DELAY	7	(2)	(6)	4	(5)	(6)	3	(4)	(5)	0			0		
INELIG	40	(12)	32)	20	(24)	31)	20	(25)	35)	0			0		
UNCONCERN	4	(1)	(3)	3	(4)	(5)	1	(1)	(2)	0			0		
NO INVOLV	3	(1)	(2)	1	(1)	(2)	2	(3)	(3)	0			0		
NA	215	(63)		20	(24)		21	(27)		96	(98)		78	(97)	
	342			85			79			98			80		

TABLE D.45 HCW CCULD COMPENSATION BOARD IMPROVE

	Claimants			Non-Claimants	
	ALL %	BKLN %	NEWK %	BKLN %	NEWK %
DELAY	21 (6) 13)	9 (11) 11)	11 (14) 14)	0	1 (1) 50)
CONCERN	16 (5) 10)	8 (9) (9)	7 (9) (9)	1 (1) 50)	0
INVOLVE.	35 (10) 21)	18 (21) 21)	17 (22) 22)	0	0
AWARD	49 (14) 29)	25 (29) 29)	23 (29) 29)	0	1 (1) 50)
ELIGIBIL	44 (13) 26)	24 (28) 28)	19 (24) 24)	1 (1) 50)	0
PROCED.	3 (1) (2)	1 (1) (1)	2 (3) (3)	0	0
NA	174 (51)	0	0	96 (98)	78 (98)
	342	85	79	98	80

APPENDIX E:
Survey Questionnaires

Victim Questionnaire

Victim name _____

Date _____

Hello, I'm a researcher from Penn State University. I'm
doing research to help make the criminal-justice system work
better. I want to find out the needs of victims and
witnesses. I would like to ask you some questions about your
experiences in the criminal process after your victimization.
Your answers will be kept strictly confidential, and you are
free to not answer any of the questions I ask.

1) First of all, can you tell me what happened in your recent
victimization?
    A) Injury
        1) none
        2) minor (no medical attention)
        3) medical attention (no hospital)
        4) hospital
    B) Property stolen/damaged?
        1) yes
        2) no (If no, skip to 1C) (If yes):
        Property recovered?
            1) yes
            2) no
            3) don't know
        If no, skip to 1C
        If yes:
            When was it returned?
                1) early in case
                2) late in case
                3) after case
        Where is property now?
            1) police
            2) court
            3) victim
            4) don't know
            5) other _____
    C) Who called the police?
        1) victim
        2) nobody
        3) don't know
        4) other _____
        If not victim: Would you have called police?
            1) yes
            2) no
            3) not sure
    D) Relationship to defendant _____

2) Have you been involved in the court system before this case?
    1) yes
    2) no
    If yes, in what way?
        1) victim
        2) witness
        3) defendant
        4) defendant and victim
        5) other
        If victim, how satisfied were you with the way you were treated in the criminal case before?
                1) satisfied
                2) somewhat satisfied
                3) dissatisfied

3) Only for those reporting this crime: In some cases a person is victimized, but decides not to report it to the police. What made you decide to report the crime?

4) Did the police arrest a suspect in your case?
    1) yes
    2) no
    If no, skip to question 20, delete questions 24, 29, 30, 32-34

5) Did you press charges?
    1) yes
    2) no
    If no, delete questions 6-9, 15-19

6) What was the most important thing you hoped to get out of taking the case to court?

7) I'm going to read you some reasons why people press charges. For each one, tell me whether it was **Very important**, **Somewhat important**, or **Not important at all**.
    A) Getting restitution or property return? _____
    B) Putting defendant in jail? _____
    C) Serving justice as citizen's duty? _____
    D) Protecting yourself/family? _____
    E) Protecting others? _____
    F) Getting revenge? _____

8) Do you know the outcome of your case?
   1) yes
   2) no
   If no, are you interested in the case outcome?
       1) yes
       2) no
       3) other _____
       (skip to question 11)
   If yes, what was the outcome of the case?
       1) victim dropped charges?
       2) dismissed
       3) acquitted
       4) convicted
       5) plead guilty
       6) other _____
       If plead guilty: Did you understand and   approve   of
the   offer   to   the   defendant   of   a guilty plea to a lesser
charge?
           1) yes
           2) no
           3) no opinion

9) Is the outcome of your case what you thought would happen?
   1) yes
   2) no

10) Are you satisfied with your case outcome?
    1) very satisfied
    2) somewhat satisfied
    3) dissatisfied
    4) don't care
    If satisfied, what makes this outcome acceptable to you?
    If dissatisfied, what would you have liked to happen as a
result of bringing this case to court?
    Did you do something else on your own to remedy the
situation?

11) Was the defendant out on bail before the case was
completed?
    1) yes
    2) no
    3) don't know

12) How did you feel about that?
    1) approved
    2) didn't care
    3) disapproved
    If Defendant released, did the fact that the defendant
wasn't in jail affect your willingness to come to court?
        1) yes
        2) no
        If yes, in what way?

were you ever threatened by the defendant or his
family and friends?
>1) yes
>2) no
>If yes, what happened?

13) Was what you had to do to pursue your case More than,
Less than, or About as much as you expected to have to do?
>1) more
>2) about as much
>3) less

14) When a complaint is first made, a witness or victim is
sometimes asked to go to the Complaint room in the
courthouse, where he is interviewed by the prosecutor.   Have
you ever been to the Complaint room?
>1) yes, in this case
>2) yes, other case
>3) no
>4) other
>If yes, what did you do there?
>If no, why didn't you show up in the Complaint room?
>>1) not asked
>>2) told not to come
>>3) unable due to crime
>>4) unable, other

15) Did you ever go to court (besides the complaint room)?
>1) yes
>2) no
>If no: skip to question 16, then 20-end, delete 32-34
>If yes: How many times did you go to court?   ____
>Were you at arraignment?
>>1) yes
>>2) no
>>If yes: Was the case settled there?
>>>1) yes
>>>2) no
>>>3) don't know
>Approximately how many days did it take for your case   to
be settled? _____
>How long were you in court on the day(s) you came?
>>1) minimum _____
>>2) maximum _____
>Were you asked to testify?
>>1) yes
>>1) no
>Did you feel it was worthwhile when you came to court?
>>1) yes
>>2) no
>>3) unsure

16) Did you drop charges against the defendant?
1) yes
2) no
3) other
If yes, is there anything that might have been different in the arrest or in court that could have persuaded you to stay with the case?

17) One problem we often hear about the court system is that the dates to be in court are scheduled at times inconvenient to the victim or witness. Were you able to make it to court each time you were asked?
1) yes
2) no
3) other

18) When people are asked to come to court, they often find it an inconvenience. Did you have any problems in the following areas?
1) taking time off from work? _____
2) transportation to court? _____
3) childcare or elderly care? _____
4) trouble finding court(room)? _____
5) place to wait? _____

19) Were you ever given any payment (witness fees) by the district attorney's office for your appearance in court?
1) yes
2) no
If yes: How much? _____
Was it adequate to cover your expenses?
1) yes
2) no
How important was payment to you in your decision to continue with the case?
1) very important
2) somewhat
3) not important
If you had received a payment, would it have affected your willingness to cooperate with the district attorney in your case?
1) yes
2) no
3) other _____
why or why not?

20) Other than inconveniences in coming to court, can you tell me some of the problems you encountered as a result of the crime?

21) Have you ever used any social service agencies (social worker, community center, counseling services, medical clinic, welfare, etc.)?
1) yes
2) no

If yes: Which ones?
    Did you ever use any of these agencies as a result of
your victimization?
    1) yes
    2) no
        If yes: How satisfied were you with their aid?
            1) satisfied
            2) somewhat
            3) dissatisfied
        If no: Why have you never used these agencies?

22) Only if mentioned above: Have you ever been helped by a
victim assistance or service agency?
    1) yes
    2) no
    If yes: How satisfied were you with their aid?
        1) satisfied
        2) somewhat
        3) dissatisfied

23) Did somebody pay your bills and other financial losses
suffered as a result of your victimization?
    1) yes
    2) no
    3) some
    If yes: Who paid you? _____
        If following not mentioned:
            Were you paid by private insurance?
                1) yes
                2) no
            Did the judge order restitution from the
offender?
                1) yes
                2) no
                If yes: Have you received it?
                    1) yes
                    2) no
        Only for payments other than victim compensation:
            Were you paid before or after the case ended?
                1) before
                2) after
            How satisfied were you with the payment you
received?
                1) satisfied
                2) somewhat
                3) dissatisfied
    If no: Why not?

24) Were you ever offered any kind of payments from either
the defendant or the defense attorney, or both?
    1) defendant
    2) attorney
    3) both
    4) no

25) Do you think that payments to crime victims to cover their losses as a result of being victimized should be provided by government?
    1) yes
    2) no
If yes: If you knew that some payments for your victimization losses were possible, would it change your willingness to cooperate with criminal-justice officials?
    1) yes
    2) no
Do you think that payments should be given to all victims, or only to poor victims?
    1) all
    2) poor only
Do you think that payments should be prohibited to people who are victimized by someone in their own household, or by a relative?
    1) yes
    2) no
Do you think that payments should be made for property losses, or only for medical and other expenses associated with being attacked?
    1) both
    2) just medical
If no: Why not?

26) The Crime Victims Compensation Board/Violent Crimes Compensation Board is a government agency that compensates victims of violent crimes for their losses. How does the availability of payments by government make you feel?

27) Have you ever heard of this agency?
    1) yes
    2) no
If yes: How?
Have you ever used it?
    1) yes
    2) no
If no: Why not?
       (Skip question 27 A-U)
 * A) Have you applied to the compensation board before?
    1) applied before
    2) first time
If before: Were you satisfied with the outcome when you used the board before?
      1) satisfied
      2) somewhat
      3) dissatisfied
      Why or why not?
  B) Why did you decide to use the compensation board in your recent case?
  C) Did you hesitate at all in using the board?
    1) yes
    2) no
    If yes: Why?

D) Was there a formal hearing in your case?
    1) yes
    2) no

E) When people apply for compensation, they are sometimes inconvenienced. Did you have any problems in the following areas?
    1) taking time off from work? ____
    2) transportation? _____
    3) childcare, elderly care? _____
    4) trouble finding where to go? ___
    5) place to wait? _____
    6) getting a lawyer? _____
    7) getting witnesses? _____
    8) hearing time? _____
    9) board procedures? _____
    10) completing forms? _____
    11) gathering evidence? _____

F) How satisfied were you with the opportunity you were given to present, and get involved in, your case?
    1) satisfied
    2) somewhat
    3) dissatisfied
    why or why not?

G) How long did your case last before the compensation board from the time you filed your claim until the case was decided?

H) How satisfied were you with the speed with which your case was decided?
    1) satisfied
    2) somewhat
    3) dissatisfied
    why or why not?

I) Did the board keep you well informed about how your case was progressing?
    1) satisfied
    2) somewhat
    3) dissatisfied

J) What was your impression of board officials?
    1) favorable
    2) neutral
    3) unfavorable

K) Do you think the board officials were fair to you?
    1) yes
    2) no
    3) no opinion

L) Do you feel that board officials are concerned about crime victims?
    1) very
    2) somewhat
    3) not at all

M) As you probably know, a person who makes a claim before the compensation board must satisfy certain requirements in order to be considered for an award. Can you tell me whether you approve, disapprove, or are unsure about the following requirements:

    1) need to report crime to police? _____

    2) need to cooperate with court? _____

    3) need to have minimum loss? _____

    4) need to limit amount applied for? _____

    5) need to miss minimum time work? _____

    6) need to subtract other payments? _____

    7) cannot have provoked the crime? _____

N) Did you get an award from the compensation board?

    1) yes

    2) no

If no: Why do you think you were denied an award?

O) Did you really expect to get an award when you first made a claim?

    1) yes

    2) no

Why or why not?

P) Were you satisfied with the outcome of your case?

    1) satisfied

    2) somewhat

    3) dissatisfied

If satisfied: Why?

If dissatisfied: Why?

    Did you appeal your case?

        1) yes

        2) no

    If yes: What happened?

Q) Were there any other remaining financial problems resulting from your victimization that would have liked the board to help you with, but it could not consider?

R) Did your hopes for compensation increase your willingness to cooperate with criminal-justice officials while the case against the defendant was still going on?

    1) yes

    2) no

S) What effect, if any, has your compensation-board experience had on your attitudes about the criminal-justice system and on your willingness to become involved in the future?

T) What could the compensation board do differently to make its activities more satisfactory?

* U) Would you ever apply to the compensation board again if you were a victim of another crime?

    1) yes

    2) no

    3) unsure

Why or why not?

28) People go through many different reactions after a crime has been committed. I'm going to read you some feelings and for each one tell me whether it applied to you <u>very much</u>, <u>somewhat</u>, or <u>not at all</u>.
    A) angry with defendant? _____
    B) angry with self? _____
    C) fear of revenge? _____
    D) desire for revenge? _____
    E) feel guilty about pursuing case? _____
    F) feel less safe? _____

29) When you were in the court system, how did you feel about the prosecutors who handled your case?
    1) favorable
    2) unfavorable

30) Did the prosecutor(s) ever consult with you about how you wanted him to handle the case?
    1) yes
    2) no
    If yes: Did he follow your suggestions?
        1) yes
        2) no

31) How do you feel prosecutors treat offenders?
    1) too easy
    2) fair
    3) too hard

32) What was your impression of the judge(s)?
    1) favorable
    2) unfavorable

33) Did the judge ask you what you wanted to happen in the case?
    1) yes
    2) no

34) Do you think the judge was fair to you?
    1) yes
    2) no
    3) no opinion

35) How do you feel judges treat offenders?
    1) too easy
    2) fair
    3) too hard

36) How do you feel the police handled your case?
    1) favorable
    2) unfavorable
    3) no opinion

37) we have been talking about what you experienced in your contacts with the court system and police. I wonder now if you could tell me how being a crime victim has affected you (life, thinking, habits)?

38) What do you think causes crime and/or causes some people to become criminals?

39) Some people feel that the crime rate in Brooklyn/Newark is high, others say it's low. How do you feel?
   1) high
   2) moderate
   3) low
   4) no opinion
   If high: Why?
   Do you have any relatives or friends who have been victimized recently?
      1) yes
      2) no

40) Do you believe government should be held responsible for crime?
   1) yes
   2) no
   Why or Why not?

42) Now that you have been through this experience, do you think you would get involved if the same thing happened to you again?
   1) yes
   2) no
   3) unsure

43) If you had known about a voluntary alternative to the court system where you and the defendant and a neutral third person would sit down and talk about what happened in the case and would then reach a binding agreement that would be backed by the courts as the settlement of your case, would you have considered using it?
   1) yes
   2) no
   3) unsure
   Why do you say that?

44) I would like to know some of your feelings about government and society. Do you agree with the statement that government is generally responsive to the needs of its citizens?
   1) usually
   2) sometimes
   3) rarely

45) If a regulation were being considered by the city council that you considered very unjust or harmful, what do you think you could do?

46) How likely is it that you would try to do something?
     1) yes
     2) no

47) Have you ever before tried to influence a local decision
such as this?
     1) yes
     2) no

48) Are you registered to vote?
     1) yes
     2) no

49) Have you ever been involved in any political campaigns?
     1) yes
     2) no

50) If you ever had some trouble with the police (a traffic
violation maybe) do you think you would be given equal
treatment? Would you be treated as well as anyone else?
     1) yes
     2) no
     3) other

51) Some people think that their prospects for the future are
hopeful,   while   others   think   their prospects are very
discouraging. How do you feel?
     1) hopeful
     2) neutral
     3) discouraging

And finally, just a few questions about your background
(remember that your answers will be kept confidential):

52) How old were you on your last birthday? _____

53) What was the last grade of school that you completed?
     1) 8th or less
     2) some high school
     3) high school graduate
     4) some college
     5) college graduate
     6) postgraduate

54) What is your marital status?
     1) single
     2) married
     3) separated/divorced
     4) widowed

55) Are you currently employed?
     1) yes, full-time
     2) yes, part-time
     3) no
     Occupation? _____

56) What is your annual income?
1) welfare, unemployment
2) 0 - 4999
3) 5000 - 7499
4) 7500 - 9999
5) 10000 - 14999
6) 15000 - 24999
7) 25000 or more

57) How many people are supported by your income, excluding yourself?

58) What is your racial background?
1) white
2) black
3) hispanic
4) oriental
5) other

59) How long have you lived at your present address? _____

60) How long have you lived in Brooklyn/Newark? _____

61) Would you mind telling me whether religion is important in your life?
1) very
2) somewhat
3) not at all

62) Do you belong to any social or community groups?
1) yes
2) no

63) What political party do you belong to?
1) Republican
2) Democratic
3) Independent
4) none

64) Sex of respondent
1) male
2) female

65) Could you make any suggestions about what would make the experience (of being a victim and being involved in the criminal process) more positive for victims in the future?

Thank you very much. You have been very helpful. Hopefully something can be done to improve the victim's treatment in the future.

* compensation questions appear between asterisks.

Official Questionnaire

1) To begin with, can you tell me the purpose of victim compensation and your compensation board?

2) What are the goals of the program?
     Probe: (restorative, victim attitudes and cooperation, crime prevention, social stability)

3) At present, do you see the program as performing any other role or function besides awarding compensation?

4) Do you think that compensation must be distributed by government?
     Probe: (why not insurance, restitution, civil suits, etc?)

5) Can you describe the underlying theory upon which the program was created? On what basis has the government become involved?
     Probe: (obligtion,   right,   social   contract   or responsibility, lack of enforcement, general welfare, cost/benefit, welfare, symbolic appeasement?)

6) A victim applying for compensation must satisfy a rather long list of eligibility requirements.
     A) Do you think that any others should be added? Which?
     B) Do you disagree with any of the requirements? Why?
          Probe: (relationship, needs test, minimum loss, maximum award, property exclusion, pain and suffering, police report, cooperation, time limits for applying and reporting, subtraction of other benefits, provocation, minimum time lost from work?)
     C) Which rule excludes the most people?

7) The state legislature seems to have purposely limited its commitment in compensating victims, since many of them are excluded from eligibility? Why has that happened?
     Probe: (do you think this is justified?)

8) Can you discuss how the program's activities are publicized?
     Probe: (what are the limitations, why do they occur, and are they justified?)

9) Can you describe for me how claims are processed?
     Probe: (victim role and involvement, criminal-justice involvement,   investigator's   role,   when decision made, hearings, respondent's role, description of his work?)

10) As an administrative agency, can you describe for me any organizational problems that hinder the board's work?
     Probe: (budget,   rules and   legislation,   personnel,

scheduling, backlogs, delays, efficiency, facilities, structure, victim's inconveniences or difficulties?)

11) I would like to better understand how board decisions are made. That is, aside from the process that you have described and the rules that provide the general guidelines for awards, what other things determine the outcome of a victim's claim?
    Probe: (cues, "normal" cases, general policy, discretion?)

12) What influences would you say affect the decisions you and the other board officials make?
    Probe: (victim characteristics, attitudes, appearances; nature of the crime; board resources; reliance on investigations vs. self-report; oversight by executive and legislative branches; police; prosecutors; judges; victim-service agencies; politicians; attorneys; public and community; fellow board officials; own background and attitudes; investigators)

13) I am very interested in the impact of the board's decisions. That impact may, however, be spread among several areas:
    A) First, what effect do you think decisions have for victims?
        Probe: (denials vs. awards, adequate compensation, improve attitudes and cooperation, appeasement, keep off welfare, prevent from resort to crime?)
    B) Next, what effect do you think decisions have for the public and the community in general?
        Probe: (denials vs. awards, visibility, appeasement, improve attitudes and cooperation?)
    C) What effect do you think decisions have for offenders?
        Probe: (increase complacency?)
    D) What effect do you think decision have for the crime rate, and for criminal-justice personnel?
    E) What effect to you think decisions have for politicians (i.e., legislators)?

14) Given the limitations on the board, would you say that the impact of your activities has been mostly psychololgical or mostly tangible?

15) Can you assess the impact of the board's work more generally? Do you think the board is achieving its objectives?

16) Can you describe for me any unanticipated consequences of the board's activities that you might know of?
    Probe: (more dissatisfaction with criminal justice than if the board had not existed at all, for those claimants who had expectations and hopes raised, only to be denied an award, or a full award?)

17) Do you think the board's presence and activities diverts our attention from the real problem of crime? Are you promoting the status quo?

18) What role do you believe the board plays, if any, in the political and criminal-justice systems?

19) Can you say anything about the future of the board's activities, and its potential role for the crime victim?

20) I wonder now if I could ask you some of your personal views of issues relevant to criminal justice and your activities on the board:
    A) What do you think is the cause of crime, and how can it be solved?
        Probe: (society, government, individual, economics, racism, etc?)
    B) Do you think that this city really has a crime problem, or has it been exaggerated by the media and some law-enforcement personnel?
    C) Do you believe that some people are more likely to become victims of violent crime than others? Why?
    D) How effective do you think criminal-justice personnel are performing their jobs? Do you think they are doing the best they can under the circumstances, or are they performing unsatisfactorily? Why or why not?
    E) What do you think generally about government today? Is the welfare state a blessing or a mistake? Do you think we are heading in the right direction with our increasing involvement of government in our everyday lives? Why or why not?

21) Finally, I would like to ask you a few questions about your background:
    A) Can you tell me a little about yourself, your origins, education, previous career? What has been its impact on your work?
    B) What made you seek/accept a position with the board?
    C) Can you describe briefly the process by which you were appointed to the board?
        Probe: (Political aspects, party, etc.?)
    D) How long have you been on the board?
    E) Do you plan to remain with the board for the foreseeable future, or will you move on?
    F) Do you have other career plans (aspirations) after you leave the board?
    G) Do you have income other than your board salary?
    H) What is your political party?
    I) How long have you lived in New York/New Jersey?
    J) What year were you born?
    K) What is you marital status?

BIBLIOGRAPHY

BOOKS

American Friends Service Committee. *Struggle for Justice.* New York: Hill & Wang, 1971.

Bachrach, Peter & Morton Barantz. *Power and Poverty: Theory and Practice.* New York: Oxford University Press, 1973.

Balbus, Isaac. *Dialectics of Legal Repression.* New Brunswick: Transaction, 1973.

Balivet, T. *Connecticut: Recommendations for Improving the Use of Restitution as a Dispositional Alternative.* Washington: American Institute for Study of Justice, 1975.

Barkas, J.L. *Victims.* New York: Scribners, 1978.

Bartell, T. *Citizen Perceptions of the Justice System.* Albuquerque: University of New Mexico Institute of Social Research & Development, 1975.

Bellow, Saul. *The Victim.* New York: Vanguard, 1947.

Biderman, Albert, et al. *Report on a Pilot Study in the District of Columbia on Victimization and Attitudes Toward Law Enforcement.* Washington: U.S. Government Printing Office, 1967.

Block, D. & A. Reiss. *Patterns of Behavior in Police-Citizen Transactions.* Washington: U.S. Government Printing Office, 1967.

Blumberg, Abraham. *Criminal Justice.* Chicago: Quadrangle, 1967.

Bolin, David R. *Evaluation and Change: Services for Victims.* Minneapolis: Minnesota Medical Research Foundation, 1980.

Boskin, Joseph. *Urban Racial Violence in the 20th Century.* Beverly Hills: Glencoe, 1969.

Boston, Guy D. *Community Crime Prevention: A Selected Bibliography.* Washington: National Criminal Justice Reference Service, 1977.

Brodyaga, Lisa. *Rape and Its Victims: A Report for Citizens, Health Facilities and Criminal Justice Agencies.* Washington: National Institute of Law Enforcement & Criminal Justice, 1975.

Brown, Wenzell. *True Story of the Interplay of Aggressor and Victim in Sexual Attacks.* Derby, CT: Monarch, 1961.

Bureau of Justice Statistics. *The Hispanic Victim: A Comparative Study of Criminal Victimization Against Hispanics and Non-Hispanics.* Washington: U.S. Government Printing Office, 1980.

Burgess, Anthony. *A Clockwork Orange.* New York: Ballantine, 1962.

Cain, Anthony A. *Victim/Witness Assistance: A Selected Bibliography.* Washington: U.S. Department of Justice, 1978.

Campbell, Donald & Julian Stanley. *Experimental and Quasi-Experimental Designs for Research.* Chicago: Rand McNally, 1963.

Campbell, R. *Justice Through Restitution: Making the Criminal Pay.* Milford, MI: Mott Media, 1974.

Cannavale, Frank. *Witness Cooperation.* Lexington: D.C. Heath, 1975.

Capote, Truman. *In Cold Blood.* New York: Signet, 1965.

Carrington, Frank. *Victims.* New Rochelle: Arlington House, 1975.

Casper, Jonathan. *American Criminal Justice.* Englewood Cliffs: Prentice Hall, 1972.

Center for Research on Criminal Justice. *The Iron Fist and the Velvet Glove: An Analysis of U.S. Police.* Berkeley: Garrett, 1977.

Chambliss, William. *Crime and the Legal Process*. New York: McGraw Hill, 1969.

Chambliss, William & Robert Seidman. *Law, Order, and Power*. Reading, MA: Addison-Wesley, 1971.

Chappell, Duncan & David Monahan, eds. *Violence and Criminal Justice*. Lexington: D.C. Heath, 1975.

Chesney, S. *Assessment of Restitution in the Minnesota Parole Services*. St. Paul: Minnesota Governor's Commission, 1976.

Clark, G. *Compensation to Victims of Crime and Restitution by Offenders*. Ottowa: Canadian Correctional Association, 1968.

Cole, George F., ed. *Criminal Justice: Law and Politics*. Belmont, CA: Wadsworth, 1972.

Commission on Victim-Witness Assistance. *Help for Victims and Witnesses*. Washington: National District Attorneys Association, 1976.

_____. *The Victim Advocate*. Washington: National District Attorneys Association, 1978.

Conklin, John. *Illegal But Not Criminal*. Englewood Cliffs: Prentice Hall, 1977.

_____. *Robbery and the Criminal Justice System*. Philadelphia: Lippincott, 1972.

_____. *The Impact of Crime*. New York: MacMillan, 1975.

Connery, Robert, ed. *Urban Riots: Violence and Social Change*. New York: Academy of Political Science, 1968.

Cooley, William W. & Paul R. Lohnes. *Multivariate Data Analysis*. New York: John Wiley, 1971.

Crime Victim Compensation. Washington: National Institute of Justice, 1980.

Crime Victims Compensation Board. *1977-78 Annual Report*. Albany: State of New York, 1978.

Crimes of Violence: A Staff Report Submitted to the National Commission on the Causes and Prevention of Violence. Washington: U.S. Government Printing Office, 1969.

Criminal Victimization in Maricopa County. Berkeley: Institute for Local Self Government, 1969.

Curtis, Lynn. *Criminal Violence: National Patterns and Behavior*. Lexington: D.C. Heath, 1974.

_____. ed. *Crimes of Violence*. Lexington: D.C. Heath, 1975.

Department of Law and Public Safety. *1975 Annual Report*. Trenton: State of New Jersey, 1976.

Dimitz, Simon & Walter Reckless. *Critical Issues in the Study of Crime*. Boston: Little, Brown, 1968.

Dismissed for Want of Prosecution. Chicago: Chicago Crime Commission, 1974.

Dolbeare, Kenneth & Murray Edelman. *American Politics: Policies, Power, and Change*. Lexington: D.C. Heath, 1977.

Douglas, Jack, ed. *Crime and Justice in American Society*. New York: Bobbs Merrill, 1971.

Downie, Leonard. *Justice Denied*. Baltimore: Penguin, 1971.

Drapkin, Israel, ed. *Victimology*. Lexington: D.C. Heath, 1976.

Drapkin, Israel and Emilio Viano, eds. *Victimology: Crimes, Victims, and Justice*. Lexington: D.C. Heath, 1976.

_____. eds. *Victimology: Society's Reaction to Victimization.* Lexington: D.C. Heath, 1976.

_____. eds. *Victimology: The Exploiters and the Exploited.* Lexington: D.C. Heath, 1976.

_____. eds. *Victimology: Theoretical Issues in Victimology.* Lexington: D.C. Heath, 1976.

_____. eds. *Victimology: Violence and Its Victims.* Lexington: D.C. Heath, 1976.

Edelhertz, Herbert. *Restitutive Justice.* Seattle: Battelle, 1974.

Edelhertz, Herbert & Gilbert Geis. *Public Compensation to Victims of Crime.* New York: Praeger, 1974.

Edelman, Murray. *The Symbolic Uses of Politics.* Urbana: University of Illinois Press, 1967.

Eisenstein, James & Herbert Jacob. *Felony Justice.* Boston: Little, Brown, 1977.

Ennis, Bruce. *Criminal Victimization in the U.S.: A Report of a National Survey.* Washington: U.S. Government Printing Office, 1967.

Esslin, Martin. *The Theatre of the Absurd.* Garden City: Anchor, 1969.

Feeley, Malcolm. *The Process Is the Punishment: Handling Cases in a Lower Court.* New York: Russell Sage, 1979.

Forer, Lois G. *Criminals and Victims: A Trial Judge Reflects on Crime and Punishment.* New York: Norton, 1980.

_____. *The Death of the Law.* New York: McKay, 1975.

Freemont Police Department. *Proposal to Conduct Program to Improve and Standardize Police Treatment of Victims and Witnesses.* Washington: Police Foundation, 1974.

Gallup Poll Index. *Compensation for Crime Victims: Report No. 5.* Princeton: American Institute of Public Opinion, 1965.

Galaway, Burt & Joe Hudson, eds. *Perspectives on Crime Victims.* St. Louis: C.V. Mosby, 1981.

Gans, Herbert. *More Equality.* New York: Vintage, 1973.

Garofalo, James. *Local Victim Surveys.* Washington: U.S. Department of Justice, 1977.

Garofalo, James & L. Paul Sutton. *Compensating Victims of Violent Crime: Potential Costs and Coverage of a National Program.* Albany: Criminal Justice Research Center, 1977.

Geis, Gilbert. *Crimes of Violence.* Washington: U.S. Government Printing Office, 1969.

Gerber, Rudolph. *Contemporary Issues in Criminal Justice.* Port Washington: Kennikat, 1976.

Gochros, Harvey & LeRoy Schultz, eds. *Human Sexuality and Social Work.* New York: Association Press, 1972.

Goldfarb, Ronald. *Jails.* New York: Simon & Schuster, 1973.

Goldfarb, Ronald & Linda Singer. *After Conviction.* New York: Simon & Schuster, 1973.

Greenberg, Edward. *Serving the Few: Corporate Capitalism and the Bias of Government Policy.* New York: John Wiley, 1974.

Grotus, Jack. *The Victims.* London: Hutchinson, 1969.

Gurr, Ted. *Rogues, Rebels, and Reformers.* Beverly Hills: Sage, 1976.

Hentig, Hans von. *The Criminal and His Victim.* New Haven: Yale University Press, 1948.

Hindelang, Michael J. *Criminal Victimization in Eight American Cities*. Cambridge: Ballinger, 1976.

Honderick, Ted. *Punishment: The Supposed Justifications*. London: Penguin, 1971.

Hudson, Joe. *Restitution in Criminal Justice*. St. Paul: Minnesota Deparment of Corrections, 1976.

Hudson, Joe & Burt Galaway, eds. *Considering the Victim: Readings in Restitution and Victim Compensation*. Springfield, IL: Chas. Thomas, 1976.

Inciardi, James, ed. *Radical Criminology*. Beverly Hills: Sage, 1980.

Ionesco, Eugene. *The Lesson*. Garden City: Anchor, 1969.

Jacob, Herbert. *Crime and Justice in Urban America.* Englewood Cliffs: Prentice Hall, 1980.

James, Howard. *Crisis in the Courts*. New York: McKay, 1971.

Jones, H. *Victim Advocate*. Washington: National District Attorneys Association, 1977.

Kalish, Carol B. *Crimes and Victims.* Washington: U.S. Department of Justice, 1974.

Katznelson, Ira & Mark Kesselman. *Politics of Power*. New York: Harcourt-Brace-Jovanovich, 1979.

Kirkendall, Richard. *A Global Power: America Since the Age of Roosevelt*. New York: Knopf, 1980.

Kirkham, D.B. *Compensation for Victims of Crime*. Edmonton: Bishop, McKenzie, 1968.

Klecka, William. *Discriminant Analysis*. Beverly Hills: Sage, 1980.

Kleinman, Paula. *Protection in a Ghetto Community*. New York: Cornell University Press, 1972.

Knutden, Mary, et al. *Crime Victims and Witnesses as Victims of the Administration of Justice*. Milwaukee: Center for Criminal Justice and Social Policy, 1975.

Knutden, Richard, et al. *Victims and Witnesses: Impact of Crime and Their Experiences with the Criminal Justice System*. Milwaukee: Center for Criminal Justice and Social Policy, 1976.

Krisberg, Barry. *Crime and Privilege*. Englewood Cliffs: Prentice Hall, 1975.

Lachenbruch, P.A. *Discriminant Analysis*. New York: Hafner, 1975.

Lacy, James L. *National Standards Concerning the Prosecution Witness*. Washington: National Center for Prosecution Managment, 1972.

Latane, Biff & Joan Dorky. *The Unresponsive Bystander*. New York: Appleton-Century-Crofts, 1970.

Leftkowitz, Bernard. *The Victims*. New York: Putnam, 1969.

Legislative Committee on Expenditure Review. *Crime Victims Compensation Program*. Albany: State of New York, 1979.

_____. *Financial Aid to Victims*. Albany: State of New York, 1975.

Leiser, Burton. *Liberty, Justice and Morals*. New York: MacMillan, 1979.

McDonald, J.M. *Murderer and His Victim.* Springfield, IL: Chas. Thomas, 1961.

_____. *Rape Offenders and Their Victims*. Springfield, IL: Chas. Thomas, 1971.

McDonald, William. *Assessing the Criminal: Restitution, Retribution, and the Legal Process*. Cambridge: Ballinger, 1977.

_____. ed. *Criminal Justice and the Victim*.Beverly Hills: Sage, 1976.

McPheters, Lee & William Strange. *The Economics of Crime and Law Enforcement*. Springfield, IL: Chas. Thomas, 1976.

Mailer, Norman. *The Executioner's Song*. New York: Ballantine, 1978.

Meiners, Roger. *Victim Compensation: Economic, Legal, and Political Aspects*. Lexington: D.C. Heath, 1978.

Menninger, Karl. *The Crime of Punishment*. New York: Viking, 1968.

Miers, David. *Response to Victimization*.Oxford: Milton Trading Estate, 1978.

Mitford, Jessica. *Kind and Usual Punishment*. New York: Knopf, 1973.

Morris, Norval & Gordon Hawkins. *Honest Politician's Guide to Crime Control*. Chicago: University of Chicago Press, 1970.

Moynihan, Daniel. *The Politics of a Guaranteed Income*. New York: Harper & Row, 1972.

Mueller, Gerard O.W. & H.H.A. Cooper. *The Criminal, Society, and the Victim*. Washington: U.S. Department of Justice, 1979.

Murphy, Paul. *The Constitution in Crisis Times*. New York: Harper & Row, 1972.

Nachmais, David. *Public Policy Evaluation: Approaches and Methods*. New York: St. Martins, 1979.

National Criminal Justice Information & Statistical Service. *Criminal Victimization in the Nation's Five Largest Cities*.Washington: U.S. Government Printing Office, 1975.

_____. *Crime in Eight American Cities*. Washington: U.S. Government Printing Office, 1974.

National District Attorneys Association. *Final Evaluation: Committee on Victim-Witness Assistance*. Washington: Arthur Little, 1979.

Nie, Norman, et al. *Statistical Package for the Social Sciences*. New York: McGraw Hill, 1975.

Office of Planning & Program Assistance. *1977 Comprehensive Crime Control Plan*. New York: Division of Criminal Justice Services, 1978.

Ostrom, E.W., et al. *The Effects of Institutional Arrangements on Citizen Evaluation of Police Performance*. Bloomington: Indiana University Press, 1977.

Parsonage, William, ed. *Perspectives in Victimology*. Beverly Hills: Sage, 1979.

Piven, Frances Fox & Richard A. Cloward. *Poor People's Movements*. New York: Vintage, 1979.

_____. *Regulating the Poor: The Functions of Public Welfare*.New York: Vintage, 1971.

President's Commission on Law Enforcement & the Administration of Justice. *Task Force Report: Crime and Its Impact--An Assessment*. Washington: U.S. Government Printing Office, 1967.

Quinney, Richard. *A Critique of Legal Order: Law and Order in America*. Boston: Little, Brown, 1969.

_____. *Class, State and Crime*. New York: Longman, 1980.

_____. ed. *Crime and Justice in Society*. Boston: Little, Brown,1969.

_____. ed. *Criminal Justice in America*.Boston: Little, Brown, 1974.

Ratcliffe, James. *The Good Samaritan and the Law*. Garden City: Doubleday, 1966.

Reckless, Walter & Charles L. Newman, eds. *Interdisciplinary Problems in Criminology.*Columbus: American Society of Criminology, 1964.

Reference Services. *Victimology: A Bibliography.* Washington: U.S. Department of Justice, 1978.

Reiff, Robert. *The Invisible Victim: The Criminal Justice System's Forgotten Responsibility.*   New York: Basic, 1979.

Reiman, Jeffrey. *The Rich Get Richer and the Poor Get Prison.*New York: John Wiley, 1979.

Reiss, Albert. *Studies in Crime and Law Enforcement in Major Metropolitan Areas.*   Washington: U.S. Government Printing Office, 1967.

Report on Why Victims Fail to Prosecute. Cincinnati: Cincinnati Police Division, 1975.

Reynolds, Philip. *Victimization in Metropolitan Regions.* Minneapolis: Center for Social Research, 1973.

Richardson, Richard J., et al. *Persepectives on the Legal Justice System: Public Attitudes and Criminal Victimization.* Chapel Hill: Institute for Research on Social Science, 1972.

Rifai, M.A.Y. *Justice and Older Americans.* Lexington: D.C. Heath, 1977.

Rossner, Judith. *Looking for Mr. Goodbar.* New York: Simon & Schuster, 1975.

Ryan, William. *Blaming the Victim.* New York: Vintage, 1971.

Sacramento Police Department. *Seven Part Program to Improve the Manner in Which Crime Victims Are Handled by Police and Other Agencies of the Criminal Justice System and the Health Care Community.*Washington: Price Waterhouse, 1974

Scammon, Richard & Ben Wattenberg. *The Real Majority.* New York: Coward, McCain, 1970.

Schafer, Stephen. *Compensation and Restitution to Victims of Crime.* Montclair, NJ: Patterson Smith, 1970.

_____. *Introduction to Criminology.* Boston: Reston, 1976.

_____. *The Victim and His Criminal.* New York: Random House, 1968.

Schmidt, Winsor C. *Legal Issues in Compensating Victims of Crime.* Raleigh: National Association of Attorneys General, 1976.

Schultz, Gladys. *How Many More Victims?* Philadelphia: Lippincott, 1965.

Schur, Edwin. *Our Criminal Society.* Englewood Cliffs: Prentice Hall, 1969.

Silver, Isadore, ed.*The Crime Control Establishment.*Englewood Cliffs: Prentice Hall, 1974.

Skinner, B.F. *About Behaviorism.* New York: Vintage, 1974.

Skogan, Wesley. *Survey Studies of the Victims of Crime.* Washington: U.S. Department of Justice, 1975.

_____., ed. *Sample Surveys of the Victims of Crime.* Cambridge: Ballinger, 1976.

Small Business Adminstration.*Crimes Against Small Business.*Washington: U.S. Government Printing Office, 1968.

Smith, Kathleen. *A Cure for Crime.* London: Duckworth, 1965.

Sparks, Richard, et al. *Surveying Victims: A Study of the Measurements of Criminal Victimization, Perceptions of Crime and Attitudes Toward Criminal Justice.* New York: John Wiley, 1977.

Steggerda, R.O. *Victim Restitution: An Assessment of Restitution in Probation Experiments Operated by the Fifth Judicial District Department of Court Services.* Des Moines: Polk County Department of Program Evaluation, 1975.

Study No. 2043. New York: Louis Harris, 1970.

Study No. 861. Princeton: American Institute of Public Opinion, 1972.

Tatsuoka, Maurice. *Multivariate Analysis.* New York: John Wiley, 1971.

Thomas, C.W. & C.C. Nelson. *Public Attitudes Toward Criminal Justice Agencies, Politics, and Levels of Criminal Victimization.* Washington: National Institute of Law Enforcement & Criminal Justice, 1975.

Thornberry, Terence & Edward Sagarin, eds. *Images of Crime: Offenders and Victims.* New York: Praeger, 1974.

Trojanowicz, Robert C. & Samual Dixon. *Criminal Justice and the Community.* Englewood Cliffs: Prentice Hall, 1974.

Van De Geer, John. *Introduction to Multivariate Analysis for the Social Sciences.* San Francisco: Freeman, 1971.

Viano, Emilio, ed. *Victims and Society.* Washington: Visage, 1978.

Violent Crimes Compensation Board. *Annual Report 1977.* Newark: State of New Jersey, 1978.

_____. *Annual Report 1978.* Newark: State of New Jersey, 1979.

Walker, Darlene & Richard J. Richardson. *Public Attitudes Toward the Police.* Chapel Hill: Institute for Research on Social Science, 1972.

Williams, Donald. *Criminal Injuries Compensation.* London: Oyez, 1972.

Wise, Edward & Gerhard O.W. Mueller. *Studies in Comparative Criminal Law.* Springfirld, IL: Chas. Thomas, 1975.

Wolfgang, Marvin. *Studies in Homicide.* New York: Harper & Row, 1967.

Wolfgang, Marvin & Franco Ferracuti. *Subculture of Violence.* London: Social Science Paperbacks, 1967.

Wolfe, Alan. *The Seamy Side of Democracy.* New York: Longman, 1978.

Wright, Eric. *Politics of Punishment.* New York: Harper & Row, 1973.

Ziegenhagen, Eduard. *Victims, Crime and Social Control.* New York: Praeger, 1977.

ARTICLES

Agopian, Michael W. "Parental Child Stealing: Participants and the Victimization Process." *Victimology* 5(1980°, 263.

Aldrich, J. & C.F. Cnudde, "Probing the Bounds of Conventional Wisdom: A Comparison of Regression, Probit and Discriminant Analysis." *American Journal of Political Science* 29(1975), 541.

Allison, John. "Economic Factors and the Rate of Crime." *Land Economics* (1972), 193.

"An Analysis of Victim Compensation in America." *Urban Lawyer* 8(1972), 17.

Arnold, Mark. "Making the Criminal Pay Back His Victim." *Christian Science Monitor* 14 February 1978, 3

Aromaa, K & S. Leppa. "A Survey of Individual Victims of Property
    Crimes." Institute of Criminology, 1973.
Ash, Michael. "On Witnesses: A Radical Critique of Criminal Court
    Procedures." *Notre Dame Lawyer* 46(1972), 382.
"A Spokesman for Victims: Past and Future." *Law Enforcement Journ-
    al* 5(1975), 4.
"A State Statute to Provide Compensation for Innocent Victims of
    Violent Crime."*Harvard Journal of Legislation* 4(1966), 127.
Astor, Gerald. "Crime Doesn't Pay Its Victims Very Well Either."
    New York Times 30 May 1976, 8.
Austern, David T. "Crime Victim Compensation Programs: The Issue of
    Costs." *Victimology* 5(1980), 61.
Avio, Kenneth. "Economic Analysis of Criminal Corrections: The Ca-
    nadian Case." *Canadian Journal of Economics* 6(1973), 24.
"Awards of the Crimes Compensation Board." *Saskatchewan Law Review*
    35(1970), 75.
Baldwin, J. "Role of the Victim in Certain Property Offenses."*Cri-
    minal Law Review* (1974), 353.
Ball, Richard A. "The Victimological Cycle."*Victimology* 1(1976),
    379.
Baluss, Mary. "Integrated Services for Victims of Crime: A County
    Based Approach." Washington: National Association of Counties
    Research Foundation, 1975.
Banfield, Laura & C. David Anderson. "Continuances in the Cook
    County Criminal Courts." *University of Chicago Law Review* 35
    (1968), 259.
Barlow, Hugh. "Crime Victims and the Sentencing Process." Unpub-
    lished paper presented at Second International Symposium on Vic-
    timology, Boston, 1976.
Barnett, Doreen S. "Victim in the Witness Box: Confronting the Ste-
    reotype." Unpublished paper presented at Second International
    Symposium on Victimology, Boston, 1976.
Barry, John. "Compensation Without Litigation."*Australian Law
    Journal* 37(1974), 347.
Baumer, Terry. "Research on the Fear of Crime in the U.S." *Victimo-
    logy* 3(1978), 274.
Bental, David J. "Selected Problems in Public Compensation to Vic-
    tims of Crime." *Issues in Crimonology* 3(1968), 217.
Beran, N.J. "Criminal Victimization in Small Town, USA." *Interna-
    tional Journal of Criminology & Penology* 2(1974), 7.
Bickman, Leonard. "Research and Evaluation: Cook County State's At-
    torney Victim Witness Assistance Project." *Victimology* 1(1976),
    454.
Biderman, A.D. "Time Distortions of Victimization Data and Mnemonic
    Effects." Washington: Bureau of Social Science Research, 1970.
Block, M.K. & G.J. Lenz "Subjective Probability of Victimization
    and Crime Levels: An Econometric Approach." *Criminology*11(1973),
    87.
Block, Richard. "Why Notify the Police: The Victim's Decision to No-
    tify the Police of an Assault." *Criminology* 11(1974), 555.
Blum, W.J. "Victims of Crime and Other Victims." *Chicago Bar Record*
    5(1971), 463.

Blumin, D. "Victims: A Study of Crime in a Boston Housing Project."
    Boston: Mayor's Safe Streets Act Advisory Commission, 1973.
Brock, H. Donnie. "Victims of Violent Crime: Should They Be An Ob-
    ject of Social Effection? *Mississippi Law Review* 40(1968), 92.
Brooks, James. "Compensating Victims of Crime: The Recommendations
    of Program Administrators." *Law & Society Review* 7(1973), 445.
_____. "Crime Compensation Programs: An Opinion Survey of Program
    Administrators." *Criminology* 11(1973), 271.
_____. "How Well Are Criminal Injury Compensation Boards Perform-
    ing?" *Crime & Delinquency* 21(1975), 50.
_____. "The Case for Creating Compensation Programs to Aid Victims
    of Violent Crimes." *Tulsa Law Journal* 11(1967), 479.
_____. "Who Gets What? An Analysis of Five Model Proposals for Cri-
    minal Injury Compensation Legislation." *State Government* (1974),
    18.
Brown, L.P. "Crime Prevention for Older Americans: Mutinomah County's
    Victimization Study." *Police Chief* 43(1976), 38.
Brownell, H. "The Forgotten Victims of Crime." *Record* 31(1976), 136.
Bryan, George J. "Compensation to Victims of Crime." *Alberta Law
    Journal* 6(1968), 202.
Buchwald, Art. "Solving the Crime Problem." *Washington Post* 5 Feb-
    ruary 1969, 34.
Buder, Leonard. "Half of 1976 Murder Victims Had Police Records." *New
    York Times* 28 August 1977, 9.
Burns, P. "Comprehensive Study of Victims of Crime Indemnification
    in Canada: British Columbia as a Microcosm." *University of Brit-
    ish Columbia Law Review* 8(1973), 105.
Busch, J.P. "Victims Rights in Stolen Property Cases in California."
    California Law Review 64(1976), 1018.
Callahan, Leo F. "The Victim Advocate: Programmed Police Response for
    the Crime Victim." *Police Chief* 42(1975), 50.
Campbell, Barbara. "More Money and Fast Action Asked for Crime Vic-
    tims." *New York Times* 26 April 1975, 14.
Cameron, B. "Compensation for Victims of Crime: The New Zealand Ex-
    perience." *Journal of Public Law* 12(1963), 375.
Cancilla, Robert. "Compensating Victims of Crime." *Crime Prevention
    Review* (1975), 286.
Castillo, Ruben, et al. "The Use of Civil Liability to Aid Crime Vic-
    tims." *Journal of Criminal Law & Criminology* 70(1979), 57.
Caudy, David & Elliott Ennson. "The Influence of the Characteristics
    of the Criminal and His Victim on the Decisions of Simulated Jur-
    ors." *Journal of Experimental Social Psychology* 5(1969), 141.
Center, Lawrence J. "Victim Assistance for the Elderly." *Victimology*
    5(1980), 374.
Chappell, Duncan. "Compensating Australian Victims of Violent Crime."
    Australian Law Journal 39(1967), 3.
_____. "Emergence of Australian Schemes to Compensate Victims of
    Crime." *Southern California Law Review* 43(1970), 69.
_____. "Providing for the Victims of Crime: Political Placebos or
    Progressive Programs?" *Adelaide Law Review* 4(1972), 294.
Chauvin, Stanley. "Compensation for Victims of Crime: An Overview."
    State Government (1974), 9.

Childres, Robert. "Compensation for Criminally Inflicted Personal Injury." *New York University Law Review* 39(1964), 445.

———. "Compensation for Criminally Inflicted Personal Injury." *Minnesota Law Review*50(1965), 271.

Chiossone, T. "Defendant's Rights to Repayment for Damage Caused by Detention Following a Verdict of Not Guilty." *Annuario del Instituto de Ciencias Penales y Criminologicas* 5(1973), 23.

Clark, G. "Compensation for Personal Injuries, Damages, and Social Insurance." *Law & Society Gazette* 64(1967), 339.

Cohn, Ellen, et al. "Crime Prevention vs. Victimization: The Psychology of Two Different Reactions." *Victimology* 3(1978), 285.

Cohn, Ellen & David B. Sugarman. "Marital Abuse: Abusing the One You Love." *Victimology* 5(1980), 203.

Commission on Victim-Witness Assistance. "No Show Survey." Washington: National District Attorneys Association, 1975.

"Compensating Crime Victims." *Justice Assistance News* 1980.

"Compensating Victims of Crime: Individualized Responsibility and Government Compensation Plans." *Maine Law Review* 26(1974), 175.

"Compensation for Victims of Crime." *University of Chicago Law Review* 33(1966), 537.

"Compensation to Victims of Violent Crime." *Northwestern University Law Review* 61(1966), 76.

Congalton, A.A. "New South Wales: Unreported Crime." New South Wales: Bureau of Crime, 1975.

———. "Who Are the Victims? New South Wales: Bureau of Crime, 1975.

Coon, T.F. "Public Defender and Victim's Compensation Legislation: Their Part in the Criminal Justice System." *Bulletin of Society of Professional Investigators* (1971), 25.

Cordrey, Joan B. "Crime Rates, Victims and Offenders." *Journal of Police Science & Administration* 3(1975), 100.

Cormier, B.M. & C.C. Angliker. "Psychodynamics of Homicide Committed in a Semi-Specific Relationship." *Canadian Journal of Crime & Corrections* 14(1972), 335.

Cosway, R. "Symposium on Recent Washington Legislation: Criminal Compensation." *University of Washington Law Review* 49(1974), 551.

Covey, Joan. "Alternatives to a Compensation Plan for Victims of Physical Violence." *Dickinson Law Review* 69(1965), 391.

"Crime Victims Advocate Urged." *Trial* 12(1976), 52.

Crime Victims Compensation Board. "Rules Governing Practice and Procedure." Albany: State of New York, 1976.

"Crime Victims: Recovery for Police Inaction and Underprotection." *Law & Social Order* (1970), 179.

"Crimes Against Aging Americans: The Kansas City Study." Kansas City: Midwest Research Institute, 1977.

"Criminal Law: Victims' Rights—Virginia Adopts Statute to Compensate Victims of Crime." *University of Richmond Law Review* 11(1977), 679.

"Criminal Victim Compensation in Maryland." *Maryland Law Review* 30 (1970), 266.

"The Curse of Violent Crime." *Time* 23 March 1981, 24.

Curtis, Lynn. "The Conservative New Criminology." *Society* 14(1977), 3.

———. "Victim Precipitation and Violent Crime." *Social Problems*21 (1973), 594.

_____. "Victims, Policy and the Dangers of a Conservative Menta-
lity." Unpublished paper presented at Second International Symposium on Victimology, Boston, 1976.
Cutter, A.S. "Why the Good Citizen Avoids Testifying." *Annals* 287
(1953), 103.
Dadrian, Vahahn N. "The Victimization of the American Indian." *Vic-
tomology* 1(1976), 517.
Davis, Robert C. & Forrest Dill. "Comparative Study of Victim Participation in Criminal Court Decision-Making." New York: Vera In-
stitute of Justice, 1978.
Deaton, Fae A. "Sexual Victimology Within the Home: A Treatment Ap-
proach." *Victimology* 5(1980), 311.
DeFrancis, V. "Protecting the Child Victim of Sex Crimes Committed
by Adults." *Federal Probation* 35(1971), 15.
Deming, R. "Correctional Restitution: A Strategy for Correctional
Conflict Management." *Federal Probation* 40(1976), 27.
_____. "When Criminals Repay Their Victims: A Survey of Restitution
Programs." *Judicature* 60(1977), 312.
Denenberg, Herbert. "Compensation for Victims of Crime: Justice for
the Victim as Well as for the Criminal." *Insurance Law Journal*
(1970), 628.
Doerner, William. "A Quasi-Experimental Analysis of Selected Victim
Compensation Programs." *Canadian Journal of Criminology* 20(1978),
239.
_____. "An Examination of the Alleged Latent Effects of Victim Com-
pensation Programs Upon Crime Reporting." *L.A.E. Journal* 41(1978),
71.
_____. "Some Critical Issues in Victimological Research." *L.A.E.
Journal* 42(1980), 17.
_____. "The Diffusion of Victim Compensation Laws in the U.S." *Vic-
timology* 4(1979), 119.
_____. et al. "An Analysis of Victim Compensation Programs as a
Time-Series Experiment." *Victimology* 1(1976), 310.
_____. et al. "Correspondence Between Crime Victim Needs and Avail-
able Public Services." *Social Service Review* 50(1976), 482.
Downey, Bernard. "Compensating Victims of Violent Crime." *British
Journal of Criminology* (1965), 92.
Drobny, Pablo. "Compensation to Victims of Crime." *St. Louis Univer-
sity Law Review* 16(1971), 201.
Dulberg, Barbara. "Social and Psychological Factors Inhibiting the Use
of Crime Victims Compensation Board." M.A. Thesis, John Jay College
of Criminal Justice, 1978.
Doplissie, A. J. "Compensating Victims of Crimes of Violence." *Inter-
national Crime & Policy Review* 24(1966), 8.
Durso, John. "Illinois Crime Victims Compensation Act." *Loyola Law
Journal* 7(1976), 351.
Edwards, J. "Compensation to Victims of Crimes of Personal Violence."
Federal Probation 30(1966), 8.
Eglash, Albert. "Creative Restitution." *Journal of Criminal Law, Cri-
minology & Police Science* 48(1958), 619.
Eremko, James. "Compensation of Criminal Injuries in Saskatchewan."
University of Toronto Law Review 19(1969), 263.

Fattah, Essat A. "The Use of the Victim as an Agent of Self-Legiti-
mation: Toward a Dynamic Explanation of Criminal Behavior." *Victimology* 1(1976), 29.

Feeney, D.T.G. "Compensation for Victims of Crime." *Canadian Journal of Corrections* 10(1968), 261.

Feeley, Malcolm. "Two Models of the Criminal Justice System: An Organizational Perspective." *Law & Society Review* 7(1973), 403.

Feyerherm, W.H. "On the Victimization of Juveniles: Some Preliminary
Results." *Journal of Research on Crime & Delinquency* 11(1974), 40.

Floyd, Glenn. "Compensation to Victims of Violent Crime." *Tulsa Law
Journal* 6(1970), 100.

_____. "Massachusetts Plan to Aid Victims of Crime." *Boston Univer-
sity Law Review* 48(1968), 380.

_____. "Victim Compensation: A Comparative Study." *Trial* 8(1972), 14.

_____. "Victim Compensation Plans." *American Bar Association Journal*
55(1969), 159.

Fogel, David, et al. "Restitution in Criminal Justice: A Minnesota
Experiment." *Criminal Law Bulletin* 8(1973), 681.

Fogelman, Sylvia. "Compensation to Victims of Violence." M.S.W. Thesis, University of Southern California, 1971.

Forston, R. "Criminal Victimization of the Aged: The Houston Model
Neighborhood Authority." Austin: Texas Criminal Justice Council,
1974.

Franklin, Clyde W. "Victimology Revisited: A Critique and Suggestions
for Future Change." *Criminology* 14(1976), 125.

"Fraudulent Advertising: The Right of a Public Attorney to Seek Restitution for Consumers." *Pacific Law Journal* 4(1973), 168.

"From State Capitols." *Concern* 1(1979), 5.

Fujii, Edwin T. "On the Compensation of Victims of Torts." *Victimology* 5(1980), 42.

Furstenberg, Frank & Charles Welford. "Calling the Police: The Evaluation of Police Service." *Law & Society Review* 8(1972), 24.

Galaway, Burt. "Is Restitution Practical?" *Federal Probation* 41(1977),
3.

Galaway, Burt & L. Rutman, "Victim Compensation: An Analysis of Substantive Issues." *Social Service Review* 48(1974), 60.

Gaguin, Diedre. "Measuring Fear of Crime: The National Crime Survey's
Attitude Data." *Victimology* 3(1978), 314.

Garofalo, James. "Victimization and the Fear of Crime." *Journal of
Research on Crime & Delinquency* (1979), 80.

Garofalo, James & John Laub. "The Fear of Crime: Broadening Our Perspectives." *Victimology* 3(1978), 242.

Garofalo, James & John McDermott. "National Victim Compensation: Its
Costs and Coverage." *Law & Policy Quarterly* 1(1979), 439.

Geis, Gilbert. "California's New Crime Victims Compensation Statute."
San Diego Law Review 24(1974), 880.

_____. "Compensation for Crime Victims and the Police." *Police* 13(1969),
55.

_____. "State Compensation for Crime." *Hospitals* 46(1976), 50.

_____. "Victims of Violent Crime: Should They Be Compensated?" *Vital Is-
sues* 20(1970), 1.

Geis, Gilbert, et al. "Public Compensation of Victims of Crime: A Survey of the New York Experience." *Criminal Law Bulletin* 9(1973), 9.

Geis, Gilbert & Herbert Sigurdson. "State Aid to Victims of Violent Crime." *State Government* 43(1970), 16.

Geis, Gilbert & Richard A. Weiner. "International Conference on Compensation to Victims of Crime." *International Review of Criminological Policy* 26(1970), 123.

Geis, Gilbert & Dorothy Zietz. "California's Program of Compensation to Crime Victims." *Legal Aid Briefcase* 25(1966), 66.

Genn, Hazel G. "Findings of a Pilot Study of Victimization in England." *Victimology* 1(1976), 253.

Gentry, Charles & Virginia Bass Eddy. "Treatment of Children in Spouse Abusive Families" *Victimology* 5(1980), 240.

Glazebrook, D. "Compensation for Victims of Crimes of Violence" *British Journal of Criminology* 2(1962), 295.

Goldberg, Arthur. "Equality and Government Action." *New York University Law Review* 39(1964), 205.

Goldsmith, Jack. "A Symposium on Crime and the Elderly." *Police Chief* 43(1976), 18.

Goodstein, Lynne & R. Lance Shotland. "The Crime Causes Crime Model: A Critical Review of the Relationship Between Fear of Crime, Bystander Surveillance, and Changes in the Crime Rate." *Victimology* 5(1980), 133.

Gordon, Margaret & Stephanie Rigor. "The Fear of Rape Prosecution." *Victimology* 3(1978), 346.

Graber, Dorothy. "Evaluating Crime-Fighting Policies: The Public's Perspective." Unpublished paper presented at American Political Science Convention, Washington, 1972.

Griew, J. "Compensation for Victims of Violence." *Criminal Law Review* (1962), 801.

Gross, R.J. "Crime Victims Compensation in North Dakota: A Year of Trial and Error." *North Dakota Law Review* 53(1976), 7.

Grossman, Allan. "Victim Compensation in Child Abuse Cases: Problems in Practical Application." *Victimology* 5(1980), 57.

Gubrium, J.F. "Victimization in Old Age: Available Evidence and Three Hypotheses." *Crime & Delinquency* 20(1974), 245.

Gulotta, Guglielmo. "Victimization and Interpersonal Misunderstandings in Dyadic Systems." *Victimology* 5(1980), 110.

Haas, Harl. "An Argument for the Enacting of Criminal Victim Compensation Legislation in Queensland." *Willamette Law Journal* 10(1974), 185.

Hall, D.J. "The Role of the Victim in the Prosecution and Disposition Stages of a Criminal Case." *Vanderbilt Law Review* 28(1975), 931.

Halleck, Seymour. "Vengeance and Victimization" *Victimology* 5(1980), 79.

Han, Robert. "Crime and the Cost of Crime: An Econometric Approach." *Journal of Research on Crime & Delinquency*(1972), 12.

Hanson, Kitty. "Billions on Criminals: How About Victims?" *New York Daily News* 4 October 1977, 28.

Harland, Alan. "Restitution by the Criminal: A Better Way of Paying for the Crime?" *Vital Issues* 27(1975), 2.

Harper, Gordon L. "Saul Bellow: The Art of Fiction--An Interview."
    Paris Review 37(1965), 48.
Harris, Duane G. "Compensating Victims of Crime: Blunting the Blow"
    Philadelphia: Philadelphia Federal Reserve Board, 1972.
Harris, John. "On the Economics of Law and Order." *Journal of Political Economy* (1970), 165.
Harrison, David. "Criminal Injuries Compensation in Britain." *American Bar Association Journal* 54(1971), 476.
Hawkins, Richard O. "Who Called the Cops? Decisions to Report Criminal Victimization." *Law & Society Review* 7(1973), 22.
Heinz, J. "Restitution or Parole: A Follow-Up Study of Adult Offenders." *Social Service Review* 50(1976), 148.
Henig, Jeffrey & Michael Maxfield. "Reducing Fear of Crime: Strategies for Intervention." *Victimology* 3(1978), 297.
Herman, Dianne. "The Politics of Rape and Wife-Beating: The Criminal Justice System's Response to Violence Against Women." Unpublished paper presented at American Political Science Association meeting, Washington, 1977.
Hook, Sidney. "The Emerging Rights of the Victims of Crime." *Florida Bar Journal* 46(1972), 192.
____. "The Rights of the Victim." *Encounter* 38(1972), 11.
Howard, M.A. "Police Reports and Victimization Survey Results: An Empirical Study." *Criminology* 12(1975), 433.
"H.R. 4267: Compensation for Victims of Crime." *Concern* 2(1980), 7.
Hudson, Joe. "Undoing the Wrong." *Social Work* 19(1974), 313.
Hudson, Paul. "A Bill of Rights for Crime Victims." *Victimology* 5 (1980), 428.
Humphrey, John & Stuart Palmer. "Stressful Life Events and Criminal Homicide Offender-Victim Relationships." *Victimology* 5(1980), 115.
In re Hollywood 124 NJ Super. 50, 304 A.2nd, 747(1973).
Inbau, F.E. "Comment on the Proposal." *Journal of Public Law* 8(1959), 201.
____. "Victim's Rights Litigation: A Wave of the Future?" *University of Richmond Law Review* 11(1977), 447.
Jacob, Bruce R. "Reparations or Restitution by the Criminal Offender to His Victim: Applicability of an Ancient Concept in the Modern Correctional Process." *Journal of Criminal Law, Criminology, & Police Science* 61(1970), 152.
Jacobson, William. "Use of Restitution in the Criminal Process: People v. Miller." *UCLA Law Review* 16(1969), 456.
Jaycox, Victoria. "The Elderly's Fear of Crime: Rational or Irrational?" *Victimology* 3(1978), 329.
Johnson, H. "Compensation for Victims of Criminal Offenses in England and the Soviet Union." *Current Legislative Problems* 17(1964), 144.
Johnson, Joan H., et al. "The Recidivist Victim: A Descriptive Study." Huntsville, TX: Institute of Contemporary Corrections & Behavioral Science, 1973.
Johnson, Knowlton W., et al. "Consumer Protection: Responsiveness of Consumer Agents to Victims of Fraud." *Victimology* 3(1978), 63.
Kappell, Sybille & Erika Leuteritz. "Wife Battering in the Federal Republic of Germany." *Victimology* 5(1980), 225.
Karmen, Andrew. "Auto Theft: Beyond Victim Blaming." *Victimology* 5 (1980), 161.

Kestenberg. "Discriminatory Practices in the German Restitution Program." *Victimology* 5(1980), 421.

Kidner, John. "Victims? Hell! We're the Victims! A Conversation with Charles "Chuckie" Crimaldi." *Victimology* 3(1978), 161.

King, Wayne. "If You Are Maimed By A Criminal, You Can Be Compensated (Maybe)."*New York Times Magazine* 26 March 1972, 8.

Kleinman, P.H. "Victimization and Perceptions of Crime in a Ghetto Community." *Criminology* 11(1973), 307.

Knutden, Mary. "Will Anyone Be Left to Testify? Disenchantment with the Criminal Justice System." Unpublished paper presented at American Sociological Association, San Francisco, 1975.

Knutden, Richard. "Crime Victims Compensation Laws and Programs." Unpublished paper, Marquette University, 1976.

Komesar, Neil S. "A Theoretical and Empirical Study of Victims of Crime." *Journal of Legal Studies* 4(1976), 301.

Kort, Fred. "Regression Analysis and Discriminant Analysis: An Application of R.A. Fisher's Theorem to Data in Political Science." *American Political Science Review* 67(1973), 555.

Kraft, Louis P., et al. "An Evaluation of the Victim-Witness Advocate Program of Puma County." Tuscon: Office of Puma County Attorney, 1979.

Kress, Jack. "The Role of the Victim at Sentencing." Unpublished paper presented at Second International Symposium on Victimology, Boston, 1976.

Kress, Susan. "Doubly Abused: The Plight of Crime Victims in Literature." Unpublished paper presented at Second International Symposium on Victimology, Boston, 1976.

Krupnick, Janice. "Brief Psychotherapy with Victims of Violent Crime." *Victimology* 5(1980), 347.

Kutner, Luis. "Crime Torts: Due Process of Compensation for Crime Victims." *Notre Dame Lawyer* 41(1966), 494.

_____. "Due Process for Crime Victims."*Trial* 8(1972), 28.

Lambert, J.L. "Compensation Orders: A Review of the Appellate Cases." *New Law Journal* 126(1976), 69.

Lamborn, LeRoy. "Crime Victim Compensation: Theory and Practice in the Second Decade." *Victimology* 1(1976), 509.

_____. "Remedies for the Victims of Crime." *Southern California Law Review* (1970), 43.

_____. "The Methods of Governmental Compensation of Crime Victims." *University of Illinois Law Forum* (1971), 696.

_____. "The Propriety of Governmental Compensation of Victims of Crime." *George Washington Law Review* 41(1973), 714.

_____. "The Scope of Programs for Governmental Compensation of the Victims of Crime." *University of Illinois Law Forum* (1973), 25.

_____. "Toward a Victim Orientation in Criminological Theory." *Rutgers Law Review* 22(1968), 760.

Laster, Richard. "Criminal Restitution: A Survey of Its Past History and An Analysis of Its Present Usefulness." *University of Richmond Law Review* 5(1970), 88.

Law Enforcement Assistance Administration. "Victims of Crime Act of 1972." Washington: U.S. Department of Justice, 1972.

LeJeune, Robert & Nicholas Alex. "On Being Mugged: The Event and
Its Aftermath." *Urban Life & Culture* 2(1973), 259.

Lens, Sidney. "Blaming the Victim." *The Progressive* August 1980, 27.

Levine, James. "The Potential for Crime Over-Reporting in Criminal
Victimization Surveys." *Criminology* 14(1976), 307.

Levine, Ken. "Empiricism in Victimological Research: A Critique."
Victimology 3(1978), 77.

Linden, H.M. "International Conference on Compensation to Victims
of Violent Crime." *Criminal Law Quarterly* 11(1969), 145.

_____. "Victims of Crime and Tort Laws." *Journal of Canadian Bar
Association* (1969), 17.

Lynch, Mitchell C. "Tough Luck If You're Ripped Off." *Wall Street
Journal* 16 December 1979, 7.

McClellan, John. "Society's Moral Obligation: Victims of Crime Act
of 1972." *Trial* 8(1972), 22.

McClure, Barbara. "Crime: Compensation for Victims." Washington:
Library of Congress, 1979.

McCormack, Geoffrey. "Revenge and Compensation in Early Law." *American Journal of Comparative Law* 21(1973), 69.

McDonald, William. "Notes on the Victim's Role in the Prosecution
and Disposition Stages of the American Criminal Process." Unpublished paper presented at Second International Symposium on Victimology, Boston, 1976.

McGowan, P.G. "Criminal Injuries Compensation Act of 1970 (W.A.)."
University of Western Australia Law Review 10(1972), 305.

McGrath, W.J. "Compensation to Victims of Crime in Canada." *Canadian Journal of Corrections* 12(1970), 11.

McKay, Heather & John Hagan. "Studying the Victim of Crime: Some Methodological Notes." *Victimology* 3(1978), 135.

McPherson, Marlys. "Realities and Perceptions of Crime at the Neighborhood Level." *Victimology* 3(1978), 319.

McPheters, Lee & William Strange. "Law Enforcement Expenditures and
Urban Crime." *National Tax Journal* (1974), 24.

Maggadino, Joseph. "Crime, Victim Compensation, and the Supply of
Offenses." *Public Policy* 54(1976), 437.

Maisch, Herbert. "The Victim in Judicial Proceedings." *International Journal of Crime & Penology* 3(1975), 63.

Mansfield, Michael. "Justice for Victims of Crime." *Houston Law Review* 9(1971), 75.

Marshall, Douglas. "Compensation: New Atonement for Old Guilt?"
Journal of Canadian Bar Association 2(1971), 24.

Martin, Glenn B. "Victim Compensation in Several States: A Comparative Analysis." M.A. Thesis, University of Texas, 1978.

Mazelan, P.M. "Stereotypes and Perceptions of the Victims of Rape."
Victimology 5(1980), 121.

Meade, Anthony, et al. "Discovery of a Forgotten Party: Trends in American Victims Compensation Legislation." *Victimology* 1(1976), 429.

Melton, Gary B. "Psychological Issues in Child Victims' Interaction
with the Legal System." *Victimology* 5(1980), 274.

Meyers, Martha. "Determinants of Conviction: The Prosecutorial Roles
of the Victim and Defendant." Unpublished paper presented at Second International Symposium on Victimology, Boston, 1976.

"Michigan Public Speaks Out" Washington: U.S. Department of Justice, 1973.

Miers, David. "Compensation for Consequential Loss Under the Malicious Injuries Code." *Irish Jurist* 6(1971), 50.

_____. "Compensation for Victims of Crimes of Violence: The Northern Ireland Model." *Criminal Law Review*(1969), 579.

_____. "Ontario Criminal Injuries Compensation Scheme." *University of Toronto Law Review* 24(1974), 347.

_____. "Victim Compensation as a Labelling Process." *Victimology* 5 (1980), 3.

Miller, Frank W. "Comment on the Proposal." *Journal of Public Law* 8(1959), 203.

Morris, Terence. "Compensating for Victims of Crimes of Violence." *Modern Law Review* 24(1961), 744.

Mueller, Gerhard O.W. "Comment on the Proposal." *Journal of Public Law* 8(1959), 218.

_____. "Compensation for Victims of Crime: Thought Before Action." *Minnesota Law Review* 50(1965), 213.

Mueller, Gerhard O.W. & H.H.A. Cooper. "Civil Alternatives for Victims of Crimes." Unpublished paper, New York University, 1973.

"New Jersey Criminal Injuries Compensation Act." *Rutgers Law Review* 27(1974), 728.

"New York Crime Victims Compensation Board: Four Years Later." *Columbia Journal of Law & Social Problems* 7(1971), 27.

Newton, Anne. "Aid to the Victim: Compensation and Restitution." *Crime & Delinquency Literature* 8(1976), 368.

_____. "Aid to the Victim: Victim Aid Programs." *Crime & Delinquency Literature* 8(1976), 368.

_____. "Alternatives to Imprisonment: Day Fines, Community Service Orders, and Restitution." *Crime & Delinquency Literature* 8(1976), 109.

Kwpa, Nwokocha K.U. "Victimization of Babies in Nigerian Urban Centers." *Victimology* 5(1980), 251.

Ostrovmov, S.S. & I.V. Frank. "On Victimology and Victimization." *Soviet Law & Government* 15(1976-77), 70.

Palmer, Geoffrey W.R. "Compensation for Personal Injury: A Requiem for the Criminal Law in New Zealand." *American Journal of Comparative Law* 21(1973), 1.

Peltoniemi, Teuvo. "Family Violence: Police House Calls in Helsinki, Finland in 1977." *Victimology* 5(1980), 213.

Perillo, J.M. "Restitution in a Contractual Context." *Columbia Law Review* (1973), 1208.

Perkins, Rollin. "The Law of Homicide." *Journal of Criminal Law, Criminology & Police Science* 36(1946), 412.

Phillips, Llad & Harold Votey. "Economic Analysis of the Deterrent Effect of Law Enforcement on Criminal Activity." *Journal of Criminal Law, Criminology & Police Science* (1972), 330.

"Pilot Complainant Survey." Unpublished paper, Vera Institute of Justice, 1976.

Pinkerton, Stewart W. "Aiding the Innocent: More States Award Cash Compensation to Victims of Crime." *Wall Street Journal* 26 August 1970, 3.

Ploog, Holly. "Tennessee's Criminal Injuries Compensation Act." *Memphis State University Law Review* 7(1977), 241.

———. "Virginia Adopts Statute to Compensate Victims of Crime." *University of Richmond Law Review* 11(1977), 679.

Polish, James. "Rehabilitation of the Victims of Crime." *UCLA Law Review* 21(1976), 335.

Pope, C.E. "The Effects of Crime on the Elderly." *Police Chief* 43 (1976), 48.

Pressman, Israel & Carol Arthur. "Crime as a Diseconomy of Scale." *Review of Sociology & Economics* (1971), 227.

Quinney, Richard. "Who Is The Victim?" *Criminology* (1972), 314.

Rajan, V.N. "Crime Victimization Research Program and Policy Planning in Developing Countries." *Victimology* 5(1980), 193.

"Random-Digit Dialing for Survey Research." Washington: Police Foundation, 1978.

Read, Bill. "How Restitution Works in Georgia." *Judicature* 60(1977), 322.

Reiss, A.J. "Discretionary Justice in the United States." *International Journal of Criminology & Penology* 2(1974), 181.

Rejda, George E. & Emil Meuer. "An Analysis of State Criminal Compensation Plans." *Journal of Risk & Insurance* (1975), 599.

Rigor, Stephanie, et al. "Women's Fear of Crime." *Victimology* 3(1978) 244.

Rogers, Theresa F. "Interviews by Telephone and In Person: An Experiment to Test the Quality of Responses and Field Performance." Unpublished paper presented at American Association of Public Opinion Research, 1975.

Rosenthal, Herbert A. "Compensation for Victims of Crimes." *American Bar Association Journal* 58(1972), 968.

Rothstein, Paul F. "State Compensation for Criminally Inflicted Injuries." *Texas Law Review* 44(1965), 38.

Rounsaville, Bruce J. "Theories in Marital Violence." *Victimology* 3 (1978), 11.

Rubel, Robert. "Victimization and Fear in Public Schools." *Victimology* 3(1978), 339.

Samuels, Alex. "Compensation for Criminal Injuries in Britain." *University of Toronto Law Journal* 17(1967), 20.

Sandler, Robert. "Compensation for Victims of Crime: Some Practical Considerations." *Buffalo Law Review* 15(1971), 645.

Savitz, Leonard, et al. "Delinquency and Gang Membership as Related to Victimization." *Victimology* 5(1980), 152.

Schafer, Stephen. "Compensation of Victims of Criminal Offenses." *Criminal Law Bulletin* 10(1974), 605.

———. "Creative Compensation." *Crime-Trial Magazine* (1972), 5.

———. "Creative Compensation." *Trial* 8(1972), 25.

———. "Restitution to Victims of Crime: An Old Correctional Aid Modernized." *Minnesota Law Review* 50(1965), 243.

———. "The Proper Role of a Victim Compensation System." *Crime & Delinquency* 21(1975), 48.

———. "Victim Compensation and Responsibility." *Southern California Law Review* 43(1970), 55.

Schmid, Calvin. "A Study of Homicides in Seattle, 1919 to 1924." *Social Forces* 4(1926), 745.

Schmidt, Randall A. "Crime Victim Compensation Legislation: A Comparative Study." *Victimology* 5(1980), 401.

Schmutz, Joan. "Compensation for the Criminally Injured Revisited: An Emphasis on the Victim?" *Notre Dame Lawyer* 47(1971), 90.

Schneider, A.L. "Methodological Approaches for Measuring Short-Term Victimization Trends." Eugene: Oregon Research Institute, 1975.

Schram, D.D. "Study of Public Opinion and Criminal Victimization in Seattle." Washington: U.S. Department of Justice, 1973.

Schultz, LeRoy. "The Violated: A Proposal to Compensate Victims of Violent Crime." *St. Louis University Law Review* 10(1965), 238.

_____. "The Victim-Offender Relationship." *St. Louis University Law Review* 18(1967), 138.

Schwind, H.D. "Interim Report on Research on Unreported Crime in Goettingen." *Kriminalistik* 28(1974), 241.

Scott, Robert. "Compensation for Victims of Violent Crimes: An Analysis." *William & Mary Law Review* 8(1967), 277.

Section on Criminal Justice, Committee on Victims. "Reducing Victim-Witness Intimidation: A Package." Washington: American Bar Association, 1979.

Serrill, M.S. "Minnesota Restitution Center." *Corrections Magazine* 1(1975), 13.

Shank, Willard. "Aid to Victims of Crime in California." *Southern California Law Review* 43(1970), 85.

Shakolsky, Sheleff. "Victim Compensation: Its History, Rationale, Implementation and Potentialities." *Crime, Punishment & Corrections* 5(1976), 8.

Shapiro, Carol. "Crime Victim Services." *Social Policy* 13(1982), 50.

Shoup, Carol S. "Standards for Distributing a Free Governmental Service: Crime Prevention." *Public Finance* 19(1964), 383.

Silverman, Susan Stelzenmuller & William Doerner. "The Effect of Victim Compensation Programs Upon Conviction Rates." *Sociological Symposium* 25(1979), 40.

Silving, Helen. "Comment on the Proposal." *Journal of Public Law* 8(1959), 236.

Sinclair, Ward & John Jacobs. "Are These America's Political Prisoners?" *Washington Post* 8 January 1978, 71.

Sjoquist, David. "Property Crime and Economic Behavior: Some Empirical Results." *American Economic Review* (1973), 439.

Skogan, Wesley G. "Comparing Measures of Crime: Police Statistics and Survey Estimates of Citizen Victimization in American Cities." Washington: American Statistical Association, 1974.

_____. "Measurement Problems in Official and Survey Crime Rates." *Journal of Criminal Justice* 3(1975), 17.

_____. "Public Policy and the Fear of Crime in Large American Cities." Unpublished paper presented to Midwest Political Science Association, Chicago, 1976.

_____. "Validity of Official Crime Statistics: An Empirical Investigation." *Social Science Quarterly* 12(1974), 15.

_____. "Victimization Surveys and Criminal Justice Planning." *University of Cincinnati Law Review* 45(1976), 167.

_____. "Victims of Crime: Some National Panel Data." Washington: U.S. Department of Justice, 1975.

Smartt, Ronald G. "Compensation for Crime Victims: Northern Ireland Perspective." *Victimology* 5(1980), 51.

Smith, P.E. "Victimization: Types of Citizen-Police Contacts and Attitudes Toward the Police." *Law & Society Review* 8(1973), 135.

Smodish, Michael. "But What About the Victim? The Forsaken Man in American Criminal Law." *University of Florida Law Review* 22(1969), 6.

Stanko, Elizabeth Anne. "The Impact of Victim Assessment on Prosecutor's Screening Decisions: The Case of the New York County District Attorney's Office." *Law & Society Review* 16(1981-82), 225.

Star, Barbara. "Comparing Battered and Non-Battered Women." *Victimology* 3(1978), 32.

Starrs, James E. "A Modest Proposal to Insure Justice for Victims of Crime." *Minnesota Law Review* 50(1965), 285.

Stephan, E. "Results of the Stuttgart Survey of Victims Taking Comparable American Data Into Account: An Interim Report." *Kriminalistik* 29(1975), 201.

Stewart, John & Stanley Rosen. "Adequacy of Compensation, Worthiness of Recipient, and Their Effects on Transgressor Compliance to Render Aid." *Journal of Social Psychology* 97(1975), 77.

Stookey, James. "The Victim's Perspective on American Criminal Justice." Minneapolis: Minnesota Department of Corrections, 1976.

Sudman, S. "New Uses of Telephone Methods in Survey Research." *Journal of Marketing Research* 3(1966), 66.

Sutton, L. Paul. "Compensation to Victims of Violent Crime in New York State." Seattle: Battelle, 1972.

Task Force on Criminal Justice Research & Development, Standards & Goals." Research on Criminal Justice Problems: Victim Research." Washington: Rand, 1976.

Thorvaldson, Sveinn & Mark Krasnick. "On Recovering Compensation Funds from Offenders." *Victimology* 5(1980), 18.

Thurow, Lester. "Equity Versus Efficiency in Law Enforcement." *Public Policy* 18(1970), 454.

"Treatment of Victims and Witnesses." *Crime & Delinquency* 21(1975),190.

Tullock, Gordon. "An Economic Approach to Crime." *Social Science Quarterly* 50(1969), 59.

U.S. House of Representatives, Committee on the Judiciary. "Crime Victims Compensation." Hearings, 94th Congress. Washington: U.S. Government Printing Office, serial no. 39, 1273.

___. "Victims of Crime Act of 1974.: Report 95-337, HR. 7010, 95th Congress. Washington: U.S. Government Printing Office, 1157.

U.S. Senate, Committee on District of Columbia. "Compensation of Victims of Crime." Hearings, 91st Congress. Washington: U.S. Government Printing Office, 1970.

"Use of Record of Criminal Conviction in Subsequent Act Arising from Same Facts as the Prosecution." *Michigan Law Review* 64(1966), 708.

Van Renssaelear, S. "A Compensation Board at Work." *Trial* 8(1972), 21.

___. "Compensating for Victims of Crime: The New York Experience." *State Government* (1974), 15.

Vaughn, Jacqueline & Richard Hofrichter. "Program Visibility in State Victim Compensation Programs." *Victimology* 5(1980), 30.

Vennard, Julie. "Victim's Views on Compensation and Criminal Justice System." London: Home Office Reprint, 1976.

"Victim Assistance Programs in Minnesota." *Victimology* 2(1976), 88.
"Victims of Crime or Victims of Justice?" Washington: American Bar Association, 1977.
"Victims Rights." *University of Richmond Law Review* 11(1977), 679.
"Victim-Witness Assistance Project Operations Report." Unpublished paper, Vera Institute of Justice, 1975.
Violent Crimes Compensation Board. "Rules and Regulations of the Violent Crimes Compensation Board." Trenton: State of New Jersey, nd.
Virkkinen, Matti. "Victim-Precipitated Pedophilia Offenses." *British Journal of Criminology* 15(1979), 175.
Vitali, Samuel. "A Year's Experience with the Massachusetts Compensation of Victims of Violent Crime Law, 1968-69." *Suffolk University Law Review* 40(1970), 175.
Wachter, S. "High Cost of Victimless Crimes." *Record* 28(1973), 354.
Walker, J.C. "Valuations of Criminal Inuries Compensation Board." *Solicitor's Journal* 110(1966), 940.
Waller, Irwin. "Victim Research, Public Policy and Criminal Justice." *Victimology* 1(1976), 240.
Walzer, Norman. "Economics of Scale and Municipal Police Services: The Illinois Experience." *Review of Economics & Statistics* (1972), 431.
Watchke, Gary. "Compensation for Victims of Crime: A Current Status Report." Madison: Wisconsin Legislative Reference Bureau, 1976.
Weeks, Kent. "The New Zealand Criminal Injuries Compensation Scheme." *Southern California Law Review* 43(1976), 107.
Weicher, Joan. "Allocation of Police Protection by Income Class." *Urban Studies* (1971), 207.
Weihofen, Henry. "Comment on the Proposal." *Journal of Public Law* 8(1959), 211.
Westling, W.T. "Some Aspects of Judicial Determinants of Compensation Payable to Victims of Crime." *Australian Law Journal* 48(1974), 428.
"Why Witnesses Cannot Be Located." Washington: National Criminal Justice Reference Service, 1977.
Williams, Glanville. "Comment on the Proposals." *Journal of Public Law* 8(1959), 194.
Wolfe, Nancy. "Victim Provocation: The Battered Wife and the Legal Definition of Self-Defense." *Sociological Symposium* 25(1979), 98.
Wolfgang, Marvin. "Victim Compensation in Crimes of Personal Violence." *Minnesota Law Review* 50(1965), 230.
Wright, Boyd L. "What About the Victims? Compensation for the Victims of Crime." *North Dakota Law Review* 48(1972), 473.
Wright, M. "Nobody Came: Criminal Justice and the Needs of Victims." *Howard Journal of Penology & Crime Prevention* 16(1977), 22.
Yarborough, Ralph. "S.2155 of 89th Congress: The Criminal Injuries Compensation Act." *Minnesota Law Review* 50(1965), 255.
_____. "The Battle for a Federal Violent Crimes Compensation Act: The Genesis of S.9." *Southern California Law Review* 43(1970), 93.
Younger, Evelyn J. "Commendable Words: A Critical Evaluation of California's Victim Compensation Law." *Journal of Beverly Hills Bar Association* 7(1973), 12.

Zagaris, Bruce. "State Victim Compensation Programs in Action." *Victimology* 2(1977), 106.

Ziegenhagen, Eduard. "The Recidivist Victim of Violent Crime." *Victimology* 1(1976), 538.

Zion, Robert. "Reducing Crime and Fear of Crime in Downtown Cleveland." *Victimology* 3(1978), 341.

DATE DUE

MAY 2 3 1989			
MAR 2 1 1994			